# HOW
# ASIA
# WORKS

## ALSO BY JOE STUDWELL

*The China Dream*
*Asian Godfathers*

# HOW ASIA WORKS

### SUCCESS AND FAILURE IN THE
### WORLD'S MOST DYNAMIC REGION

## JOE
## STUDWELL

Grove Press
*New York*

For Tiffany

# Contents

*I went out in the heat of the moment, and in the bitterness of my heart . . .*

William Gladstone, Midlothian campaign

# Author's Note

Two key data sources I have used are the International Monetary Fund's World Economic Outlook database, which starts from 1980, and the World Bank's World Development Indicators database, which starts from 1960. If no source is given for a data point, it has been taken from one of these two databases. The decision to not always quote the IMF and World Bank sources aims to reduce the number of endnotes.

The World Bank has changed its terminology and now refers to Gross National Product (GNP) as Gross National Income (GNI). While some readers may be used to the older term, GNP, GNI has been used throughout this book. According to the World Bank, there is no methodological difference between the two. The methodological difference that readers should take note of is that between GNI, which covers a country's income from both domestic and international sources, and GDP, which reflects income in the domestic economy alone.

Despite my efforts to contain the number of endnotes, there are still a good many that are necessary to elucidate a point or show that there is a substantive source for what I am saying. It is not expected or intended that readers will look up all the notes. The best way to proceed for many people will be to only turn to the endnotes if the point being made is one you consider particularly important or controversial. For those interested, I hope to publish more of the academic research that supports what I say in a separate addendum. Any progress on this front will be reported at www.howasiaworks.com.

Unless otherwise noted, exchange rates are those that applied in the year or period that is being discussed.

Finally, pretty much every country in Asia has produced competing systems of romanisation of Asian languages. In writing names of people and places, I have attempted to use the romanised forms that are most familiar to contemporary English language readers. Hence Deng Xiaoping is rendered in the mainland Chinese pinyin system, whereas Chiang Kai-shek is rendered in the Wade-Giles system favoured in Taiwan. In South Korea, a degree of romanisation anarchy reigns. The McCune-Reischauer system, the Yale system, the new Revised Romanisation system and more exist concurrently and Koreans take their pick when romanising their names. Moreover, there is no accepted convention for the hyphenation and capitalisation of given names. I have therefore followed expressed preference or what appears to be the most common usage. Park Chung Hee preferred to be styled thus. Ha-Joon Chang writes his name thus. Byung-kook Kim is styled thus. And South Korea's first president insisted on, and is still known as, Syngman Rhee (if I called him the more standard Lee Seung Man, no one would know him.) In North Korea, there is unanimity that Kim Il Sung is the way to style a name. In Indonesia I have avoided the older, Dutch-influenced spellings such as Soeharto, since post-colonial spelling, such as Suharto, is now very widely accepted. I apologise in the knowledge that in dealing with eight countries there will be some romanisation choices, and some name stylings, that readers disagree with.

# Introduction

This is a book about how rapid economic transformation is, or is not, achieved. It argues that there are three critical interventions that governments can use to speed up economic development. Where these interventions have been employed most effectively in east Asia – in Japan, South Korea, Taiwan and now China – they have produced the quickest progressions from poverty to wealth that the world has seen. When, by contrast, other east Asian states have set off with the same ambitions and equal or better endowments, but have not followed the same policies, they have achieved fast growth for a period but the progress has proved to be unsustainable.

The first intervention – and the most overlooked – is to maximise output from agriculture, which employs the vast majority of people in poor countries. Successful east Asian states have shown that the way to do this is to restructure agriculture as highly labour-intensive household farming – a slightly larger-scale form of gardening. This makes use of all available labour in a poor economy and pushes up yields and output to the highest possible levels, albeit on the basis of tiny gains per person employed. The overall result is an initial productive surplus that primes demand for goods and services.

The second intervention – in many respects, a second 'stage' – is to direct investment and entrepreneurs towards manufacturing. This is because manufacturing industry makes the most effective use of the limited productive skills of the workforce of a developing economy, as workers begin to migrate out of agriculture. Relatively unskilled labourers create value in factories by working with machines that can be easily purchased on the world market. In addition, in east Asia successful governments pioneered new ways to promote accelerated technological upgrading in manufacturing through subsidies that were conditioned on export performance. This combination of subsidy and what I call 'export discipline' took the pace of industrialisation to a level never before seen.

Finally, interventions in the financial sector to focus capital on intensive, small-scale agriculture and on manufacturing development provide the third key to accelerated economic transformation. The state's role is to keep money targeted at a development strategy that produces the fastest possible technological learning, and hence the promise of high future profits, rather than on short-term returns and individual consumption. This tends to pit the state against many businessmen, and also against consumers, who have shorter strategic horizons.

The policy prescription for rapid economic development was confused for a time in east Asia by the presence of other fast-growing economies that did not conform to the pattern of Japan, Korea, Taiwan and China. In the 1980s and early 1990s, the World Bank seized on the performance of the offshore financial centres of Hong Kong and Singapore, and the suddenly faster-growing south-east Asian economies of Indonesia, Malaysia and Thailand, to argue that economic development was in fact fostered by *laissez-faire* policies, with a minimal role for government. Despite the fact that the offshore centres, with their tiny, dense populations and absence of agricultural sectors to drag on productivity, are not really comparable to regular countries, the World Bank used Hong Kong and Singapore as two of its three 'proving' case studies in a highly controversial 1987 report.[1] After widespread academic criticism of the report, the World Bank followed up with another one in 1993, *The East Asian Miracle,* which admitted the existence of industrial policy and infant industry protection in some states. But it downplayed the significance of such policies, avoided discussion of agriculture altogether, and added Hong Kong and Singapore to Malaysia, Indonesia and Thailand, thereby leaving Japan, Korea and Taiwan as the statistical minority among its 'High Performing Asian Economies'. (China was omitted from the report.)[2]

This was the ideologically charged era of the so-called Washington Consensus, when the World Bank, the International Monetary Fund and the US

Treasury were united in their determination that the free market policies coming into vogue in the US and Britain were appropriate to all economies, no matter what their level of development.[3] The vitriol of the debate was such that academic rigour was frequently a victim, as with the World Bank reports. Indeed, even the academic specialists on Japan, Korea and Taiwan who opposed the Washington Consensus position on economic development made suspect claims in order to bolster their case. This only added to confusion. Chalmers Johnson wrote in the preface to his seminal study of Japanese development, published in 1982: '[The Japanese development model] is being repeated today in newly industrializing states of East Asia – Taiwan and South Korea – and in Singapore and South and Southeast Asian countries.' Alice Amsden, who produced the defining deconstruction of Korean development, referred in the introduction to a follow-up book to 'the model used by Japan, Korea, Taiwan and Thailand'. Even W. W. Rostow, author of one of the earliest and most historically informed post-war books on economic development, *The Stages of Economic Growth*, declaimed in the foreword to a new edition in 1991 that Malaysia and Thailand were following Korea and Taiwan towards technological maturity.[4] In the argument over east Asia, everyone started to talk beyond their turf in an effort to win the debate.

The disagreement about the nature of economic development was only made possible by continued fast growth rates around the region. In the early 1980s, however, Brazil – the outstanding fast growth story of 1960s' and 1970s' Latin America – had shown how dangerous it is to judge economic progress by growth rates alone. Brazil is the only major economy outside east Asia which has managed to grow by more than 7 per cent a year for more than a quarter of a century.[5] But, with the onset of the Latin American debt crisis in 1982, Brazil crumbled amid currency depreciation, inflation and years of zero growth. It turned out that too much of Brazil's earlier growth had been generated by debt that did not translate into a more genuinely productive and competitive economy.

Beginning in 1997, with seven economies that have expanded at least 7 per cent a year for a quarter century – Japan, Korea, Taiwan, China, Malaysia, Indonesia and Thailand – east Asia entered a period of reckoning of its own, as the Asian financial crisis took hold. By this point Japan had long since become a mature economy that faced a new set of post-developmental structural problems, ones it showed much less capacity to address than the original challenge of becoming rich. Korea, Taiwan and China, however, were still in the developmental catch-up phase. These states were either unaffected by the Asian crisis or recovered quickly from it, and returned to brisk growth and technological progress. But Malaysia, Indonesia and Thailand were knocked completely off course. They suffered currency depreciation, inflation and much reduced growth. It is indicative that today Indonesia and Thailand report GDP per capita of only USD3,000 and USD5,000 respectively, and feature significant levels of poverty, where Korea and Taiwan report GDP per capita around USD20,000. At the end of the Second World War, all these countries were similarly poor.[6]

What the Asian crisis clarified was that a consistent set of government policy interventions had indeed made the difference between long-run success and failure in economic development in east Asia. In Japan, Korea, Taiwan and China, governments radically restructured agriculture after the Second World War, focused their modernisation efforts on manufacturing, and made their financial systems slaves to these two objectives. They thereby changed the structures of their economies in a manner that made it all but impossible to return to an earlier stage of development. In the south-east Asian states – despite their long periods of impressive growth – governments did not fundamentally reorganise agriculture, did not create globally competitive manufacturing firms, and *did* accept bad advice from already rich countries to open up financial sectors at an early stage. The Japanese economist Yoshihara Kunio had warned in the 1980s that south-east Asian states risked becoming 'technology-less' developing nations. This is exactly what happened, and they slid backwards when their investment funds dried up. In short, different policy choices created – and will probably further widen – a developmental gulf in the Asian region.[7]

### The reality of two East Asias

The strategies – agricultural, manufacturing and financial – that determine success and failure were set in train decades before the Asian 'miracle' debate of the 1980s and 1990s took place. It is those strategies that this book explores. It begins with the radical redistribution of agricultural land in Japan, Korea, Taiwan and China in the late 1940s and early 1950s. Land was the biggest political issue in east Asia after the Second World War and promises of land reform were fundamental to the communist victories in China, North Korea and Vietnam. However, in these socialist states, family farming was later substituted, for ideological reasons, by collectivisation, which caused yields to stagnate or fall. In Japan, South Korea and Taiwan, household-based land redistribution programmes were implemented peacefully, and sustained. It was this that led to prolonged rural booms that catalysed overall economic transformation.

In south-east Asia there was also much post-war talk about more equitable land distribution, new agricultural extension services to support farmers and the provision of affordable rural credit. A good many reform programmes were launched. But the actual implemented effects were a fraction of what they were in the north-east of the region. This is where east Asian divergence began. The failure of the leaders of south-east Asian states to get to grips with the problems of agriculture both made development in general much more difficult and presaged other policy failures. It is instructive that sixty years later land is still a major political issue in the Philippines, Indonesia and Thailand, and only less so in Malaysia because the country's natural resource wealth mitigates its poor agricultural performance. Part 1 of this book explores why agriculture is so important. It does so partly through journeys to Japan and the Philippines.

Part 2 moves on to the role of manufacturing. It investigates how Japan, Korea, Taiwan and China perfected ways to marry subsidies and protection for manufacturers – so as to nurture their development – with competition and 'export discipline', which forced them to sell their products internationally and thereby become globally competitive. This overcame the traditional problem with subsidy and protection policies, whereby entrepreneurs pocketed financial incentives but failed to do the hard work of producing competitive products. Firms were not able to hide behind tariff and other barriers and sell only to a protected domestic market because protection, subsidies and credit were conditioned on export growth. Firms that did not meet the export benchmark were cut off from state largesse, forced to merge with more successful companies, or occasionally even bankrupted. Governments thereby ended up with world-beating firms to justify their considerable investments of public funds.

This is the second point at which there has been a sharp divergence of policy in south-east Asia and north-east Asia and China. In south-east Asian nations, leading entrepreneurs were no less capable than those in other countries, but governments failed to constrain them to manufacture and did not subject them to export discipline. Instead, there were state-sector manufacturing projects, but with little competition between firms and no requirement to export. As a result, governments obtained a very low return on all forms of industrial policy investment. In the boom years of the 1980s and 1990s, the failure to generate indigenous manufacturing and technological capacity was hidden by the arrival of high levels of foreign direct investment, much of it concentrated on processing operations within quite advanced manufacturing sectors. With the onset of the Asian crisis, however, the industrial difference between south-east and north-east Asia became starkly apparent. South-east Asia has almost no popularly recognisable, globally competitive manufacturing companies. Singapore's Tiger Beer and Thailand's Singha Beer and Chang Beer are about as close as we can get to widely recognised south-east Asian industrial brands, and these brewers are not really *manufacturers* at all. Without successful large, branded companies of their own, south-east Asian economies remain technologically dependent on multinationals, eking out a living as contractors for the lower-margin parts of international production chains. The manner in which states did, or did not, become masters of their industrial destinies is explored in part 2 during journeys to Korea and Malaysia, visiting the sites of their respective efforts to learn how to make steel and cars.

Part 3 looks at financial policy. In successful east Asian states, the structure of finance was determined by the need to achieve the objectives of high-yield, small-scale agriculture and the acquisition of manufacturing skills. To this end, financial systems in Japan, Korea, Taiwan and China were kept under close state supervision, and controls on international capital flows were maintained until an advanced stage of development. The main mechanism for making finance support state policy objectives was bank lending, which was manipulated to force export discipline on manufacturers. Firms had to demonstrate export orders in order to secure credit. In a neat circle, export performance also provided signals to banks about whether their loans would eventually be repaid, because exporters were almost by definition better businesses than firms that sold only at home. In order to fund development, interest on bank deposits in north-east Asia and China was set well below market rates, a form of stealth taxation that helped pay for subsidies to agriculture and industry. This encouraged the setting up of illegal deposit-taking institutions; however, these so-called 'kerb' markets never drained money from banks to a point that became destabilising.

In south-east Asia, countries were blessed with high levels of savings in their banking systems just as in north-east Asia. But governments directed the hefty investments this made possible to the wrong ends – to lower-yield, large-scale agriculture, and to companies that were either not focused on manufacturing or only on manufacturing for protected domestic markets. South-east Asian states then made their developmental prospects even worse by following rich country advice to deregulate banking, to open up other financial markets, and to lift capital controls. The same advice had been proffered to Japan, Korea, Taiwan and China in the early stages of their development, but they sensibly resisted for as long as possible. Premature financial deregulation in south-east Asia led to a proliferation of family-business-controlled banks which did nothing to support export-able manufacturing and which indulged in vast amounts of illegal related-party lending. It was a story of banks being captured by narrow, private sector interests whose aims were almost completely unaligned with those of national economic development. The process was one which has also been observed in Latin America and, more recently, in Russia. The detail of how financial liberalisation went wrong in south-east Asia is explored on a journey to Indonesia's capital Jakarta, where a new financial district grew like a mushroom in the run-up to the Asian financial crisis.

## The countries covered

I have made a number of simplifications in this book so as not to dilute its central messages and to enable its story to be told (endnotes excepted) in just over 200 pages. One of these involved choosing which east Asian countries to leave out of the narrative. Since the book is about developmental strategies that have achieved a modicum of success, the region's failed states do not appear. North Korea, Laos, Cambodia, Myanmar and Papua New Guinea, all of which are found near the bottom of the United Nations' Human Development Index (HDI) rankings,[8] are not discussed. The reasons for the failure of these states are varied, but one common characteristic leaps out: they are all politically and economically introverted. In varying degrees, these countries are re-learning the old lesson of pre-1978 China, pre-1989 Soviet Union and pre-1991 India: that if a country does not trade and interact with the world, it is all but impossible to get ahead in the development game.

This book also restricts itself to the developmental challenges facing what I would call 'proper countries'. It ignores east Asia's two main offshore financial centres – Hong Kong and Singapore. (A more accurate description of these two is port-offshore financial centres because of their dual role as shipping hubs.) The micro oil state of Brunei and east Asia's traditional gambling centre, Macau, are also left out. As noted, much pointless and deeply misleading debate has been promoted over the years by comparing the development of, say, Hong Kong with that of China, or that of Singapore with Indonesia's. The World Bank has been the prime offender and I aim not to add to the detritus. Offshore centres are not normal states. Around the world, they compete by specialising in trade and financial services while enjoying lower structural overheads than other countries, which have larger, more dispersed populations, and agricultural sectors that drag on productivity.[9] Offshore centres' lower overheads mean that they also have a built-in fiscal advantage. Yet they can never exist in isolation – they are in a strict sense parasitic, because they have to have their host or hosts to feed on.[10]

The island of Taiwan is discussed – in politically incorrect but economically essential fashion – as a standalone state. Despite being recognised by most governments as a province of the People's Republic of China, Taiwan has functioned as an independent political and economic entity since 1949. Before that, the island was a colony of Japan for half a century. With its population of 23 million, Taiwan has a developmental story that is both distinct from that of mainland China, and one which exhibits some striking and underreported policy similarities – reflecting the shared experiences of Kuomintang and Communist politicians and bureaucrats on the mainland in the 1930s and 1940s. The book's structure allows both facets of Taiwan's economic history to be discussed.

The omission of failed states and offshore centres, and the adjustment with respect to Taiwan, means that we are left with nine significant east Asian economies: a north-east Asian group of Japan and its two former colonies, South Korea and Taiwan; a south-east Asian group of Thailand, Malaysia, Indonesia and the Philippines; and China and Vietnam. Vietnam, however, is omitted from this third 'post-communist' group in order to further to simplify the structure of the book. Forgiveness is begged from Vietnamese readers, whose country is no way deemed to have anything more in common with China than a certain structural economic framework that results from its being a gradually reforming communist state.

China, and the question of how different the country's economic development strategy really is from those of Japan, Korea and Taiwan, is mostly dealt with in part 4, which is dedicated to the rise of what is now Asia's largest economy. However, some historical aspects of China's development are addressed earlier, because they can only be fitted into the broader history of east Asian development. The Communist Party of China's land reform campaign and early household farming strategy, followed by its switch to agricultural collectivisation, are dealt with in part 1. The post-1978 agricultural story is picked up again in part 4. China's industrial policy strategy prior to 1949 is dealt with part 2, because it connects directly with Taiwan's later experience via the flight of the Kuomintang and various senior planning officials to the island at the end of the Chinese civil war. Mainland China's separate industrialisation story after 1949 is discussed in part 4. Almost all aspects of China's finance policy story are dealt with in part 4 alone.

## In the background

In terms of influences on economic development that are not directly addressed by the policy focus on agriculture, manufacturing and finance in this book, the most important is probably demographics. The size and age profile of a country's population has a huge impact on its developmental potential. Labour is an input into an economy – a form of 'capital' – just like money, and a large working-age population relative to the cohorts of children and retired people increases the possibilities for fast growth. Rapidly declining death rates – particularly for children – and rapidly rising working-age populations have been a big part of the east Asian developmental story since the Second World War. These demographic trends, largely the result of advances in medicine and sanitation, have facilitated unprecedented growth. The phenomenon is sometimes referred to as the 'demographic dividend'. The flip side of this dividend is that it is followed by the faster ageing of populations – by which we really mean the increase of retired people relative to workers. After a tipping point, workforces start to shrink quickly, and older people consume their savings, devouring what were previously funds for investment. Japan's problems since the 1980s have been bound up with acute demographic challenges in an only recently matured industrial economy. In China, the very fast growth of the working-age population that accompanied economic take-off is peaking already, and the country's demographic headwinds will slowly increase this decade.

Demographics are important. However, a certain demographic profile has been part and parcel of the developmental experience of all east Asian states. In this sense the demographic story is a given. The only attempt to manage demographics as an element of economic policy occurred in China, but this has not been a major determinant of that country's performance. Mao Zedong proselytised a baby boom that was already occurring, telling Chinese people there was strength in numbers. Then Deng Xiaoping and his successors put the brakes on the birth rate, which was already slowing, with an often brutally enforced policy to limit child-bearing. Yet despite the misery induced by these *Brave New World*-style interventions, China's developmental performance has been shaped by the same policy choices in agriculture, manufacturing and finance that have made the difference elsewhere. In the end the size of your working-age population is still less important to your developmental progress than what you do with that population.

The other influence on development that is given only a background role in this book is education. Here, the reason is that the evidence of a positive correlation between total years of education and GDP growth is much weaker than most people imagine.[11] The strongest evidence globally concerns primary schooling, but even with respect to that formative period of education when people learn basic literacy and numeracy skills there are states like South Korea and Taiwan that took off economically with educational capital that was well below average. Fifty-five per cent of Taiwanese were illiterate at the end of the Second World War; the figure was still 45 per cent in 1960. Literacy in South Korea in 1950 was lower than in contemporary Ethiopia. It may be that, more than education leading to economic progress, economic progress leads families to educate their children, which in turn makes more economic progress possible.

In the Philippines, the US colonial government placed great emphasis on investment in schooling in the early twentieth century. Even today the Philippines has the highest level of tertiary-educated students in south-east Asia. But because more important policy choices were flunked, the country is on the cusp of being a failed state. Looking further afield, Cuba has the world's second-highest literacy rate for children over age fifteen, and the sixth highest rate of school enrolment. Education has been a top priority there since the revolution in 1960. Yet the country ranks only ninety-fifth in GDP per capita in the world. Cuba has a surfeit of university graduates and inadequate employment opportunities for them – one reason why 25,000 Cuban physicians undertake state-subsidised work overseas.[12] In the former Soviet Union, too, output of highly trained personnel was never matched by economic development.

There are two, related explanations for the patchy connection between education and economic growth. The one heard about most often is that, from a developmental perspective, there is too much education of the wrong kind. In east Asia there exists a marked contrast between the emphasis on vocational training of secondary and tertiary level students in Japan, Korea, Taiwan and China, versus the less trades-focused education systems of former European and US colonial states in south-east Asia. The engineering qualification of a Taiwanese student may be more appropriate to the initial task of economic advancement than the accountancy qualification of the Malaysian student. By the late 1980s, vocational training (mostly focused on manufacturing) constituted 55 per cent of tertiary education in Taiwan, while less than 10 per cent of students were taking humanities subjects. In the 1980s, relative to population, Taiwan had 70 per cent more engineers than the US.[13] Like Korea and Japan, which established the model in east Asia, the Taiwanese education system came to resemble those of the manufacturing-based economies of Germany and Italy in Europe. South-east Asian states, in the Anglo-Saxon tradition, placed more emphasis on the humanities and on 'pure science'.

A shortfall of vocational training and engineers, however, cannot be more than a tiny part of the explanation for the laggardly performances of south-east Asian states and others with educational profiles like them. To begin with, in north-east Asia most of the engineers were trained after fast growth took off. The early success of Meiji Japan was achieved with surprisingly few engineers – the country only began to step up its vocational and scientific and technical education in the 1930s.[14] In countries like Cuba and Russia, by contrast, vast numbers of engineers have been churned out without positive results. All this points to the second, and almost certainly more important, reason why data about formal education and development do not jibe well. It is that a lot of critical learning in the most successful developing countries takes place outside the formal education sector. It occurs, instead, inside firms.

This intra-firm learning helps explain the relative failure of the former Soviet Union and its satellites, where investment in education and research was focused on elite universities and state research institutions rather than inside businesses. The situation has been not too dissimilar in south-east Asia, which combined the Anglo-Saxon tradition of elitist tertiary education with a major post-independence expansion of public sector research institutions. In Japan, Korea, Taiwan and post-1978 China, by contrast, a lot of highly effective educational investment and research has been concentrated not in the formal education sector but within companies, and by definition – unlike the Soviet situation – within companies that are competing internationally. This may be critical to the rapid acquisition of technological capacity. As the Japanese scholar Masayuki Kondo put it when describing Malaysia's failure to develop indigenous technological capacity despite a lot of investment in higher education and research: 'The main context for industrial technology development is firms, not public institutions.'[15] Technology policy, not science policy, is the key to the early stages of industrial development. As a result, a government's industrial strategy is the most powerful determinant of success. If a state does not force the creation of firms that can be the vehicles for industrial learning – and then nurture them – all efforts at formal education may go to waste. The only caveat is that once a country reaches the 'technological frontier' in manufacturing, its optimal educational mix –and the relationship between institutions of formal education and learning within firms – changes. But that is not the focus of this book. Here we are concerned with what gets you into the rich man's club in the first place.

## Not part of the package

Demographics and 'learning', then, are woven into the fabric of this book as and when necessary and appropriate. Three other considerations which are frequently deemed to affect economic development, however, are left out.

The first is political pluralism and democracy. There are those who try to construct a compelling case that democracy either prevents – or makes possible – economic development. It is hard to see any very clear pattern in east Asia. At a national level, nineteenth-century Japan followed a slow but steady course towards a more democratic political structure and an increasing franchise, and initiated the region's first – and, until the Second World War, sole – successful modernisation programme. Only during the global depression of the 1920s, and under considerable racist pressure from the 'white' powers, did the political system descend into chaos and, later, military dictatorship. In South Korea and Taiwan, by contrast, many people point to the authoritarian success of generals Park Chung Hee and Chiang Kai-shek respectively. But they conveniently forget the authoritarian disaster of Chiang Kai-shek in mainland China before 1949 under a different set of economic policies. In south-east Asia, in Indonesia after the Second World War, Sukarno ran a chaotic democratic administration before switching to authoritarian 'guided democracy' with even more chaos. Suharto took over in a military coup, and brought greater stability and development under authoritarianism, but his family ended up plundering the country. In the Philippines, a democratically elected Ferdinand

Marcos announced in 1972 that he needed martial law in order to make vital reforms that would expedite development, and then went on to set a new standard of plunder.

At a micro, sub-national level it is equally difficult to find a consistent correlation between either authoritarianism or democracy on the one hand, and policies required to promote economic development on the other. There are moments, as with General Park Chung Hee's temporary imprisonment of business leaders and re-nationalisation of the Korean banking system in 1961, when actions of an extremely authoritarian nature have produced clear dividends. But there are also policy interventions where a democratic approach has been essential. In communist-controlled areas of China in the mid and late 1940s, the success of land reform was bound up with elected village committees whose functioning was in stark contrast to the authoritarianism we associate with China today. Likewise, the representative – usually elected – land reform committees employed in Japan and Taiwan were vital to their unprecedented success.[16] South Korea's more centralised, authoritarian land reform was less effective. And in southeast Asia an absence of democratic process was a hallmark of the abject failure of land reform attempts by states in that region. Democracy and authoritarianism, in sum, have not been consistent explanatory variables of economic development in east Asia.

Perhaps most important, it is hard to ignore the reasoning – associated with, among others, the Indian Nobel Prize-winning economist Amartya Sen – that the question of whether democracy encourages or retards development is based on a false distinction. Democracy and institutional development are *part of* development and so are not to be judged as drivers of it. After living in China and Italy – states where institutional development has trailed economic development with a considerable lag – I believe this not only intellectually but based on twenty years of personal experience. The miseries visited on ordinary people by a lack of attention to institutional progress deserve attention in their own right. Economic development is the subject of this book, but economic development alone is not a recipe for human happiness.

Another lately fashionable institution – 'rule of law' – belongs in the same category as democracy in being a part of development rather than a prerequisite of economic progress. In recent years Western governments and academics – British and American, in particular – have tried desperately to persuade the Communist Party of China that rule of law is a critical requirement of economic development. They have not been successful in this, mainly because evidence for the argument in east Asia has been distinctly mixed – and China has been the source of much of the negative evidence. As the Chinese economy developed after 1978, its government left questions of property rights deliberately opaque, and gave legal sanction to many activities only after they occurred. The outcomes of important legal cases continue to be decided in advance by Political and Legal Affairs Committees of the Communist Party. Yet China has boomed. In South Korea, the courts, the police and the secret police did the bidding of big business in intimidating, beating and imprisoning union leaders and other labour activists into the 1990s (not wholly different, it must be said, from what happened in the late nineteenth century in the United States or, a little earlier, in Britain). On the other hand, there have been somewhat better legal protections in Japan, which is the region's greatest economic success story. And in the Philippines and Indonesia, where court verdicts often go to the highest bidder, an absence of rule of law has been associated with weaker economic performance. As with democracy, it is better to admit that the rule of law is not a principal driver of economic development, but rather is an integral part of overall development. We should expect developing countries to pursue both.

Finally, there is the old chestnut that geography and climate are major determinants of economic development. There is no shortage of people who believe that geographical south-east Asia is relatively backward simply because it is 'too hot' or that north-east Asia is in the vanguard because, like northern Europe, it enjoys a temperate climate. Confronted with such prejudices I find myself imagining a bar-room commentator in the early eighth century who, noting that the Arab ascendancy of that era was based in what is today Iraq and north Africa, and that the magnificent Tang dynasty operated out of boiling hot Xi'an, announced that Europeans, north Americans, Japanese and Koreans would always be backward because their climates were too cold. The case for geography and climate as key drivers of economic development is given little succour by what follows.

Despite a very real tendency of countries to copy their neighbours, geography fits sufficiently poorly with economic success and failure in east Asia that it has had to be treated with considerable licence in this book. Taiwan, which is a three-and-a-half hour flight south of Tokyo, enjoys a subtropical climate, but is placed in this book's north-east Asia group. Equally, Vietnam is geographically just as much south-east Asian as Thailand or Malaysia, but I would group it with China. It is only the very loose geographic economic convergence of two different parts of east Asia that allows believers in geographic pre-destination to argue that there is 'nothing to be done'.

This book indicates that there is plenty to be done. It focuses down on the three areas of policy choice where political decisions make the biggest difference to developmental outcomes. What follows is not a set of detailed policy recommendations because the conditions of each country vary. But it does claim a degree of historical accuracy in describing what happened in east Asia. That history reminds us that, however fleetingly, the developmental destiny of a nation is in its government's hands.

# Part I

# Land: The Triumph of Gardening

*'I am the son of peasants and I know what is happening in the villages. That is why I wanted to take revenge, and I regret nothing.'*

Gavrilo Princip, assassin of Archduke Franz Ferdinand of Austria[1]

Why should land policy be so important to development? The simple answer is that in a country in the early stages of development, typically three-quarters of the population is employed in agriculture and lives on the land. East Asia after the Second World War was no exception. Even in Japan, which began its development in the 1870s with a three-quarters rural population, almost half the workforce was still farm-based at the start of the war. With most resources concentrated in agriculture, the sector offers poor countries the most immediate opportunity to increase their economic output.

The problem with agriculture in pre-industrial states with rising populations, however, is that when market forces are left to themselves agricultural yields tend to stagnate or even fall. This happens because demand for land increases faster than supply, and so landlords lease out land at increasing rents. They also act as money lenders at high rates of interest. Tenants, facing stiff rents and expensive debts and with little security of tenure, are unable to make the investments – for instance, in improving irrigation or buying fertiliser – that will increase yields on the land they farm. Landlords could make the investments to increase yields, but they make money more easily by exacting the highest possible rents and by usury, which adds to their land holdings when debts cannot be paid and they take over plots that have been pledged as collateral. A situation arises where 'the market' fails to maximise output. At the time of the Second World War, this scenario was present – in varying degrees – everywhere in east Asia, from Japan to China to Indonesia.

In conditions of a growing population, low security of tenure and no restrictions on the charging of interest, a market in land arises in which concentration of ownership trumps improvement of yields as the easiest source of income for land owners. The problem has plagued agriculture in poor countries around the world. What is different in some states in east Asia is that after the Second World War they made radical changes to land distribution and structured a different kind of agricultural market. It was a rural

3

arrangement in which market forces tended to maximise output. There has
been no equivalent policy change of such magnitude and effect anywhere else.

The vehicle for the change was a series of land reform programmes undertaken in China, Japan, Korea and Taiwan. Although the first was orchestrated
by communists, and the second, third and fourth by anti-communists, the
objective was the same in all cases. It was, roughly speaking, to take available
agricultural land and to divide it up on an equal basis (once variation in land
quality was allowed for) among the farming population. This, backed by
government support for rural credit and marketing institutions, agronomic
training and other support services, created a new type of market. It was a
market in which owners of small household farms were incentivised to invest
their labour and the surplus they generated towards maximising production.
The result was hugely increased yields in all four countries.

Output booms occurred in conditions in which farming was essentially a
form of large-scale gardening. Families of five, six or seven people tended plots
of not more than one hectare. To most economists, theory dictates that such
an arrangement must be inefficient. So-called 'free marketers' and Marxists
are united in insisting that scale is fundamental to efficiency. For Marxists
in China, North Korea, Vietnam (and Russia before them) this – fatally for
millions of people – meant switching household farming to large collectives.

In reality, the question of efficiency depends on what outcome you are
looking for. Big capitalist farms may produce the highest return on cash
invested. But that is not the agricultural 'efficiency' that is appropriate to a
developing state. At an early stage, a poor country with a surfeit of labour
is better served by maximising its crop production until the return on
any more labour falls to zero. Put another way, you might as well use the
labour you have – even if the return per man hour looks terribly low on
paper – because that is the only use you have for your workers. A gardening approach delivers the maximum crop output, as any gardener knows.

**Try this at home**

Fruit and vegetable gardeners will tell you (indeed they may already have
done, at length) just how much you can produce on a tiny plot of land if you
put your mind to it. What they omit to mention is the grotesque amount of

labour involved. The techniques that maximise output in a backyard garden of a hundred square metres are also broadly those that will maximise yields on a small family farm of 10,000 square metres (one hectare, or 2.47 acres).

The list of time-consuming interventions is almost endless. One of the most effective is to start off seeds in trays indoors so that they are only put in the ground for the more rapid maturation process. Soil-bed temperature also greatly affects yields and can be regulated by using raised beds in temperate climates or pits in tropical climates. Compost is most effective when applied with diligence – high-yield fruit and vegetable gardeners deploy fertiliser on a plant-by-plant basis. Targeted watering (taller plants, for instance, tend to need more) and constant weeding also have a big effect on crop size.[2] The most productive plots utilise an almost solid leaf canopy because close planting minimises water loss and discourages weeds; but this rules out access for machines. The use of trellises, nets, strings and poles – all set up by hand – maximises yields through 'vertical' gardening; a single tomato plant can produce 20 kg of fruit. Inter-growing of plants with different maturities saves more space (the *cognoscenti* place radishes and carrots in the same furrow because the radishes mature before the carrots begin to crowd them out; but then the radishes can only be harvested by hand). Equally, shade-tolerant vegetables like spinach or celery can be raised in the shadows of taller plants to ensure that no space is wasted; but again, this must be done by hand.

The world of the home fruit and vegetable gardener – including that of the contemporary, rich-world family growing its own organic produce – is very familiar to the post-war east Asian peasant family with its mini-farm. Of course each person in the Asian family tends an area of soil thirty or more times greater than that of the hobby kitchen gardener. But the logic of the labour-intensive gardening approach to cultivation is the same wherever you do it: it gets more out of a given plot of land than anything else.

In the United States, as one example, well-managed vegetable gardens yield 5–10kg of food per square metre (1–2lbs per square foot) per year, which equates to USD11–22 per square metre at shop prices. In 2009 Roger Doiron, a blogger for the popular website Kitchen Gardeners International, weighed and checked the retail prices of all 380kg of the fruit and vegetables that his 160-square-metre kitchen garden produced; the garden's retail value was USD16.50 per square metre. That meant a total value from his plot of USD2,200 – equivalent to USD135,000 per hectare (USD55,000 per acre). As a very loose benchmark, the *wholesale* price of the US's most common and successful crop from large-scale farming, corn, equated to USD2,500 per hectare in 2010.[3]

So why doesn't everyone do it? The problem is that the gardening level of output needs so much labour. If Mr Doiron gardened full time, he might be able to maintain his yields for 1,000 square metres of land. But that would still require ten Mr Doirons to earn USD135,000 across one hectare before costs. Consequently, American farmers are sensible and use big tractors to grow corn on farms that average 170 hectares. Indeed, the agglomeration of US farms, which started out – except in the southern plantation belt – as much smaller units in the early nineteenth century when the country was opened up by immigrants, is the story of gradually rising labour costs and the consequent pressure for mechanisation over two centuries.

After the Second World War, China and the north-east Asian states were countries in which agricultural labour was far more abundant than in nineteenth-century America, and about to become more abundant because of rapidly rising populations. These countries were ready-made for high-output gardening. In Taiwan, for instance, surveys before and after the shift to equalised household farms showed that there was an increase of more than 50 per cent in the work days invested in each hectare of land after the shift.[4] Although the island continued to produce large volumes of rice and sugar, its new boom crops of the 1950s and early 1960s were asparagus and mushrooms – two of the most labour-intensive crops there are. Taiwan, the most successful agricultural development story in the whole of Asia, really is a story that vegetable gardeners can relate to.

Some economists – again, principally dogmatic free marketers and Marxists – argue that even if small-scale household farming can sometimes work, then its principles do not apply to 'cash crops' grown on plantations in some parts of Asia, such as sugar, bananas, rubber and palm oil. It is certainly true that the plants involved require different types of nurture to household vegetables or subsistence crops like corn and rice. Sugar cane, for instance, takes almost a year to grow to maturity and benefits from deep ploughing that can only be done by a tractor. It seems plausible that this kind of crop should be grown on larger, more mechanised plantations. Yet, the sugar yield on small household farms in Taiwan or China has traditionally been 50 per cent more than on pre- or post-colonial plantations in the Philippines or Indonesia.[5] From the 1960s, Taiwan's household farmers were also more successful on the world banana market than those from Asian plantation economies. In colonial Malaysia, surveys of natural rubber production revealed in the 1920s that the yields of smallholders were far higher than those of plantations. Most agronomic requirements which suggest a need for large farms can, on inspection, be overcome quite easily – for instance, by leasing a tractor or sharing one through a co-operative in order to plough sugar land or replant rubber trees. It is striking that in so many countries in both Asia and Africa, such as Malaysia, Kenya and Zimbabwe, where European colonists introduced large-scale agriculture, they actively discouraged smallholder competition by native farmers and subsidised large-scale production, either directly or more indirectly, by funnelling tax revenues to infrastructure that supported plantations.[6] If scale plantation agriculture was so efficient, this should not have been necessary.

The arguments about the efficiency of small-scale farms are not without their complexities. The very high yields achieved in Japan, Korea, Taiwan and China are not simply the outcome of farm size, but of farm size combined with complicated infrastructures that have been set up to deliver inputs like fertilisers and seeds, and to facilitate storage, marketing and sales. Without adequate supporting infrastructure, small farms struggle anywhere, as has been the case after failed land reform attempts in places like the Philippines. It is impossible to say with absolute certainty that radical land reform would have produced the stunning yield increases it facilitated in north-east Asia for every country and every crop grown in east Asia. However, the evidence of what occurred in China, Japan, Korea and Taiwan is powerful: good land policy, centred on egalitarian household farming, set up the world's most impressive post-war development stories.

**The merits of abundance**

In the first ten to fifteen years following the shift to small-scale household agriculture in successful east Asian states, gross output of foodstuffs increased by somewhere between half (in Japan, which was already the most productive country) and three-quarters (Taiwan). Increases in agricultural output are traditionally represented as important by economists because they lead to increased surplus, which implies more savings which can then be used to finance industrial investment.[7]

However, big yield gains also mean big increases in rural consumption – something that may be even more important when farmers create demand for consumer goods. Famous east Asian corporations from Meiji Japan to post-war Korea and contemporary China made their first millions adapting products to the exigencies of extensive but cash-limited rural markets. Local firms learned critical lessons about marketing from rural populations with whom they had a natural cultural affinity. Examples from Japan include Toyota and Nissan building robust cars for unpaved roads on small truck chassis after the Second World War, or Honda's early 50cc engines being used to convert cycles into motorcycles. More recently, in China, firms have grown to scale through rural markets for rooftop solar water heaters and cut-price mobile phone systems that use existing fixed-line infrastructure.[8]

A third way of thinking about the benefits of agricultural output maximisation is from the perspective of foreign trade. States beginning their economic development never have enough foreign exchange, and one of the easiest ways to fritter it away is to spend more than is necessary on imported food. This erodes a country's capacity to import the technology – usually, machines for making things – that is essential to development and learning. For instance, although poorly understood at the time, a large part of what undermined Latin America's efforts to industrialise after the Second World War was that the region proved itself much better at increasing manufacturing exports than at increasing agricultural output. As a result, as incomes rose and people ate more food – including meat, which is more land-intensive to produce than vegetable crops – different Latin American countries either reduced their agricultural exports or increased their agricultural imports. Either way, the net effect was that agriculture tended to bleed away any foreign exchange that industrial exports (or reduced imports) created. Latin America was undone in the 1950s, 1960s and 1970s by a developmental strategy characterised by what the economist Michael Lipton dubbed 'urban bias', or the tendency of the urban elites that run poor countries to undervalue farmers.[9] Like most developing countries – there are strong echoes of this scenario in south-east Asia today – Latin American states paid far too little attention to agriculture. This wasn't just bad for farmers, it was bad for development overall.[10]

Finally, household farms play a vital, and much under-remarked, welfare role. Poor countries do not offer unemployment benefits or other welfare payments. In periods of economic downturn, the opportunity for laid-off migrant factory workers to return to their family farms is therefore of great importance. In Taiwan, an estimated 200,000 factory workers returned to farming during the first oil crisis in the mid 1970s; similar, temporary de-migrations have occurred in slack periods in recent years in China.[11] Asian countries where land reform has worked have avoided the legions of indigent poor or acres of squatter camps that have characterised nations with larger scale farming, ranging from eighteenth-century Britain to the contemporary Philippines.

North-east Asian states gave themselves the best possible start in their economic development by the attention they paid to agriculture. However, the impetus to development was greater still because of the means by which maximisation of agricultural output was achieved. By giving rural families equal amounts of land to farm, governments created conditions of almost perfect, laboratory-like competition. This was the kind of competition involving large numbers, no barriers to entry and freely available information about which mathematical economists fantasise (and at which many other people scoff because it occurs so rarely). But in this case conditions akin to those assumed by textbook economics were indeed created.

Every family had its bit of capital – its land – along with the ability to access technical support, credit and markets, and so competed on a remarkably equal basis with its neighbour. In the United States, American government support for land reform in Japan, Korea and Taiwan was attacked domestically in the 1950s as socialism by the back door. But it was quite the opposite. It represented the creation in north-east Asia of the most idealised capitalist free market ever established for developing economies. For once, there were no landlords born with silver spoons in their mouths and (almost) no landless peasants without capital; everyone was given the chance to compete.

Klaus Deininger, one of the world's leading authorities on land policy and development, has spent decades assembling data that show how the nature of land distribution in poor countries predicts future economic performance. Using global land surveys done by the United Nations' Food and Agriculture Organisation (FAO), he has worked out that only one significant developing country has managed a long-term growth rate of over 2.5 per cent with a very unequal distribution of land. That country is Brazil, the false prophet of fast growth which collapsed in a debt crisis in the 1980s in large part because of its failure to increase agricultural output. Deininger's two big conclusions are that land inequality leads to low long-term growth and that low growth reduces income for the poor but not for the rich.[12]

In short, if poor countries are to become rich, then the equitable division of land at the outset of development is a huge help. Japan, Korea and Taiwan put this in place. The problem for most countries, however, in practice is that efforts to create an equitable distribution of land, and an equitable supply of resources to support the land, usually fail. To understand why this is the case – as well as the extraordinary examples of land reform success in north-east Asia – we must look more closely at the history of land policy.

**A very old idea**

The most advanced ancient Asian states used 'reformed' land systems more than a thousand years ago. As the world's most sophisticated civilisation in the seventh and eighth centuries, Tang dynasty China operated an agricultural bureaucracy which allocated and rotated household farming plots among families to ensure fair access to natural resources, while the ownership of most land was retained by the state. By contemporary standards, yields were very high.[13] What is called the Taika Reform in seventh-century Japan attempted to copy Tang land policy, but with more limited – and declining – success. Elites in both countries resisted interventions based on fair play, even if they led to higher yields. It was an attempt by China's Song dynasty, which followed Tang, to re-nationalise some farmland in the thirteenth century that convinced many aristocrats to throw in their lot with Kublai Khan and the Mongol invaders when they overran the country.

Modern land reform in north-east Asia has been based on the rediscovery in Meiji Japan of the wisdom of an earlier era. The process began with the overthrow of the Tokugawa shogunate and the formation of a progressive Japanese government under the restored emperor in 1868. Although land in Japan technically still belonged to the state, the system had long since ceased to deliver any kind of protection or equity to ordinary farmers. Instead, quasi-feudal lords known as *daimyo* (literally 'big land') operated vast estates farmed by smallholders who were, in effect, their serf tenants. The *daimyo* also controlled the grain-trading system, and hence were in a position to rig the market.

In its most important early reform, the Meiji administration pensioned off the *daimyo* (generously), gave them seats in Japan's new House of Peers in Tokyo, and gave small farmers title to their lands. One hundred and nine million certificates of ownership were issued in three years. For the first time, land could be mortgaged and sold legally. Taxes were also fixed in cash terms, so farmers kept more of the income from higher yields rather than splitting their physical crop with their landlords through sharecropping. As a result, farmers were incentivised to invest in their land while more liquid markets for crops came into being. The Meiji leadership squeezed farmers quite hard, obtaining a peak of four-fifths of its revenues from land tax in the late nineteenth century, but the tax squeeze was no harder – and probably a little less hard – than under the shogunate.[14]

Overall, these changes produced a spurt in yields and output that ran from the Meiji restoration until around the time of the First World War. Japan's production of rice – its staple food – roughly doubled, a little ahead of a rapidly increasing population. As the industrial economy took off, there was no need to import food.[15] And not only did agriculture feed more mouths, it also supplied the leading export (and hence foreign exchange earner) of Japan's early development era – silk, produced by worms that were fed on mulberry leaves from trees that were planted on the most marginal, hilly agricultural land.

The central government hired American specialists to introduce new farming techniques, and supported the construction of a national network of training services – or what agronomists call 'extension'. The spread of fertiliser use and higher-yield rice varieties was an important driver of output growth. In addition, by the time of the First World War, Japan had brought into cultivation pretty much every acre of cultivable land, including many plots that were converted to farming through considerable investment in clearing, terracing, irrigation and so forth.

Prior to this, no country had begun a period of industrialisation with such an overwhelmingly rural population. The populations of rich European and north American countries were at least 35 per cent urban before industrialisation took off.[16] However, by throwing off feudalism in short order, switching to private smallholder agriculture and mobilising an impressive level of national bureaucratic support, Japan was able to begin industrialisation despite having a three-quarters rural populace. In turn agriculture undergirded what was already becoming, at the start of the twentieth century, the most rapid economic transformation the world had seen. The pace of development in Germany and the United States was put in the shade by Japan. In just three decades after the Meiji restoration, Japanese modernisation was such that the country could defeat China (1895) and Russia (1905) in wars, be welcomed into a bilateral military alliance by Great Britain (1902), and begin to export its goods around the world. None of this could have occurred without the food, taxes and foreign exchange supplied by the countryside. The Meiji government discovered the developmental trick encapsulated in Michael Lipton's dictum as: 'If you wish for industrialisation, prepare to develop agriculture.'[17]

## Not yet perfect

Despite this early success, the rural reforms of the Meiji government were limited in their scope. Although the more feudal, absentee, large-scale landlord was swept away and small farmers were given private title, within farming communities considerable variation in landholding remained. In the context of a rising population and limited finance and marketing support, there was always the risk that returns from renting out land and lending money would again outstrip returns from investing in order to increase yields.

This, gradually, is what happened. The data are not clear enough to establish a precise chronology, but there was a tipping point around the time of the First World War. The supply of new agricultural land stopped growing, while population continued to increase. At the same time, the so-called 'terms of trade' between agriculture and manufacturing – what a unit of agricultural output could buy in terms of manufactures or vice versa – began to favour manufacturing, where in the early reform era farmers had done better. This made life relatively more expensive for the rural population. And whereas early industrial development provided lots of extra income for female members of farm families through work in textile factories in rural towns, most new jobs after the First World War were created in larger-scale industry in cities.

In a country where, between the world wars, there was an average of just 1.1 hectares of cultivable land per farm household, these cumulative changes began to tell in the lives of those families that held a little less land or had fewer able-bodied members. There was an increase in money-lending to those who could not make ends meet, and when debts could not be repaid, land was forfeited. There were few really big landlords – even in 1940, less than 100,000 of 1.7 million Japanese landlords held more than five hectares.[18] It was small-time landlordism by attrition – adding a few *tan* (0.01 hectares) every year or two at the expense of some less fortunate villager. Those with too little land, or rented land, or both, often had to sell their crops as soon as they were harvested, when the market was flooded and prices were low. Landlords stored their rice, and sold it later for better prices, before offering money at interest to those who sold early and now had no money left. Between the world wars, farmer debt in Japan rose eight-fold.[19]

Tenanted land as a share of all cultivated land was around 20 per cent in the first years after the Meiji government instituted its land reform. By the time of the Second World War, almost half of arable land was under tenancy and 70 per cent of Japanese farmers rented some or all of their fields. Despite the global depression, tenant rents did not fall below 50–60 per cent of crops (and this was after the renter had paid the cost of seeds, fertiliser, implements and all taxes and levies bar the main land tax). It was hardly surprising that output stopped rising in the 1920s. A senior official at the Ministry of Agriculture noted in 1928: 'There is a great difference between the productivity of owner-farmer land and that of tenanted land. My officials who go out into the villages tell me that even they – men who have never used a plough in their lives – can tell at a glance by the look of the crop whether the land is farmed by an owner or by a tenant.'[20] It was in this context that in the 1930s the Japanese military pitched itself as the champion of the downtrodden rural populace, recruiting its most fervent supporters from farming communities. Japanese agriculture swung back from post-feudal abundance to brutal conditions of rural capitalist exploitation.

### Journey 1: Tokyo to Niigata

*You can begin to understand much about Japan's agricultural history simply by driving around, because that history is so heavily dependent on topography. A journey from Tokyo north-west across the main island of Honshu to Niigata prefecture, producer of the country's finest rice, highlights the basic challenges.*

First, however, you must exit from Tokyo's urban sprawl. The capital, with its silent, strange residential suburbs, its little lanes and its religiously maintained road markings, ends only in theory. In practice it merges into a series of other, less prosperous towns in a seamless continuum of low-rise clapboard houses, malls, discount stores, fast-food restaurants and car showrooms. Not only has Japan developed with an impossibly small supply of cultivable land per capita, but large swathes of that land have been relentlessly gobbled up by its urban and industrial development. This trend has long been exacerbated by a cultural aversion to high-rise building. The insistence on low-rise, sadly, has done nothing to make modern Japanese construction more attractive.

Avoiding expressways, it is a 40-kilometre, two- to three-hour grind through spirit-sapping urban sprawl, past the vast American Yokota air base, before you see anything remotely rural to the north-west of Tokyo. What happens is that eventually the hills become too steep to build on or, indeed, to farm. And that is the reason why Japan has so little cultivable land – the country is covered in hills and mountains, which in turn are covered in forests. Inside a car, the smell of pine trees announces the ascent. Japan has a lower cultivable land share than any country in east Asia – just 14 per cent of its total area. Even Korea is 20 per cent cultivable, while Taiwan is 25 per cent.[21]

Entering the forest north-west of Tokyo, highway 299 winds up through the hills until it reaches Chichibu, a sleepy, nondescript town with no definable centre. Chichibu's name is synonymous in Japan with the largest farmer rebellion of the Meiji era, put down by state police and troops in 1884. As in other marginal rural areas, the farmers here had little to farm. Forested hills rise steeply on every side. There are a few fields along tiny local rivers and streams, the possibility of some mulberry orchards on steeper slopes. A sharp, temporary drop in agricultural prices in the early 1880s – as the government battled an early bout of inflation – left the people of the area close to starvation. Several thousand poorly armed men took a desperate swipe at authority. The leaders were hanged, and hundreds more convicted of felonies. North of Chichibu, at Minano, a side road drops away past old corrugated metal shacks and crosses a railway line; at the bottom of the road is a reconstructed shrine, where the farmers assembled.[22]

North of Chichibu and Minano, the Kan-Etsu expressway now tunnels its way under the peaks of central Honshu. Speeding along this highway, the pattern you will notice is that whenever a flattish area occurs among the hills and mountains and forest, it is filled to bursting with urban and industrial construction. This recurs for well over a hundred kilometres as the expressway snakes its way north-north-west towards Niigata and Honshu's western shore. Only when the road descends to a suddenly much broader stretch of the Shinano river – at a town called Ojiya – does the coastal delta begin and the scenery change. This is just thirty kilometres from the Sea of Japan.

Suddenly, everything bar essential human structures is rice paddy. Packed in between the mountains and the sea is the rice basket of Japan's most populous island. The Shinano river delta is much the biggest area of cultivable land around the city of Niigata; elsewhere, paddy is pinned into a coastal strip a few kilometres wide. In the Meiji era, the Niigata prefecture was itself one of the most populous in the country, initially providing the labour to produce large yield increases, then later the surplus population to make conditions ripe for increased tenancy and high-rent landlordism. Today what you see are the houses that farmers have built for themselves in the past fifty years, after the deeper, post-Second World War land reform: concrete structures with ersatz, mock-vernacular tiled roofs, double glazing and even – when kitsch breaks completely loose – brown, 'wood-look', plastic cladding.

Nestled at the edge of one village, however, there remains one of the few fully preserved historical relics of life in pre-war rural Japan. The home of the Ito family is an extreme example of what was a tale of rising, near-ubiquitous petty landlordism in the run-up to Japan's second round of land reform. Indeed, the house is preserved as an exaggerated reminder of the bad old days. It is now a museum to rural exploitation. The Itos, through high rents and money-lending, became some of the biggest landlords in Japan. Their lands multiplied in the late nineteenth and early twentieth centuries until by the 1920s they owned 1,370 hectares of paddy and another 1,000 hectares of forest. They had 2,800 tenants. The family were not typical landlords, but they were typical of the trend towards ever greater landlordism. Their former home occupies a 3-hectare site – the size of two average Japanese family farms today – and contains sixty rooms.[23]

Compared with the average European castle or stately home, the house at first appears to involve a less aggressive statement of power. Its 'walking' garden, rice warehouse (with inscribed *haiku* poem), tea pavilions and reception rooms that look on to an ornamental, koi-filled stream, a becalming, susurrant waterfall and an exquisitely crafted, enclosed garden all seem to point, aesthetically, to some higher form of landlordism. How could anyone with such sublime taste be putting the squeeze on anyone? Yet, on inspection, the tell-tale signs are there: reception rooms of different levels of grandeur for receiving persons of different ranks; entrances of different types through which persons of a given rank must pass; pile after pile of beautifully inscribed and annotated tenant ledgers and loan books. The Ito family employed around eighty manager go-betweens – known as *banto* – to oversee their tenants. Like the big landlords of today's southeast Asia, they never had to deal with their tenants direct and any requests, such as for rent reductions, were passed up through a hierarchical chain. The beauty of the property is breathtaking, but it does not reflect any softness of human relations. The Ito home, built around 1885 on the family's revenues from its ever-expanding roster of tenants, is in fact a monument to the agricultural market failure that slowly asphyxiated liberal, reformist Japan and helped pave the way for the country's military dictatorship. In the end, Japan's halfway house land reform crumbled.

## Chinese Communists take the lead

The Itos would lose their estates, along with their home, in 1946 when Japan implemented a more permanent revolution in agricultural relations. Before that, however, it was the Chinese communists who began to claim the role of vanguard in Asian rural reform. If Japan in the early twentieth century was a place where farmers faced a return to the hardships they had temporarily escaped under the Meiji reforms, China was a place where ordinary farmers had known nothing but the cruellest suffering for centuries.

In the 1920s, when 85 per cent of Chinese people lived in the countryside, life expectancy at birth for rural dwellers was 20–25 years. Three-quarters of farming families had plots of less than one hectare, while perhaps one-tenth of the population owned seven-tenths of the cultivable land. As in Japan, there were few really big landlords, but there was sufficient inequality of land distribution and easily enough population pressure to induce high-rent tenancy and stagnant output. A rather typical landlord of the era was Deng Wenming, father of future Chinese leader Deng Xiaoping, who owned ten hectares in Paifang village in the hinterland of Chongqing in Sichuan province. Deng Wenming lived in a 22-room house on the edge of his village and leased out two-thirds of his fields. He, like so many other landlords, was not a man of limitless wealth. But he controlled the land of more than half a dozen average families.[24]

R.H. Tawney, the British economic historian, wrote after a visit to China in the late 1920s that the precariousness of Chinese agriculture was such that: 'There are districts in which the position of the rural population is that of a man standing permanently up to the neck in water, so that even a ripple is sufficient to drown him ... An eminent Chinese official stated that in Shanxi province at the beginning of 1931, three million persons had died of hunger in the last few years, and the misery had been such that 400,000 women and children had changed hands by sale.'[25]

It was William Hinton, an American Marxist writer conducting research in the 1940s, who produced the classic outsider-insider's tale of life in a Chinese farming village, one that was also located in Shanxi province. Hinton wrote about the mundane realities of death by starvation during the annual 'spring hunger' when food reserves ran out, and of the slavery (mostly of girls), landlord violence, domestic violence, usury, endemic mafia-style secret societies and other assorted brutalities that characterised everyday life. One of the most striking aspects was the attention paid to faeces, the key fertiliser. Children and old people constantly scoured public areas for animal droppings. Landlords demanded that day labourers defecate only in their landlords' privies; out-of-village labourers were preferred by some because they could not skip off to their own toilets.26

Hinton called his book *Fanshen*, meaning 'to turn the body'. This was an expression that the Communist Party of China (CPC) and farmers came to use to denote the effects of land reform, the term being a metaphor for a revolution in one's life. The CPC began to expropriate selected landlords and redistribute land in areas it controlled in the late 1920s. This 'land to the tiller' policy expanded in the communists' southern China base area in Jiangxi province. However, when a full-scale war with Japan broke out in 1937, the CPC pulled back from forced land redistribution, demanding instead a so-called 'double reduction' by landlords, of both rents and interest. The new policy was part of a 'united front' with Chiang Kai-shek's Nationalist Party, which counted on many landlords for political support.

In reality, however, when the communists took control of a village during the Japanese war of 1937–45, and again during the Chinese civil war that resumed between communists and nationalists in 1946, bottom-up demand for land redistribution was so great that it happened anyway. This was especially the case at the end of the conflict with Japan in 1945, because most landlords had thrown in their lot with the Japanese occupiers and those Chinese who did their bidding. Revenge against Japan, land redistribution and the politicisation of the peasantry by CPC cadres were rolled up into a single struggle at the local level. In the village called Long Bow in which Hinton lived, and in many like it, when the CPC published its Draft Agrarian Law legislating land reform in December 1947 there were no landlords left to dispossess.27

None the less, the Draft Agrarian Law committed the CPC to universal uncompensated expropriation of land and to the cancellation of all pre-existing rural debts. The first lines of the succinct and pointed resolution which prefaced the law are worth restating:

> China's agrarian system is unjust in the extreme. Speaking of general conditions, landlords and rich peasants who make up less than 10 per cent of the rural population hold approximately 70 to 80 per cent of the land, cruelly exploiting the peasantry. Farm labourers, poor peasants, middle peasants, and other people however, who make up over 90 per cent of the rural population, hold a total of approximately only 20 to 30 per cent of the land, toiling throughout the whole year, knowing neither warmth nor full stomach. These grave conditions are the root of our country's being the victim of aggression, oppression, poverty, backwardness, and the basic obstacles to our country's democratisation, industrialisation, independence, unity, strength and prosperity.
>
> In order to change these conditions, it is necessary, on the basis of the demands of the peasantry, to wipe out the agrarian system of feudal and semi-feudal exploitation, and realise the system of 'land to the tillers'.[28]

## Not a dinner party

In line with Mao Zedong's dictum that 'a revolution is not the same as inviting people to dinner', the land expropriation that Hinton studied in Long Bow village was often violent. Of some 250 families, twenty-six had their lands expropriated immediately after the Japanese surrender in August 1945. Erstwhile landlords were subject to repeated, all-day 'struggle sessions' by villagers and CPC cadres and their land and goods were divided among the most needy. Several were beaten to death; others died later from starvation. By spring 1946, about one-quarter of the land in Long Bow had changed hands, along with draft animals and many sections of housing (which, being wooden, could be dismantled and moved). Villagers dug up the homes and courtyards of landlords, searching for the profits of usury that were traditionally buried for safe-keeping.

All this preceded the founding of a formal CPC village branch in April 1946. When the civil war against the nationalists resumed in the summer, another round of intensified struggle broke out, with physical attacks on the remaining family members of landlords and 'middle peasants' (people who owned slightly larger than average plots and occasionally used hired labour). Two 'middle peasants' were beaten to death. Still more violence, as well as theft and rape, occurred as a minority of CPC cadres began to exploit their new position of power; members of the local militia celebrated Chinese New Year in 1947 with the gang rape of the daughter-in-law of a former 'bad element'. All this happened before the publication of the Draft Agrarian Law at the end of 1947.

Nationally, estimates of the death toll related to land reform in China range from hundreds of thousands of people to several million.[29] The campaign continued until 1952, as areas which only came under CPC control in 1948 and 1949 were made subject to redistribution. Overall, as Hinton observed, land reform was critical to the communist victory itself. The People's Liberation Army secured many recruits during the civil war, first by giving their families confiscated land and then by organising supporters to farm it while the young men were away at the front. 'Only the satisfaction of the peasants' demand for land,' he wrote, 'could provide during the coming period of the civil war the kind of inspiration and cohesion that the spirit of resistance to national subjugation had provided during the war against Japan.'[30]

Despite the dislocations of war, the economic benefits of land reform began to be felt rather quickly. The CPC introduced a more progressive tax system whereby, instead of taking a fixed share of whatever was produced, the state exempted an initial quota of output from tax and subjected the rest to levies based on average local yields. Anyone who beat the average got to retain the upside. Household ownership of land, fairer tax, mutual aid groups to share machinery and draft animals, village land reclamation and irrigation that had never taken place under tenancy, along with the first rural co-operative banks, all began to push up yields.

There was, in the second half of the 1940s and the first half of the 1950s, a very substantial increase in agricultural output in China. The available data are of poor quality, but the increase is widely agreed to have been in the range of 40–70 per cent, taking grain output from a pre-Second World War peak of less than 140 million tonnes to close to 200 million tonnes.[31] For a brief moment, Chinese farmers experienced an unprecedented holiday from want, not to mention a boom in rural textile, handicraft and manufacturing output. There is no reason this state of affairs should not have lasted. No reason, that is, except Marxist dogma, and the obsession with large scale, which soon destroyed much of the progress that China had made through household farming.

In 1956, following the Russian and North Korean examples, Mao Zedong led a drive to create agricultural collectives in which hundreds of families pooled their land, tools and labour in units of production. These changes, together with an industrialisation drive, were presented as China's Great Leap Forward. In reality, the disruption to agricultural output in the late 1950s was such that a famine occurred in 1959–61 in which an estimated 30–40 million people (slightly less than 10 per cent of the population) died.

After the famine, a modified collective agriculture system was introduced whereby labour was rewarded with 'work points' handed out by bureaucrats. But food output under collectivisation barely kept up with the growth in population, and standards of nutrition in China in the 1970s were little better on average than in the 1930s.[32] China waited until the revolutionary son of a landlord, Deng Xiaoping, rose to power in 1978 to rediscover what household farming could do for a developing country. By then, two decades of development had been lost.

## The American response

The perversion of Chinese land reform by collectivisation did not occur until the late 1950s. Prior to that, for a decade after the Second World War, China was a beacon to the rest of the region for communist-organised land reform leading to small-scale household farming. In neighbouring North Korea, which was occupied by Soviet forces at the end of the war, another communist party, headed by Kim Il Sung, organised a sweeping land reform programme in 1946. This one achieved its objectives with much less violence than occurred in China. In both countries – at least until North Korea began its collectivisation in 1954 – the communists were hugely popular with farmers. Their agricultural reforms threw down the political gauntlet to the region. The challenge required a response from the pre-eminent power in east Asia, the United States.

American politicians and bureaucrats struggled to reach a consensus about how to respond. On the one hand, despite the longstanding legal right of Americans to claim homesteads, the mandatory redistribution of other people's private property was decidedly un-American. On the other hand, Washington's more liberal foreign policy specialists argued that land reform was necessary to make Asian societies fairer and – in the context of an incipient Cold War – less susceptible to the rising tide of communism. (There was no significant body of empirical evidence, as of 1945, to show that land reform would inevitably lead to faster economic growth.) The tensions between the property rights camp and those who viewed land reform as the key to stabilising US allies in Asia were never resolved; this led to a see-sawing of policy for several years, followed by a retreat from support for redistribution despite its manifest successes.

At the end of a world war in which 50 million people had died, there was more appetite than usual for bold policy and the land reformers won a crucial early victory with respect to Japan in the winter of 1945–6. General Douglas MacArthur, Supreme Commander for the Allied Powers (SCAP) that were occupying Japan, was persuaded to make 'land to the tiller' official policy. However, the momentum for change in other US-influenced states quickly hit a road block in South Korea. There the US military commander on the ground was vehemently opposed to land redistribution and the Washington political elite was less interested in forcing the issue. It was Kim Il Sung's spring 1946 land reform in the north which put the US and its favoured political stooge in Seoul, Syngman Rhee, on the spot. Reform legislation was passed, but President Rhee dragged his heels on implementation and Washington did not press him. The issue was eventually brought to a head for the second time by the 1950–3 Korean civil war, after which land redistribution was instituted.

In mainland China, the American response to the land reform issue during the 1946–9 civil war was hopelessly and embarrassingly belated. The US government sponsored the setting up of a Joint Commission on Rural Reconstruction (JCRR) with its Kuomintang (Nationalist Party) allies in October 1948 – long after most communist-controlled areas had completed land reform. The JCRR funded some small 'land to the tiller' experiments in that bit of central China still under nationalist sway in the last twelve months of the civil war.[33] However, once the nationalists had been defeated and fled to Taiwan, the negligible US intervention on the mainland gave way to much greater political determination. The work of the JCRR was transferred to Taiwan, where it was greatly expanded. When Chiang Kai-shek's resolve to redistribute private property showed signs of flagging in the early 1950s, it was his US ally that insisted he should move ahead. This, however, was the last time Washington used its influence to make land reform happen in east Asia. America's south-east Asian allies were never put under the same pressure.

The US contribution was a fitful one, reflecting the mixed emotions that land reform inspired among American politicians and their military commanders. There was early, decisive action over defeated Japan, vacillation in South Korea until events forced the US hand, far too little too late in mainland China, and a belated but important intervention in Taiwan. The victory of communism in China and North Korea demanded clear American leadership. In the end, enough of it was provided to stabilise the political situation in north-east Asia and to fix the boundaries of the incipient Cold War. But such leadership was born of necessity and did not come from any real conviction in Washington. That is why the impetus for land reform proved so fleeting; indeed, too fleeting for south-east Asia – including the US colony of the Philippines and the US orphan colony of South Vietnam – to taste the benefits of US-backed land redistribution. The political will that existed in the early 1950s came not from the US polity as a whole, but from a few clear-thinking individuals. Among these, one of the greatest was Wolf Ladejinsky.

### A few brave men

Ladejinsky was the most important adviser to the US government on agricultural issues in Asia. A naturalised American born in the Ukraine in 1899, who had fled the Russian Revolution, he recalled that: 'I came to this [work] chiefly as a result of a lesson I learned from my experience before

I left Russia in early 1921, namely that the communists would never have attained political power if they had not dealt with the land question resolutely, by turning the land over to the peasants.'[34] Ladejinsky also noted, however, that the Russian communists, having won popular support with a transition to household farming, then switched to forced collectivisation. He predicted, correctly, that the same pattern would occur in China, where he was sent in 1949 by the US Department of Agriculture as part of the JCRR's belated attempt at land reform in the final months of the Chinese civil war.[35]

Four years before that, in 1945, Ladejinsky had been seconded to General MacArthur's SCAP staff, which administered the defeated Japan. It was in this role that he provided the technical input for an October 1945 US State Department memorandum to MacArthur which made the case for the expropriation of all tenanted farmland.[36] Many people around MacArthur were arguing for the lesser policy of rent reductions but Ladejinsky insisted that a radical policy was necessary to undermine local communist support. He also argued that forced rent reductions would lead many landlords to farm land themselves, and thereby create more landless peasants. Ladejinsky and his allies persuaded MacArthur – whose instincts were conservative and who had showed no previous interest in the subject – to insist on land reform legislation in Japan.

The instruction MacArthur sent to the Japanese government neatly echoed the Communist Party of China's preamble to its Draft Agrarian Law of 1947:

> In order that the Imperial Japanese Government shall remove economic
> obstacles to the revival and strengthening of democratic tendencies,
> establish respect for the dignity of man, and destroy the economic
> bondage which has enslaved the Japanese farmer to centuries of
> feudal oppression, the Japanese Imperial Government is directed
> to take measures to ensure that those who till the soil of Japan shall
> have more equal opportunity to enjoy the fruits of their labor ... The
> Japanese Imperial Government is therefore ordered to submit to this
> Headquarters on or before 15 March 1946 a programme of rural land
> reform.[37]

There was already a move by progressive politicians in the Japanese parliament to introduce new land reform legislation. Indeed, a first Land Reform Bill was passed in late 1945. However, this contained a higher retention limit for landlords than was likely to be effective, as well as numerous legal loopholes for land owners to exploit. MacArthur and his SCAP staff, with Soviet and British representatives on the Allied Council for Japan urging them on, demanded that parliament write a second, more radical and more watertight bill, which was passed in October 1946. While the bill itself originated in the Japanese parliament, much of its technical detail came from Wolf Ladejinsky and his team.[38] And so it was that Japan's remarkable second phase of development began.

## Theory into practice

The reform involved a maximum 3-hectare limit for farms in almost all areas of the country. The critical mechanism to implement this was the creation of land committees on which local tenants and owner-farmers outnumbered landlords. These committees had the adjudicating power in what for landlords was a distinctly painful process: they would lose their land in return for 30-year bonds paying 3.6 per cent interest on below-market valuations, despite an inflation rate so high that it would render the payment almost worthless.[39] Approximately 2 million families stood to lose by the land reform and 4 million to gain.

In the months before redistribution began, the Ministry of Agriculture estimated there were 250,000 cases of landlords attempting to retain their land by taking it back from their tenants. But the land committees, which were required to review all transfers that attempted to circumvent land reform, managed to reverse almost all of them. Despite this, only 110 incidents of violence between landlords and tenants were reported in the reform years 1947–8 and not one life was lost. The agricultural historian Ronald Dore remarks: 'The very fact that it [the reform] was imposed from outside was a powerful factor in making the land reform a peaceful and orderly one. Tenants could take over the land, not with the light of revolution in their eyes but half-apologetically, as if it hurt them more than it hurt their landlords, for the cause was not in themselves but in a law for which they bore no responsibility either personally or collectively.'[40]

As well as requiring land redistribution, the Agricultural Land Law placed numerous restrictions on land sales once the reform was complete. Land was not to return to tenancy as it had after the Meiji reforms. Almost two-fifths (just under 2 million hectares) of cultivable land changed hands, and by the mid 1950s less than one-tenth of farmland was tenanted. Most rental payments disappeared, while post-war inflation wiped out farmer debts – just as it destroyed the value of the bonds given to landlords – and led to high prices for farm products sold on black markets outside of official government procurement. It was a good time to be a farmer.

Rural output and consumption raced far ahead of pre-war levels in the early 1950s, even as Japan's urbanites were still struggling to get back to a 1930s standard of living.[41] The government spent heavily on rural infrastructure, offering scores of different subsidies and grants-in-aid to farmers and providing an average of one agricultural extension worker per village. Relatively low-interest credit was also offered through village co-operatives. As a result, agricultural production rose by a robust 3 per cent a year from 1955 to 1970.[42] Japan was self-sufficient in food and rural employment boomed.

Agriculture was still the provider of two-fifths of employment and almost one-fifth of national income in 1955. The introduction of a more deep-rooted, enduring land reform – which kept the agricultural economy focused on yield gains rather than tenancy profits – set the stage for Japan's post-war miracle. It made possible economic development with high levels of income equality and supported the growth of manufacturing capacity in rural towns. However, the impact of comprehensive land reform in Japan must be considered in the context of a country which had already progressed further in its economic modernisation than any other Asian state by the time of the Second World War. The results were far more interesting when the same land reforms were repeated in South Korea and Taiwan. These were states starting from the lowest rungs of the developmental ladder. Their ascent under the impetus of radical land policy provided a clearer laboratory study of its potential.

## The rise of stir-fried development

Land ownership in South Korea prior to reform was the most unequal among the north-east Asian states. Wolf Ladejinsky, writing about Korean agriculture before partition in 1945, quoted a 1928 US State Department research report which said that less than 4 per cent of households owned 55 per cent of agricultural land, while there were a quarter of a million landless squatter families.[43] Relatively less public investment went to agriculture when compared with Taiwan during the colonial period. Japan operated a more repressive regime in Korea in the face of greater political opposition to her rule than she faced in Taiwan. By the end of the colonial era in 1945, Japanese interests owned about one-fifth of all Korean land and the majority of farmers were pure tenants.

The American Military Government (AMG) that became the occupying force in South Korea from September 1945 instituted rent controls and requirements for written leases on previously Japanese-controlled land. However the US military governor, General Archer L. Lerch, was not disposed to land reform, regarding it as a socialist policy; his concern was to keep the Soviets north of the 38th parallel and to suppress communism in the south. The attentions of pro-land reform US liberals in Washington, meanwhile, were focused on Japan.

The American hand was forced by events. From March 1946, land reform with a (generous) retention of five hectares was introduced in North Korea. There was little violence and grass-roots support for the emerging communist government increased markedly. In the south, resentment against heavy-handed government by the AMG and its barely legitimate local ally Syngman Rhee – an elitist, long-time expatriate who had only recently returned – increased. In the autumn of 1946, the US State Department concluded that land reform had to be pushed. None the less, General Lerch and Syngman Rhee continued to resist.

After the former died in 1947, the AMG organised redistribution of lands formerly controlled by Japanese interests. The reform affected only a little over 10 per cent of South Korea's cultivable land. However, it raised expectations. In 1948, South Korea became a sovereign state, and the following year, despite being heavily linked to landlord interests, the new Korean parliament passed a substantive land reform bill. The bill was significantly more radical than President Rhee wanted. He vetoed it only to have his veto overridden by the legislators.

Rhee was forced to sign the Land Reform Act in June 1949. A legislature with considerable vested interests in land took a principled stand on the question of redistribution – a reminder that democracy is not always inimical to development.[44] Rhee himself continued to prevaricate over the implementation of reform, which finally began the week before the Korean War broke out in June 1950. The opening of the war involved a North Korean invasion, in the wake of which northern forces quickly set up farmers' committees in most parts of the south, redistributing more than half a million hectares of land for free to more than 1 million families. After US–UN forces reoccupied the south in late 1950, the communist land reform was declared illegal and Rhee – urged on by the US – belatedly moved to implement the south's own programme. This was completed by the end of 1952.

The formal terms of the Korean reforms were much like those which had already been enforced in Japan and which were to come in Taiwan. There was a 3-hectare retention limit. Remuneration to landlords was particularly ungenerous, with some losing 90 per cent of the value of their assets. However, the reform was more centrally managed and there was much less farmer participation in the process than in Japan and Taiwan. This helps explain a number of variations in outcomes. First, a large amount of land was sold by landlords outside the formal land reform process, sometimes to third-party tenants but sometimes to relatives. Second, tenancy – much of it illegal under the terms of the land reform law – reappeared in South Korea and by the late 1970s affected about a quarter of agricultural land. None the less, owners increased from not much more than one-tenth of farm households in 1945 to over seven-tenths in 1964.[45] After land reform, almost 50 per cent of farmers farmed less than half a hectare.

Korean agricultural output did not increase as fast as that in Japan. Syngman Rhee's government in the 1950s forcibly procured rice at less than the cost of production; under the circumstances, farm households increased output somewhat, but preferred to eat the extra themselves than sell at a loss. In the late 1950s, Korea became dependent on US food aid to avoid famine. Then, following the 1961 military coup of General Park Chung Hee, government raised procurement prices and increased investment in rural infrastructure and domestic fertiliser plants. It was in the 1960s and 1970s, when the state provided household agriculture with the kind of support seen in Japan and Taiwan in the 1950s, that yields increased appreciably. Rice paddy yields rose from an average 3 tonnes per hectare in the mid 1950s to 5.3 tonnes per hectare in the mid 1970s – less than in Japan or Taiwan, but one-and-a-half to two times what was achieved in south-east Asian states, or in 1970s China under collective farming.

The Korean state was less able to extract wealth from its relatively less productive agriculture in order to fund industrialisation than either Meiji Japan or post-Second World War Japan and Taiwan. When it came to finance, the Korean government relied heavily on foreign borrowing. Still, agriculture delivered a great deal to national development: it gainfully employed vast numbers of people until industry was ready to absorb them; it provided cheap food – via subsidised state procurement – to urban workers; it generated considerable local consumption for the early output of Korean manufacturers; and it staved off what could have been a much more serious food import dependency. Korea's post-reform agricultural performance was a world apart from what the country had known before the Second World War, or what less successful east Asian states continued to endure after it.

### The one to beat

Taiwan is the most interesting agricultural story in north-east Asia, for two reasons. First, the island produced the most remarkable developmental results as a consequence of land reform. Second, with its subtropical climate Taiwan is geographically more south-east Asian than north-east Asian and hence the success of land reform there gives us a powerful reminder that geography is not destiny in development. The less successful agricultural economies of other south-east Asian states are the outcomes of policies, not climatic conditions. Indeed, climate in geographic south-east Asia is generally much more favourable to agriculture than in north-east Asia because of a year-round growing season and abundant, regular rainfall.

The worst climatic and soil conditions for agriculture in the region are to be found in South Korea and parts of Japan.

At the end of the Chinese civil war in 1949, the defeated Nationalist government under Chiang Kai-shek retreated to Taiwan. Around a million refugees from the mainland moved to the island, pushing up its population from 6 million people to well over 7 million in a matter of months. Under Japanese colonial occupation, which ended in 1945, considerable investment had been made in rural infrastructure, particularly in irrigation works and in land reclamation – Japan used its Taiwanese colony as a supplier of rice and cane sugar. The promotion of fertiliser use and the introduction of new seed varieties also led to impressive increases in yields, and real per capita income in agriculture probably doubled under the Japanese occupation.[46] However, as in Japan, tenancy tended to increase in the run-up to the Second World War; rents, if anything, were higher than in Japan – reaching 70 per cent of output for high-quality land, with frequent demands for payment in advance and for high minimum rents irrespective of the size of the year's crop.

Chiang Kai-shek's Kuomintang government, which could see the end of the civil war coming well before its formal defeat, introduced legislation on Taiwan to limit rents to 37.5 per cent of crops at the beginning of 1949. The Kuomintang had just started working with the American-sponsored JCRR on the mainland, and Taiwan rent control represented an act of ingratiation towards the rural population of an island that was not universally thrilled by the idea that the Nationalist military and political machine might be coming to stay. Landlords were also required to sign written tenancy agreements of a minimum of six years, under which the requirements for repossession of land were onerous.

Beginning in 1951, the Nationalists offered a second prize to Taiwan's rural constituency by starting the sell-off of lands confiscated from former Japanese owners. By the end of the decade, 140,000 families had benefited from this programme, buying an average of half a hectare. The case for fully-fledged land reform, however, was not addressed.

It was the JCRR, now operating in Taiwan, and the US government that sponsored it, which pushed for a more radical policy. American policymakers wanted the Kuomintang to build a genuinely popular support base and were encouraged by the non-violent implementation of land reform in Japan. Chiang Kai-shek's government – which had studiously avoided land reform on the mainland for decades – was persuaded to change its approach. If the desire to win the support of Taiwan's rural population was the major driver, the fact that the Nationalist elite had few vested interests on the island was the facilitating consideration.

The government passed land reform legislation in 1953. The terms were similar to those employed in Japan and South Korea: expropriation of land in excess of approximately three hectares; landlord compensation amounting to two and a half years' average crop (compared with three to eight years on the open market); payment to landlords mostly in low-yield bonds; purchase of the land by tenants in instalments over ten years. In the event, half of landlords were required to sell less than a hectare and fewer than a fifth sold more than three hectares.[47] As in Japan, there were few big landlords – but the effects would prove to be enormous all the same.

Wolf Ladejinsky's influence continued to be felt. It was he who recommended that the Kuomintang set up tenancy committees, which adjudicated thousands of land sales and purchases at the village level. The participation of tenants, as well as of owner-farmers and landlords, helped prevent widespread evasion of the rules, just as the activities of similar committees had done in Japan. In contrast to what was to occur in southeast Asia, popular participation in the process was at the root of successful implementation.

Whereas a little over 30 per cent of agricultural land in Taiwan was farmed by owner-cultivators in 1945, the proportion by 1960 was 64 per cent.[48] Farmers who gained new land in effect paid nothing for it because their payments to the government were offset by their not having to pay rent. As in Japan, it was forced sellers who lost. By one estimate, the transfer of wealth involved in the land reform was equivalent to 13 per cent of Taiwan's GDP passing from one group of people to another.[49]

The structural effects were the creation of a textbook market environment in which everybody had a small amount of capital, and an evening out of income distribution. When the share of property income in a society falls (here because fewer people were renting out land), income from current work is relatively more important and overall incomes diverge less.

Household income surveys in Taiwan showed that the country moved from a Gini coefficient – the standard measure of equality, where 0 is perfect equality and 1 is perfect inequality – on a par with Brazil in the early 1950s (scoring 0.56) to a level in the mid 1960s that was unprecedented for a developing country (0.33).[50]

Greater equality was welcomed by the average Taiwanese, but it was the impact of land reform and a more incentivising market structure on output which was truly revolutionary. Taiwanese agriculture in the 1950s needed to provide a vast amount of additional food and employment – the population increased faster than anywhere else in the region – and to generate foreign exchange in order to plug a large gap in the state's balance of payments. All this was achieved. Yields of traditional crops like rice and sugar went up by half, and those of specialist fruit and vegetables doubled. In the 1950s, raw and processed agricultural goods produced two-thirds of Taiwan's export receipts.[51] To begin with, sugar was the dominant foreign exchange earner. The government nationalised formerly Japanese-owned sugar refineries under the Taiwan Sugar Corporation, but bought sugar cane from household farmers.[52] From the 1960s, family farms also diversified into new, value-added and highly labour-intensive crops, including mushrooms and asparagus and, in the south, bananas.

As in every instance where it succeeds, land reform was coupled with state investments in rural infrastructure, agricultural extension services and marketing support. The JCRR – which had been a monument to US foreign policy failure in mainland China – was hugely important in supporting these initiatives in Taiwan. By one estimate, the agency handled one-third of US aid to the island between 1951 and 1965, running 6,000 projects and accounting for a little over half of net investment in Taiwanese farming. Through it, Taiwan acquired the world's proportionately largest cohort of agricultural research and extension workers.[53]

The JCRR was instrumental in developing high-yield varieties for existing crops and in publicising alternative high-value crops, while the Taiwanese government frequently guaranteed minimum prices for export-oriented produce to limit farmer risk. To take one example of a popular new export vegetable, asparagus was calculated to require 2,900 times as much labour per hectare as rice, providing ample work in a country where industrial job creation did not begin to exceed the rate of population growth until the end of the 1950s. Processing of foodstuffs, which began with sugar and moved on to asparagus, mushrooms, tropical fruits and other crops, was Taiwan's first 'manufacturing' export industry. The textile business did not begin to kick in until the second half of the 1950s.

Taiwan stands out among north-east Asian states for the extent to which agricultural goods drove and dominated exports at the beginning of the country's development process. The experience was testament to just what a powerful catalyst labour-intensive, private household farming can be. Indeed, such was the contribution of the agricultural sector to Taiwan's economy that government was able to squeeze considerable financial resources out of it without apparently undermining farmers' incentives to produce more. The state operated a fertiliser monopoly which sold different fertilisers to farmers at a premium of 10–30 per cent over world market prices, and also bought around a quarter of rice output by compulsory purchase at significantly less than market rates. Yet still the sector continued to operate efficiently.

There is much debate about how hard agriculture was squeezed in the aggregate, since government was also putting investment into the sector, but there is no doubt that the Taiwanese farmers helped to fund their country's early industrialisation. And not only did their household savings pay to build factories, they also provided the key market for early manufactures as farm incomes more than doubled in real terms in the 1950s.[54]

Taiwan set a high-water mark for agricultural input into development. Moreover, early industrial development echoed that in Meiji Japan (and to a lesser extent that in post-Second World War Japan) and in post-1978 China by being concentrated in rural areas. In other words, agricultural progress became bound up with industrial progress not only financially – because the former was the early generator of new wealth and markets – but also geographically, because rural areas were home to many new manufacturing enterprises and produced many industrial entrepreneurs. In this respect, it is artificial to separate the rural and manufacturing stories of Japan, China and Taiwan. These states, however, are not typical of the developing world. The more common developmental tale is one of 'urban bias', in which town and country, agriculture and manufacturing, remain worlds apart.

That is what happened in south-east Asia. There, post-colonial governments toyed with land reform, but never followed through to fundamentally restructure their rural economies. And the United States failed to apply the external political pressure that it used to such positive effect in north-east Asia. This lack of domestic and international political conviction over the importance of household farming in development was the first step towards the relative economic underperformance of the south-east Asian region. No country bears this out more painfully than the Philippines.

### *Journey 2: Negros Occidental*

*Out on the runway of Manila's Ninoy Aquino airport, a large private jet comes in to land in the afternoon sun. It is a useful reminder, if you have travelled down from north-east Asia, that you have left the world of 0.3 Gini coefficients and entered the world of 0.5 Gini coefficients – that is, a different kind of 'developing' economy. The plane I am on is travelling to Bacolod, the dominant city in Negros Occidental, the western half of the island of Negros. It is an area of the Philippines sometimes referred to as 'Sugarlandia', because of its historical role as the epicentre of the plantation sugar industry.*

It is a brief one-hour flight. On the descent, light green fields shimmer up and down the coastal plain. Only a few darker wooded areas remain of what was once forest. Plumes of smoke rise from fields where sugar cane stubble is being burned; it is November, the middle of the harvest season. Around the new airport, sugar cane grows right up to the airfield apron. On the ride into town we pass by one sugar cane field after another, while large trucks fully laden with harvested brown canes trundle off to refineries. Skinny *sacadas*, the seasonal cane-cutters and the lowest of the low in the pecking order of agricultural labour, are dotted around the fields or loading trucks, each with his long machete.

Bacolod is well past its heyday, which came in the 1970s. Back then, a large US import quota gave sugar producers in the former colony access to the heavily protected US market, where sugar prices – despite America's free market claims – are among the highest in the world.[55] In the 1960s and early 1970s, sugar barons rode around Bacolod in the latest American stretch open-top sedans. In photographs of the era downtown seems more California than Asia. Today, Bacolod still has its casino with security guards toting sawn-off shotguns, but the old swagger has gone.

The fundamentals of Third World agriculture, however, are intact: land-lords are ascendant; most farming is conducted by landless peasants;[56] farm-ers who have been granted plots through poorly conceived, half-cocked land reform initiatives have mostly leased them back to landlords or lost control of them through indebtedness; yields are low (and on many farms are lower than in the 1970s); and the going wage for a farm labourer is PHP120 (USD2.60) a day.[57]

It was not meant to be thus. Nowhere in Asia has produced more plans for land reform than the Philippines. But, equally, no ruling elite in Asia has come up with as many ways to avoid implementing genuine land reform as the Filipino one. Back in 1904, a new US colonial government – imposed after the American defeat of Spain in a war of 1898 – promised to help tenants with a first land reform affecting estates owned by the Catholic church. However the Americans insisted on a full market price, making the tenants' right of first refusal to purchase meaningless – they didn't have the money. Almost all of the 165,000 hectares in question ended up in the hands of businessmen.[58]

In the 1930s, the periodic agrarian unrest born of poverty that has afflicted the Philippines for centuries became permanent armed resist-ance with the development of the communist-led Huk rebel movement in Luzon, the largest island in the Philippines. Local politicians (power had been devolved by Washington in 1916) responded with a new tenancy law, which was not enforced, and undertook resettlement of a few thousand landless farmers. The Huk rebellion increased in scale and spread through the archipelago. After the Second World War, when General MacArthur had retaken the Philippines, many landlords recovered their land from Huk rebels by raising private forces; the country was awash with weapons left over from conflict. Following independence in 1946, the Huk rebel-lion reached a new level of intensity. The US, still heavily involved in the Philippines through its military bases, commissioned two reports in 1950 and 1951, both of which stated that redistributive land reform was the only way to end agrarian unrest.[59]

However, while radical land reform was supported by the US embassy in Manila, it did not win support in Washington – unlike the reforms in Japan, South Korea and Taiwan. A Philippine Rural Reconstruction Movement was set up and funded by various US agencies, including the Central Intelligence Agency, but it did not promote compulsory land redistribution. In 1954–5, the Philippine government gave rice and corn farmers the right to demand written tenancy agreements, legislated to expropriate private tenanted estates over 300 hectares, and began a more aggressive programme to settle landless farmers and rebels on public lands (even though this frequently displaced defenceless tribal groups). Combined with US training for the Filipino military and an anti-insurgency drive, these very limited agricultural reforms were enough to take the heat out of the Huk rebellion. In 1963, there was a further 'enhancement' of the mid-1950s reforms when the expropriation limit for rice and corn land was reduced from 300 hectares to 75 hectares. However, compulsory purchase only occurred when a specific locality was declared a 'land reform area'.[60]

A pattern was established whereby government undertook the absolute minimum amount of agricultural reform needed to head off outright civil war. There was no shift to a fundamentally more productive rural economy. It is a pattern that has persisted. In 1969, the remnants of the Huk movement resurfaced, together with a reformed Communist Party of the Philippines, to create the New People's Army (NPA). In the early 1970s, the NPA began to co-operate with Christian socialist activists who, despairing of peaceful reform, set up rural base areas inspired by the Chinese revolution. The NPA enforced rent and interest reductions, and occasionally the redistribution of land, in areas it controlled, just as the Chinese communists had in the 1930s and 1940s.

It was during the early rise of the NPA that Ferdinand Marcos declared martial law, in September 1972. He repeatedly justified military rule on the basis that authoritarian government was the only means by which land reform could be achieved. In a speech on the first anniversary of martial law in which he talked about his promise of a 'New Society' (Chiang Kai-shek had promised the Chinese something similar in the 1930s with his New Life Movement), Marcos opined: 'Land reform is the only gauge for the success or failure of the New Society ... If land reform fails, there is no New

Society.' As with Chiang in China, there was very little land reform and there was no new society. The land reform that Marcos did pursue remained limited to corn and rice land, involved a high, 7-hectare retention limit, and was largely targeted at property belonging to his political enemies.[61]

By the time of Marcos's fall in 1986, he had achieved less than a quarter of his own, very limited targets. The Philippine military, meanwhile, estimated that the NPA had 25,000 members and was present in one in eight villages in the country. In January 1986, a month before Marcos fled, in an act of desperation the government began handing out thousands of land reform 'Emancipation Patents' – titles to plots of land – to farmers who had not even completed the land reform application process. Just as when the United States formed the JCRR to support land reform in Nationalist China in the winter of 1948–9, or when Washington finally backed land reform in South Vietnam under Nguyen Van Thieu in 1969, it was far, far too late. By one calculation, the cumulative achievement of land reform in the Philippines between 1900 and 1986 was the redistribution of 315,000 hectares, or about 4 per cent of the cultivated area.[62]

## The revolution that wasn't

If Ferdy failed land reformers, his successor Cory Aquino – brought to power by 'people power' – did little better. To be fair, she was the wife of an assassinated political leader (Ninoy, shot by Marcos's agents at Manila airport in 1983) and more used to making small talk with her husband's guests than dealing with the snake-pit of Philippine politics. She was the figurehead for anti-Marcos protest, but she had no political party of her own. She was also from a landed family, the Cojuangcos, one of whose main assets is a 6,400-hectare estate in Tarlac in central Luzon; her brother, Jose Cojuangco Jr, was one of the anti-reform leaders of the landowner bloc in congress. Cory Aquino only confronted the land reform question when a huge farmer demonstration in Manila in January 1987 ended with police killing at least thirteen people and wounding ninety – what came to be known as the Mendiola Massacre, for the bridge around which the killing took place. Her response was to ask the Philippine congress to work out the details of a new land reform law, rather than taking the lead herself.

The result was a law that was long-winded, unduly complex, insufficiently radical, with many loopholes and with an absurdly extended timetable for implementation. A quarter of a century and two extensions later, the Comprehensive Agrarian Reform Law (CARL) of 1988 is still being implemented. Despite this, the effects of a change of government, the *promise* of radical reform and another of the Philippines' periodic counter-insurgency drives were enough to undermine the NPA. The movement lost both active and passive support, and splintered internally.

During the land reform legislation debate, Cory Aquino produced some of the Philippines' most famous political last words: 'I shall ask no greater sacrifices,' she told her countrymen, 'than I myself am prepared to make.'[63] When her family's vast estate sought and received permission to avoid break-up under the new land reform law, it was clear that radical reform under people power was not going to happen. Hacienda Luisita, as the Aquino–Cojuangco *latifundia* is called, exploited a clause in the Comprehensive Agrarian Reform Law called the Stock Distribution Option (SDO) which allowed the family to give its tenants equity in a new farming business rather than family plots.

SDO, like other loophole mechanisms in the CARL such as Voluntary Land Transfer and Voluntary Offer of Sale, broke one of the cardinal rules of successful land reform as implemented in north-east Asia: do not let landlords negotiate directly with tenants. In such circumstances, landlords almost invariably manage to negotiate arrangements that are not favourable to tenants. In an SDO case, for instance, a landowner can overvalue non-land inputs and management expenses in a business and undervalue land, meaning that his or her shareholders work for very little return. Luisita has been plagued with strikes and unrest ever since it became a 'shareholder business'; farmers say their 'dividends' are as little as PHP2,000 (USD43) a year.

To those who know their Luisita history, this is one more chapter in a story that is fatally emblematic of the bigger history of Filipino land. The Cojuangcos originally built up their agricultural holdings in Tarlac in the nineteenth and early twentieth centuries through agricultural usury. Then, in 1957, the family acquired Hacienda Luisita with a government loan on the specific condition that the farmland would be resold 'at reasonable terms and conditions' to the tenants.[64] The Cojuangcos were supposed to retain only the large sugar mill on the estate. But the undertaking to sell off the land was never honoured and the Cojuangcos were never held to account. That such people can become presidents – Cory's son Noynoy is the current president, as this book goes to press – places a glass ceiling above the possibilities for Filipino development.

**Official success**

The Philippine government claims that the implementation of the Comprehensive Agrarian Reform Law has met most of its national targets. According to official data, by the end of 2006, 6.8 million hectares of a targeted 8.2 million hectares of farmland were subjected to land reform to the benefit of 4.1 million rural households.[65] This sounds like north-east Asia. But it is not.

To begin with, the Filipino statistics count all kinds of new land titles that have been issued, not practical and physical changes in ownership. One-third of new titles are collective (and almost by definition incomplete), often covering hundreds or thousands of supposed beneficiaries. Much of the land which on paper has been redistributed has been leased back, or sold illegally, to the original owners or to others. Moreover, only one-third of the targeted 8.2 million hectares under land reform is private land – the rest is publicly owned forest where some farming takes place, or new farmer resettlement projects, or other non-private categories. The CARL objective was originally 10.3 million hectares and covered much more private land, but a couple of million hectares of private estates have been dropped from the target without explanation.[66]

Commercial farms like Luisita have hardly been affected. Prior to the reforms, no reliable land survey was conducted, guaranteeing perpetual confusion about both objectives and outcomes. Land reform has been overseen not by tenant committees but by government bureaucrats, who are under-resourced and frequently bribed. Most private land has been 'redistributed' through direct negotiations between owners and tenants – Voluntary Land Transfer and Voluntary Offer of Sale and other related categories – sometimes on terms so unfair to farmers that the process has involved a transfer of wealth from poor to rich.[67]

The hardest number that exists in the Philippines to define meaningful land reform is that for compulsory acquisition, reflecting the kind of forced land redistribution that occurred in north-east Asia. By 2006, compulsory acquisition under the CARL affected just under 300,000 hectares of land – 5 per cent of the area the government says has been reformed, and 2.5 per cent of the Philippines' total cultivable land area.

These data are even worse when one considers the land retention limit under the CARL was set too high – at five hectares plus three more hectares for every owner's child over fifteen years of age; some land owners turned out to have a remarkable number of kids. Today, an estimated 8.5 million of 11.2 million rural workers in the Philippines are landless.[68] The majority of people in the countryside live in poverty. Yields are also shockingly low and not increasing. And all this in a country where cultivable land is one-third of the land mass – far more than in Japan, Korea or Taiwan – and climate and soil quality are more naturally conducive to high yields. In the Philippines, man's capacity to seize failure from the jaws of opportunity is writ large.

### A world of lords ...

A drive south of Bacolod, into the heart of the Negros countryside, soon reveals the realities of Filipino agriculture.[69] Despite the official data extolling the extent of land redistribution to households, it is not long before we are trundling past kilometre after kilometre of commercial mango, pili nut (used in foods from chocolate to ice cream), rambutan (a relative of the lychee), banana, jackfruit and durian plantations. From time to time, groups of labourers come into sight. If there has been land reform in the Philippines, then the average plantation landlord has not noticed. In this part of Negros we are entering the world of the man known to his employees as 'Boss Danding', the biggest landowner in the area.

Eduardo 'Danding' Cojuangco is Cory Aquino's estranged first cousin and one of the Philippines' richest businessmen. He is also the most powerful agricultural and political force in Negros Occidental. In recent years, Danding converted much of his land away from sugar cultivation to other plantation crops. Despite the theory that there is ongoing land redistribution, he continues to build up estates that currently total at least 6,000 hectares and stretch between six Negros towns.[70] Near one of these towns, Pontevedra, he lives in a secluded mansion known locally as the White House. Boss Danding's recreational tastes are standard playboy-billionaire fare: vintage luxury cars, big motorbikes, racehorses, private jets – plus two Filipino specialities: guns and cock fighting. Hundreds of his prize-fighting cocks strut in individual cages in large, manicured fields. They are worth PHP5,000 (USD108) each, the same as the monthly income that constitutes the Philippine poverty line. Ascending a hilltop in the nearby Raphael Salas Nature Park, one sees the full extent of Danding's local estates – the orchards dark green, the sugar a lighter green. This elevated position used to be a New People's Army guerrilla base. Today, with armed struggle in one of its periodic lulls, thugs from an NPA splinter group are employed to guard Danding's land. The arrangement is much cheaper than keeping a standing army. At the height of the insurgency in the mid 1980s Danding was reckoned to have 1,600 fighters on his payroll.[71]

It is hard to believe that Danding is at liberty in the Philippines, let alone acquiring more and more land in Negros Occidental and other parts of the archipelago. He was Ferdinand Marcos's number one crony and accompanied Ferdy and Imelda when they were evacuated by the US military in February 1986. Under Marcos's protection, Danding was governor of the Development Bank of the Philippines (lending money to his own firms); ran a coconut marketing monopoly (taxing the leading 1970s export industry to fund the growth of his personal business empire, including the takeover of the nation's leading firm, San Miguel Corp.); and set up the United Coconut Planters Bank (which deployed even more of other people's money to Danding's ends).[72]

Despite all this, after a period of exile, Danding was able to return to the Philippines in November 1991. Other Marcos cronies who fled and returned were forced to cut deals with Cory Aquino's government to give up part of their assets; Danding never gave up anything. On his return, he settled down in Negros Occidental, where his wife comes from and where he now controls his own political party and most of the local mayors and congressmen.[73]

Danding's response to the Comprehensive Agrarian Reform Law was a variant on the Stock Distribution Option used by his cousin Cory's side of the family to evade the aims of the law at Hacienda Luisita. He proposed 'corporative land reform', a joint venture with his tenants which involved the nominal transfer of land to them over which he retained management control. Indeed, accepting Danding's continuing control was a precondition of the ownership 'transfer'.[74]

The joint venture was negotiated direct between Danding and farmers without government oversight. Under its terms, workers are paid the going rate for day labour plus a minority, 35 per cent share of profits after all Danding's costs. Needless to say, outsiders are not invited to pore over the books. When Danding needs to talk to his tenant 'partners' in Negros, he has them assemble at the giant cock-fighting arena, called Gallera Balbina, which he has constructed near the White House. The central government has never challenged the questionable legality of Boss Danding's 'corporative land reform'. Indeed, former president Joseph Estrada lauded him publicly, and apparently without irony, as 'the godfather of agrarian reform'.

### ... and a world of serfs

We drive up to the confines of an estate of another Marcos crony that is nestled in among Danding's lands. Roberto Benedicto, now deceased, was almost, but not quite, as close to the former dictator as Danding. He ran a Philippine sugar marketing monopoly similar to Danding's coconut trading monopoly and is remembered in Negros for having funded local vigilante groups which murdered people hostile to the Marcos regime.[75] This 564-hectare estate is called Hacienda Esperanza.

Danding offered to buy Esperanza after his return from exile. However, a group of estate workers applied for land reform under the CARL. The story that then unfolded is illustrative of the failings of the reform mechanism. The Benedicto family responded to the CARL application by setting up a 'union' among their more deferential employees, who declared themselves opposed to land redistribution. Lobbying groups became involved on both sides and the case featured in the national media. After a long campaign, central government determined to move ahead with that relatively rare

event, compulsory land reform, and issued Certificates of Land Ownership Awards (CLOAs) to the hacienda's farmers. The Secretary of Agrarian
Reform himself travelled to Negros to lead the 'installation' of the emancipated workers on their plots. However, he was refused access to the estate
by armed guards and members of the Benedictos' union. The holders of
CLOAs then tried to occupy by force the land they had been granted. The
guards shot dead one of them and wounded two others.[76]

Ultimately, compulsory land reform was enforced. It was impossible
to avoid after the shootings. However, like most Philippine land reform,
the Esperanza tale does not have a happy ending for most of the farmers.
The reason is a complete lack of state support for those who were granted
plots. The new title holders were too poor to be able to farm independently and most immediately leased their plots back to the Benedicto
family for just PHP12,000 (USD240) a year, becoming wage labourers
once more.

Some individuals, more stoic, struggled to make a go of independent
farming, borrowing working capital from informal lenders at interest rates
of 50–120 per cent a year . The Benedictos' estate manager, for instance,
lends at 10 per cent a month. With the Benedictos controlling the local
sugar mill as the sole buyer of sugar cane, the maths almost never summed
to a positive return. Farmers found themselves mortgaging their sugar canes
at an earlier point in the growing season each year, and not replanting the
canes after the optimum three years to avoid borrowing more money, which
led instead to declining yields and to yet more debt by another route. When
a debt situation runs out of control, the money lender takes possession
of the land and controls it until the debt and interest are repaid – if ever.
The process has followed exactly the same form as the unravelling of land
reform in 1920s and 1930s Japan.

Only the usurers are happy: the independent farmers are mired in poverty while the sugar yield on the land farmed by the Benedictos is a paltry
52 tonnes per hectare, more than 50 per cent less than post-land reform
sugar farmers in Taiwan and China (after 1978) achieved. As elsewhere in
the Philippines, the beneficiaries of land reform have even greater need of
credit, marketing and agricultural extension support than those in north-east
Asia did. They are almost always farm labourers, used to being told what to

do, rather than the more autonomous tenants who were given the right to buy land in Japan, Korea and Taiwan, or occupy it rent-free in China. Yet where credit and technical support was present in every village in north-east Asia, the Filipinos get almost nothing. Ninety-seven per cent of land reform beneficiaries in Negros told a provincial survey they have received zero support.[77] It is hardly surprising that an emblematic image one sees in Negros is the 'reform' family that immediately leased its land back to the landowner and now sits around a karaoke TV set bought with the proceeds of the rental advance. In the absence of any real chance of household farming success, people put their capital into a KTV machine and sing in a shack.

### Sticking plasters for state failure

The only occasions on which land reform has worked in the Philippines have been when non-government organisations (NGOs) have stepped into the breach left by the state and provided lending, extension, crop processing and marketing support that household agriculture needs to prosper. Otherwise, families like the Benedictos, who have dominated agricultural workers as feudal estate owners, have continued to do so even where they have theoretically given up title.

Within Esperanza, there is a small group of twenty-one farming families which have obtained NGO support. Needless to say, these farmers are more politicised, better educated and more articulate than the 250 other farming families which do not have NGO support. Lito, the group's leader, came down to the hacienda boundary to guide us past the Benedictos' armed guards to their 20-hectare enclave; along the way we saw a wooden cross erected to the farmer the guards killed when he tried to claim his CLOA land. Sitting under a tree in front of a meeting hut, Lito explains that a PHP1.2 million (USD24,000) rotating credit facility, at 20 per cent interest per annum, is what separates his group from the other independent farmers – 95 per cent of whom, he claims, are mired in insurmountable usurious debt.

The NGO lender, Alter Trade, also provided extension support to help the farmers convert to organic sugar and new crops. They now produce most of their own food and no longer face the prospect of hunger if something goes wrong with the sugar harvest. The sugar itself is sold by the NGO through the Fair Trade movement in Europe and equivalent groups in north-east Asia. Ironically, it is bourgeois consumers made rich in Japan and Korea off the back of proper land reform who are now the most significant buyers of the premium brown *mascobado* sugar sold by these Filipino farmers.

Since agreeing terms with Alter Trade in 2004, Lito's group has paid all its interest and made enough profit to buy a 20-year-old tractor, a truck and ten bull carts. The group achieves a 25 per cent higher sugar yield than the Benedicto-farmed land and is saving for irrigation equipment that should push its yield – helped by the Philippines' more favourable agronomic conditions – up to or beyond Taiwanese and Chinese output levels.

Not far away, on a hacienda called Isabel, another group supported by Alter Trade does even better. Eighty holders of Certificates of Land Ownership Awards, supporting a total population of 500, farm eighty hectares of sugar and food crops as a collective enterprise. The leaders of that group proudly show off a large, brand new tractor, which cost them PHP1.5 million (USD30,000). They have already bought another, mid-size tractor and a truck from retained earnings. By local standards, they are rich; four-fifths of the group's adolescent children attend secondary school, and some are going on to college.

Like Lito's group, however, this one is thoroughly atypical – mainly because it is politically organised. Some members were political officers and medics in the NPA and so were able to hold together the kind of collective enterprise that does not occur spontaneously in a society of impoverished and cowed agricultural labourers. These farmers fought for and took the things their government failed to provide. They lobbied for and obtained a compulsory land reform order. They are pursuing the hacienda family in court, asking for more land which they say was illegally retained by registering entitlements for seven heirs when the family has only two children. In addition to a working capital facility from AlterTrade, they secured a loan for their new tractor from a Dutch church-based charity. They electrified members' properties with a grant from a sympathetic German supermarket. And, in the winter of 2009–10, they were building a 20-room boarding house for the rich Japanese and Korean consumers who fly down to Bacolod because they want to meet the people who grow their organic brown sugar. In short, they know how to work the NGO system.

The Esperanza and Isabel farmers are a source both of optimism – for what some people and some NGOs can achieve despite the odds – and of pessimism, because the resourcefulness of the collectives and the size of the NGO's input simply bring into focus the extraordinary impotence of the Philippine state. The reality is that most agricultural labourers will never be able to organise themselves as effectively as these groups, while NGOs in Negros are able to support farmers who number in the hundreds, versus an official tally of 120,000 local people the government claims have been 'beneficiaries' of land reform. The NGOs quite sensibly target the farmers they believe are most capable of succeeding, leaving the weakest to fend for themselves.

It is a matter of sticking plasters for the open wound that is Philippine agriculture. Charity can take the edge off, but never substitute for, the state's developmental failure. In north-east Asia, the remarkable growth of agricultural output was the result of the state itself mobilising effectively to redistribute land quickly and fairly and then to provide the credit, extension and sales support necessary to enable and incentivise households to maximise output. There has never been any equivalent focused effort in the Philippines. Instead, the weakest state among the major economies of east Asia has given rise, proportionately, to the largest number of NGOs – an estimated 60,000–100,000. Typically tiny, they scramble around desperately trying to make up for the state's hopelessness.

### Inefficient by every measure that counts

Back on the road, heading south-east towards the town of La Castellana, we cross the estates of some more elite Filipino families. Powerful irrigation pumps watering sugar cane mark out land of the Arroyo family of recently defeated Philippine president Gloria Macapagal Arroyo; the family has several Negros estates. Gloria's landowner husband is Mike Arroyo and her brother-in-law is Ignacio 'Iggy' Arroyo, member of congress for the Negros Fifth District, where we are driving. Back in 2001, Gloria promised that the Arroyo land would be placed under land reform; it didn't happen. A tour of rural Negros Occidental takes us past estates that read like a *Who's Who* of the families which helped bring the country to its knees in the post-independence era: Cojuangco, Benedicto, Arroyo, Cuenca, Lopez ... Task Force Mapalad, the biggest of the pro-land reform groups in the Philippines, estimated in 2005 that, after more than fifteen years of the CARL, seventeen families still controlled 78 per cent of all sugar land in Negros Occidental.[78]

Filipino farming remains grotesquely inefficient. Despite the insistence of Negros landlords that sugar growing can only be competitive on plantations of a minimum scale, yields have always been less than in the family-farmed areas of southern Taiwan and China: around 56 tonnes per hectare on average, compared with 85–90 tonnes. Land redistributed under the Comprehensive Agrarian Reform Law in Negros fails to lead to increased yields because the state provides no support for the household farming it claims to be implementing and because landlords undermine the reform process.

A 2007 survey of the province referred to the 'dismal income of agricultural reform beneficiaries and minimal increase in terms of agricultural productivity'; seven in ten agricultural reform beneficiaries in Negros said they were no better off than before reform.[79] Even the Alter Trade-supported groups at haciendas Esperanza and Isabel operate at well below Taiwanese and Chinese yields (although they are, at around 70 tonnes per hectare, a quarter above the average Negros yield). The Alter Trade farmers are still saving for the irrigation systems that in north-east Asia would typically be a part of the state's infrastructural support service. When all they seem to do in rural Negros is ford rivers, it is absurd that most sugar cane is unirrigated. The traveller is constantly reminded that the greatest rural poverty in east Asia is concentrated in the areas of greatest natural abundance.

The mesmerising poverty of the Philippines does not make its agricultural output cheap. The final cost of producing sugar in Negros, inclusive of refining expenses, is US15 cents per pound versus a world market wholesale price (before a spike in the summer of 2009) that has ranged between 10 and 12 US cents per pound in recent years. Negros' twelve sugar mills, known as 'centrals', feature some of the global industry's most outdated equipment; sugar extraction rates in the Philippines were higher fifty years ago. With the Philippines having moved to tariff-free sugar imports in 2010, the outlook for the local industry is not good. Landlords conspire to do relatively well only because they have access to the formal banking system and to the remaining US sugar quota, which guarantees a minimum of 18 US cents per pound. As Michael Billig, historian of the Philippine sugar industry, observes, a planter with sixty hectares will still keep a dozen servants at his house in Bacolod and maintain an apartment in Manila.[80]

The inefficiency of Filipino sugar farming extends to other crops. Average yields of rice and corn – the two biggest crops – are 3.8 tonnes and 2.6 tonnes per hectare respectively; in Taiwan they are 4.8 tonnes and 3.8 tonnes. A survey of total agricultural value-added in various Asian countries in the 1980s, which counted output across both crops and agricultural livestock, produced figures of USD655 per hectare for the Philippines, USD2,500 for China, USD5,000 for Taiwan, USD7,000 for Korea and USD10,000 for Japan. By this point the numbers for the north-east Asian states included considerable subsidies that were being paid to support agricultural prices in already prosperous societies. But the enormous difference between the Philippines and China, which had returned to high-yield household farming at the end of the 1970s, tells a clear story.[81]

Wolf Ladejinsky made several visits to the Philippines, witnessing the reality of early land reform attempts in the countryside, and as ever had wise observations. After a trip in December 1962 he wrote that 'I couldn't forbear from telling Mr Perez [the acting minister of finance] that, as I listened to him, the fundamentally richly endowed Philippines reminded me of the more depressed areas of India.' Ladejinsky noted the same conversations 'in the stately homes of the rich of Manila' that one still hears today – that Filipino farmers are congenitally 'lazy' and hence beyond salvation. He visited the International Rice Research Institute at the 'Nature and Science City' of Los Baños, in Laguna, which launched the green revolution in Asia. Ladejinsky observed that high-yield rice seed varieties from Los Baños changed the lives of millions in north-east Asia but could do little in the Philippines where the mechanisms to put irrigation, fertiliser, credit and marketing supports in place were absent. With respect to the true character of the Filipino farmer, he concluded: 'A tenant in prevailing Philippine conditions would act as an irrational economic man if he tried to apply to the land practices that make for higher production, knowing full well that a lion's share of this would go to the landlord, moneylender or merchant.' Ladejinsky's observation holds true half a century later.[82]

## Sukarno talks the talk

The Philippines is perhaps the most extreme example of land policy dysfunction in south-east Asia. None the less if you proceed, clockwise, around the rest of the region, you will see a pattern of agricultural development elsewhere that is not dissimilar, although it occurs in paler and less pale imitations.

In Indonesia, following independence in 1945, President Sukarno promised increasingly radical agricultural development policies during the 1950s. In 1957, foreign-owned (mostly Dutch) plantations were nationalised. In 1960, a general programme of land reform was announced. However, while the Marxist-influenced Sukarno talked revolution, his personal ignorance of rural issues and the defensive manoeuvrings of the land-owning elite rendered his policies ineffective. The Indonesian land reform legislation and implementing regulations followed the Filipino model.

By 1960, the principal island of Java was already one of the most densely populated parts of Asia, with the average landholding of those fortunate enough to have land at all of under half a hectare, and 60 per cent of the rural population landless.[83] Despite this, Indonesia's minimum retention allowance for landowners was set at five hectares, and could be as high as twenty hectares because of loopholes. A widespread, kulak-type class of richer peasants – known as *sikep* – was left untouched by land reform. And larger-scale, absentee landlords were given a six-month window in which they could either claim residency on their land or sell it to a resident in order to reduce or avoid expropriation.[84] Implementation of the land reform was rife with anticipatory transfers and very little land changed hands. There were land reform committees, but these were run by the landlords, who unsurprisingly tended to block land redistribution.

Wolf Ladejinsky made three trips to Indonesia in the early 1960s, involving several months of field observation. Describing the land reform programme as over-complex, inefficient and very slow, he estimated that Java was redistributing less than 2 per cent of its cultivable land and Bali perhaps 4 per cent. He wrote to a US government colleague that 'only a miracle can help them to make some sense out of their voluminous, disjointed, contradictory, and altogether too politically, conservatively inspired agrarian reform legislation'.[85]

There was no miracle. Proof of failure was found in yields that did not rise. Despite the extraordinarily rich, volcanic soil of Java, Ladejinsky noted after a long visit in 1963 that rice output per hectare was still one-third that of Japan. The government did orchestrate extension campaigns to raise crop yields, providing fertiliser, improved seeds and funds for infrastructure, but in the absence of land reform these had little impact on yields. Indebted tenants and agricultural labourers were not incentivised to produce more when most of the upside would go to landlords. Moreover landlords and other local elites pilfered a large part of the development funds.

After Suharto became president in 1967, there was a more focused push to increase yields through agricultural extension support, which initially led to more edifying results. Part of the reason was that the Suharto regime introduced minimum price guarantees for rice. None the less, yield gains tailed off in the mid 1970s amid widespread evidence that extension and other funds were again being misappropriated, not least by government marketing co-operatives at village level which, instead of paying the mandated minimum prices to peasants for their crops, pocketed the money.[86]

Indonesia failed to change its landholding pattern, and it also failed to escape from south-east Asia's colonial approach to food policy which had long emphasised the provision of cheap food for consumers rather than higher food prices to incentivise small farmers. The policy made sense to colonial governments whose constituency was plantation and mine operators wanting to keep down labour costs.[87] It was not conducive to rural development in an independent state. Post-independence leaders, however, consistently prioritised their urban populations ahead of their rural ones, a mix of the old colonial bias and the urban bias of the new indigenous elite. As the population rose, low agricultural yields meant that Indonesia was forced to import huge volumes of rice and wheat, draining away foreign exchange for which it had more pressing developmental uses. Rice self-sufficiency was eventually achieved in the mid 1980s, but general food self-sufficiency remained beyond reach.

The story of the nationalised plantations in Indonesia is no happier. Most of the formerly foreign-controlled estates were taken over by state-owned companies and run inefficiently. In the 1960s sugar plantations – which covered the largest area – saw yields fall to half pre-Second World War levels, posting heavy losses.[88] Again, government was guilty of urban bias, determined to keep domestic sugar prices low and to tax the plantations heavily. Under Suharto, a radical shift to smallholder sugar growing was proposed in 1975 as a means to raise yields.[89] However, smallholders were compelled to take up sugar farming, their commercial relationship with the sugar mills was not put on attractive terms, there was no provision of adequate credit and extension services, and sugar continued to be more heavily taxed than other crops. The predictable outcome was that farmers grew sugar against their will at low yields.

Ultimately, Indonesia switched to what Michael Lipton has dubbed one of the 'two great evasions'[90] of developmental land policy – a farmer resettlement programme. (The other one, says Lipton, is when a government focuses purely on tenancy issues without any land redistribution.) As Java's population pushed up to 80 million in the 1970s, the Suharto administration began shipping tens of thousands of families off to new farming areas on less populous islands, in particular Sumatra. By far the most intense period of sponsored migration was between 1979 and 1984, when 1.5 million settlers were paid by the government to move.[91] The policy did not address the fundamental problems of land reform or effective agricultural extension – and the relocation costs to the state were very high – but it did manage temporarily to alleviate pressure in some of Indonesia's poorest areas.

Ironically, for those millions of landless and subsistence farmers who remain on Java, the one thing which often keeps them from starvation is the garden around their dwelling. It is the same for inhabitants of other equatorial countries in Asia, Latin America and the Caribbean. The equatorial climate means that some form of foodstuff can always be in season. Studies in Java show that food output per square metre of domestic gardens is far higher than in paddy fields or other areas that are given over to formal agriculture and are farmed by tenants or day labourers. It turns out that the high yields of north-east Asian agriculture are present in places like Java – but only on the tiniest of scales in the micro-plots cultivated for personal consumption.[92]

### The British view of agricultural efficiency

In the colonial era, Indonesia was the most profitable colony for the Dutch. For the British, Malaysia was even more profitable. The reason for this was that Malaysian farming was structured even more heavily in the interests of plantation agriculture, which put profit per hectare for small numbers of third-party investors ahead of output per hectare and food self-sufficiency. By the time of the First World War, about 400,000 hectares of Malaysia had been converted to plantations, a far higher proportion of available land than in Indonesia.[93]

The land belonged in theory to the Malay sultans, but was leased out at the discretion of British 'Residents', or advisers. Better quality land, and land which fronted on to the extensive road network constructed during this time – essential to the marketing of produce – went to plantations. Government infrastructure investments beyond the road network, from irrigation and electrification to agricultural extension services, were also largely targeted at plantations. And colonial banks dealt only with plantations. These considerations amounted to a hefty subsidy to the plantation sector. As Malaysia's leading agricultural historian, Lim Teck Ghee, put it: 'Peasant producers were thought to be inefficient and backward, and so they were relegated to a subsidiary role in the development of the Malay States.'[94] The only investment support given to smallholders encouraged them to grow rice in order to limit the country's food import requirement necessitated by its plantation economy.

The fallacy of the claims about plantation efficiency, however, was unexpectedly exposed in Malaysia in the 1920s, when British officials were forced to conduct yield surveys. The country was then the world's biggest rubber producer. The story began when global rubber prices began to fall precipitously in 1920 as demand waned after the First World War. It was not long before the mostly European owners of supposedly efficient plantations were demanding output controls to shore up prices. Despite the imprecations of the colonial government to focus on rice, Malay smallholders had also piled into rubber growing and accounted for one-third of production. However, they did not join the campaign to restrict output. A committee of inquiry chaired by Sir James Stevenson was appointed by the Secretary of State for the Colonies, Winston Churchill. This committee found in favour of limits on rubber output and, from November 1922, the Stevenson Restriction Scheme came into force in Malaysia and in Sri Lanka, Britain's other main rubber-growing colony. For plantations, the system restricted output based on their historic records. For smallholders, most of whom could not produce formal production records, it limited them on the basis of an arbitrary government estimate of expected smallholder yields. The estimate, at 320 pounds per acre per year, was well below that of plantations, which was typically around 400 pounds.[95]

The announcement of the details of the Stevenson scheme almost caused a peasant rebellion. Violent protests occurred around Malaysia. The reason was that the smallholder yield estimate bore no relation to reality. A new investigation was quickly announced. This revealed, much to the colonial government's embarrassment, that smallholder rubber yields were consistently higher than plantation ones. Indeed, the average smallholder yield was more than 50 per cent higher than that of the average plantation, and in some cases several multiples higher. Evidence submitted to the Stevenson committee showed that, on surveyed smallholdings, yields ranged between 600 pounds and 1,200 pounds per acre per year.[96]

The reasons for the higher smallholder yields were the usual 'gardening' ones. Peasants planted their trees more densely – often 200 per acre versus 100 on a plantation – and they tapped them daily, maximising their output at the expense of extra labour. The peasants were also far more resilient than the plantations to the global commodities depression, because they intercropped foodstuffs with their rubber and frequently also had secondary non-farming occupations. Without the overheads of the plantation owners, they were willing and able to take lower prices. Yet they were forced to accept output restrictions in order to stop the plantations going bust.

The Stevenson committee recommended an increase in the smallholding average estimated yield from 320 pounds to 533 pounds, which was still too low but was at least no worse than that of the more efficient plantations. However, both the colonial government and the British government failed to support the proposal and the peasants were allocated an average yield of 426 pounds per acre, of which their allowed production was then a fraction. The Stevenson restriction ran until 1928. A second, international restriction agreement made in 1934 was also biased against smallholder interests.

A British government-commissioned report published after the Second World War estimated the loss to Malaysian smallholder rubber growers from the two schemes had been GBP40 million, or around GBP2.1 billion at today's prices – equivalent to two years of rubber output for the whole of Malaysia. The report's author, P.T Bauer, condemned the bias of the restriction schemes against smallholders as 'a clear breach of certain definite moral obligations'.[97] The farmers received no compensation.

The rubber market in colonial Malaysia was a simple case of a market being rigged in such a way that higher-yield family farmers subsidised lower-yield big business. Under the Stevenson scheme, the colonial government even put plantation operators in charge of assessing the size of smallholder plots, leading to many more complaints that the sizes as well as the yields of the household farms were being systematically under-assessed. There was no way that the government was going to be convinced by mere sampling evidence that smallholders were substantially more productive than large plantations which had general managers and London stock listings. Yet, despite all the state assistance given to the plantation sector before and during the depression, this was incontrovertibly the case.

A further example of smallholder efficiency became apparent in the 1920s and 1930s in tin mining areas. As thousands of ethnic Chinese miners were laid off during the depression, large numbers of them turned for survival to market gardening. Food commanded a good price in Malaysia because so much of it was imported, and government noticed that family plots were beginning to supply a high proportion of urban food requirements. Restrictions on the growing of crops on mining land were suspended to further encourage the practice.[98] But there was no rethinking of basic agricultural policy, which continued to favour plantation profit over output maximisation and Malaysian development.

## The British view becomes the Malaysian view

The end of the Second World War and Malaysian independence in 1957 augured no significant change in land policy. Unlike the Philippines and Indonesia, Malaysia did not even attempt land reform, although the spirit of the times required some greater sensibility to peasant interests. Legislation passed in 1955 and 1967 was supposed to increase tenant security and ban tenant cash deposits known as 'tea money', but the laws were weak and enforcement was left up to individual states, largely run by landed elites. Subsidies were introduced for agricultural essentials such as fertiliser, but again their distribution favoured large farms over small. A government fund to support rubber replanting was established, but the contributions it required from its recipients were often reckoned to exceed the value of the support offered.[99] As in Indonesia, government fell back on expensive resettlement schemes, run by institutions like the Federal Land Development Agency (FELDA). Many of the European-owned plantations were bought out during the 1970s using petrodollars but were run no more, and often less, efficiently by Malaysian state companies.

In the post-independence era land concentration in Malaysia increased and, as a corollary, tenancy and landlessness increased. As ever, tenancy and landlessness were associated with poverty and indebtedness and, frequently, falling yields.[100] One exasperated observer stated in the mid 1970s: 'Despite some inadequate and half-hearted legislation, tenancy and share-cropping, with all the attending insecurity, exists substantially and the concentration of smallholdings in the hands of speculators, investors, and money-lenders is spreading.'[101]

From 1981, the Mahathir administration brought some relief to rice cultivators by guaranteeing minimum prices. However, most poverty reduction in rural areas in Malaysia since the 1980s has been achieved not by increasing smallholder farming incomes, but instead by farmers finding non-agricultural work related to the export processing economy. Malaysia is not, it should be stressed, a country that faces a shortage of agricultural land. Most local agronomists say there are still several hundred thousand hectares that could be opened up to agriculture, while in periods of recession like the early 1980s thousands of hectares of existing agricultural land have

lain idle. Instead, Malaysia is a country that has found a sub-optimal structure for its agricultural economy despite a surfeit of land. This is another
reminder that, in order to thrive, smallholders require not only their fields,
but also the extension, marketing and credit infrastructure that allows them
to compete.[102]

**For anyone who missed the point, Thailand puts on a show**

The agricultural economist Ronald Herring noted that the most common
defence for doing the minimum possible to enforce land redistribution – as
has been the case throughout south-east Asia – is that one must be realistic
about the difficulty of doing more. The counter to this argument, Herring
pointed out, is that 'the political realists seem to assume, rather curiously,
that it is politically realistic to leave the *status quo* in place'.[103]

In south-east Asia, the agricultural *status quo* has proven to have very
high costs. In the Philippines, the state has repeatedly been confronted
by peasant-based revolutionary and terrorist groups. In Indonesia in the
1960s, Suharto suppressed a rural-based communist movement with the
loss of hundreds of thousands of lives. In Malaysia, the British fought a
ruthless campaign in the countryside to suppress a communist insurgency
in the late 1940s and early 1950s. And in Thailand, land policy failure is
contributing to a state of near civil war even as this book is being written.

In May 2010, the Thai military killed scores of 'Red Shirt' anti-gov-
ernment protesters, whose base is Thailand's impoverished north-east, in
street battles in Bangkok. The confrontation came only a few years after a
renewed insurgency in the poorest areas of southern Thailand was brutally
put down. In the last decade, Thailand has witnessed the worst rural-driven
violence since the military fought a long campaign against guerrillas of the
Communist Party of Thailand in the north and north-east of the country
in the late 1960s and 1970s. As in the past, at the root of the latest violence
is a cyclical upsurge in rural poverty – this time associated with the post-
boom era after the Asian financial crisis.

The agricultural history of Thailand – which, unlike other south-east
Asian states, remained nominally independent in the colonial era – can
crudely be divided into two geographically defined parts. The first is the

rice-dominated economy of the coastal areas and central plain. Like Malaysia, the Philippines prior to the 1950s and Java in the nineteenth century, Thailand has for most of its modern history been land-abundant. With the spread of colonial mining and cash crop agriculture in other parts of the region in the nineteenth century, the driver for Thai agriculture was a regional demand for rice exports to colonies that were concentrating on growing commodities like rubber and sugar. The Thai plain was drained to create ever more rice paddy. The central government built key drainage canals, but did little more. Land around Bangkok tended to be accumulated into large estates by allies of the royal family, but most of the land further afield was farmed by smallholders who cleared it themselves. Yields were low, but the abundance of land relative to population made this unimportant. For a long time, it was more fruitful for farmers to farm a larger area through broadcast sowing than by careful transplanting of seedlings. By the 1930s, Thailand was exporting 1.5 million tons of rice a year, despite yields of only about 1,200 kilogrammes per hectare – one-fifth of post-land reform north-east Asian yields.[104]

At the Thai court (the country was an absolute monarchy until 1932), the myth grew up of a happy, loyal peasantry tending rice in the provinces. When a minister of finance wrote Thailand's first formal treatise on economics in 1906–7, and had the temerity to argue that credit and other support were necessary for smallholders who were struggling, King Vajiravudh was outraged. 'I am able to attest,' he pronounced, 'that no other country has fewer poor or needy people than Siam.' Both the finance minister's work and the study of economics were banned.[105]

In reality, there was already rising tenancy, landlessness and indebtedness in the lead-up to the Second World War. However, since most land outside the Bangkok area could not be officially taken by creditors because of the absence of formal title, and because peasants could simply disappear and find new land, there were some limits to rural suffering.

After the Second World War, as the population growth rate rose to 3 per cent a year and tenancy, landlessness and wage-based labour increased further, there was a big jump in income inequality in rural areas. The government increased expenditure on rural infrastructure, but its overall policy remained heavily urban-biased. The proof of this was the setting-up of a monopoly state buyer of rice for export, or a monopsony, which pushed down domestic rice prices received by farmers, creating instead trading profits for government that in some years amounted to one-third of total state income. At the same time, the government charged so heavily for imported fertiliser that the cost, expressed in terms of kilos of rice equivalent, was five times what it was for contemporary Japanese farmers.[106]

The exactions on the rice economy were gradually reduced during the 1960s and 1970s as Thailand's rural insurgency expanded. But there were already tenancy rates of 30–50 per cent among rice farmers. The independent smallholder ceased to be the basis of the rice economy, throttled by population growth and state policy. State-organised credit was available from the 1960s, but it went to mid- and large-scale farmers with formal titles and to agribusiness. A Land Reform Act of 1975 led to almost no land redistribution.[107] Thailand's two best-known economic historians, Pasuk Phongpaichit and Chris Baker, conclude: 'Beyond the basic drainage works, the government provided no support for development of the rice economy. With very basic technology and virtually no access to capital, the frontier evolved the most low-tech, low-intensity, and low-yield paddy regime in Asia.'[108]

### The even less good bit

This is the first part of the Thai story. The second concerns the push into the less fertile regions of north and, especially, north-east Thailand (the area which borders Laos and Cambodia) after the Second World War.[109] As has already been mentioned, the government's state bank financing favoured large-scale agribusiness, but this became particularly the case in the north-east as the area was opened up at breakneck speed from the 1960s.

In the Philippines, Indonesia and Malaysia, the post-independence governments had inherited plantations and scale agriculture from their colonisers. In Thailand, it was a state that had not been formally colonised that created and nurtured this sector. It did so both by backing domestic agribusiness firms like Charoen Pokphand (now known as CP Group), and by welcoming foreign direct investment from companies like America's Dole.[110]

The creation from scratch of domestic agribusiness firms may have generated greater agricultural and industrial learning for large companies in Thailand than was the case with the takeovers of originally foreign-dominated plantation sectors in former colonies.[111] However, the support for agribusiness, as elsewhere, was very much at the expense of the smallholder sector. Individual Thai farmers tended to clear land in the north (following in the trail of loggers) and farm it, but they were heavily dependent on agribusiness for inputs and sales. And without formal title to their plots they had no access to bank credit.

It was not long before individual farmers were working as captive suppliers to state-bank-supported agribusinesses, which built sugar mills, cassava yards, animal feed mills and pineapple canneries, and other infrastructure necessary for industrial agriculture. CP Group developed a huge business supplying new-born chicks to peasant farmers who then raised them and sold chickens back to CP, which was a near-monopsonistic buyer. With little state investment in irrigation or other supports for smallholders, an impoverished rural economy developed in which many farmers worked at rain-fed agriculture for part of the year and then spent the off-season migrating in search of casual labour. By the 1980s, the north-east contained half of Thailand's poor.[112]

As in Malaysia and Indonesia, what kept the lid on the rural situation in the 1980s and 1990s was the rise of the labour-intensive export processing economy serving foreign multinationals which provided more and more off-farm employment. The agricultural situation was dire, but it was masked. Hundreds of thousands of young, rural Thais migrated from *ban* to *muang* – from village to city, from the north-east to Bangkok. They even created their own highly popular country music genre, *phleng luk thung*, singing lonesome tunes about the hardships of migrant life; a survey of popular titles in the late 1980s noted that one-fifth dealt with prostitution. On the eve of the Asian financial crisis, government income surveys showed that more than four-fifths of agricultural household income in the north-east was coming not from farming but from wages and remittances. This said as much about the failure of Thai land policy as it did about the growth of the export processing economy.[113]

Then came the Asian crisis, factory lay-offs, and spiralling rural poverty. It was in these conditions that a high-born urban tycoon, Thaksin Shinawatra, mobilised rural voters in the north-east behind a new political party, Thai Rak Thai. The resonance of his electoral strategy based on rural discontent was such that Thaksin was catapulted to the premiership in 2001. However, his ascent split the Bangkok military and civilian elite and threatened a national political breakdown. Thaksin was eventually chased into exile by the military in 2006 ending a brief – and rather disingenuous – attempt to give greater recognition to the rural masses. Thai Rak Thai threw the villages a bit of money; but it never promoted any radical change to land policy.[114]

A chasm-like division between Bangkok and the countryside, and an extreme urban bias in policymaking, have been a constant in Thailand. In the 1970s the agricultural economist Zahir Ahmed described the political view from the capital as follows:

> Here are all the trappings of modern civilisation – night clubs, bars, miniskirted girls, long-haired boys, narcotics, prostitution and perversion ... The villages where more than 75 percent of the people live, remain poor, congested and insanitary and the people there toil from day to day in a merciless, lifelong grind ... Here is a society of men with no social vision, living on the toil of the peasant, and striving to hold on to power.[115]

Almost nothing has changed. Today, Thailand, and south-east Asia generally, are still farmed by 'peasants', and still exist in a condition of political instability because of rural poverty. By not squarely confronting the agricultural aspects of development, the region's governments have consigned the bulk of their populations to economically fruitless lives and made industrialisation much more difficult. The vastly greater output that would be possible under properly supported household farming has been foregone. Rural populations which could have provided the basis of demand for manufactures and a source of industrial entrepreneurship are instead a dead weight. There has been a straightforward failure of developmental policy.

**No good policy lasts for ever**

North-east Asia, unlike south-east Asia, no longer has 'peasants'. In Japan, Korea, Taiwan (and, from 1978, China), land reform – backed by the necessary institutional support – unleashed unprecedented agricultural growth, created markets and unlocked very considerable social mobility. However, this does not mean these states managed their agricultural development to perfection. Even the best policy is only a solution to the developmental challenges of a particular moment in time. As the economic environment unfolds, good policies that remain unchanged eventually turn into bad ones.

In agriculture, the initial developmental challenge is to maximise yields and output by utilising all the labour in an economy. Gardening-style cultivation achieves this. However, as industry takes off and rural dwellers begin to move into better-paid industrial and service jobs, farming needs to rebalance towards a greater emphasis on productivity and profit. Gradually, this requires a shift towards larger, more mechanised farms, allowing the incomes of the remaining farmers to rise beyond what is permitted by the cultivation of equalised small plots. There is no reason for tenancy to reappear if surplus farm labour is employed in industry and services, and credit and marketing institutions for family farming remain in place. In the land-abundant United States, average farm size has increased in line with gross domestic product growth from around fifty hectares in the late nineteenth century to nearly 200 hectares today. Yet, three-quarters of farm labour continues to come from families. American farmers steadily used more and bigger machines on expanding farms, accepting lower potential yields per hectare in return for higher profits per farmer.[116]

As a country develops, like its industry its agriculture needs to specialise by activity. Most states do not have high natural resource to population endowments such that farming can remain a large part of their economies, as in the anomalous cases of New Zealand or Denmark. They will have greater competitive strengths in manufacturing or services. But states with good policies will find globally competitive niches that allow farmer incomes to continue to rise as labour leaves the countryside This involves a move away from agricultural protection and guaranteed minimum farm prices. From a global development perspective, reduced protection in already-developed countries also gives other poor countries in turn the opportunity, in turn, to export their agricultural surplus in the period when their labour is cheapest; it keeps the developmental drawbridge down.

Unfortunately, in north-east Asia, governments in Japan, Korea and, to a lesser extent, Taiwan failed to make the transition to larger farms, greater specialisation and reduced protectionism. They gradually eased legal restrictions on the leasing and sale of agricultural land to allow consolidation of farms. But they then undermined incentives to consolidate and specialise by paying increasing, world-beating subsidies to farmers. The main reason for this was that family farms in north-east Asia substituted for welfare systems. Moreover, once they could afford to, governments wanted to show their fiscal appreciation for agricultural sectors that had primed economic take-off. The household farming country in east Asia that largely gave up subsidies *and* kept farms small – China – has seen urban incomes rise to more than three times rural ones. This level of inequality was never acceptable to governments in Japan, Korea and Taiwan. However, the determination to maintain parity between urban and rural incomes substituted an extreme form of welfare policy for economic development policy.

In Japan, whose industrial boom kicked in at the start of the 1950s, agricultural incomes had begun to decline relative to urban ones by the middle of the decade. The government started immediately to use a crop purchasing system set up during the Second World War to pay farmers above-market prices for part of their output. The core focus of price support was – as has been the case throughout north-east Asia – rice. The price the government paid for rice doubled in the 1960s and doubled again in the 1970s. A combination of rising subsidies, an effective ban on agricultural imports and plentiful off-farm employment opportunities meant that by the mid 1970s the average rural family was earning more than the average urban one – a situation unthinkable in other developing countries.[117] The result was that, instead of scaling up, fewer and older members of farm families cultivated unchanged plots using small-scale machinery. The average age of farmers across north-east Asia has been over fifty years since 1990; in essence, the first land reform generation stayed put on their small plots while their children left for the cities.

A rare rural diary kept by a farmer in Niigata prefecture, near to the former Ito family estate, gives a sense of the transition from poverty to abundance to state indulgence. Nishiyama Kōichi, the diarist, was born into a family of impoverished and indebted tenants in 1902. He grew up in the depression pursuing one failed sideline activity after another – each financed with borrowed money – in his struggle with destitution. At the end of the Second World War, Nishiyama became a farmer representative on his area's land committee during land reform. Following land redistribution, his diary relates how emancipated farmers co-operated on paddy and irrigation improvements, drained marshes and started a collective rice research group. Yields and output shot up. Nishiyama became the archetypal land reform success story. Then, in the 1960s, subsidy payments started to become substantial. The first local farmland was re-zoned for housing development and villagers enjoyed a windfall from the sale of a communal plot to a local politician. Thereafter, Nishiyama's diary entries are less concerned with farming issues and more with the outlook for further commercial re-zoning. With money to pay for all sorts of fancy tools, and land values soaring, Nishiyama was able to retire, leaving his eldest son in charge of family affairs. The son, however, was barely interested in farming. He began to play the stock market and, by 1987, lost JPY300 million (just over USD2 million in today's money[118]), borrowed against the hugely inflated value of Nishiyama's land. The family turned in one generation from impoverished tenant peasantry to super-intensive, frugal household farmers to subsidised – and bankrupted – stock market day traders.[119]

South Korea moved to increasing subsidy and protection of domestic agriculture in the 1970s and 1980s. The government bought larger and larger quantities of rice at above-market prices, which it then sold on to consumers at a discount of up to 50 per cent. A state monopoly on fertiliser supply, which early in the country's development was used to squeeze money out of farmers by charging them above-world-market rates, was redeployed to further subsidise input costs by providing fertiliser cheap. The government acquired a large 'rice mountain' because farmers were encouraged to grow more rice than people wanted to eat and almost every crop benefited from import protection. Of the 547 standard product categories which faced quantitative import restrictions in Korea by the late 1980s, all but a few dozen were agricultural products.[120]

Taiwan's farmers were both the most successful and the least protected in the region. During the island's early agricultural boom, farm exports were almost 60 per cent of the value of all exports in the mid 1960s. The proportion dropped quickly to less than 20 per cent in 1975, as rural and urban industrialisation took off and, in line with this shift, rural incomes fell from near-parity with urban ones to a level one-quarter below urban ones.[121] As in Korea, from the 1970s government adjusted the selling prices of a state fertiliser monopoly to stop squeezing and start subsidising farmers. It also began to buy part of the rice harvest at high prices. Similar supports were put in place for sugar farmers. However, protection was relatively less than in Japan and Korea, and Taiwanese farmers were therefore forced to diversify more and to develop more internationally competitive products. They became, for instance, important regional exporters of pork products.

Everywhere in north-east Asia, agricultural subsidies were paid for by consumers through higher prices and higher taxes. Even after reductions in recent years, the share of farm incomes in Japan and Korea accounted for by subsidies is one-half. This compares with one-quarter in Taiwan, one-fifth in Europe and one-tenth in the United States.[122] The annual direct agricultural subsidy expenditures of the Japanese and Korean governments are well over 1 per cent of GDP – even though in Japan agriculture now accounts for less than 1 per cent of GDP. And there are many indirect costs associated with protecting tiny farms beyond their developmental due date. For the consumer, food prices in Japan are 60 per cent higher than world market prices, and the price of rice is a multiple of the world price. A sense of the extremity of the situation is given by the fact that a single apple in Japan can cost USD5. On my trip from Tokyo to Niigata, I bought apples in convenience stores in Tokyo and Chichibu for USD4 and USD3 respectively, although I balked at paying USD10 for ten strawberries.[123] You know that something is wrong when a few strawberries cost what Japan's lowest-paid temporary workers now make in an hour.

The ossification of agricultural policy presaged many other challenges in the outperforming east Asian states. In general, it pointed to a distinctly limited political capacity to cope with the dynamic nature of economic development. The fact that governments were able to institute land reform and its necessary supporting infrastructure as their strategy for take-off did not mean they were natural experts in the subsequent stages of the development process. They discovered – as have the fast-growth emerging economies of Europe since the Second World War – that knowing how to regulate and how to deregulate are two different things. And while the difficulty of the first is such that few states even get into the ballpark of successful developing countries, the difficulty of the second is no less great.

**Credit where due**

Despite the recent farm policy woes of north-east Asia, nothing can detract from the impact that the initial household land reform had on rural, and in turn industrial, economies. Household farming produced two enormously beneficial effects that could not have been achieved through other policies. The first was the fullest possible use of labour in rural economies in order to maximise output. As Michael Lipton put it: 'In *early development*, with labour plentiful and the ability to save scarce, small farming is especially promising, because it is the part of the economy in which a given amount of scarce investible resources will be supported by the most human effort.'[124] Increased agricultural production then translated into rural purchasing power to buy early manufactures. Land reform created a kind of 'consumption shock' as waves of spending power for basic, domestically manufactured consumer goods spread through the economy. Increased farm output also helped countries to pay for the imported technology they needed to industrialise.

The second effect of land reform was separate from the output and consumption shock effect, but combined with it to produce yet more economic virtue. It was the creation of a high level of social mobility as the result of an equal initial distribution of society's most basic non-human asset – land. People not only competed on equal terms but they could realistically believe that they had a chance of success. They did. It is emblematic that in South Korea two key historical figures who appear in the next chapter, President Park Chung Hee and Hyundai founder Chung Ju Yung, were both the sons of farmers; and that a third key character who led the struggle for democracy and institutional development, Kim Dae Jung, was also a farmer's son. In Taiwan, the best-known industrialist, Wang Yung-ching of the Formosa Plastics Group, was a farmer's son, as were many of his entrepreneurial peers. Chen Shui-bian, a leader of the pro-democracy movement who in 2000 became the first non-Nationalist Party president, was a peasant's son. In mainland China, the pioneering entrepreneurs of the 1980s were overwhelmingly from farming backgrounds.[125] This type of social mobility in business and political life is almost unheard of in south-east Asia, where elites still rule the roost from one generation to the next. A major reason is that fairness in land distribution has never been established there and therefore has never led to societies of broadly based opportunity. In terms of social mobility, south-east Asian states are much more like Latin American ones, where land reform has also failed.

In the wake of the Second World War, progressive politicians in north-east Asia, and outsiders like Wolf Ladejinsky, recognised the capacity of land reform to deliver simultaneously on both the economic and political fronts. Land redistribution primed the most impressive economic development performances the world has seen *and* undercut the attractions of militant communism and other insurgencies. Yet despite being both pro-market and pro-democratic, the land reform case was never taken up with any conviction by the political elite of the world's pre-eminent power, the United States. After Taiwan in the early 1950s, the US never again pushed comprehensive land reform in Asia – excepting the far-too-late programme announced in South Vietnam in 1969, when Washington was already looking to cut and run. South Vietnamese land reform echoed the superficial US intervention in China in 1948. Elsewhere in south-east Asia, America went with the *status quo*, even though the *status quo* has meant terrorism and insurgency in each of the major south-east Asian states, and those states remain today as much problems as allies to US foreign policy and national interest. Land reform continues to be dismissed as too difficult, even though land inequality and agricultural dysfunction are at the heart of the world's most dangerous societies. Pakistan is perhaps the outstanding case in point.

In the US domestic politics of the 1950s, the pro-market ideas of Ladejinsky and his ilk were represented by the country's insular right-wing politicians as socialism by the back door. After the victory of the Republican Dwight D. Eisenhower in November 1952, the political atmosphere in Washington swung decisively against those supporting forced land redistribution. Joe McCarthy's 'anti-communist' cabal had been growing in strength since 1950 and Eisenhower's election lent it support. In November 1954, Ladejinsky was turned down for a routine job reassignment at the Department of Agriculture on 'security' grounds. The reasons cited for this by the Secretary of Agriculture, Ezra Taft Benson, were that Ladejinsky had three sisters in the Soviet Union (making him, it was argued, a potential subject of coercion), that he had visited there in 1939, and that he had worked briefly as a translator for the American office of a Soviet trading firm after he first arrived in the US. Benson also made clear to journalists that he did not like the idea of land reform, though he conceded that he understood little of the details of its implementation in north-east Asia.[126] Ladejinsky refused to resign and was fired, although he was defended by some more thoughtful Republicans, who stood up for him against Benson and Eisenhower. For instance, Walter Judd, a Republican congressman, described Ladejinsky's work as 'about the only successful anti-communist step we have taken in Asia'.[127] Ladejinsky went on to take up a job resettling refugees in south Vietnam, and later to positions at the Ford Foundation and the World Bank. He died in 1975.

**Poor excuses**

Two main excuses are used by those countries in south-east Asia which have failed to institute effective land reform. Neither bears close scrutiny. The first is that the cash crops grown in south-east Asia are unsuited to household production. The plantation managers who reflexively offer up this excuse are usually unaware of the success of household sugar and banana farming during Taiwan's early development, of household sugar cultivation in China today, or indeed of any other hard evidence. The colonial history of smallholder rubber production in Malaysia has also been conveniently forgotten. There, and in Indonesia, the producers of south-east Asia's most important contemporary cash crop – palm oil – insist that it can only be grown effectively on plantations. Yet the large farms' perennial complaints about the price of labour suggest that this might be another crop suitable for household cultivation given the right supporting infrastructure for processing and marketing. Palm oil yields are highly sensitive to labour input. The fruits in oil palm bunches ripen unevenly and have to be surgically cut out at least every ten days to avoid rotting and pest infestation. Engineers have never been able to mechanise the task and the work can only be done by hand. There is no reason why plantation agriculture should have a natural yield advantage over household farms; yields on Malaysian and Indonesian plantations have barely increased in the past two decades. Malaysia's plantations now require imported cheap labour to turn a profit – just like the indentured 'Indian rubber man' who became essential to the profitability of colonial rubber plantations.[128]

Almost anything – and perhaps everything – that grows is able to benefit from increased human attention. This is why there is so much evidence from so many countries that farm yields per hectare are in inverse proportion to farm size.[129] It has been too easy for too long for plantation operators to argue that the case for their crops is otherwise, because most people know little about the agronomy of the crops they grow. However, the basic arguments about why home gardening produces high yields are also applicable to cash crops. Plant exceptionalism, like human exceptionalism, is pronounced more often than it occurs. The economies of scale that exist in agriculture in south-east Asia are not in cultivation, but in processing and marketing, which means that household farming is no less viable there than in north-east Asia.

The second south-east Asian excuse is the political one that successful land reform in north-east Asia was the unrepeatable product of historical circumstances, and of the intervention of the United States. Superficially, this looks to be a more credible argument. Land reform was indeed instituted in Japan, South Korea and Taiwan in the context of military defeat in the Second World War, and against landed interests which were closely identified with defeated forces (in Korea and Taiwan, as in mainland China, landlords had co-operated closely with the Japanese). The United States pressed land reform on the north-east Asian states to varying degrees, and supported its implementation with considerable financial and technical aid. None the less, in Japan and South Korea, and to a lesser extent in Taiwan, domestic politicians also played a significant role in pushing through land reform legislation and its implementation. Ladejinsky wrote that in Japan the socialist Minister of Agriculture, Hiroo Wada, was the single most important person in ensuring that land reform happened.[130] In South Korea, a left-leaning Minister of Agriculture, Cho Pong-am, organised the drafting of the first land reform law in November 1948 and confronted the anti-reform president Syngman Rhee so aggressively it cost him his life; he was denounced as a North Korean spy and executed.[131] On the question of US aid, it should be noted that large amounts of financial support were also given to the Philippines and Thailand, and to Indonesia after Sukarno's fall, but that the governments of those countries chose to spend little of it on rural development.

The political excuse for inaction on land reform is subtle and pernicious. It suggests countries cannot control their own developmental destinies. However, while it may be difficult – and far more land reform attempts around the world have failed than have succeeded – they can. Meiji Japan instituted a first land reform without any external political direction or funding. In India, the state governments of Kerala and West Bengal pushed through land reforms in the 1960s and 1970s despite the rest of the nation's failure to do so. Developing countries are not just little ships blown about on the developmental ocean by the winds of rich states. In agriculture they have a greater capacity to chart their own course than in any other sector of the economy because land policy is entirely a domestic affair. In this respect, land policy is the acid test of the government of a poor country. It measures the extent to which leaders are in touch with the bulk of their population – farmers – and the extent to which they are willing to shake up society to produce positive developmental outcomes. In short, land policy tells you how much the leaders know and care about their populations. On both counts, north-east Asian leaders scored far better than south-east Asian ones, and this goes a long way to explaining why their countries are richer.

The only real defence for south-east Asia is that the influence of European and American colonialism made it harder for politicians there to see what kind of policies they needed. It is incontrovertible that colonialism did a lot of damage to south-east Asia. However it did not *guarantee* countries' inability to make good development choices. The heart of the problem was that elites in south-east Asia were sufficiently co-opted by colonial rulers (before and after independence) that they lost their ability – or perhaps their desire – to think clearly about national economic development. In Korea and Taiwan, anger at Japanese colonialism and humiliation from the communist victory in mainland China made leaders think more clearly about how to raise their nations up. The only really angry leaders that south-east Asian states produced were Sukarno, who was utterly dissolute, and Mahathir Mohamad, who knew too little economic history to make informed policy choices for his country.

It is now time to move forward, but without ever forgetting the profound importance of agriculture to rapid economic transformation. The sector that employs the vast majority of the population of a poor country cannot be underestimated.

# Part 2

# Manufacturing: The Victory of the Historians

*'If I had to summarise the essence of what economic history can contribute to economic science, I would say that there exist no "laws" or rules in economics which are valid for all periods of history.'*

Paul Bairoch, *Mythes et paradoxes de l'histoire économique*[1]

Agricultural policy is important in poor countries because most people are farmers, and household farming can deliver big output and consumption boosts that can get an economy moving briskly forwards. However, a country cannot sustain growth on agriculture alone. Returns from land reform and other agricultural improvements begin to taper off after only a decade or so, and emerging economies have to transition into another phase of development. That phase has historically revolved around manufacturing. Today, even though the service sectors have come to dominate the economies of rich countries, manufacturing remains critical to the rapid economic transformation of poor countries.

There are two main reasons why this is the case. The first is that manufacturing is based on the use of machines, and so it allows poor countries to mitigate their biggest constraint at the earliest stage of development – a shortfall of productive *human* skills. In manufacturing, a small number of entrepreneurs and technicians is able, through the medium of machines (imported to begin with), to have an outsized impact on economic development by focusing on mechanised production that employs large cohorts of unskilled and semi-skilled labour. Workers can add value in basic manufacturing tasks after minimal training; they can then learn more skills on the job. Many service sector activities are not like this, because productivity gains depend on educating and changing people before they can be productive. A person has to learn software code, for instance, before he or she can write even one line of software. Furthermore, it is less common for machines to 'scale up' what people do in service jobs than in manufacturing. This point becomes clear if you think of the difference between a person overseeing a robotic production line in a factory, where the person's work adds value via himself *and* several machines, and a person who provides a service that has to be delivered to each customer discretely, as when a telephone operator can speak to only one customer at a time. In short, productivity gains in services are inherently slower than in manufacturing because there is greater dependence in the former on people and on enhancing human skills.[2]

73

The second reason why manufacturing is so important is another relative advantage that it has over the service sector. This is that manufactures are much more freely traded in the world than services. Most manufactures can be put in containers and shipped to anyone willing to pay for them. Trade in services faces more practical and political impediments. In practical terms, some services – like call centres or software – are sold at distance down phone and computer lines. But most services require goods or people to travel in two directions, adding time and cost. It is not typically viable, for instance, to send bicycles to India for repairs, or to fly heart-attack patients around the world before operating on them. Politically, there are still greater constraints on trade in services. Genuine free trade in services would require free movement of labour around the world, so that any service could be performed where it was required. However not even neoliberal economists want to let labour migrate at will. Evangelists of the free market do not really believe in free trade when it comes to unrestricted movement of people, and nor do rich country governments. Partly for this reason, in international trade agreements trade in services is opened up more slowly than that in manufactures. Consequently, any country which bases its development policy on its service sector faces higher barriers to exports than one with a traditional manufacturing-oriented policy. It should be no surprise that the share of services in total world trade has been stuck at around one-fifth for the past two decades.[3]

Manufacturing allows for trade, and trade is essential to rapid economic development. Through it, poor countries learn productive skills from more advanced economies and acquire new technologies. Non-trading ('autarkic') developing states such as the former Soviet Union, China before 1978 and India before 1991 made painfully slow technological progress; indeed, so much so that their populations lost faith in the possibilities of economic advancement. For states that want to get into the developmental fast lane, the global market in manufactures is the natural conduit for a quick technological learning process. Home markets are important because local firms understand their local customers instinctively. But international markets and international trade force companies to shape up in unique ways, adjusting their products to meet different demands and increasing their potential aggregate market by many times. Learning about manufactured products that foreigners like also paves the way to more demanding services exports at a later stage.

It is difficult for people in rich countries to recognise the importance of manufacturing in development because in our economies services are now so dominant and manufacturing employs so few people. Most of us are also unaware that, because of the extraordinary productivity gains that are possible in manufacturing, even the comparatively shrunken manufacturing sectors in rich countries today produce more goods than ever. In a manufacturing laggard such as the United Kingdom, the real value of manufacturing output is currently two and a half times what it was at the end of the Second World War. This expanded output is produced by less than one-tenth of the British workforce, compared with the one-third of employees who worked in manufacturing as recently as 1960.[4]

None the less, the productivity gains do not mean it is easy for a country like Britain to further expand its manufacturing sector. This is because many machine-based tasks are most efficiently undertaken by the kind of low-skilled, cheap workers that rich countries are short of. And that is precisely where the opportunities lie for emerging nations. Their manufacturing is nothing like as efficient as it is in advanced economies, but nor does it need to be because poor countries can throw highly motivated, cut-price, fresh-off-the-farm labour at the task.

### Caveat imperium

Manufacturing and trade drive the second phase of rapid economic development. The challenge to policymakers is therefore to direct entrepreneurial talent towards manufacturing rather than services, and in particular towards large-scale manufacturing with the heft to compete globally. Manufacturing firms are nurtured by the state in two ways: through protection and through subsidy. These interventions create breathing space for entrepreneurs while they learn to manufacture competitively.

Unfortunately, protection and subsidy also bring with them a well-known risk – one which economists call 'rent seeking'. In a developing country, rent seeking refers to the propensity of entrepreneurs to concentrate their efforts on obtaining protection and subsidies (rents) from the state without delivering the technological progress and competitiveness that economic development requires. The problem is a very real one and has undermined industrial development efforts in many poor countries. The solution to the problem is to find mechanisms that force manufacturing entrepreneurs to become globally competitive *at the same time as* they are allowed to make profits for themselves. In other words, the interests of national development and business have to be forcibly aligned.

Governments in all the major economies of east Asia tried at some stage to nurture domestic manufacturers. That those in north-east Asia succeeded, while those in south-east Asia failed miserably, turned on a small number of policy differences. By far the most important of these was the presence – or absence – of what I call 'export discipline'. This term refers to a policy of continually testing and benchmarking domestic manufacturers that are given subsidies and market protection by forcing them to export their goods and hence face global competition. It is their level of exports that reveals whether they merit state support or not.

International sales have been the feedback mechanism by which successful governments have known whether the manufacturing businesses they have nurtured are approaching global standards, and whether firms have invested the billions of dollars it takes to create, for instance, a viable steel maker or car firm efficiently. Where export discipline has not been present, development policy has become a game of charades, with local firms able to pretend that they have been achieving world-class standards without having to prove it in the global market place. In south-east Asia, the energies of entrepreneurs were directed towards fooling politicians rather than exporting. In these circumstances, they demonstrated all the proverbial finesse required to sell sand to Arabs or snow to Eskimos. They also drained away nations' developmental capital, redirecting much of it into excessive real estate development that culminated in the property bubbles associated with the Asian financial crisis.

The capacity to export told politicians in Japan, South Korea and Taiwan what worked and what didn't and they responded accordingly. Since exports have to pass through customs, they were relatively easy to check up on. In Japan, the amount of depreciation firms were allowed to charge to their accounts – effectively, a tax break – was determined by their exports.

In Korea, firms had to report export performance to the government on a monthly basis, and the numbers determined their access to bank credit. In Taiwan, everything from cash subsidies to preferential exchange rates was used to encourage exporters.

North-east Asian politicians then improved their industrial policy returns through a second intervention – culling those firms which did not measure up. This might have meant a forced merger with a more successful firm, the withdrawal of capital by a state-directed financial system, withholding – or threatening to withhold – production licences, or even the ultimate capitalist sanction, bankruptcy. Since the 1970s, there has been much talk about state industrial policy in western countries being an attempt to 'pick winners' among firms, something that most people would agree is extremely difficult. But this term does not describe what happened in successful developing states in east Asia.[5] In Japan, Korea, Taiwan and China, the state did not so much pick winners as weed out losers.

Japan developed a government agency as early as the 1930s to 'rationalise' different manufacturing sectors through mergers after studying German practice, and reintroduced a similar agency after the Second World War.[6] The South Korean state was still more direct in its disciplining of under-achieving businesses. Most of the top ten *chaebol* (conglomerates) of the mid 1960s had disappeared through forced mergers and bankruptcy by the mid 1970s, and half of the new group had disappeared by the early 1980s.[7] Few Koreans, let alone foreigners, now know the names of some of the biggest *chaebol* of the post-war era, such as Samho, Gaepong, Donglip, Shinjin and Dongmyung – and that is because they are long dead. Another group of huge firms, including Daewoo, Hanbo, Halla and Sammi, was culled by a process of state negotiation and fiat during the Asian financial crisis. In the car industry, half a dozen auto makers were set up in Korea with the help of direct and indirect state subsidies in the 1970s and 1980s. Over the next three decades, most of these firms were killed off. Today only one purely Korean car firm survives, Hyundai (with Kia as its subsidiary). However, the last company standing is the fastest-growing and one of the most successful car firms in the world.

The fact that north-east Asian governments concentrated on weeding out losers rather than picking winners also helps to explain the existence of large businesses which grew up without significant direct state support and outside state plans – like Sony and Honda in Japan, or Acer and HTC in Taiwan – in addition to ones which received more state largesse. Businesses that worked were always allowed to survive.

A third intervention in north-east Asia was to provide a great deal of bureaucratic support to manufacturers which exported successfully. In addition to domestic market protection and a supply of credit, states provided important assistance in the field of technology acquisition. Governments in Japan, Korea, Taiwan and China have variously undertaken collective bargaining operations to buy foreign technology – often forcing foreign firms to hand over know-how or to lower their price for it in return for local market access – and organised public sector or joint public–private research initiatives where individual firms were unable to undertake research and development investments alone. One infamous intervention occurred when Sahashi Shigeru, head of Japan's Ministry of International Trade and Industry's Enterprises Bureau,[8] told IBM in the late 1950s that he would block Big Blue's business unless it licensed its technology to local firms at a maximum 5 per cent royalty. He also informed the US firm that it would have to accept 'administrative guidance' – a euphemism for government instructions – as to how many computers it could sell in Japan each year. Desperate for access to the burgeoning Japanese market, IBM agreed.

Such ruthless bureaucratic support of domestic manufacturing was aided in each state by the concentration of key industrial and foreign trade policy decisions in a single government agency: the Ministry of International Trade and Industry (MITI) in Japan; the Economic Planning Board (EPB) in Korea; the Industrial Development Bureau (IDB) in Taiwan; and the National Development and Reform Commission (NDRC) in China.[9] Considerable attention has been paid to these bureaucracies over the years, in part because the most famous and influential academic book about north-east Asian industrial development, Chalmers Johnson's *MITI and the Japanese Miracle,* is all about bureaucrats. However, comparisons with south-east Asia show that the significance of bureaucracies ultimately depends on the more fundamental governmental decision to force entrepreneurs to manufacture for export and then to cull firms which fail to perform adequately. Bureaucracies are only as good as the policies they implement.

Above all, developing states must force their most powerful and resourceful entrepreneurs to export, typically against their will. Firms that can make money at home in a protected environment are always reluctant to compete globally. Other policies tend to be induced by this basic framework. That said, the framework was not rationalised in east Asia by policy makers, but rather copied by nineteenth-century Japan from historical example.

## Unspeakable reality

To the modern economic ear, accustomed to ideas of free markets that are supposed to be 'win–win' for all participants, policies to protect local industry and create a forced march for exports may sound more like a list of crimes. In rich countries, we are raised to believe that all wealth is the product of competition. The shocking truth, however, is that every economically successful society has been guilty, in its formative stages, of protectionism. Outside of the anomalous offshore port financial havens such as Hong Kong and Singapore, there are no economies in the world that have developed to the first rank through policies of free trade.[10]

It was Tudor Britain that pioneered protectionism and subsidies as a means to industrialisation in the sixteenth century. Government taxed exports of raw wool and imports of clothing in order to nurture Britain's export-oriented woollen textiles industry.[11] France introduced similar strategies in the seventeenth century. The independent United States fought back the objections of southern plantation owners – who preferred to export cash crops and import manufactures – to pursue protectionist industrial policies and high tariffs from the time of the Founding Father and first Treasury Secretary Alexander Hamilton until the early twentieth century. Indeed, the economic historian Paul Bairoch has dubbed the United States 'the mother country and bastion of modern protectionism'.[12] Prussia from the time of Frederick the Great in the eighteenth century, and then the unified Germany refined and expanded interventionist industrial policy in Europe. In turn, German protectionism had a profound influence on Meiji Japan.

The policies deployed by countries in Europe and north America when they were industrialising included heavy tariff and non-tariff restrictions on imports; controls on trading rights (such as Britain's Navigation Acts, which from 1651 allowed only British-flagged vessels to trade in British and British colonial ports); special subsidies or 'bounties' for manufactured exports and processed commodities; taxes and quantitative restrictions to discourage unprocessed raw material exports; state infrastructure support for exporters through the construction of canals and railways; state projects set up to obtain foreign technology (usually by acquiring advanced machinery and wooing foreign technicians, often in contravention of the laws of other nations); state provision of subsidised raw materials; and state export-quality inspection regimes designed to build national brands and reputations for product reliability. Overarching all of this, countries focused a lot of state support on small groups of large firms – monopolies and oligopolies – which had the heft to make large capital investments and compete internationally. Examples range from Britain's first chartered trade monopoly, the East India Company, to Germany's giant industrial cartels of the late nineteenth century.

In short, protectionism has always been the rich man's entry ticket to industrial development. Historians enjoy considerable consensus on this point. Most economists, however, find it impossible to admit that protectionism could be a precondition of industrial upgrading. The problem is that protectionism involves another of the temporary trade-offs that economics is at a loss to explain. Measured by economists at a single moment in time, protectionism is expensive and inefficient because it adds cost, punishes consumers and invites retaliation. However, as a means to the long-term end of industrial learning, protectionism makes possible the acquisition of strategically vital knowledge at a cost that is only temporary. The subsidies inherent in protection help shift the structure of an industrialising economy from a lower level of value-adding to a higher one. When the new level is reached, economists still say that protectionism is inefficient because of its costs, but without conceding that it was protectionism that changed the economy's structure.

The learning role of state industrial policy and industrial protection has, over the centuries, been reflected in the many child-rearing analogies that practitioners have used. Alexander Hamilton, who as Treasury Secretary was responsible for shaping the early manufacturing policy of the independent United States, coined the expression 'infant industry' when setting out his arguments in favour of protection. The term was then picked up and widely employed in nineteenth-century Germany. The Meiji development theorist Sugi Kōji wrote of the need for Japanese businesses to be 'protected until they are mature, just as children are by their parents and students by their teachers'.[13] Ha-Joon Chang, a contemporary Korean economist, has argued that a developing country's investment in industrial learning follows exactly the same logic as parents' investment in their children's education. Just as nineteenth-century European parents who could legally send 10-year-old children to work in factories avoided this if they could afford to, and kept their children in school until they were better educated, so successful governments of developing countries have focused on learning and higher future returns.[14] In manufacturing, the route to higher returns is through learning a range of basic production techniques that have been digested by developed states throughout the world. The only exceptions to this have been offshore financial centres with very small and mobile populations and a handful of super-specialised agricultural economies such as Denmark, New Zealand and, up to a point, Australia, which have instead focused on processing agricultural products (which is, anyway, another form of manufacturing).

The mechanism for acquiring manufacturing capability, like the means for acquiring all practical skills, has always been 'learning by doing' – that is, making things again and again until you make them well.[15] Like any kind of learning, it is somewhat hit and miss and involves many disappointments. But, just as we do not reject the idea of school if a child frequently gets his or her homework wrong, so it is not the case that individual failures mean that industrial learning is a flawed process. Moreover, learning to manufacture things like steel, petrochemicals, plastics, semiconductors and so on is like anything studied at school in that others have gone before you and there is a curriculum. Technology scholars refer to this as working and learning 'within the technological frontier'. For at least a couple of decades, developing states learn, modify and steal skills which have been established by others. Throughout history, it has always been thus. It is this learning around a set of established manufacturing skills which makes the role of governments and government policy important. Governments can push firms and economies towards desired objectives precisely because those objectives are established. Later – as the present-day economies of countries from Japan to Italy testify by their low growth and stagnant technological progress – too much, or the wrong sort of, government interference becomes a problem. However, this is a problem for rich countries after they have used government policy to modernise quickly. What we are concerned with here is becoming rich in the first place – something that seems a whole lot more important when you are poor.

**What goes around ...**

The way to understand successful manufacturing policy in east Asia is to trace the manner in which lessons learned by other countries were imported into the region. North-east Asian industrial policy was not invented out of thin air. Instead it was copied from examples of successful economic modernisation in the United States and Europe. Most directly, manufacturing policy was copied from the example of Germany, which in the late nineteenth and early twentieth centuries provided Meiji Japan with a contemporaneous case study of successful industrialisation.

From Japan, ideas spread to the Japanese colonies of Korea and Taiwan, and also to China, whose modern development started about two decades behind that of Japan.[16] However, China's leaders were also influenced by an eclectic mix of Russian industrialisation under Lenin and Stalin and inter-war fascist Germany, which became a special adviser to Chiang Kai-shek on industrial and military modernisation until Hitler abandoned the relationship in favour of Japan in 1938. The influence of communist socialism and national socialism, combined with the first president Sun Yat-sen's deep-rooted prejudices against private industry, meant that there was a particularly heavy emphasis on the role of state companies in both pre- and post-1949 China and Taiwan.

In south-east Asian states, cut off from the direct influence of Japanese industrialisation, learning about developmental manufacturing policy had to wait until the post-colonial, post-Second World War era, when a set of international agencies (notably the World Bank) was created to assist newly independent countries. These agencies offered up a new, 'approved' set of ideas about what to do. To begin with, the ideas were drawn from the historical developmental experiences of already rich countries. In time, however, more abstract economic theory took over, predicated on a belief that all economies, irrespective of their levels of development, are subject to similar rules. This had less than salutary outcomes for states which lost touch with the lessons of history and accepted instead the dictates of the 'science' of economics.

## Japan goes German–American–British

In the nineteenth century, Meiji Japan's leaders latched instinctively on to the German example. The Meiji Restoration of 1868 took place three years before the Prussian-led unification of Germany – even if Japan's level of development lagged. The oligarchs who ruled the new Japan were also a temperamental match for the Prussians who drove the modernisation of Germany. Both groups were politically conservative, both were committed to industrialisation, and both were concerned by territorial security. The Prussians sought military security by drawing other German-speaking states into their orbit, and dreamed of avenging past defeats and territorial losses to Napoleon Bonaparte.[17] Similarly, the samurai warrior class launched its coup against the Tokugawa shogunate with the aim of stitching together all of Japan's *han* – its large, semi-feudal domains – in a unitary nation that would be able to fight back against colonial encroachment. The means to military security in both places was economic development.

Nineteenth-century Germany was the first state to articulate clearly a set of conclusions about development that had been reached by the Americans when they had split from the British Empire. The German view was put forward by the so-called Historical School, an informal affiliation of intellectuals that was the dominant force in the political economy and jurisprudence departments of German universities in the mid nineteenth century. The group held that the history of Britain showed that a successful developing state had to deploy protectionist industrial policies in order to nurture its manufacturers. The School rejected the newly fashionable pro-free market theories associated with Adam Smith and David Ricardo as inappropriate to Germany's stage of development. Friedrich List, the group's greatest luminary, contended that the free market evangelism emanating from Britain was motivated largely by opportunism based on the country's global technological leadership. In an attack on the new profession of 'economics', he wrote:

> Any nation which by means of protective duties and restrictions on navigation has raised her manufacturing power and her navigation to such a degree of development that no other nation can sustain free competition with her can do nothing wiser than to throw away these ladders of her greatness, to preach to other nations the benefits of free trade, and to declare in penitent tones that she has hitherto wandered in the paths of error, and has now for the first time succeeded in discovering the truth.[18]

List's views on development had formed while he was living in the United States between 1825 and 1832, when he had studied the arguments for a protectionist industrial policy to nurture 'infant industries' set out by Alexander Hamilton in his *Report on the Subject of Manufactures* submitted to Congress in 1791. From the early nineteenth century onwards, many of the report's recommendations – including selective high tariffs – were adopted in America.[19] Hamilton, born to a Scottish father in the British West Indies, was a keen observer of the extreme protectionism that had characterised Britain's rise to global pre-eminence – not least its policy of preventing colonies from competing with British manufacturers.[20]

Friedrich List always maintained that free trade should be a country's ultimate goal. But that goal was only feasible after manufacturing capacities were first raised up through protection. 'The system of protection,' he wrote, 'inasmuch as it forms the only means of placing those nations which are far behind in civilisation on equal terms with the one predominating nation [Britain], appears to be the most efficient means of furthering the final union of nations, and hence also of promoting true freedom of trade.'[21] It was an historical argument based on stages of economic development that challenged the universal claims of the economists – an argument that has subsequently been proven beyond doubt by the experiences of east Asia. On his return to Germany, List became the most influential political scientist of the nineteenth century after Karl Marx. He offered the non-communist solution to development. What List figured out in America, the Japanese then learned from List and his Historical School colleagues.

The Japanese, moreover, were an extraordinarily attentive audience. Most of the senior leadership travelled to Europe and north America in the 1870s and 1880s. The first Japanese mission, departing in 1871, contained three serving ministers and was used to decide on an initial group of industrial pilot projects.[22] Although England, France and the United States were much visited, Germany was the favourite destination. Ito Hirobumi, Japan's first (and multiple) prime minister, spent two months in Berlin in 1882, meeting the Iron Chancellor, Otto von Bismarck. Among the second generation of Meiji leaders, several studied in Germany for periods of years. Hirata Tosuke, Minister of Agriculture and Commerce and then Interior Minister in the 1890s, was the first Japanese to obtain a German doctorate, in 1875; Hirata also undertook one of several translations of List into Japanese.[23] Kanai Noboru, who studied in Germany in the 1880s under almost all the key scholars of the Historical School, returned to a professorship at Tokyo Imperial University and trained a generation of bureaucrats at what remains Japan's most elite school for government officials. Several important German scholars were also recruited to teach in Japan and to advise the government.

The diaries and other papers of leading Japanese statesmen contain repeated references to the suitability of Prussian ideas and institutions for their country. The historian Kenneth Pyle called the notion of copying the development trajectories of advanced states the '*idée fixe*' of Meiji development.[24] The economic historian Robert Wade noted that in the Japanese language the concept was often communicated in the metaphor that all developing countries and their economies are ultimately 'descending the same stretch of the river'. This was the Historical School message writ large.

## Beg, borrow, steal ...

Meiji Japan began to implement its industrial policy in the 1870s just as Prussia had in the late eighteenth century, by opening a series of state pilot factories in basic industries. Most of these lost money but, as in Prussia, the government was prepared to subsidise an initial learning process at a time when private investors were unwilling to risk their capital in poorly understood businesses. Just as the Prussians had bought and copied English machines and convinced English engineers to work for them – despite British criminal laws which forbade this – Japan re-engineered imported machinery and hired foreigners with essential technical knowledge. There were 400 foreigners at work in Japan within a decade of the Meiji Restoration and this number rose to several thousand.

Britain abolished her last legal restraints on the export of manufacturing machinery in 1843, and governments and town guilds in the rest of Europe began to lift similar restrictions, so the global availability of technology was less constrained for Meiji Japan than it had been for continental European states.[25] The Japanese were pressured into signing international patent and copyright agreements, but they ignored them. 'That [the agreements] posed no effective obstacle to Japanese copying of foreign designs,' wrote the Japan historian William Lockwood, 'was a constant complaint of manufacturers abroad.'[26] As would be the case again and again in rising states in post-Second World War east Asia, Meiji Japanese knock-offs were typically low-cost, low-tech product adaptations which were mocked as cheap and tacky by foreigners. In fact, they were usually goods evolved with Japan's tight-fisted rural consumers in mind – the key early market. Less frequently, foreign technology was copied and cleverly upgraded, as with the Toyoda automatic loom, which was sold back to the home of modern textiles, Britain.[27] Like Prussia, Japan discouraged foreigners from making direct investments in its economy.

In the 1880s, the Japanese government sold off most of its pilot firms – in businesses like mining, cotton spinning, woollen thread production, silk reeling, shipbuilding, plate glass and cement – to private entrepreneurs at low prices. Subsequently, many of the ventures became highly profitable.[28] In 1889, a modified Prussian constitution was promulgated in Japan which put much of the business of actually running government in the hands of a professional bureaucracy.[29] These bureaucrats then nurtured an early generation of entrepreneurs, not only through the sales of pilot factories, but also with licences to operate firms that faced limited competition – oligopolies – and with minimum profit guarantees in mining, shipping and infrastructure projects. Builders of railways, for instance, were guaranteed a return of not less than 7 per cent. Mitsubishi, founded by a politically well-connected trader, Iwasaki Yataro, in 1870, was given government vessels and huge subsidies until the firm was finally able to break the foreign stranglehold on shipping. Exports, which at the outset were mainly raw silk and the simple manufactures of small-scale firms, began to take off from their low base, rising eight times between 1880 and 1913.

### ... and scale up

In Germany, there had been little real industrial innovation until the final stages of the country's ascent to modernity, in the late nineteenth and early twentieth centuries. This proved even more the case in Japan. The Prussian, and then German, key to progress had been to increase the scale of investments, often by merging firms, while making only incremental modifications to old technologies. The industrial techniques Germany employed during take-off were mostly developed in England and France: the Gilchrist–Thomas system for producing phosphorous-free pig iron, the commercial production technique for aniline dyestuffs, and an assortment of technologies for electricity generation and transmission. The unprecedented scale of Germany's output meant that unit costs became lower than those of established industrial powers like Britain, whose earlier investments in smaller-scale plants became a liability. Germany's economies of scale were such that its iron and steel works were able to soak up the transportation costs of importing half their iron ore (at a time when per-unit freight rates were far higher than they are today) and still remain Europe's most efficient producers. It was a game of targeted industrial development in which Germany pushed total annual investment in its economy to one quarter of GNI, a rate never seen before.[30]

Only in the 1880s, after two decades of relying on raw silk as her main foreign currency earner, was Japan ready to emulate Germany by building factories on a grand scale. She began, as has every significant developing economy, with textiles, a business with limited capital requirements and ubiquitous markets. In 1882, the legendary Meiji entrepreneur Shibusawa Eiichi put a technician he had sent to Manchester to study cotton spinning together with a consortium of financiers and opened a steam-powered mill with 10,500 spindles. The capital outlay was more than six times any investment in the Japanese cotton industry to date. A year after it commenced production, the factory paid out to its shareholders an 18 per cent dividend. Economies of scale had arrived in Japan and the country began to reduce its reliance on imported cotton thread and cloth, which had accounted for one-third of all imports in the late 1870s.[31]

Shibusawa next convinced government to lift import duties on raw cotton and moved Japan on to the German-style approach of scale processing of imported raw materials. He saw that scale producers ideally seek protection at home but also free access to the cheapest, highest-quality raw materials on the world market. The government sacrificed the interests of previously protected Japanese cotton farmers to those of industry, and by 1914 various textiles accounted for 60 per cent of all Japanese exports. The country's chronic trade deficits ended. The First World War then disrupted European industrial output, allowing Japanese firms to move in on colonial Asian markets for all kinds of basic goods: textiles, bicycles, canned foods, and so on. There was an unprecedented export boom. (In European style, Japan also took Taiwan, in 1895, and Korea, in 1910, as captive colony markets for itself.)

### More export discipline needed

Despite Japanese success, however, there was a latent problem with the development model, and one that Germany had also experienced. This was that Japan's biggest companies managed to avoid doing much exporting, leaving it up to smaller firms. The so-called *zaibatsu* family conglomerates which came to dominate the Japanese economy in the inter-war years focused on mining, shipping and infrastructure concessions and on upstream, domestic-oriented manufacturing businesses, all of which allowed them to charge high prices to the rest of the economy without having to bother with the export market. The *zaibatsu* became huge – by 1928 the Big Four (Mitsui, Mitsubishi, Sumitomo, Yasuda) accounted for about 15 per cent of all the paid-up capital in the Japanese economy[32] – but they frequently profited by putting the squeeze on downstream manufacturers. This meant that in the good times the manufacturers survived on thin margins and lacked the cash flows to move on to more complex activities; and when the bad times hit, they went bust.

With the onset of domestic recession in Japan in 1920, thousands of manufacturers started to go out of business. As the recession endured, government was eventually driven to discover the final, essential modification to its industrialisation policy: a subsidy system that forced big business to behave in the interests of national development, and to export. The process of discovery was a very gradual one that spanned the Second World War. It was also a process that Germany had gone through when that country descended the same stretch of the economic river in the late nineteenth century.

Germany had hit its problems in the two-decade deflationary downturn that occurred in Europe after a financial crisis in 1873. The German economy was affected much like the Japanese one in the 1920s, with thousands of smaller, downstream manufacturers driven to bankruptcy. Firms which survived often did so by creating production cartels which sought to prevent price cutting. However these cartels – and the mergers they encouraged as big firms bought up small ones to capture production quotas that were set by cartel boards – only exacerbated a long-run trend for the biggest, most upstream players in the economy to bilk both downstream manufacturers and individual consumers.

The situation came to a head when a government inquiry into cartels was held in 1903, covering some 400 groupings and 12,000 factories. The inquiry roundly criticised raw material producers for exploiting domestic manufacturers. However, it recognised the need to sell excess manufacturing output in overseas markets to keep production capacity in use and Germans in jobs. The solution suggested by the cartel groups was a rebate system that gave raw material and component cost reductions only to production that was destined, directly or indirectly, for export. In effect this meant that German domestic prices – kept artificially high by tariffs – subsidised the development of manufacturing export markets. It marked the birth of a series of cartel-managed export subsidy regimes that triggered what the economic historian Clive Trebilcock called 'the exuberant German export drive of the 1900s'.[33]

The first such cartel was put into force by the Steel Works Association in 1904.[34] Export subsidies focused economic activity on capital-intensive manufacturing and helped propel Germany to the highest rank of contemporary technological development. Weaker members of export cartels were forced to get rid of obsolete production machinery because the international market was less forgiving of lower-quality production than the protected domestic one. This was export discipline at work. German exporters scaled up further and further to a point where they could fund radical technological innovations. They opened up and dominated entire new industries like electrical engineering, chemicals and petrochemicals with vast investments in research and development.[35]

Japan refined its industrial policy around the export discipline of large manufacturers over a long period between 1925 and 1954. The process spanned the Depression and the fascist, war and early post-war eras.[36] It began in 1925, when the Japanese government created the Ministry of Commerce and Industry (MCI) with legal authority to oversee the pricing and quality of important exports.[37] Following a devastating banking crisis in 1927, the Commerce and Industry Deliberation Council was set up to lead mergers of industrial firms that were facing bankruptcy. The term *sangyō gōrika* – 'industrial rationalisation' – came into use to signify the need for the state to cull weaker industrial firms within the context of a protectionist environment that nurtured industrial development.[38] In 1930 a senior MCI official, Kishi Nobosuke, spent seven months in Germany studying how cartels operated there. In 1931, after Kishi published his report, a new law allowed for a cartel in any business where two-thirds of entrants wanted one; it also provided the government with clear powers to enforce cartel agreements.[39] By the mid 1930s cartels existed in twenty-six industries, from iron and steel to silk thread. However, as in Germany before the introduction of export subsidies, these measures only tended to strengthen the great *zaibatsu* whose activities were concentrated in upstream businesses, while downstream manufacturers remained under the *zaibatsu* kosh (albeit in an expanding economy in the 1930s as militarisation pumped up economic growth).[40] Before the Second World War, the Ministry of Commerce and Industry remained focused on protecting manufacturers from the predations of the *zaibatsu*, rather than imposing export discipline on the whole industrial structure.

The final pieces of Japan's manufacturing policy puzzle had to wait until the arrival of the Supreme Commander for the Allied Powers

(SCAP), Douglas MacArthur, after the Second World War. It was the American-led government which dispossessed the *zaibatsu* families (they had been too close to the military), banned their holding companies and instead enhanced the powers of the Ministry of Commerce and Industry. MITI was born out of the MCI in 1949. It obtained extraordinary controls over both industrial policy and trade policy – powers intended only as temporary post-war measures by the SCAP – which allowed it to combine export discipline with culling losers to a degree never before seen.[41] After Japan's independence was restored in 1952, and a somewhat timorous pro-American government led by Yoshida Shigeru fell in 1954, MITI went to work.

The rest, as they say, is history. MITI ran a protectionist pro-manufacturing policy built around rigorous export discipline. The big industrial firms of post-war Japan were beholden not to *zaibatsu* bosses, but to MITI bureaucrats who focused them on exports by exempting up to 80 per cent of their export revenues from taxation. When Japan was forced under the General Agreement on Tariffs and Trade (GATT) to stop tax exemption of export earnings in 1964, MITI instead based firms' depreciation allowances on export performance – an equivalent tax rebate by a back door. In the 1950s MITI officials, still working far inside the global technological frontier, systematically researched and built the foundations of a world-class manufacturing economy. They moved year by year through steel, shipping, fertilisers, synthetic textiles, plastics, petrochemicals, automobiles and electronics. MITI's Enterprises Bureau licensed the acquisition of all foreign technology, involving 2,487 contracts between 1950 and 1963. An Industrial Structure Council – an enhanced version of the 1927 Commerce and Industry Deliberation Council – was set up with forty-five committees to oversee every major industry. The bureaucrats who ran the committees hammered out agreements with business leaders on export targets, quality control standards, productivity, capacity changes and mergers.[42] Firms that did not co-operate with MITI found that they had no foreign exchange allocation to buy raw materials and equipment. Favoured manufacturers were given not only subsidies and tax breaks but also publicly funded infrastructure investment and free land.[43] Most business leaders loathed being told what to do, but they had little choice but to co-operate.

All this represented the raising to a new level of the infant industry policies that had spread from Britain to the independent United States to Prussia and the rest of continental Europe in the nineteenth century. Of course, impressive and effective refinements of state-led industrial policy were seen in West Germany, France and Italy after the Second World War. However, it was the aggressive application of infant industry techniques in a relatively poorer country, Japan, that caught the world's attention most forcefully. From 1952 Japanese manufacturing and mining output increased more than tenfold in only two decades. Japan became the first state to close in on sustained double-digit economic growth.[44] Many people thought the country had discovered a new and unbeatable form of economic management. (The US and Japanese bestseller *Japan as Number One* came out in 1979.) In fact Japan had merely rediscovered old ideas, and built on earlier German refinements thereof. Moreover, while the Japanese capacity to burnish and improve those ideas was impressive, it was put in the shade by South Korea and Taiwan. Meiji Japan was a relatively powerful, stable state – soon to be a colonial power – when it began implementing its industrialisation programme in the nineteenth century. Its two former colonies were small, repressed and, particularly in South Korea's case, dirt poor when they started out on their journeys in the early 1950s.

### Historian and general

The means by which effective manufacturing policy came to South Korea was simple. The man who defined Korea's modernisation era was General Park Chung Hee, who came to power in a coup on 16 May 1961. Park had served as a lieutenant in the Japanese colonial military, in the elite Kwangtung army when it oversaw a huge industrialisation drive in Korea and Chinese Manchuria in the 1930s. Unlike European colonists, Japan belatedly built manufacturing plants in its colonies and the result was an industrialisation example that post-colonial leaderships could follow.[45] (In European and American colonies, there were no medium- or heavy- industrial plants because all but the most basic industrial goods were supplied from the home country.)

General Park therefore had Japanese ideas about how to run his country. However, he was also an amateur historian who specialised in the histories of rising powers. He was well read on German development, and followed closely that country's swift, state-led re-industrialisation after the Second World War. He also knew in detail the stories of Sun Yat-sen, Turkey's Kemal Pasha and Egypt's Gamal Abdel Nasser and their efforts to nurture modern, large-scale industries. Nine months after taking power in Korea, the peasant-born Park published a book of his own, *Our Nation's Path: Ideology for Social Reconstruction*, which contained a road map for what Park described as 'co-ordination and supervisory guidance, by the state, of mammoth economic strength'.[46] The next year Park published *The Country, the Revolution and I*, with chapters on 'The Miracle on the Rhine' and 'Various Forms of Revolution' in which he discussed different historical revolutions from an economic and developmental perspective. (He always referred to his own coup as a revolution.) In both his books, in a reference to the river that runs through Seoul, Park promised his countrymen a 'miracle on the Han'.

Because Park had been a member of a communist cell in the South Korean army in the 1940s, South Korea's American allies were nervous that he might still be a closet communist. But he stressed that, as in Japan, the Korean state would do the planning while the private sector would lead the investment: 'The economic planning or long-range development programme must not be allowed to stifle creativity or spontaneity of private enterprise,' Park wrote. 'We should utilise to the maximum extent the merits usually introduced by the price machinery of free competition, thus avoiding the possible damages accompanying a monopoly system. There can be and will be no economic planning for the sake of planning itself.' He gave as his historical cue the co-opting of private capitalism by the Meiji oligarchs: 'Millionaires ... were allowed to enter the central stage, both politically and economically, thus encouraging national capitalism,' he wrote. 'The case of the Meiji imperial restoration will be of great help to the performance of our own revolution.'[47]

Park knew his history and his books also show that he had a fine grasp of the basic economic condition and resources of his country. He was a very well informed peasant. Like the Meiji oligarchs in Japan in the 1930s, however, Park had not yet worked out the role of export subsidies. But he quickly discovered the power of these when, desperate for foreign exchange, his regime created a textile cartel on the Japanese model, furnishing it with cheap loans, tax exemptions and tariff exemptions on its raw materials.[48] Overseas sales increased and precious foreign exchange started to flow in. In 1962 Korea's merchandise exports were worth USD56 million; three years later they were worth over USD170 million.[49] Park was so happy that he declared that from 1964 every 30 November would be Korea National Export Day. He needed the hard currency to import equipment for the massive industrial investments he planned. 'Thereafter,' the scholar Alice Amsden noted, 'the Park regime increasingly made exports a compulsion rather than a choice.'[50] Indeed, Korea became the most export-dependent developmental state the world had seen, with the government giving subsidised credit to any firm that sold abroad. The interest rate paid by exporters ranged between a quarter and a half of the rate paid by everybody else. In the high-inflation 1970s, the real, inflation-adjusted interest rate given to exporters was between −10 per cent and −20 per cent per annum. So long as they could raise their sale prices in line with inflation, exporters were being paid to borrow money.[51]

With merchandise exports rising around twentyfold in the 1960s to USD836 million in 1970, Park doled out production licences and credit lines to entrepreneurs whose exports impressed, giving them the opportunity to pursue his vast infrastructural and industrial developments. Many people have likened the *chaebol* business groups that were thus nurtured – the biggest like Hyundai, Daewoo and Samsung each absorbed one-tenth of bank credit in peak years – to Japan's pre-war *zaibatsu*. However, whereas the old *zaibatsu* were adept at avoiding export obligations, Park's *chaebol* were compelled to lead the export campaign. Korea thereby avoided the problem of export-shy big business that had for a long time constrained both Japan and Germany. The country went straight to a more effective form of infant industry promotion.

Of course, it was not all Park's doing. He was ably assisted by other Koreans who had also observed Japan's pre-war industrialisation. Among these was an important group that had worked for the colonial Industrial Bank of Chosen,[52] led by Chang Ki-Yong, who headed the Economic Planning

Board. Park gave the EPB powers which, like those of MITI in Japan, strad-
dled both trade and industry; its director's political rank was that of vice
prime minister. In the 1970s the EPB set out a massive heavy and chemical
industries (HCI) investment programme. Juicy subsidies, including cheap
credit and land, were offered to entrepreneurs who were prepared to build
export-capable plants for petrochemicals, machine building, steel, shipbuilding, electronics and non-ferrous metals. Most professional economists
said the HCI plan was lunacy. Even record-setting Japan had three-quarters
of a century of industrial experience behind it when it undertook its heavy
industrial drive in the 1950s. The World Bank's 1974 report on South Korea
expressed 'grave reservations about the practicability of many of the export
goals set for individual heavy industries' and recommended the country
stick with textiles.[53] The warning looked prescient at the start of the 1980s
when Korea was saddled with extreme overcapacity in heavy industry. Yet,
even at the nadir, the firms that Park backed were slowly breaking into
export markets and in the mid-1980s boom in US and European markets,
Korea emerged as a global force in steel and shipbuilding, and later in
semiconductors and autos. By 1987 the World Bank was writing that the
vast, integrated Korean steel plant, Pohang Iron and Steel (now known as
POSCO), was 'arguably the world's most efficient producer';[54] the Bank
had refused to finance the plant. As of 1984, three-fifths of Korean exports
came from the heavy and chemical industries Park had demanded, versus
less than one-quarter at the start of the HCI drive in 1973.

Along the way, Korean bureaucrats were reading not the rising American
stars of neo-liberal economics, or even Adam Smith, but instead Friedrich
List. The Korea and Taiwan scholar Robert Wade observed when he was
teaching in Korea in the late 1970s that 'whole shelves' of List's books could
be found in the university bookshops of Seoul. When he moved to the
Massachussetts Insitute of Technology, Wade found that a solitary copy of
List's main work had last been taken out of the library in 1966.[55] Such are
the different economics appropriate to different stages of development. In
Korea, List's ideas for a national system of development were being adapted
to a country with a population far smaller than Germany's or Japan's, and
with a mid-1970s GDP per capita on par with Guatemala.[56] The ideas were
implemented in the teeth of the worst international trading conditions for

a generation featuring two unprecedented energy crises. It did not matter. Park motored on regardless. Each time the US, the World Bank and the IMF urged him to back away from his state-led industrial policy he agreed – and then did precisely nothing (or occasionally a very little).[57] Park was a leader of conviction, and his convictions were based in history.

## Public sector variants

China and Taiwan's approaches to industrialisation differed from Japan and Korea's because of the different roles played in these economies by public ownership. On the mainland after 1949, the Communist Party of China (CPC) nationalised everything. In Taiwan, where the defeated Kuomintang (KMT) party set itself up, a big role was also given to state ownership. The reason was the common legacy of republican China from 1911 to 1949. Sun Yat-sen's abiding antipathy to private ownership, the influence of Russia on the republican government until 1927 (when Chiang Kai-shek split with Russian and Chinese communists) and the subsequent influence of Germany and then German national socialism in the 1930s meant that, before 1949, public ownership of industry in China was already the norm.[58]

The vehicle for state ownership in China before 1949 was an industrial planning bureaucracy that was far bigger, and more sophisticated, than almost anyone, including Chinese people, realises. From 1935, following earlier, smaller-scale experiments with planning, industrial policy was directed by the now-forgotten National Resources Commission (NRC). Under Kuomintang leadership, the NRC became a huge planning agency in the 1930s, responsible for strategic civilian and defence industries. In 1936, it implemented an ambitious barter deal with Nazi Germany that traded Chinese minerals for German industrial technology; the arrangement only ended because of Hitler's decision to side with Japan after Japan launched an all-out war against China in 1937.[59] Under military mobilisation against the Japanese, the NRC continued to grow and to expand its control over industry. By 1944 it had 12,000 staff and 160,000 dependent workers in mining, manufacturing and electricity generating enterprises. Some businesses were set up as state firms and others were nationalised from the private sector. As of the Second World War, almost seven-tenths of the paid-up capital of registered businesses in China belonged to state firms, most of them managed by the NRC.[60]

During the Second World War, the agency produced an enormously detailed, 20-volume plan for the industrialisation of China once the conflict ended. But with the resumption of the Chinese civil war in 1946, and much less US aid than Chiang Kai-shek had hoped for, the NRC's grand ambitions were not realised. The agency continued to expand, to a record head count of 33,000 staff and nearly a quarter of a million workers in its enterprises by late 1947, but it was unable to put most of its developmental plans into action. NRC bureaucrats in republican China had a reputation for relative competence and professionalism. Most of them stayed in communist China after 1949 and helped to hand over control of already state-run companies to the CPC; many went on to work in Mao's state planning apparatus. The State Planning Commission (SPC) was created in 1953 and implemented numerous projects that had been conceived by the NRC – although personnel who had been employed under the Kuomintang later suffered persecution in political campaigns. The SPC is today called the National Development and Reform Commission (NDRC).

A much smaller number of NRC staffers, most of whom had been posted to the NRC's Taiwan regional office when Japan gave up the island in 1945, went on to work there. They were allowed far greater influence than their peers on the mainland, and supplied a generation of Taiwanese economic leadership – including eight of the fourteen ministers of economic affairs prior to 1985, under whom the critical Industrial Development Bureau operated.[61] These were the senior officials who enacted a manufacturing policy that gave heavy preference to public companies. They created a Taiwanese state sector concentrated in the same businesses that had been targeted by the NRC – petrochemicals, steel, shipbuilding, heavy machinery and other types of engineering – and then they expanded the coverage. Former NRC employees also ran many of the state firms. By the early 1980s, India and Burma were the only countries in contemporary non-communist Asia that had public sectors of comparable scale.[62]

Unlike Maoist China (or India or Burma), however, state ownership in Taiwan had limited impact on growth and technological upgrading because government stressed the role of exports in development. It targeted specific sectors for export promotion from the early 1950s (starting with processed foodstuffs and then textiles), allowed exporters to retain a share of the foreign exchange they earned (all other foreign exchange had to be handed over to the central bank), offered direct cash subsidies to exporters for a period, organised export cartels in order to 'manage' competition, and introduced a limited amount of concessionary export credit which, from 1957 to the mid 1970s, provided short-term export loans at rates around 50 per cent cheaper than non-exporters paid.[63] In the 1970s, Taiwan pushed further into heavy industry, into synthetic textiles and into the electronics sector for which it is today best known. The government set up the Industrial Technology Research Institute (ITRI) in 1973, and the Electronic Research and Service Organisation (ERSO) in 1974, in order to license foreign technology, undertake publicly funded research and development, and select public and private firms to utilise the research and make new products. Where Korea targeted mass-production memory chips, Taiwan went after application-specific integrated circuits (ASICs), which are developed with specific consumer electronic products in mind. By the mid 1980s ITRI and ERSO combined had well over 5,000 staff, as well as huge state-controlled production subsidiaries.[64]

**That lurking problem**

Export discipline in Taiwan was ostensibly highly effective. In 1952, the value of Taiwan's exports was equivalent to only 9 per cent of GDP; by 1979, the figure was 50 per cent. Through the 1970s exports grew so fast that one study found they accounted for almost 70 per cent of overall manufacturing expansion.[65] However, on close inspection Taiwan grew up with an export economy that had some similar structural weaknesses to those of nineteenth-century Germany and pre-Second World War Japan. In 1985, it was small and medium-sized enterprises with fewer than 300 employees which accounted for 65 per cent of exports, the same ratio as in Japan in the 1920s. Whereas the situations in Germany and Japan were the results of a failure to make big private firms export, in Taiwan there was a failure to impose rigorous export discipline on big state firms. It was a new twist to an old problem.[66] At the same time, Taiwan also failed to support its exporting private entrepreneurs as effectively as post-Second World War Japan and Korea.

For several decades, nobody paid much attention to Taiwan's export structure. The island consistently boasted a higher GDP per capita than South Korea – USD8,000 in 1990 versus USD6,300 for Korea. Part of the differential is explained by the fact that Taiwan got moving faster with its development in the 1950s, when Korean policy under Syngman Rhee was much less focused. It was also the case that Taiwan's land reform was the most effective the world has seen, and provided a strong boost to early manufacturing growth. However, Taiwan's manufacturing policy was very much second best to Korea's, and failed to impose adequate export discipline on its biggest businesses. This policy lapse eventually caught up with the island's economy. In the 1990s, Korea closed its GDP per capita gap with Taiwan before being temporarily knocked back by the Asian financial crisis. Then it quickly caught up again, and today boasts a USD2,000 GDP per capita lead over Taiwan.[67]

Being state-owned was not the only reason why big Taiwanese state firms failed to become as globally competitive as Korean *chaebol*. (Public ownership is often associated with poor performance, but it does not guarantee it.) Taiwanese state enterprises underperformed Korean corporations because they faced less export discipline and less competition. They were allowed to be more dependent on foreign equity joint ventures for technology, and this weakened their capacity to originate their own technology. An example of the phenomenon is the telecommunications sector, where local firms were unable to break their dependency on US multinational partners ITT and GTE.[68] Meanwhile, Taiwan's leading private companies, like the computer manufacturer Acer, were denied the level of export subsidy, domestic protection and financial support given to their Korean cousins, and so were forced to live off thinner margins, consequently becoming less technologically competitive and smaller in scale.[69] By the start of the 1980s, Korea already had ten firms in the Fortune 500 list of leading industrial companies; Taiwan had two.[70] Compared with Korean firms, Taiwan's exporters do more low-margin manufacturing as suppliers to American and European multinationals – making, for instance, all of the world's iPhones and iPads – and less higher-margin manufacturing under their own brands, whereas Korea has Samsung selling its own smart phones and leading the world by sales, and Hyundai among the top five global auto makers.[71] Taiwan may be structurally 'stuck' one level below the branded, high-margin top layer of economic activity where the richest countries exist.

## The triumph of the historians

Despite the relative failings of industrial policy in Taiwan, it remains the case that Japan, Korea and Taiwan are all examples of states that have successfully managed to develop their manufacturing businesses. Each of their governments exercised the minimum necessary level of export discipline. Korea and Taiwan went from being the world's 33rd and 28th leading exporters in 1965 to being the 13th and 10th respectively twenty years later. At that point, both economies boasted greater manufacturing exports than the whole of Latin America.[72] The heavy industrialisation drives pursued by Korea and Taiwan took the ratio of their light to heavy manufacturing from 4:1 to 1:1 in only fifteen years.

Of course, manufacturing policy throughout north-east Asia was based on the solid foundation of highly productive, expanding agricultural sectors. Meiji Japan had developed faster than early nineteenth-century Prussia or eighteenth-century Britain in large part because its agricultural output had also increased faster, creating a domestic market for basic manufactures which firms later exported. In the 1950s, Japanese farm output increased by another half in one decade, and once more a booming rural market demanded manufacturing products which went on to become export staples.[73] Chalmers Johnson reckoned that in the 1950s and 1960s transistor radios and cameras were the only two important Japanese export goods which had not first been honed in the domestic market.[74] In the same vein Korea and, especially, Taiwan were able to build out manufacturing economies from their agricultural sectors. Each north-east Asian state bore out the truism set down by the Japanologists Kazushi Ohkawa and Henry Rosovsky when analysing the original Meiji lift-off: 'If there had been no increase in the output of the traditional economy, there could hardly have existed any domestic market for the output of modern industry.'[75]

At the industrial policy-making level, what stands out with the benefit of hindsight is that there was almost no role played in Japan, Korea or Taiwan by economists. Meiji Japan blazed its trail by following the Prussian, and earlier American, model which rejected the modern classical economics that began with Adam Smith and David Ricardo. The framers of the Meiji revolution were trained in Germany and at Tokyo University's law school, which focused not so much on law as on European-style public administration.[76] There was a strong prejudice against the theoretical approach associated with modern economics, and in favour of practical problem-solving. Yoshino Shinji, vice minister of the Ministry of Commerce and Industry in the 1930s, said of Japan's implementation of German industrial planning techniques that: 'Concerning the idea of control, there are many complex explanations of it in terms of logical principles, but all one really needs to understand it is common sense.'[77] Japan exalted the educated generalist – its government bureaucracy distinguished between administrative officers and technical officers, and the former always outranked the latter. At the height of its powers in the 1960s, MITI had just two employees with PhDs in economics among its senior staff.[78]

A similar disposition carried over into South Korea, where until at least the 1970s almost all the senior leaders and bureaucrats, including Park Chung Hee and planning chief Chang Ki-yong, were Japanese trained. The main difference was one of class: many senior personnel in the 1960s and 1970s came, like Park himself, from peasant stock. The Korea scholar Jung-en Woo referred to them as 'men of peasant origin ... when they thought of capitalism, they thought of a conspiracy of the rich'. In Taiwan, the constructors of industrial policy were not generalist administrators as in Japan, but engineers. Almost all Taiwan's ministers of economic affairs, most of whom started out in the mainland's National Resources Commission, had engineering or other science degrees. K. Y. Yin, who defined industrial policy more than anyone and started out at the Industrial Development Bureau in the 1950s, was an electrical engineer. The IDB did not employ any economists until 1981.[79]

The most prominent economists in circulation in north-east Asia in the 1950s and 1960s were the ones sent by the US government to try to 'straighten out' its new allies. Among these was Joseph Dodge, who was despatched to occupied Japan in 1949 to enforce fiscal austerity.[80] His policies induced a deep, deflationary recession in the winter of 1949–50. The country only recovered with the onset of the Korean War from June 1950 and the concomitant demand for war-related supplies. In 1952, Japan regained its sovereignty and MITI then followed its own, history-oriented instincts. In South Korea in the 1950s and early 1960s, US-despatched economists demanded the privatisation of banks, increases in interest rates and import liberalisation. The banks were briefly privatised, but Park Chung Hee renationalised them after his coup. Under pressure, he gave some ground on interest rates and import controls, but most changes were cosmetic and designed to get the Americans off his back. As exports picked up from the mid 1960s, Park's regime became increasingly confident in resisting the demands of free market economists.[81]

It would be wrong, however, to think that only economists of a neo-classical stripe were providing advice from Washington. After the Second World War a historical view of development was still contending with a rising neo-liberal one in the economics profession. Just as Wolf Ladejinsky enjoyed a few post-war years of great influence over agricultural policy, so a handful of historically literate advisers were being taken seriously in the US capital on matters of industrial development. The most important of these was Walt Rostow. Like Ladejinsky, Rostow was from an immigrant Russian family. Unlike Ladejinsky, he wore his anti-communist sentiments on his sleeve, meaning he prospered through the Cold War, becoming a senior adviser to three successive presidents: Eisenhower, Kennedy and Johnson. As an economic historian, Rostow brought a classic Listian perspective to Washington. His key work, *The Stages of Economic Growth*, is about how developing states all descend, as the Japanese phrase has it, the same stretch of the economic river; Taiwan's chief planner, K. Y. Yin, was among the book's fans.[82]

The US appetite for land reform in east Asia disappeared in the early 1950s with the sidelining of Ladejinsky. But Rostow and his supporters continued to press US governments to accommodate the industrialisation of friendly states like Korea and Taiwan, and infant industry manufacturing programmes were grudgingly tolerated. Indeed, the US often paid for such policies with its vast military and civilian aid budgets. Non-repayable grants were cut back in the late 1950s, but other money continued to flow through the US Development Loan Fund, whose explicit Rostovian aim was to support the industrialisation of Cold War allies. The governments in Seoul and Taipei not only structured infant industry programmes on the US buck, they made American consultants fit in with their objectives. In Taiwan, for example, the New York engineering firm J. G. White was used to screen scores of state sector heavy industrial projects. And US consultancy Arthur D. Little was tasked with identifying new manufacturing products to promote, while advising on tax breaks to subsidise exporters (the latter a policy that would today be illegal under World Trade Organisation rules).[83]

North-east Asian states, unlike south-east Asian ones, used money proffered by the US to strengthen industrial policy. At the same time, neoclassical economists in north-east Asia were, as Robert Wade put it, 'held at a distance so that their preoccupation with efficiency criteria would not subvert the process of identifying industries and products for intensified growth'.[84] When such economists did start to appear in positions of influence in Korea and Taiwan in the 1980s, 'efficiency' issues were becoming more pressing – large firms brought into being by the state were increasingly abusive of their oligopoly positions, and consumers were growing weary of being on the wrong end of state industrial policy, with its high domestic prices subsidising export competitiveness. In Korea, economists 'with their newly minted US PhDs', as Jung-En Woo disparagingly put it, wrought havoc with the financial system in the 1980s, setting the stage for Korea's 1998 financial meltdown.[85] However, their entry on to the policy stage was becoming necessary at a time when Korea was already globally competitive in a number of manufacturing sectors, and needed to deregulate to progress further.

In south-east Asia, by contrast, the historian's understanding of the development process never got a look-in. Newly independent countries fiddled around with industrial policy, and then moved precipitously to taking advice from efficiency-oriented economists. Sometimes these were local economists trained abroad – as with the so-called 'Berkeley Mafia' of five leading advisers to Suharto in Indonesia, who had all studied at the University of California.[86] More often, the economic advice came from the World Bank and the IMF, which were ready with their free market prescriptions for development, despite the fact that these prescriptions have never produced a successful industrial state. In recent years it has become fashionable to heap much of the blame for the developing world's ills on the World Bank and the IMF. However, it is more constructive to digest the principal lesson of Meiji Japan: that, hard as it may be, a developing state does not have to depend on the advice of others. It can take control of its own destiny, look out at the world with open eyes, and figure out what really goes on. As the fifth and final article of the Meiji Charter Oath, promulgated at the new emperor's enthronement in April 1868, read: 'Knowledge shall be sought throughout the world so as to strengthen the foundation of imperial rule.'[87]

**Off to Korea and Malaysia**

In order to understand how industrial policy works close up, it is necessary to see how different manufacturing sectors were managed in north-east Asian versus south-east Asian countries. One of the most interesting country comparisons is between Korea and Malaysia, because under Mahathir Mohamad the latter made a unique political commitment within south-east Asia to industrialisation based on north-east Asian experience. Yet the outcome was far from what was hoped for. The reasons illuminate some of the most important lessons about industrial policy. Korea and Malaysia set out with not dissimilar domestic business structures. But they ended up completely different. In Korea, effective policy changed the very nature of the economy; in Malaysia, key features of its old colonial economy remained intact.

Korea's industrial development experience is particularly instructive in north-east Asia because it is fresher than Japan's and, in terms of the export discipline applied to big firms, purer than Taiwan's. Whereas Japan after the Second World War built on its earlier developmental gains, Korea rose through a far rawer developmental experience. The country started out after independence from Japan in 1945 with a tiny entrepreneurial class of compradores who had acted as commercial go-betweens for the colonial power. In the 1950s, these men were allowed to buy state assets cheaply, and to acquire many monopoly concessions, from Syngman Rhee's government. There was no concomitant pressure to manufacture for export, and Korea remained dependent on American aid. But after Park Chung Hee's 1961 coup, the new regime began to apply export discipline with a vengeance, and to cull underperforming firms. In place of a hotch-potch of domestic economy-oriented businesses, Korea went on to produce a group of huge, manufacturing-based conglomerates with brand names – typified by Hyundai and Samsung – that are known around the world. Both types of company – pre- and post-Park – were family-run, but state industrial policy completely changed how these firms behaved.

After Malaysia gained its independence from Britain in 1957, its economy exhibited important structural similarities to that of Syngman Rhee's Korea.[88] The old colonial compradore class which operated between the British and the Malay sultans continued to dominate private business, enjoyed an enlarged share of state concessions for new investments like food processing plants, and faced minimal pressure to manufacture or export. In the 1970s, the government used state entities to buy out various mining and plantation interests still owned by British companies. But there was no shift to an export manufacturing strategy for domestic firms. Instead, government invited foreign companies to set up export processing operations in Malaysia. Then, with the ascent to the premiership of Mahathir Mohamad in 1981, came a belated recognition that Malaysia had gone through twenty years of independence without starting to build an industrial structure worthy of the name.

Mahathir announced a 'Look East' policy in which he said Malaysia would emulate the manufacturing development programmes of northeast Asia. He had taken a keen interest in Japan and Korea as Minister for Trade and Industry, immediately before he became prime minister. It seemed for a moment that, just as Korea had learned from Japan which had learned from Germany, so Malaysia was going to learn the lessons of history, too. Yet despite sending thousands of Malaysians to Japan for training, and even taking his cabinet on a course to learn Japanese tea-drinking etiquette, Mahathir failed to understand the most basic prerequisites of infant industry policy: export discipline and sanctions for failure. He tried to make state-owned firms do more than they were capable of, and completely failed to discipline Malaysia's leading entrepreneurs, who socked away billions of dollars without making any serious developmental contribution. Mahathir's 1980s adventure became a tragi-comedy in which he told cabinet colleagues to read a wholly inappropriate book on economic development, and substituted overwrought cultural theories for simple, structural explanations of economic cause and effect. Despite this, even Mahathir's half-baked industrial policy left Malaysia better off than a country like the Philippines, which did nothing effective to enhance its manufacturing capacity. Malaysia is a manufacturing failure, but it is a reminder that it is better to fail trying than never to try at all.

Among the different industrial sectors that provide useful comparisons between developing states, the most fundamental one is steel making. Steel has been an important part of the early industrialisation process of all rich states bar financial havens and low-population agricultural specialists. Steel was critical to the economic development of Britain, the United States, Germany and other continental European states, as well as to each of the three north-east Asian success stories. It continues to be an essential input into all manufacturing economies. The capability to make steel efficiently has, historically, signalled that a country will go on to make other things efficiently – a sort of entry-level test for the economic big time. Park Chung Hee seemed to know this when he inscribed the Chinese characters *gangtie guo li* – 'Iron and Steel is National Strength' – that hang on the wall at the headquarters of Pohang Iron and Steel, Korea's first big steel plant.

Success in steel making depends on scale, on organising a limited number of inputs, and on constant incremental improvements to a core technology that has been the same for a very long time. This bureaucratic, organisational challenge means steel making can be tackled under state ownership. In Japan, Korea and Taiwan, governments initially owned steel plants, in addition to deciding at a state policy level what products to make, which technology to buy and how much capital to commit. The role of the private entrepreneur was usurped, but in each case steel was produced extremely efficiently. Japan and Korea eventually privatised their steel makers; Taiwan never has. Malaysia opted for the same combination of state direction of strategy and public ownership as Taiwan. Yet Malaysia's efforts to deliver a public sector steel champion came up very short.

In most businesses, the state is not cut out to replace entirely the private entrepreneur. Other sectors involve a greater number of inputs and supplier relationships than steel, as well as a much bigger marketing challenge. Such is the case with car making, which Korea, Malaysia and every major east Asian economy apart from the Philippines tried to break into. The marketing requirement in particular favours the talents and energy of the private entrepreneur because of the need for flexibility and for swift responses to changing market tastes. As a result, the state's most effective role is not to take over all aspects of entrepreneurial activity, but rather to channel the private entrepreneur towards its developmental ends. In particular, the entrepreneur must be compelled to compete internationally in a business that is a cut-throat and highly cyclical. In Korea, government achieved this by attracting half a dozen hungry businessmen with the subsidies, only to whittle them down over thirty years to a single, world-beating Hyundai–Kia colossus. The process was far from tidy – in fact, it was often chaotic – but with the anchor of export discipline it was ultimately successful. Malaysia, by contrast, first tried to enter the car business with a single state-owned firm – so that it was impossible to threaten to favour another entrant – and with no serious export discipline. Then it added a second public–private joint venture, focusing on a different segment of the market, again with no real export discipline. Malaysia's most successful private entrepreneurs were not tapped for the effort, and were instead allowed to carry on building their empires in non-manufacturing, protected activities such as mobile telephony services or power generation. Today Malaysia's car industry, like all its large-scale manufacturing industry, is a state sector headache, while its private entrepreneurs exist in a parallel, non-manufacturing universe.

Korea and Malaysia point up the single most important commonality of all developing states in terms of manufacturing policy: that in most large-scale businesses the critical variable is the relationship between the state and private entrepreneurs. A government can try to circumvent the private sector by running every firm itself. But such an approach is not recommended by history. Instead, governments must use their power – particularly their discretion over state-controlled assets, business licences, credit and scarce foreign exchange – to make private entrepreneurs do what industrial development requires. In so doing, governments need to take a realistic view of entrepreneurs. Rather than plead with them to move voluntarily to some higher moral plane, it is better to accept the existence of the entrepreneur's 'animal spirits',[89] and use his desire to make as much money as possible to control him. The entrepreneur seeks to 'get in and grab', as the term indicates. The state has to force him to fulfill developmental objectives while this is going on.

Development is therefore a thoroughly political undertaking. If governments allow entrepreneurs access to what economists call 'rents' – sources of income at government discretion – without contributing to developmental objectives, this is a political dereliction of duty. What south-east Asians were the first to call 'crony capitalism', whereby businessmen are granted concessions without developmental strings attached, is a political failure rather than an entrepreneurial one. The term originates in the Philippines, where the political class has been the most selfish and culpable among all the major states in east Asia. Neo-liberal economists argue that developing countries should avoid the risk of crony capitalism by getting rid of economic rents. But while this might make sense in rich countries, in aspiring states it simply begs the question: How, in that case, will you get entrepreneurs to do what you need them to do in order to develop your economy? Were Park Chung Hee – who nurtured world-beating entrepreneurs but never trusted them – still alive, his answer would quite certainly be: You won't. Rents are the bait with which the successful developing state catches and controls its entrepreneurs.

## Journey 3: Seoul to Pohang and Ulsan

*South Korea's capital Seoul, like South Korea generally, is a bit of a mess. The city's hilly setting gives it a certain topographical charm. But apart from some tidy bits around City Hall, the place has the hallmarks of a job done cheaply, not that cheerfully and all too quickly. In a very un-Japanese fashion, people are prone to leave rubbish out on the street. In the suburbs, the monotonous high-rises look about right for the OECD country with the highest suicide rate. The food, however, is superb, and the taxis relatively cheaper than in Taiwan and Japan thanks to Korea's less than punctilious commitment to north-east Asian social equality.[90]*

The epicentre of Seoul is the top of a circle of which the bottom half is formed by a U-bend in the Han river. Here are City Hall, big business and the main public spaces. It is around this epicentre that three locations in the city quickly explain the nature of the relationship that was formed in the 1960s between Park Chung Hee and the businessmen who industrialised Korea. The first location is the presidential residence, a couple of kilometres to the north of the centre. It was here that, in the wake of the May 1961 coup, Park made the 60-acre Blue House compound his command post for Korean development; it has remained the centre of government ever since. Park abandoned the now-demolished, Japanese-built capitol for all but ceremonial occasions and instead consolidated key offices of his regime in a modest battery of low-rise satellite buildings around the blue-roofed – hence 'Blue House' – main pavilion. There was an annexe for Park's much-feared Korean Central Intelligence Agency (KCIA), whose chief would in 1979 assassinate him, and offices for the powerful Blue House Economic Secretariat.

Park kept his key people very close at hand; the main reason he needed to go out was for a daily visit to the downtown Economic Planning Bureau, whose staff could not all be accommodated at the Blue House. The general's modus operandi was reflected in words he wrote in 1963: 'We need wordless deeds and ambitious construction programmes.'[91] His public explanation of what he was doing was his books. The rest of the time he was getting on with the job of making bureaucrats and businessmen interact in such a way as to achieve his industrial objectives. Leading entrepreneurs were summoned to the Blue House on a regular basis to report on their activities. The most successful, like Hyundai founder Chung Ju Yung, were received weekly. Chung (who died in 2001) usually dined with Park on a Thursday evening; his construction subsidiary undertook many of Park's modifications to the Blue House.

Chung himself lived not far away at a second site of interest: a relatively modest, seven-room house built on a hill near what is left of the imperial Kyongbok Palace. The house, which Chung always said was built on the cheap with surplus materials that his construction firm had to hand, was completed in 1958, three years before Park's coup. Chung never traded up when he became a billionaire. In part his public disdain for the trappings of wealth – for thirty years he walked the four kilometres to his top-floor

office in the city centre each morning, setting off at 7 a.m. with his sons and
bodyguards in tow – was framed by the culture of austerity introduced by
Park. But above and beyond this, Chung was the archetypical tight-fisted
entrepreneur, conserving his capital and expecting his minions to do the
same.

Chung was a driven man, getting up at 4 a.m. to exercise, hold meetings
and call managers before having breakfast at 6 a.m, at which he held court
over his family. He was also autocratic, and known on occasion to slap
or punch his managers. His main hobby was his mistresses: several of his
eight acknowledged sons were by different mothers and he had numerous
unacknowledged sons and daughters.[92] But most prototypical of all, Chung
had the developing country entrepreneur's ability to spot where money was
going to be made whichever way the political winds shifted. Under the Japanese he went into auto repair (one of a very limited number of businesses
Koreans were allowed to operate). When the Americans arrived in 1945,
he did construction work for the US military, using his English-speaking
brother to tout for work.[93] Under Syngman Rhee's congenitally corrupt
administration, he tendered successfully for civil construction projects,
including the first bridge across the Han river, finished in 1958.

Chung's family business structure, the nature of his business activities
and his personal foibles were the same as those of the oligarchs who have
dominated south-east Asian economies. In the 1950s in particular he operated in a cronyistic environment in which kickbacks and bid rigging, known
locally as 'tea-housing', were endemic. By the time of Park Chung Hee's
coup, Hyundai Construction was one of the Big Five Korean building
firms. Chung had never made or exported anything. He was just a politically astute entrepreneur with a reputation for getting construction jobs
done. In post-independence south-east Asia, he would have carried on
doing construction work and added more domestic business concessions
to his portfolio as the state offered them up. But under Park Chung Hee in
Korea, Chung was to become a global force in manufacturing and a major
exporter, first of his construction services, and later of manufactured goods
from cars to semiconductors.

Something happened to make Chung's business develop differently.[94]
The clue as to what is found at a third Seoul location, a couple of kilometres

south-west of the Blue House compound. It is Seodaemun, a small prison nestled between a park and a group of more recently built high-rises. Constructed originally by the Japanese, Seodaemun is maintained today as a museum of Japanese colonial brutality. However, under Park Chung Hee it continued to serve as a convenient downtown lock-up for people who failed to adhere to his plans for Korea's development.

Most developing state dictators just lock up political dissidents. Park also locked up businessmen whose attention he wanted to grasp. Seodaemun's cells and torture chambers now feature waxwork models of Japanese guards from the colonial era – 'nail picking and tortures with boxes and electricity', according to the English language guide; there are even looped recordings of agonised shrieks of pain to enhance the visitor experience. However, Seodaemun's work continued after the Japanese departed in 1945. The prison, and the execution room in the grounds, played a leading role in Park Chung Hee's ruthless campaign to re-orient the course of Korean economic development.[95] Park had no more success than any other dictator in cowing those fighting for transparency and institutional development – including democracy. But he discovered that entrepreneurs, so long as they were still allowed to make money, could be bent to his will quite easily.

It was twelve days after the 1961 coup, on 28 May, that Park and his colleagues[96] began arresting businessmen. They did so under a Special Measure for the Control of Illicit Profiteering. There are conflicting accounts of how many businessmen were held, where and for how long. But it is clear that scores of the country's most senior entrepreneurs were locked up.[97] Seodaemun was one detention point. A few top figures, including Samsung's founder, Lee Byung Chull, had the good fortune – or, more likely, the forewarning – to be in Japan. But the great majority of the country's business elite was taken in. Park put the frighteners on the business community in a manner unprecedented in a capitalist developing country. He declared that the days of what he termed 'liberation aristocrats' – crony capitalists who bought favours from Syngman Rhee's government and did nothing for their country in return – were over.

Imprisoned businessmen were required to sign agreements which stated: 'I will donate all my property when the government requires it for national construction.'[98] In effect, this put the entrepreneurs on parole to do whatever

Park required. The most senior group, including Lee Byung Chull after he returned from Japan, quickly agreed to pursue investments in industries – mostly manufacturing ones – that the military and a handful of bureaucrats familiar with Japanese industrialisation wanted to develop: fertiliser, synthetic fibres, cement, iron and steel, electricity generation, and so on. They formed the Promotional Committee for Economic Reconstruction (PCER), later to become the Federation of Korean Businessmen, as the formal channel through which big business communicated with government and aligned itself with state objectives. Samsung's Lee was the first chairman. The leading business families also agreed to the renationalisation of banks which had been privatised to them, under US pressure, in 1957. The banks had become a destabilising source of illegal lending to their owners' firms, a problem that has afflicted privatised banking systems in developing states from Meiji Japan to post-Second World War south-east Asia and Latin America.

Once he established the basic rules of the game, Park informed Korea's businessmen that they were free to make as much money as they could so long as they stuck by the rules. Most of the businessmen were released from prison during 1961. But if they thought Park's regime would ease off once they were out, it soon became clear that this was not the case. One early exchange that sent a crystal clear message occurred after the chief of Lucky-Goldstar (now known as LG), Koo In Hwoi, was released. One of Park's colonels responsible for industrial policy told him to organise a foreign loan (which the government would guarantee) and technology transfer for a cable factory. When Koo tried to wriggle out of the task, pleading that he knew nothing about the cable business, the colonel told him that whereas he had been thinking of making Koo sort the whole thing out in a week, as a special dispensation he would let him do it in two weeks. Ten days later, Koo was sufficiently chastised to produce a technology transfer deal with a West German firm and the requisite financing arrangements.[99] One of Korea's richest businessmen had gotten the message.

**We always wanted to manufacture ...**

Chung Ju Yung avoided arrest in May 1961. However, he and his business were put under scrutiny by the new junta. Not to worry: Chung proved to be another quick convert to the causes of manufacturing and exports. He lobbied for, and was given, a manufacturing project in 1962 when Hyundai Construction was allowed to build the third of three Korean cement plants financed by US concessionary loans. It was Chung's first factory. Until this point, most cement had been imported from Japan. One year after the factory began production, Hyundai Construction was not only producing cement for Korea, it had started exporting it to Vietnam, where the US was ramping up its military involvement. It was a requirement of the US funding for Hyundai's first cement factory that the firm buy all its equipment from American suppliers. However an even greater measure of the changes that were occurring in Korea was that, having mastered cement making, Chung then went on to master the engineering behind his cement plant. Within a few years, Hyundai was building cement plants on a turnkey basis in countries like Saudi Arabia.[100]

The export discipline message was not one that businessmen could miss since the Economic Planning Board demanded the monthly reporting of export revenues. In 1964, Chung sent one of his five brothers to Thailand to look for construction projects, thinking to sell the one thing he really understood – construction services – overseas. The family put in a low-ball bid, backed by Korean government debt guarantees, for the 58-mile Pattani–Narathiwat highway in southern Thailand. They won it, although Chung went on to lose millions of dollars on the project, having made all kinds of rash assumptions about the equipment needed, Thai weather patterns and the difficulties attached to cutting through a jungle. But through undertaking the project, Hyundai Construction learned from its mistakes, and in the next few years the firm picked up contracts in Vietnam, Guam, Papua New Guinea and Australia.[101]

Export success drew attention. In 1967, Chung obtained the first of many one-on-one audiences with Park Chung Hee.[102] The two men talked about a putative 266-mile Seoul–Pusan expressway, a project that would link one end of South Korea to the other and which had been discussed, but never pursued, for years. Chung, now with twenty years of experience of increasingly complex infrastructure projects, volunteered a low-cost option with steeper gradients and less tunneling. The plan was accepted and he went on to win tenders for half the road, built between 1968 and

1970. It was the biggest construction project ever undertaken in Korea. It was also the project that led to Chung being invited to his weekly dinners with Park. He was on the inside track.

The same year the expressway deal came through, Chung obtained permission to assemble complete knock-down (CKD) car kits in a joint venture with Ford. He bought an 82-acre site for a car assembly plant at Ulsan in south-east Korea – part of General Park's Ulsan Industrial Complex, his favoured location for the promotion of new industrial projects. Park called the complex Korea's 'Aswan Dam'. For Chung, the car venture was a toe in the water. The government was encouraging domestic firms to go into kit assembly of cars as a first step to building finished vehicles from scratch. In 1967, Park had published a second five-year plan which made the automotive sector a priority for development. Like other businessmen, Chung was learning to pay close attention to the policy documents put out by the Blue House and the EPB, because they determined where domestic bank finance, overseas loan guarantees, export subsidies, tax exemptions, reduced utility rates, tariff rebates and more would be directed. Within five years of Park's coup, business was listening to government as it never had before. Meanwhile, GDP growth between 1962 and 1971 averaged 10 per cent a year and the manufacturing share of exports rose from one-quarter to more than four-fifths.[103] Government and business were forging an effective partnership for development, a shotgun marriage in which Park held the weapon.

**The Road to Somewhere**

Driving down the Number One expressway that Hyundai Construction helped build in a Hyundai Avante, one can still see how this road – a bell-weather for Korea's industrial take-off – was imposed on the rural society of the late 1960s. The expressway cuts through mile after mile of closely tended farmland. Nearer to Seoul there are fields of fruit trees and tobacco, which appear to be farmed on a commercial basis, but further into the South Korean heartland evidence of the intensive household farming that supported the country's industrial development is unmistakeable. Small plastic greenhouses and neat wooden frames with black awnings (employed to expedite plant growth) are everywhere. The rice paddies are livid green, stuffed to the gills with fertiliser. Along the banks of the paddies, families plant their home vegetable crops: maize, courgettes, potatoes, salad leaves and the inevitable radish, onion and cabbage required for that Korean staple, *kimchi*. Below an elevated section of the expressway a man with a spraying unit on his back is applying a chemical treatment to his rice. Among the forested hills, which appear to have no topographical pattern, every inch of cultivable farmland is in use. Even the land in the loop of an expressway slip road is farmed.

The urban centres, when they come, feature identical high-rise apartment blocks. These places could easily be mistaken for Stalinist factory towns, except that here the market is very much alive. The sight of low-cost, red brick churches with spires – 30 per cent of Koreans are Christians – is also a reminder that this is not Soviet Russia. Koreans – like the builders of their presidential residence – have a weakness for blue roofs. Whether using tiles or corrugated sheets of plastic or iron, houses and low-rise factories throughout Korea go with the blue. Combined with vast amounts of concrete, it does not look good. In a rather beautiful, undulating setting, Korea's remarkable economic development has come at an aesthetic cost that is rarely out of mind during the five-hour drive from Seoul to the great industrial centres of the south-east. At the end of the Number One expressway is Pusan, the nation's second metropolis and biggest port. A little to the north of Pusan is Ulsan, now sometimes referred to as 'Hyundai City', such is the local dominance of that firm. But my first stop is a little further north again, at Pohang, site of one of the world's most efficient steel factories.

In the 1960s Pohang was an agricultural town of 67,000 inhabitants. Today it is an industrial city of half a million people and home to the world's third biggest – and most profitable – steel producer. The urban area is unremittingly bland and shabby, and separated from the steel works by a river. Outside the main gates of the Pohang Iron and Steel Company is a big, dirty blue sign announcing 'Clean and Green POSCO'. A researcher from POSCO's own university and two of his colleagues wait outside to accompany me on a tour.[104] Once inside we drive to the reception building where Park Chung Hee's original inscription, 'Iron and Steel is National

Strength' (written in the Chinese calligraphy favoured for such formal pronouncements), hangs on the wall of a central office tower.

The official POSCO history movie is shown on the top floor. Then, with the press of a button, curtains around the room are raised to reveal a panoramic view over the 9 million square metre plant, with its 320 kilometres of internal roads. The compound is in the shape of a huge horseshoe encircling a bay on the sea. At one end I can see a 20-day, 2 million tonne supply of raw materials that has been offloaded from one lot of ships, and at the other the finished steel to be loaded on to another lot of ships. It is instantly clear that the place was set up as an import–export machine. Tracking my eye clockwise from one end of the horseshoe to the other I see: plants for sintering the iron ore and limestone and preparing the coke; a series of 100 metre tall blast furnaces; torpedo cars that each carries 300 tonnes of molten iron to furnaces which oxidise impurities; continuous casting plants that create semi-finished steel; and rolling mills that turn out finished product. Cars which drive around the plant have '8282' written down the side – the sound of the numbers in Korean is a homonym of 'quickly, quickly'. Iron ore travels round the horseshoe and becomes finished goods ready for shipping in thirteen hours; Pohang turns out 16 million tonnes of product a year. The company's newer plant, 200 kilometres away at Gwangyang on the south coast, puts out 19 million tonnes of steel a year in a process that takes only seven hours.

It was not easy getting the Pohang plant financed and built. The Korean government tried three times in the 1960s to move the project ahead, presenting different, detailed plans. But equipment suppliers would not advance credit and financiers – including the World Bank – would not lend to the kind of large-scale, integrated operation that the Koreans wanted. A World Bank report published in November 1968 cited the failures of major integrated steel projects in Brazil, Mexico, Turkey and Venezuela.[105] In the end, Park financed Pohang by using Japanese war reparations. He put his favourite student from his teaching days at the Korean Military Academy, a 43-year-old general called Park Tae Joon, in charge. The younger Park had already turned around a state mining company. Each day workers at Pohang were lined up in front of the main, corrugated-iron site office and told that Japanese reparations money was being used for the project and that it was preferable to die rather than suffer the humiliation of wasting the money.

The success of Pohang was down to much more than sweat, tears and anger, however. First there was the combination of huge scale with a step-by-step approach. Pohang was planned as much the most expensive investment in Korea, with a 9 million tonne capacity (versus a recommendation from Japanese technical advisers of 2.6 million tonnes). However, the first phase was opened at 1 million tonnes capacity, and then expanded in four end-to-end stages. Tougher technologies were left to later in the learning process – for instance, there was no continuous casting of steel in phase one as the Koreans focused on the simpler, more upstream tasks. To start with, they built a single blast furnace. Once each construction phase was launched, POSCO moved at breakneck speed, building around the clock so as to start earning a return on precious investment capital as soon as possible. Construction speed ought to be a comparative advantage of the developing state, not least because of much lower health and safety standards. At Pohang, 24-hour building contributed to a construction cost per tonne of steel capacity that was one-quarter that of Brazil.[106]

A second driver of success was that there was constant checking of the technical advice being received. Nippon Steel was the main provider of technology. Even though Japanese reparations financed much of Pohang, POSCO went to the Australian mining firm BHP to review all the Japanese engineering reports and to provide independent advice on equipment procurement. An ethnic Korean steel specialist who lived in Japan was then asked to review the reports of both the Japanese advisers and BHP.[107] POSCO listened to everyone, and trusted no one.

Third, the firm showed a relentless application to the job of learning everything there is to know about a steel plant. During the first and second phases of its construction, POSCO management refused to employ the computerised control systems recommended by their Japanese consultants lest they did not fully understand the equipment they were buying.

A hot rolling mill that opened in 1978 is still in use at Pohang today. As huge slabs of steel are passed back and forth and pressed at 1,200 degrees centigrade – throwing off heat that makes you sweat on a gangway twenty metres above – you can still see the original manual dials on the side of the production line indicating the gap between the top and bottom rollers. Today the operation is computerised, but for several years engineers collected all production line measurements by hand. By the time that POSCO wanted to build a second mega-facility at Gwangyang in the 1980s, Japanese suppliers had lost so much intellectual property to POSCO that they were unwilling to become involved. The imported equipment at Gwangyang came from Europe. By the time the final stages of Gwangyang were completed, over half the production lines were being manufactured domestically, compared with just over one-tenth of the equipment at the outset at Pohang.

Overarching all these reasons for success, of course, was export discipline. Unlike other big, failed steel projects, Pohang was always required to export. It was encouraged to do so through export subsidies, plus it needed foreign exchange in order to service the international debts that financed its later phases of expansion. POSCO has always shipped 30–40 per cent of its steel overseas. On paper, the firm has been profitable every year since it began production in 1973, but this should not disguise the scale of the subsidies that got it moving. An Iron and Steel Industry Promotion Law of 1970, which echoes the single industry laws that were employed in Japan, laid the basis for POSCO to enjoy cheap electricity, water and gas, as well as subsidised port and rail services. The central government paid for much of Pohang's supporting infrastructure. Through the 1970s and 1980s, Korea also levied a 25 per cent tariff on imported steel that was not destined for re-export, guaranteeing POSCO surplus demand at home so long as it achieved a reasonable level of efficiency.

Employee hours per tonne of steel shipped from Pohang dropped from 33 in 1975 to 10 in 1984 (though this was still well behind Japan, at 6.5 hours in 1984). With its huge scale, POSCO had the resources gradually to begin to innovate. The company opened a research and development centre in 1977 and by 1986 exported its first technology to the United States, when it provided the main technical input for a joint venture to make cold-rolled sheets with US Steel in California. More recently, POSCO patented its Finex production technique, which produces molten iron directly from iron ore fines and coal without the need to sinter the ore or cook the coal into coke. The company operates at a scale where it is a player not just in production, but also in technology. Stripped of its subsidy support in the 1990s and 2000s, and now fully privatised, POSCO needs no further helping hand. In recent years its net income has been a very healthy 15 per cent of sales, which are in turn targeted to rise from USD30 billion in 2009 to USD100 billion by 2018. Warren Buffet's Berkshire Hathaway bought a substantial chunk of POSCO equity – a solid indicator of its long-term profitability.

In 2003, the company opened its own museum in which it tells its side of history. On one wall there is a proud discourse about how wrong the World Bank was about the POSCO plan. The original corrugated-iron site office has been preserved. And there are more waxworks. This time POSCO president Park Tae Joon stands next to 'The Rat' – as Park Chung Hee's rodent-like appearance led him to be known behind his back – while they detonate a charge during site preparation. After the first steel was poured on 9 June 1973, Park Chung Hee declared an annual National Steel Day to go with the annual National Export Day he had inaugurated in 1964. This being Korea, these were working holidays. Today POSCO vies with China's Baogang as the world's number two steel producer, behind the giant, Indian-controlled ArcelorMittal combine.[108] But POSCO's profitability, and hence market value, is relatively far superior to either. In technical terms, it trails only the most advanced Japanese mills. At the Pohang site, 7,000 workers are now employed – less than half the number who worked there a decade ago when output was far lower. Among the next workers to go are rumoured to be the drivers who sit below the load beds of vast, strange trucks that move coils of finished steel around. They are expected to be replaced by robots.

### Doing, learning

Given the role that learning plays in economic development, factories like Pohang become the schools in which successful developing nations learn. POSCO is a kind of vocational college that doubles as a steel maker. In the 1970s and 1980s it educated a first generation of Korean steel specialists and did so while POSCO was already producing and exporting product. The role of factory-based – as opposed to school-based – learning becomes

clearer still at Hyundai's manufacturing hub at Ulsan, only seventy kilometres to the south of Pohang. Back on the expressway, the Hyundai Avante is
returning – as it speeds past more of those bland low- and high-rise blocks
and red and brown brick churches – to the place of its birth. Most of the
apartment blocks in Ulsan have the Hyundai logo – a sort of heavy, stylised
C – painted on the side. As in Pohang, it is not the city area that I head
for but the docks, built on the estuary of the Taehwa river, once known as
'the river of death' for all the industrial effluent poured into it, but now a
little cleaner. Just like POSCO's two great steel plants, all Hyundai's major
factories were conceived with international trade in mind and stand at the
water's edge. Following the course of the river towards the sea, I know I
have arrived at the headquarters of Hyundai Motor Company (HMC), not
because I can see a car factory but because I can see three huge car-carrier
ships moored up on the docks next to a car park the size of multiple football
fields. Eight hundred and fifty-two thousand out of 1.5 million vehicles built
in Ulsan in 2009 went through this car park and on to the boats.

I check into the Hyundai Hotel, located next door to the Hyundai
Department Store and opposite Hyundai Heavy Industries (HHI) –
Chung Ju Yung's shipyard, the world's biggest. My room has a panoramic
view of some of the massive cranes of HHI. Not far away is the HMC compound, now stretching well beyond the original eighty-two acres Chung
bought back in 1967 to start the business. Today, HMC covers 1,225 acres
and contains five separate factories making small cars, big cars, SUVs, hybrid
energy cars and light commercial vehicles. On top of its vehicle production
capacity of 1.6 million cars and trucks, Ulsan turns out 2 million engines
and 2.5 million transmissions each year. It is the biggest integrated car
manufacturing facility in the world.[109]

Exploring the HMC compound with a manager, I soon realise that it is
impossible to reconstruct the firm's development by looking at the production lines.[110] The original factories have all been torn down. Unlike POSCO,
there is no museum and almost no older technology still in use to give clues as
to the learning process. The only nostalgic curiosity is the modified Korean
tricycles, fitted with crates, into which an assembly line worker will occasionally toss a part that has some quality defect. These go back a long way.
Otherwise, there are ever more robots. Two of them simultaneously fit the

front and rear windscreens of an Avante (known as an Elantra outside of Korea); the actions take thirty-five seconds. Immediately, two other robots grab front seats from a conveyor belt above the vehicle and place them in the car. The operations left for the humans are so monotonous that even in Korea – which developed off the back of a 50-hour work week – assembly line workers are permitted to change places and do something different every two hours and ten minutes.[111]

As at POSCO, each year that industrial learning has taken place, fewer people have turned out more product. There are presently 34,000 HMC employees in Ulsan making 1.6 million vehicles. It took 41,000 people to make 1 million in 1994, and vastly more again to make just 400,000 in 1986. The vehicles are also infinitely more complex than the cheap and cheerful products of the past. We sit in the back of a 5-litre, 300 brake horsepower Equus model. It is the new top-of–the-line luxury sedan designed to compete with the Lexus 460. The manager demonstrates Hyundai's proprietary voice-activated radio and satellite navigation systems. He points out the new hybrid petrol–electric vehicles. It is all very modern, and almost impossible to connect back to the company founded in the 1960s by Chung Ju Yung and his brothers with zero industrial experience.

Back in the day Chung had run a car repair shop but, as his biographer Donald Kirk noted, he 'had never manufactured so much as a bolt or a bearing'. The brother he put in day-to-day charge of HMC, Se Yung, always said he had no natural interest in cars.[112] None the less, the Chungs' entrepreneurial hunger, focused by strong state incentives to learn to manufacture cars, was enough to ensure success. From a first five-year plan in 1962 that encouraged kit assembly deals with foreign partners, Park Chung Hee's government never wavered in its intention to build a globally competitive automotive sector. From 1967, a second five-year plan jacked up the requirement for locally made parts from 20 per cent of a car's value to 60 per cent. In 1973, as the government launched its heavy and chemical industries (HCI) drive, a plan was issued that called for 'citizens' cars' made entirely from Korean parts. Finally, in 1979, came a national machinery export promotion policy which made autos a key export target.

The state's screw was turned in the normal ways. Access to bank finance was progressively conditioned on building a truly Korean car and exporting it. (In HMC's case, in the mid 1970s this meant state loan approvals worth twenty times the firm's paid-in capital.)[113] Firms which failed to meet local content requirements faced insuperable tariff barriers to importing components, while firms which did play the state's game were offered a protected domestic market in which the government set mouth-wateringly high car prices by bureaucratic fiat.[114] Wrapped around all this was non-negotiable export discipline. In Chung Ju Yung's case, he promised Park he would export 5,000 cars in his first full production year, 1976, if he was given funding for a Korean 'citizens' car'. He dared not admit his promise to the foreign managers he hired for technical assistance until production began. Donald Kirk observed: 'Then, as later, export pressure forced [technological] upgrades that would never have happened if HMC were manufacturing only for protected domestic consumption.'[115]

The only wobble in the government's commitment to the auto sector came after Park's 1979 assassination, during the global recession of the early 1980s. Kia, which had come into car making from motorcycle and truck manufacturing, was forced by the central government to suspend car production for a couple of years. HMC sold a minority stake to its main technology supplier, the Japanese company Mitsubishi, to raise cash.[116] However, as the HCI investments orchestrated by Park in steel and shipbuilding started to turn profitable in the mid 1980s, government support for the auto industry strengthened again. The longevity of this support was critical. HMC chose the second half of the 1980s to break into the US market, which it did by selling a compact model called the Excel as a loss leader. As each wave of growing pain was endured, the government and the banking system it controlled stood by Korea's car makers. It was a long, long struggle. HMC only produced its first genuinely in-house engine, dubbed the Alpha, in 1991, twenty-four years after the firm was founded. Toeholds in international markets were won battle by battle. In Europe, for instance, the Korean government told the protectionist French government that French train makers would have a better chance of supplying the Train de Grande Vitesse (TGV) for the Seoul–Pusan rail route if France bought Korean cars. After weighing the competing interests of its train and car producers, Paris eventually came up with a quota of 20,000 imports a year.

That the Korean government stayed the course on its industrial policy despite the doubts of some senior bureaucrats[117] and the rising fury of trade partners, was essential to its building of a globally competitive auto sector. The same was true in shipbuilding, where Hyundai was supported by a monopoly on Korean sales of offshore steel structures (such as ones required by the oil and gas industry), a state directive that only Hyundai ships could be used to import crude oil, and state-guaranteed loans not only for shipbuilding, but also to finance Hyundai's own merchant marine subsidiary – which bought the company's vessels to smooth out market demand.[118] Shipbuilding, which is a less complex business than car making, began to throw off substantial positive cash flow in the mid 1980s and the Hyundai group then spirited much of this cash away to support its auto efforts. If controlling interests in the businesses had been listed on stock markets, investors would never have tolerated such behaviour. Yet it was the right thing to do from a technological learning perspective.

A second key to HMC's manufacturing success was its ability to obtain foreign technology in such a way that the firm learned skills – and eventually learned how to originate its own technology – without becoming dependent on foreign multinationals. In the automotive industry, developing country car makers around the world have found it almost impossible to gain technological independence after going into equity joint ventures with global auto firms. In joint ventures, it is too easy and too comfortable for the local entrant to become dependent on drip-fed technology from a foreign partner, while multinationals have no interest in helping local firms export.[119] The Chungs, under the kosh of export discipline, saw that joint ventures impeded technological independence and so avoided them. They started out by putting together Ford Cortinas from kits in 1968, but when the Americans said they would not provide further technology without an equity stake in the business, Chung Ju Yung sent family members to scour the planet for better offers.[120]

The solution to the technology problem was to split up the challenge into several pieces. First there was a 1973 technology licensing deal with Japan's weakest scale car maker, Mitsubishi. The larger Japanese firms would not enter into such an arrangement given the risk of creating a competitor. Mitsubishi Motor Company (MMC) provided the key technologies

HMC needed to produce the original own-brand Hyundai car – the Pony – in return for licensing fees and revenue from parts sales. The technologies included designs for an engine, transmission and rear axle. Next, the Chungs hired George Turnbull, the former boss of failing English car maker British Leyland, to run their production line. Turnbull, in turn, hired six European chief engineers to plan a factory and to undertake design, testing and production roles. If Mitsubishi managers were thinking they could control the Chungs, they soon discovered otherwise. One of the first things the Turnbull team did was to reject the engine that MMC wanted HMC to use. It would have underpowered the Pony. The Chungs insisted on having the same engine that Mitsubishi was using in its equivalent vehicle.[121] Then the brothers went to Italian car designer ItalDesign to give them an independent look for the Pony's body. And finally they picked up all kinds of other peripheral ideas from visiting any international car maker that would receive them, including GM, VW and Alfa Romeo.

HMC put its new car into production in less than two years. The production line operated for as little as one-fifth of the day early on because of workers' errors and supplier problems, and initial output featured plastic parts that snapped in the summer heat, door handles that came off, dodgy brakes and paint that faded in weeks. The early exports that Chung Ju Yung promised General Park were offloaded at a loss in countries like Nigeria, Saudi Arabia, Peru and Ecuador.[122] Even after ten years' production, in 1978 HMC was selling less than 60,000 cars. However, the firm was digesting technology and it was learning. By 1981, HMC built a much larger factory and was limbering up for a big export push. It was at this point that the firm sold a minority stake to Mitsubishi, ceding no management control but gaining new designs and an agreement to take around 30,000 Excels a year badged as the Mitsubishi Precis. The Koreans were starting to win a little respect. Next, they set their sights on the biggest car market in the world, the United States, hiring a US marketing team away from Toyota. It was a period when the US government was beginning to force Japan to rein in its car exports under so-called 'voluntary restraint' agreements. With Japanese car prices rising as a result, HMC attacked the US market with the Excel, a small car that was priced one-fifth cheaper than any of its competitors.

HMC's US managers, backed by aggressive pricing and an advertising blitz, delivered a remarkable feat. They made the Excel the top imported compact model in the US in its first two years, selling more than 260,000 units per year in both 1987 and 1988.[123] Overnight, piddly HMC became a volume player. However, the company was taking huge losses on the exports. If the American managers thought their Korean bosses could afford this for long, they were wrong. After creating a beach-head in the US, HMC moved ruthlessly to further cut its imported component bill in Ulsan and to reduce US sales expenses. Just as Turnbull and the costly European managers taken on in 1974 were thrown a party and sent home in 1977, so the US marketing managers and distributors who made the US launch a success experienced swingeing budget cuts and firings in 1989 and 1990. Annual sales in north America fell by over half as HMC fought to break even. Finally, in the mid 1990s, the business stabilised and became profitable. Sales began to rise again, and HMC was established as a feature of the world's most competitive car market. This presaged the firm's swifter success in the less competitive and higher-margin markets of Europe.[124]

As of 1991, when HMC produced the first genuinely Korean engine, its productivity levels were, by its own analysis, still only half those of Toyota and Honda. But it was in control of its technological destiny. The symbols of HMC's technology acquisition were not foreign joint ventures, but the Hyundai bungalows and the Hyundai hotel (where I stayed on my visit, known formerly as the Diamond hotel) in which temporary foreign consultants were housed while their knowledge was absorbed. Once HMC and other Hyundai firms in Ulsan had what was needed, the consultants were sent home with a bit of money in their pockets, hazy memories of Filipina bands from the ersatz English 'pub' in the hotel basement, and perhaps even hazier memories of the seedy bars that cater to foreigners' needs in the area. From the HMC perspective, the firm built on the foundation of government support by borrowing and learning to develop technology rather than becoming a junky for a joint venture partner's technology. All that remained to do beyond this was to outlast domestic rivals and gobble up their capacity when they went out of business.

In the Korea of 1973 – which at the time boasted a car market of just 30,000 vehicles per annum – government had offered protection and subsidies to not one but three putative makers of 'citizens' cars': HMC, Shinjin and Kia. Inasmuch as the market was too small for one producer, the licensing of three companies was ridiculous. HMC posted losses every year from 1972 to 1978, despite very high domestic car prices. However, the government sanctioned multiple car makers not to make short-term profits – which would have come much sooner to a monopoly manufacturer – but rather to force the pace of technological learning through competition. With car prices fixed by the EPB, the firms had to compete on quality in the domestic market, and then on exports. The market leader in the earliest phase of development was not HMC, but the now-forgotten Shinjin *chaebol*, operating in a joint venture with General Motors under the brand Saehan. But the conglomerate took on more debt than it could handle, and the government put it out of business, allowing Daewoo to take over its car-making assets in 1982. Daewoo claimed that it would find a way to develop exportable cars despite having only 50 per cent equity in the GM joint venture.[125] The third original entrant, Kia, started out as a bicycle and motorcycle maker and obtained its earliest technology from Honda, but like HMC refused to share management control.

As the domestic car market grew to hundreds of thousands of units a year in the 1980s, other *chaebol* demanded the right to get into the car business. The government let them, but remained ruthless to any which could not service their debts. Asia Motors entered and failed in the 1980s; its carcass was thrown to an improving Kia. By the early 1990s, there were four players: HMC, Daewoo, Kia–Asia Motors and SsangYong, a four-wheel drive specialist. Samsung was demanding to join the fray. After the demise of Shinjin, HMC managed to remain the market leader, accounting for around half of all Korean automotive output in the 1980s, and hitting 1 million units of annual production for the first time in 1994. It was a position of considerable relative strength. Yet Daewoo was gaining market share in the mid 1990s, while Chung Ju Yung fell out of political favour.[126]

In the end, the Asian financial crisis, which began in 1997, was rather well timed from HMC's perspective. The Daewoo group was too heavily leveraged – despite much-improved products like its Matiz mini car – and went bust. After the IMF's intervention in Korea, Daewoo's car assets were sold to the company's former partner, GM. HMC was able to take over

Kia in 1998, giving it an unassailable three-quarters of the domestic Korean market (Chung Ju Yung's political woes were suddenly a secondary issue during the crisis). SsangYong was first reshuffled into the Daewoo Motor business, and then subject to a disastrous takeover by the state-owned Chinese auto firm Shanghai Automotive Industry Corp (SAIC). And Samsung focused down on electronics, contenting itself with a minority stake in an automotive joint venture in which it accepted its complete technological dependence on Renault–Nissan.[127] 'They just rent out the [Samsung] badge,' said my guide at HMC with gleeful contempt as we wandered through the factory.[128]

By 2000, HMC was clearly the Korean automotive winner. It had survived savage domestic competition to become the domestic market leader for a quarter of a century, and hit the export benchmarks set by the Korean state. The takeover of Kia signalled the emergence of a global powerhouse. After 2000 HMC also timed its entry into the critical global growth markets in China and India almost to perfection. In 2010 HMC, along with Kia, sold 5.7 million vehicles around the world, meaning it tied with Ford as the fourth biggest global auto group.[129] A family business with no previous industrial experience had created one of the world's most successful car companies. And the primary reason that it was able to do so was state industrial policy.

**Paler imitations**

It had taken Japan's Toyota thirty-six years to sell its first 10 million vehicles. It took HMC, based in a much poorer country with one-third the population, twenty-eight years.[130] This is a reminder of both the extraordinary success of Korea's manufacturing development policy and of the fact that the world is speeding up – the country with the right policy mix has at least the theoretical potential to develop its economy faster than ever. Korea, however, had an easy ride inasmuch as Park Chung Hee and other leaders had imbibed the fundamentals of effective industrial policy from their former colonial masters in Japan. In south-east Asia, there was no local success story to be copied. The region required one of its states to produce the path-breaking performance delivered in north-east Asia by

Meiji Japan. Of all the countries in the region, Malaysia under Mahathir Mohamad perhaps came the closest, but nowhere near close enough.[131]

In political terms, Malaysia is not a difficult country to understand. It was put together in its modern incarnation from a patchwork of sultan-ruled states which had been subjected to modestly varying colonial arrangements by the British. The colonialism was always of the 'light' variety in the sense that it did not take many Britons to run what is now Malaysia, and the local aristocracy was heavily co-opted. From 1957, the first post-independence prime minister, known to his countrymen as the Tunku ('The Prince'), was Abdul Rahman Putra Al-Haj, a rich, clubbable, Anglicised, upper-class, womanising dilettante who took a particularly long time to complete his undergraduate degree at Cambridge. He did little to change the colonial shape of the economy, letting British firms maintain their mining and plantation interests, and was soon in the habit of taking cash kickbacks from leading businessmen.[132] The second post independence leader, Abdul Razak, and the third, Hussein Onn, were also of royal lineage. Hussein Onn, who was congenitally indecisive, was perhaps the worst of the lot. By the time of his term in office (1976–81), Malaysia had suffered major race riots against the economically better-off Chinese population. The government began to use part of its new-found petroleum wealth to nationalise former British assets but, with the exception of some very ineffective 'import substitution industrialisation' – which typically amounted to joint venture kit assembly behind protective tariffs, there was no serious or effective industrial policy. This is where Mahathir Mohamad came in.

Mahathir was born in Kedah in the north of Malaysia in 1925. The Tunku – who was the son of the Sultan of Kedah – attended the English-language secondary school run by Mahathir's father. However, the Tunku subsequently claimed that he never knew the future premier in adolescence because 'he was a nobody'.[133] Mahathir, a quarter Indian through his grandfather,[134] was an outsider who grew up somewhat angry and increasingly politicised. He did not like the entitled snobbery of the Malaysian aristocracy (after being elected to parliament, he claimed that the Tunku referred to him as 'that Pakistani [sic]' because of his Indian ancestry) and he was determined to prove himself. He joined the dominant United Malay

National Organisation when it was formed in 1946, and went to university in Singapore to study medicine. He made the improvement of ordinary Malays his cause, although he grew up with a race-based view of the world that was stereotypical of the colonial era; the Malays, for Mahathir, were genetically constrained. Mahathir's judgement of developmental issues would forever be clouded by the fact that he spent too much time worrying about race and not enough time understanding the basic structural requirements of technological learning. His best-known book, *The Malay Dilemma*, is a rambling discourse on the plight of the Malays that contrasts powerfully with Park Chung Hee's two books of the early 1960s, which contained much more practical analysis of what Korea needed to do to in order to ascend the industrial learning curve.[135]

Mahathir had had his political reckoning with the Tunku after the anti-Chinese riots in Kuala Lumpur in May 1969 left around 200 people dead.[136] He wrote an open letter to the prime minister blaming his witless premiership for the killings and suggesting he was likely playing poker – the Tunku, like many members of the Malaysian upper class, was fond of gambling – while KL burned. As a result Mahathir was expelled from UMNO. The Tunku, however, had become a political liability and was eased out of power by other senior politicians. In 1971, Malaysia introduced an affirmative action plan called the New Economic Policy to ease racial tensions. With the Tunku gone, Mahathir was readmitted to UMNO after only three years, and a year after that he became Minister of Education. When the second prime minister, Razak, and his deputy both died prematurely of natural causes, Hussein Onn took over and in 1976 turned, quite unexpectedly, to Mahathir to be his deputy.

The entrepreneurial Mahathir then grabbed the job he wanted in order to figure out how to change Malaysia – Minister for Trade and Industry. He spent three years visiting north-east Asia and developing ideas about industrial policy.[137] Asmat Kamaludin, who accompanied Mahathir on a trip to Korea, recalls him charging round 'about fifteen' factories in a day and delivering an emotionally charged speech in which he said 'he hoped Malaysia could be like [Korea] one day'.[138] At the time Malaysia and Korea had almost exactly the same GNI per capita – just under USD1600 – but Mahathir could see that the Koreans were far ahead in creating the

industrial basis for further progress.[139] At home he got to know Japanese
and Korean businessmen working in Malaysia and began a lifelong friend-
ship with Kazumasa Suzuki, the local representative of the Japanese trading
house Mitsui.[140] A development plan began to form that Mahathir would
dub 'Look East', in deference to the remarkable industrial success of north-
east Asia. The models were the heavy industrialisation programmes of the
north-east Asian states, most obviously Park Chung Hee's HCI drive which
was just drawing to a close.[141] Then, in summer 1981, prime minister Hussein Onn, not up to his job and recovering from heart surgery, decided to
step aside. Mahathir suddenly became Malaysia's first commoner premier,
and its first leader to have a cohesive development strategy.

It was Malaysia's Park Chung Hee moment, without the coup. Mahathir,
from an ordinary background, with a no-nonsense attitude, took over from
the last in a line of a discredited, self-serving elite.[142] As Minister for Trade
and Industry he had already created a state holding company, Heavy Industries Corporation of Malaysia (HICOM), for an industrial 'big push' that
would encompass cement, steel, cars, motorcycles, shipbuilding, fertiliser,
petrochemicals, paper and more.[143] Mahathir also planned to build an
expressway down the more developed west coast of Malaysia, a longer version of the Seoul–Pusan link that had opened up South Korea. He thought
Malaysia should have its own *sogo shosha* – as Japan's giant trading groups
are called – which, as in Japan, would seek out markets and raw materials
around the world for domestic manufacturers, and provide them with
trade credit. As in Korea, Mahathir was ready and willing to borrow heavily
overseas to pay for his country's modernisation. He understood that, to
learn, Malaysia would first have to pay.

### The devil in the detail

Unfortunately, there were to be fundamental policy differences in Malaysia
when compared with Japan, Korea and Taiwan. Compounded by an already
lacklustre performance in unreformed agriculture,[144] these differences were
more than enough to derail Mahathir's industrial ambitions. The new leader
failed to grasp the need for export discipline, and on trips to north-east
Asia his Korean and Japanese hosts did not explain the dirty secrets of

protectionism to him. This was hardly surprising when the self-interest of these states was now in selling turnkey industrial plants and construction services to countries like Malaysia. In fairness to Mahathir, however, when it came to implementing effective industrial policy, he had no appropriate regional example to follow; all the countries around Malaysia in south-east Asia were making bad development policy choices. Mahathir could have read the first of the great academic analyses of Japanese industrial policy, Chalmers Johnson's *MITI and the Japanese Miracle*, which was published in 1982 just as Look East was being launched. Unfortunately, he did not. Nor did Mahathir read Park Chung Hee's books about development policy in Korea.[145] Instead, he would later read – and tell his underlings to read – a fashionable, pro-globalisation book that was wholly irrelevant to his country's needs: Kenichi Ohmae's 1990 tome *The Borderless World*. Mahathir was mercurial. He launched his biggest industrialisation projects, and then began to sour on Japanese joint venture partners, even before Malaysian bureaucrats had completed a detailed Industrial Master Plan.[146]

Mahathir's neglect of export discipline was his first error, and had effects that were quickly apparent. To help pay for its investment programme, the Malaysian government increased its foreign debt from 10 per cent of GDP in 1980 to 38 per cent in 1986.[147] But, unlike Korea, Malaysia's export earnings from manufactured goods grew only slowly. This not only engendered an acute balance of payments problem, it left Mahathir to make critical investment decisions without the market-based information that export performance provided to Park Chung Hee. Instead of counting exports, Mahathir trusted his own judgement about the firms and managers he was backing. He tried to know more than the market.

The second divergence from Korean experience was that Mahathir rarely employed the private sector to lead his industrial investments and did not create competing ventures. He preferred one-off investments in state enterprises.[148] By not licensing more entrants in businesses like car making, Mahathir threw away the power to cull losers. All he could do was change the management of state enterprises – firms he could not afford to let go bust because he had nowhere else to turn. Without realising it, Mahathir did just what critics of industrial policy have often falsely accused successful industrialising states of doing: he set out to pick winners when the effective approach was to create competition and then weed out the weak. Mahathir further compounded this problem by forcing putative national champions into equity joint ventures with multinational firms. The arrangements made it all too easy for Malaysian firms to develop long-term technological dependencies on their partners.[149] In sum, Mahathir unwittingly set his pet companies up for a fall. When the fall came, he blamed the managers.

A third complication was that Mahathir mixed up industrial policy with affirmative action. He came to power promising to raise up the indigenous *bumiputera*[150] population. In so doing, he painted himself into a racial corner where he decided he could not use Malaysia's mostly ethnic Chinese and Tamil established entrepreneurs to run his new heavy industrial investments. Instead, he tried to implement effective industrial policy and create a new generation of Malay entrepreneurs at the same time. This was always going to be difficult. In the absence of export discipline and private sector competition, it was impossible.

Affirmative action led to the cruellest irony of Mahathir's industrialisation programme. He sent *bumiputeras* with minimal business experience – frequently civil servants – to run industrial ventures which were supposed to achieve global levels of competitiveness. Meanwhile, Malaysia's proven and established Chinese and Tamil private sector entrepreneurs were not pushed into manufacturing or exports. They were left to gorge themselves on oligopolistic licences controlling services and commodities in the domestic economy. Of course these entrepreneurs had to impress Mahathir. But with no manufacturing or export requirement, this was not difficult. The oligarchs simply showed the premier an efficient power station built by Siemens, or a mobile phone service based on Ericsson technology, or giant towers designed by an American architect and built with north-east Asian steel, and collected the rent for being able to use that imported technology efficiently. Mahathir could be a pain to work for, but ultimately Malaysia's billionaire elite ran rings around him. They, and their peers elsewhere in south-east Asia, remained what Park Chung Hee had condemned after the end of Japanese colonialism in Korea as 'liberation aristocrats'.

Mahathir's fourth deviation from best practice was to emasculate the Malaysian bureaucracy. Industrialisation in Malaysia was all too often a one-man show. As the bureaucrat Asmat Kamaludin says: 'It became very difficult to put your view forward.'[151] Another person who worked closely with Mahathir over many years, and who retains considerable respect for him, is more forthright: 'Mahathir has this supreme confidence which is very frightening.'[152] No successful developmental leader in Japan, Korea, Taiwan (or China) circumvented the national bureaucracy to the extent that Mahathir did. He wanted to conceive the strategy, do the due diligence and cut the deals all on his own.

Finally, when debt and balance of payments problems mounted, Mahathir began to lose his nerve and flip-flopped into a rather confused hybrid economic policy. In 1985 and 1986, facing a fiscal crunch and a regional recession, he introduced aggressive tax breaks and incentives for foreign investment.[153] These changes, combined with a falling exchange rate, led to a wave of inward investment in low value-added export processing, particularly (and ironically) by Japanese and Korean companies. Exports had increased by only USD7 billion in the five years from 1980 to 1985, but they shot up USD14 billion in three years from 1985 to 1988.[154] From 1987, Malaysia began to show a current account surplus. However, instead of ploughing on with its industrialisation big push as the Koreans did through oil crises and global recessions in the 1970s and 1980s – Mahathir cut back on new projects and sought to balance the government's books.[155] A regional boom driven heavily by foreign investment took hold in the late 1980s and early 1990s, and the GDP growth rate shot up. It was tempting to believe in these circumstances that Malaysia was making real progress in its industrial development. Indeed, it appears that Mahathir did think this. In 1991, he announced his 'Vision 2020' – that Malaysia could, and would, be an industrialised developed country by 2020. Unfortunately, as Mahathir's ardour for old-fashioned infant industry policy waned, Malaysia was barely ascending the technological learning curve at all. This would become apparent in the very cold light shed on the country by the Asian financial crisis.

In the meantime, Mahathir found himself a new and influential friend in the McKinsey management consultant, futurologist and author Kenichi Ohmae. Although Japanese, Ohmae was a vehement critic of old-school *dirigiste* Japan. He looked forward to a globalised world in which national identity would be unimportant, bureaucrats would be pushed aside and open markets would be win–win for all-comers. This sanguine outlook was an early conceptualisation of the view now associated with Thomas Friedman's 2005 book *The World is Flat*. Despite its being entirely at odds with the industrial policies that made Japan rich – policies which Mahathir was supposed to be imitating – the prime minister was so taken with Ohmae's book *The Borderless World* that he ordered all around him to read it. Asmat Kamaludin, who became the top bureaucrat at Malaysia's Ministry of International Trade and Industry in this period, recalls: 'You felt safe if you were walking around with that book.'[156]

However, with the benefit of hindsight, the rather hasty, under-researched and breathless tone of *The Borderless World* was a pointer to the unlikelihood of its prediction that the world was becoming more favourable to the development of poor countries. It was not a good replacement for the work of Friedrich List. Hard-nosed infant industry protection of the kind recommended by List remains the only proven way of pushing a rising state up the technological ladder. In the 1990s, by contrast, Ohmae and Mahathir went on to plan and launch the futuristic and widely ridiculed Multimedia Super Corridor and Cyberjaya investment park projects around Kuala Lumpur. These were supposed to foster indigenous high technology through free market, win–win cross-border cooperation, but have done no such thing.[157] Instead, the white elephant projects stand as testaments to the naivete – albeit well-meaning naivete – of books like *The Borderless World* and *The World is Flat* that suggest that we are moving towards a new developmental paradigm in which the interests of rich and poor nations neatly coincide.

### Journey 4: Across Malaysia

*Once again we need to take a drive. This being Malaysia, with a Gini coefficient of around 0.5, the car hire firm despatches a couple of peons to bring a vehicle to the house where I am staying on the west side of Kuala Lumpur. The car is a Proton Waja – the name means 'strong' – built by Mahathir's beloved national car company. He put more money over more time into Proton than into any other industrial project. The Waja was the first real Malaysian car, designed by Malaysians, with a Proton engine, and it went into production in 2001.*

To my untrained eye, the Waja is no less attractive than the first generation Hyundai Elantra, built after the Korean firm had developed its own engine.[158] The one mechanical problem I had with the Waja in the course of a week was that the windshield wiper speed adjuster was not working. Apart from this the car had good acceleration, a decent ride and went much faster than the signs at the side of the road recommended. The Waja, in short, is nothing to be ashamed of. It was put on the road with a proprietary engine in less time than Hyundai took to develop a Korean car with a Korean engine.[159] Yet the Waja and the models which came immediately after it represent an industrial development peak that Malaysia has been unable to surpass.

In order to understand why, it is first necessary to understand the degree to which Mahathir failed to compel Malaysia's private entrepreneurs to make a developmental contribution to their country – a failing common throughout south-east Asia. You can do this by driving up a single street in Kuala Lumpur, the south–north downtown artery called Jalan Sultan Ismail. Here you will survey the headquarters of the billionaire oligarchs who were left out of Mahathir's manufacturing industrialisation plans. The basis of the fortunes of these entrepreneurs tells us much about what went wrong with development policy. We begin at the south end of Jalan Sultan Ismail, at the Star Hill traffic lights, an intersection that can reasonably be referred to as 'Francis Yeoh Junction', after the garrulous, ethnic Chinese billionaire who owns all the major real estate around it – shopping centres, five-star hotel, office blocks.

Yeoh is one of two local entrepreneurs who, because of their construction backgrounds, are analogues for Korea's Chung Ju Yung. His father started out building schools, hospitals and more for the government, and had made his first fortune by the 1970s. Thereafter Francis and his brothers took over. Unlike the Chungs, however, the Yeohs were not forced by government policy into manufacturing. Instead, while Mahathir launched public sector industrial projects in 1980s, they obtained untendered domestic service sector privatisations in sectors like power generation. These were offered as part of the prime minister's confused vision of infant industry protection plus privatisation and deregulation. In 1992 the Yeohs obtained, without a public tender, the first independent power producer (IPP) contract in Malaysia. The terms forced the state electricity monopoly to buy their power at a very high price and this and other infrastructure service deals brought them a river of cash without any manufacturing or export constraint.[160] Everything they needed they bought from firms like General Electric and Siemens. When domestic real estate investment was no longer able to soak up the earnings from this government largesse, the Yeohs looked offshore and in 2002 bought British water utility Wessex Water for USD1.8 billion, followed by electricity assets in Australia, Indonesia and Singapore. In the past three decades the Yeohs' company, YTL, has built a big, passive, profitable investment business that is, from Malaysia's technological learning perspective, almost entirely inconsequential.[161]

A little further up Jalan Sultan Ismail from Francis Yeoh Junction, on the right at the Jalan Raja Chulan intersection, is Wisma Genting, headquarters of the business built by Lim Goh Tong. Lim, who passed away in 2007, is the second Malaysian analogue for Chung Ju Yung. Indeed, he is an even closer one. Lim made his first fortune not just from construction, but earlier, like Chung, from trading with the Japanese during the Second World War and then by buying and selling war surplus civil engineering equipment. Lim and his partners rigged bids at British auctions of bulldozers and other heavy construction gear after the war.[162] He then reconditioned the machinery, sold some of it and used the rest to go into mining and the building of post-independence infrastructure including dams, bridges, roads and sewage systems. Like Chung, Lim was a robustly built man who joined in manual labour with his work teams and camped out at construction sites. Both had little beyond secondary education, but both were good with numbers. Neither brooked much advice from juniors and both knew how and when to charm or pay off politicians. Just as Chung Ju Yung made the transition from Syngman Rhee to his post-coup successors Generals Park Chung Hee and Chun Doo Hwan, so Lim Goh Tong got along famously with every post-independence Malaysian leader, including Mahathir.

When Mahathir became premier in 1981, Lim could have built the ambitious bridge link to Penang island on the west coast, a key project on Mahathir's to-do list. In the early 1960s Lim had already built the 850-metre Sultan Yayha Putra bridge near the Thai border, then the country's longest. This being Malaysia, however, by the 1980s Lim was already out of the infrastructure game. He had never been pressed to export construction services or to go into manufacturing. Instead, while Chung Ju Yung was, at Park Chung Hee's behest, beginning to take on the world's leading firms in auto making, shipbuilding and semiconductors, Lim shifted his resources into a giant casino development. In 1969, he persuaded the Tunku to give him a licence to operate Muslim-ruled Malaysia's first, vast and only casino at Genting Highlands outside Kuala Lumpur.[163] Genting brought Lim not so much a river of cash as a flood, running into billions of US dollars. Yet despite his making enough money to fund a major industrial business group, no requirement was ever put on him to make or export anything. Under Mahathir's regime, Lim's group continued to receive state concessions including IPP and oil and gas deals, but with no developmental quid pro quo. The cash piled up, and when largely passive domestic real estate and plantation investments could no longer consume it, the Lims began to invest in cruise ships, gaming businesses and casinos around the world; these include, in Singapore, a USD3.4 billion casino resort.[164]

Mahathir's Penang bridge, in a telling irony, was built not by Lim Goh Tong's construction firm, but instead by Chung Ju Yung's Hyundai Engineering and Construction, which remained under perennial pressure to export construction services, even in the 1980s.[165] Mahathir's strategy was to learn not by doing but by giving construction projects to firms from Japan and Korea. In 1984 he awarded what was then the biggest construction deal in Malaysia's history – for the Dayabumi complex in Kuala Lumpur – to two Japanese firms, despite the fact that local companies put in lower bids. The Malaysian taxpayer footed the bill, but Malaysians learned nothing.[166] Meanwhile Lim Goh Tong and his fellow Malaysian entrepreneurs grew fat on a diet of government-provided concessions. In 2003 Mahathir wrote a foreword for Lim's hagiographic biography in which he stated: 'He is an exemplary corporate citizen. He has complied with perhaps every rule and regulation and policy made in Malaysia.'[167] The tragedy of Malaysia is that this is largely true. Unlike the Chungs of Hyundai, or the Lees of

Samsung, Malaysian businessmen were never compelled by the state to make any form of developmental contribution.

## The crisis that changed nothing

As the Waja crawls through the dense traffic of Jalan Sultan Ismail, the next major landmark on my right serves to point up that nothing has changed in the wake of the devastating Asian financial crisis that began in 1997. The Crowne Plaza (formerly Hilton) hotel is owned by Syed Mokhtar al-Bukhary and his headquarters is Complex Antarabangsar next door. Syed Mokhtar became Mahathir's pet entrepreneur in the wake of the financial crisis. In the final years of his premiership, before he resigned in 2003, Mahathir lavished Syed Mokhtar with electricity generation deals and state financing to build a new container port at Tanjung Pelepas. But once again it was without any export or manufacturing quid pro quo. In time-honoured fashion, the grateful billionaire took the cash flow and poured it into relatively passive investments in mining, plantations, hotels and real estate – a small part of which I am looking at now from my car window.[168]

A little further north, on the west side of the Jalan P. Ramlee intersection, is Menara Hap Seng, formerly MUI Plaza, which for decades was the headquarters of fallen billionaire Khoo Kay Peng. Khoo got on the wrong side of Mahathir in the 1980s, and stopped receiving state concessions. The fall of Khoo is a reminder that state discipline was not absent in Malaysia, just that it was not directed to appropriate ends.[169] On the right, beyond the strip of girlie bars, is Rohas Perkasa, a large development put up by Wan Azmi Wan Hamzah, a fallen *bumiputera* tycoon from before the Asian financial crisis.[170] Like so many, Wan Azmi rose and fell in real estate. The next block to the south is Quek Leng Chan's Wisma Hong Leong headquarters. Quek is a banking and real estate billionaire, although over the years he has done as much manufacturing as any Malaysian oligarch – from an air-conditioner business to downstream steel rolling to downstream finishing of semiconductors. For some reason a London-trained lawyer is the closest thing to a private Malaysian manufacturing entrepreneur of scale, though by Korean standards he is not close at all.

Towering above the cigar-sucking Quek's lair are the world-famous Petronas Twin Towers that were built by a man who has never got his hands dirty.[171] Ananda Krishnan, a gifted entrepreneur, is the second-richest person in Malaysia. Over the years he has stacked up a remarkable pile of untendered government concessions that include a monopoly on racetrack betting, oil and gas franchises, IPPs, mobile telephony licences, private television licences and redevelopment rights to a city-centre racecourse where the Twin Towers now stand. When, during the Asian financial crisis, the billions of dollars that flow annually from these state-provided franchises were insufficient for Krishnan's needs, Mahathir's government stepped in and had the state oil company buy out his towers development. Krishnan represents the apotheosis of the developmental model created by Mahathir: he runs his businesses well enough to beat the local competition; he almost never manufactures or competes internationally; and, in the absence of the export benchmark, he has been unsurpassed in convincing different political leaders that he merits their attention and favour.[172] What Krishnan needs technologically – from an American architect to design the Twin Towers to the steel to support them to the base stations for his mobile phone business – he buys offshore. As of 2011, he was worth an estimated USD15 billion. His developmental contribution has been considerably less.[173]

The Waja rolls across the Jalan P. Ramlee intersection, past UBN Tower to the west (for many years the most expensive office space in Kuala Lumpur) and the Shangri-la hotel. This is Robert Kuok's turf.[174] Kuok is the man who modernised the colonial rentier system in Malaysia, accumulating plantations and commodity trading operations, and winning early government concessions to trade and process protected staple foodstuffs. Worth an estimated USD16 billion, he is the richest Malaysian, albeit one who moved his base out of Malaysia in the 1970s and expanded his fortune through similar businesses all over south-east Asia. Indeed, Kuok is a unique, regional exemplar of the south-east Asian entrepreneur. About the most he has ever manufactured is a flour sack.

I am at the Jalan Ampang junction which leads, on the right, to the villas of Kuala Lumpur's main billionaire and royalty residential ghetto, behind the Twin Towers.[175] Staying north on Jalan Sultan Ismail, I see coming into view the architectural tombstones of the Asian financial crisis – projects which were intended to extend this key thoroughfare northwards, but which remain unfinished fifteen years after the crash. Unlike Korea, south-east Asia did not pick up where it left off in the wake of the crisis. Next to the Concorde hotel is the floor plate of the putative Ritz Carlton hotel, dream-thing of Vincent Tan, another gambling and real estate oligarch.[176] To the left, down Jalan Ampang, is the half-finished Duta Grand Hyatt hotel site. North of the junction, to the east, are the few completed elements of what was to have been RHB Vision City, a name almost as unfortunate as Mahathir's Vision 2020. Vision City was the mid-1990s real estate entrée of financial services tycoon Rashid Hussain. It was a colossal, five-hectare joint venture with Daewoo, in which the South Korean firm was to have supplied all the construction know-how.[177] The most capable Muslim entre-preneur of his generation, Hussain was never, like his peers, required to manufacture anything.[178] The graveyard stretch of Jalan Sultan Ismail ends at the Jalan Abdul Rahman crossroads, known as Maju Junction. Here on the left is the Maju tower of Abu Sahid Mohamed, the tycoon known for his pink stretch limo who took over Mahathir's Perwaja steel plant after the near-total failure of the prime minister's industrial policy. The Perwaja plant is to be our next stop, located on the other side of the peninsula.

### It's a jungle out there

The Waja picks up the ring road on the north side of the city and heads through the patch of beautiful rainforest that still exists to the north-east of the capital at the start of the cross-peninsular Karak expressway. At the petrol station near the turn-off to the Genting casino, a troop of cheeky monkeys steals whatever they can from any motorist foolish enough to leave possessions unattended. Soon after is the exit for Vincent Tan's Berjaya Hills Resort at Bukit Tinggi, where Mahathir took his cabinet for a day's retreat to learn Japanese social etiquette and tea drinking manners in the early, heady days of Look East.[179] A little further on again is the road to the town of Bentong, beyond which in October 1951 the Communist Party of Malaya ambushed and killed the British High Commissioner, Sir Henry Gurney.[180] On the south side of Bentong is the model land reform village of

Lurah Bilut, built for 600 *bumiputera*, Chinese and Indian families in the late 1950s, and which is now home to a small Federal Land Development Authority (FELDA) museum. A prominently displayed quotation from second premier Abdul Razak promises 'the best land for the best people', something which was palpably never more than a pipedream in Malaysia. The nearby Lee Rubber factory,[181] with its acrid smell and mountains of raw rubber balls, reminds us that the government always allowed private sector middlemen to extract most of the profit from the household farmers it feigned to support. Back on the Karak expressway, the miles of large-scale oil palm plantations – which replace the jungle after Bentong and continue to the east coast – is the real story of Malaysian agriculture: in essence, the opposite of the commercially integrated household farming of north-east Asia and China. This is the flimsy foundation on which Mahathir built his industrial policy.

It takes three to four hours to traverse the middle of Malaysia from Kuala Lumpur to the shore of the South China Sea. Then, turning north, the Waja crosses the state border into Trengganu. Along the sleepy white sand beaches sit under-utilised, low-rise hotels; inland are yet more oil palm plantations. It is here on the coast, outside the small town of Kemaman, that Mahathir decided to build Malaysia's biggest steel plant, Perwaja. What you notice first about the factory is that, unlike the original POSCO plant at Pohang, Korea, it does not have an immediate visual logic.[182] Pohang forms a horseshoe shape on a bay where the raw materials that arrive at one end have become ship-loaded steel exports by the time they have reached the other end. Perwaja's Kemaman site, by contrast, is simply a big steel factory stuck in a field, surrounded by jungle and scrub and set back from the sea. It did not begin life with export competitiveness as its driving ambition. The choice of the east coast was also commercially dubious because most steel in Malaysia is consumed on the much more populous and industrialised west coast. It would have made more business sense to pipe the gas fuel supply from the nearby offshore fields to the west side of the peninsula and to make steel where it is needed.

None the less, Mahathir's determination to marry affirmative action – by building the plant in what is called 'the Malay heartland' – with industrial policy was not of itself enough to wreck this project. Instead, he made a series of compounding errors. The most egregious of these were to have no export requirement and to fail to critique the project recommended by Perwaja's Japanese partner, a consortium led by Nippon Steel (the same partner the Koreans had). POSCO and the Korean government paid the Australian mining firm BHP to check the Japanese engineering plans at Pohang, and a Korean consultant from Japan to double-check the Australians. Mahathir and the Implementation and Co-ordination Unit through which he micro-managed his industrial policy took no such precautions, accepting at face value a Japanese proposal to produce Direct Reduced Iron (DRI) with a new, gas-based technology that turns ore directly into high-grade sponge iron ready for steel-making without going through the traditional iron ore sintering and blast furnace procedures.

Nippon Steel had zero operational experience of the gas technology it was selling. Where the Koreans had rejected Nippon Steel's computerised production systems in favour of manual ones until they understood the nuts and bolts of the most basic iron- and steel-making processes, Mahathir went straight to the bleeding edge with technology Nippon Steel had not used before.[183] Instead of Malaysia learning from the Japanese, many industry experts concluded that it was the Japanese who learned about a new technology on the Malaysian dollar. Although Mahathir's team was not so naive that there were no compensation clauses – after the technology failed the Japanese consortium paid back in 1987 about one-third of the initial project costs[184] – the failure of the DRI technology immediately stalled the momentum of Malaysia's entire development effort. Perwaja was forced to operate for several years using scrap metal, of which there is very little on the east coast, and so piled up unnecessary operating losses. Dr Tan Tat Wai, one of three industry experts assembled into an emergency task force by the government when the plant hit trouble, concludes: 'I think Mahathir got taken for a ride by the Japanese.'[185]

Having found himself in a hole, Mahathir then started digging. As would be the case with other projects, he saw Perwaja's problems in terms of management failure. 'Unfortunately, the first CEO was quite unable to manage,' Mahathir says.[186] In his determination to change management, the prime minister could have turned to one of several proven Malaysian entrepreneurs in downstream steel businesses, or to one of the leading entrepreneurs outside steel. Instead, he chose Eric Chia, a bluff salesman and the son of the founder of a car trading business, who was now involved in the firm that sold Proton cars. If the premier had been led a dance by Nippon Steel, he was to be led a much merrier one by Chia.

Given total discretion by Mahathir, the new Perwaja boss ordered up two expensive replacement DRI plants from Mexico and some new electric arc furnaces. It appears he continued to tell Mahathir that Perwaja would produce the highest grades of steel, including automotive sheet, for which very pure DRI sponge iron would be needed. But the downstream facility Chia actually added – 400 kilometres away, in Mahathir's home state of Kedah – was a large section plant for I-beams and bars needed in the domestic construction industry.[187] Perwaja has never made any high-grade industrial or automotive steel of the kind that a country climbing the global technology ladder requires. Instead it produced, at the second attempt, DRI sponge iron of a quality that fell well below world standards, took it halfway across the country and cast it into low-grade construction steel which was then sold only in the protected domestic market. The original DRI plant cost RM1.3 billion. By the time Chia was done, Perwaja had soaked up at least RM10 billion (USD4 billion at the then exchange rate) of public money.[188]

**Just for you, doctor**

Chia had claimed publicly he was taking on Perwaja as an act of 'national service' – as Malaysian billionaires often dub their faux development contributions – and that he would work out of a temporary cabin at the Kemaman site on a nominal salary of RM1. It was the kind of talk that Mahathir loved and, with no export requirement to benchmark progress, it was possible for the supremely self-confident premier to believe his acolyte was turning the business around. In reality, however, Chia went to Kemaman as little as possible and was usually to be found in his luxury office in UBN Tower on Jalan Sultan Ismail. Moreover, while he was failing to deliver any serious technological learning at Perwaja, Chia was also bilking the business. Two separate reports commissioned by the government when Chia resigned amid rumours of huge hidden losses in 1995 (and which were subsequently leaked) revealed suspect contracts with parties connected to Chia, contracts with firms which had no business experience relevant to what they were paid to do, purchase and sale contracts inside and outside Malaysia which appeared contrary to Perwaja's commercial interests, and payments for which no paperwork existed. Different scams accumulated for seven years while Mahathir, having denied himself the verdict of the export markets, trusted his own deeply flawed ability to judge people.[189]

In 1996 the government took a colossal RM9.9 billion charge against Perwaja to clear the bulk of the firm's debts. The bizarre postscript to this was that, despite the evidence that Chia had conducted scores of suspect transactions with related parties over the years, Mahathir then privatised Perwaja into the hands of close Chia associates.[190] Abu Sahid Mohamed, who has led the group controlling the business since 1996 and operates out of Maju Tower at the top of Jalan Sultan Ismail, is an old friend of Chia's who was granted exclusive transportation contracts for Perwaja when Chia was in charge. His long-time associate and partner, Pheng Yin Huah, was in turn Perwaja's exclusive supplier of scrap metal under Chia. And Abu Sahid's accountant elder brother, Abu Talib, was Eric Chia's chief operating officer and one of his closest confidants. No one has ever suggested that Mahathir did anything other than what he thought was right for Perwaja, or that he behaved in any sense improperly. The point is that, without commercial feedback from the international market, Malaysia's most visionary leader made a series of disastrous decisions.

Abu Sahid took over pristine assets that were almost completely paid down by the state because Perwaja's second-phase investments came on line just as Eric Chia left the business. Abu Sahid agreed to pay RM1.3 billion in cash and assumed debt for Perwaja, but only handed over RM50 million. The rest was to come, interest-free, at RM4 million a month over ten years.[191] With the Perwaja shares in hand, according to his own staff as well as government sources, Abu Sahid then successfully pressured his main state-owned creditor to take a reduction on its debt and failed to make his payments to the government on time.[192] He also stopped paying Perwaja's electricity bills, calculating – quite rightly – that the state-owned provider, Tenaga, would not cut off the national steel project. After a period of limbo in which he reduced Perwaja's operating costs, a cyclical upswing led to rising steel prices in the 2000s. Abu Sahid sold off some Perwaja equity to associates and managed in August 2008, just before the global financial crisis, to list more on the Kuala Lumpur stock exchange.[193] Despite the listing, a decade after he 'bought' Perwaja, Abu Sahid and his associates still owed the government for it.

In manipulating the Malaysian government, Abu Sahid showed at least as much entrepreneurial flair as Nippon Steel or Eric Chia had. He is proof positive that Malaysia's *bumiputeras* have no less entrepreneurial capability than any other racial group. The problem is that, because of government policy failure, Malaysian private entrepreneurship is directed to ends that do not benefit the country at large. Abu Sahid, like the rest of the country's big-time entrepreneurs, is an asset trader, not a developer of technological capacity. From the outset, he handed over operational control of Perwaja to his steel trading associates, the Pheng family.[194] They in turn, as traders rather than manufacturers, left the original on-site management in place. The general manager of plant operations at Kemaman has been there since inception in 1984. The general manager of the DRI plant has been there since the replacement facility was planned in 1991.[195] The operational staff – and the technological learning process – have remained cocooned for decades while an entrepreneurial pantomime has developed around them.

In Korea, POSCO started production in 1973 with a 1 million tonne a year operation at Pohang, ramping up to 9 million tonnes of world-class output by 1983, and involving an investment of USD20 billion at today's prices. In Malaysia, Perwaja started out with 1.5 million tonnes of output and got stuck, both in volume and quality terms. With no export discipline, a succession of carpet-baggers filled their boots as the taxpayer shelled out the equivalent of USD6–8 billion in today's money in order for the country to learn next to nothing.[196]

## Things could only get better

The failure of Perwaja broke the potential link between high-grade steel output and Mahathir's other ambitions for value-added manufacturing. The most obvious of these was car making, where Malaysia has had to continue to import sheet steel. With more than 5 million cars sold by

Malaysian firms between the first Proton in 1986 and 2010, a lot of potential business went begging, even without considering demand from other users of high-grade flat steel products, such as foreign car assemblers and the large, foreign-dominated consumer electronics industry.

The Waja heads back past the plantations that blanket the country's orange earth to the industrial west coast. Here, three different sites account for the domestic car industry. Seventy kilometres north of Kuala Lumpur, off Mahathir's north–south expressway at Tanjung Malim, is Proton City, a manufacturing plant that was opened in 2004, shortly before political support for the 'national car project' fell apart. (The political trigger was Mahathir's 2003 resignation.) Closer to the capital, but still on its north side in a rural area outside Rawang, is the plant of Perodua, a second auto manufacturer that was set up in 1993 to make mini cars, as a complement to Proton's larger passenger vehicles. Finally, on the south-west side of Kuala Lumpur, in the capital's key commercial district of Shah Alam, is the original Proton manufacturing facility, which still acts as the firm's headquarters.

Each of these three destinations sends the same message: that, unlike Hyundai's Ulsan complex with the giant car carriers tied up on the docks outside, none was chosen with exports in mind. Moreover, the car models displayed in the headquarters of Proton and Perodua make it clear that little competition between the firms is envisaged: Proton makes bigger cars, Perodua makes smaller cars. Korea began its automotive industrialisation drive in 1973 with an annual domestic car market of only 30,000 units, but set up three private firms to compete directly with one another. When Malaysia kicked off its national car project in 1983, it already had a domestic market of 90,000 units a year, yet government sanctioned a single state-owned manufacturer.[197] A decade later, a second manufacturer was added, but one making vehicles that were explicitly intended not to compete against those of the first firm.[198] In both cases Mahathir, negotiating personally,[199] insisted on equity joint ventures with Japanese car makers: Mitsubishi (the same partner Hyundai managed to obtain its technology from without an equity joint venture)[200] for Proton, and Toyota's small-car affiliate Daihatsu for Perodua. Mahathir claims that 'I decided to adopt Japanese and Korean strategies and methods for developing Malaysia.'[201] But what he did was completely different.

At Hyundai, Chung Ju Yung was persistently suspicious of MMC's objectives. He brought in independent European engineers who alerted him to the Japanese firm's attempt to supply Hyundai with a second-rate engine. Mahathir was less hard-headed. The difference may be that Chung was a proven business entrepreneur, whereas Mahathir was someone who had meddled in various businesses in his youth but was really a political entrepreneur.[202] Whichever, in Malaysia, having signed a deal to build a variant of the Mitsubishi Lancer rebranded as a Proton Saga, MMC was able to: sell the joint venture superannuated production equipment; slow down the pace of content localisation; keep prices of its own components far above world market prices; and build a car which Japanese managers knew would not meet safety standards for export to developed country markets. When Mitsubishi was forced to localise components, it frequently did so through Japanese joint ventures which kept most technological learning out of Malaysian hands.[203] It appears that Mahathir did not include specific export requirements in the original MMC contract; when he did begin to demand overseas sales, the Japanese partner was less than helpful, saying it would take two years to incorporate the safety changes necessary to enter the US market.[204]

Proton–Mitsubishi was a classic example of how equity joint ventures with multinationals have failed to impart adequate technological learning to aspiring car makers around the world. The interests of the two parties were necessarily conflicting. As with Perwaja, when things went wrong at Proton Mahathir turned his wrath on management. After only two years of production, in 1988 he got rid of his senior *bumiputera* managers and asked the Japanese to take charge. MMC executives then happily shelved plans to export to the United States and concentrated instead on making money out of the protected domestic market.[205] They had no interest in selling at a loss in America in order to develop a globally competitive business; they preferred instead to sell in Malaysia at artificially high prices to support their bottom line.

## Outstripping Perwaja

Mahathir maintained that his industrial policy copied those of Japan and Korea, but what he was actually doing was closer to the import substitution industrialisation (ISI) which had failed to deliver substantial technological learning in south-east Asia in the 1950s and early 1960s. Without domestic competition and a strong export focus he was repeating past mistakes – ones that north-east Asian states had figured out how to avoid. None the less, even Mahathir's pale imitation of Hyundai produced some positive results. His constant imprecations to localise production saw local content of both Proton cars and other brands assembled in Malaysia increase substantially, from only 10 per cent before 1980 to over 60 per cent by 1990. Former assemblers of imported car kits went into parts manufacturing, and some of them began to export components. Mitsubishi buried the plan to sell Protons in the US, telling the Malaysians to look instead at small Third World markets like Jamaica, Bangladesh and Sri Lanka, but Mahathir's government obtained tariff-free access to the United Kingdom for 14,000 cars a year off its own bat. The premier lacked direction, but not energy. When Proton sold more than 10,000 units in its first year in the UK and the Saga was named one of the ten best economy cars by a British national newspaper, it was a faint echo of Hyundai's remarkable early success in the United States.[206]

By 1993 Mahathir had tired of Mitsubishi's high costs and technological foot-dragging and decided to return Proton to Malaysian management. This time he turned to a private sector *bumiputera* entrepreneur, Yahaya Ahmad, whom he eventually allowed to buy out the government's controlling interest in Proton. Yahaya turned out to be a more serious proposition than either Eric Chia or Abu Sahid. Just as Chung Ju Yung had in Korea, he began looking to outside consultants and third party technical collaborators to reduce Proton's dependence on Mitsubishi. He bought British specialist auto firm Lotus, not because he wanted a maker of sports cars, but in order to learn through the firm's successful Lotus Engineering consultancy arm.[207] After Yahaya was killed in a helicopter crash in 1997, his deputy, Mahaleel Bin Tengku Ariff, took over and continued the strategy. Lotus Engineering helped to redesign the Saga and to develop new models with a more distinctive Proton look. The first car designed by Proton itself, the Waja, was launched in 2001 and soon after it was running on a Proton Campro engine developed in conjunction with Lotus. In 2004, with a domestic car market surpassing 400,000 units a year, Proton boasted a 60 per cent market share and opened the first phase of its Proton City manufacturing operation. Management envisaged an integrated automotive town with a quarter of a million inhabitants where the company could consolidate its activities along with those of its suppliers. Between 2000 and 2005, Proton cut its annual parts spend with Mitsubishi from around RM1 billion to RM600 million. In 2004, the firm also acquired Italian motorcycle maker MV Agusta, which provided technical consultancy on a mini car project incorporating motorcycle-related technology.[208]

This, however, was a high-water mark that was not to be surpassed. Although Proton had developed a domestic business turning over billions of dollars a year, and had much increased its technological capacity since the mid 1990s, it did little more than flirt with international markets and still lacked global competitiveness. It was, for instance, able to avoid putting airbags or anti-lock braking systems (ABS) in cars sold in the protected domestic market, even though a lack of them made the cars unexportable to many markets. Whereas, by manufacturing more cars for export and so reducing unit costs for all production, Hyundai was able to produce its Elantra not just with front airbags, but with lateral ones as well, in all models and all markets. Mahaleel insists that an all-out Hyundai-style export drive was impossible because other areas of Malaysian industrial policy, especially steel, had failed, rendering supplier costs too high. 'Korean industry was working simultaneously,' he says. 'Malaysia could not do it ... Perwaja was supposed to do sheet steel and never did.'[209] Proton's current chairman and one of the original project members from the early 1980s, Nadzmi Mohd Salleh, disagrees. He suggests that Mahaleel's nine-year tenure without an export assault was fatal: '[His strategy] was niche and domestic,' says Nadzmi. 'In my opinion it was the biggest mistake.'[210] By the end of his tenure, Mahaleel had six different car platforms in place and was ready to produce twenty different models, but overseas sales remained an afterthought.

## Return of the political aristocracy

In the end, Proton's ongoing investment demands and the wider costs of the Asian financial crisis – which not only saw Mahathir renationalise the car firm but also bail out a roster of far less productive business cronies (including his own family)[211] with billions of dollars of public money – began to sap the Malaysian will to carry on with the national car project. There was also the looming challenge of the Association of South-east Asian Nations (ASEAN) free trade area (AFTA), which since 2003 has given preferential tariffs to goods with only 40 per cent local ASEAN content. This threatened a potentially murderous blow to infant industry projects competing with Japanese plants located in ASEAN, although Proton and Perodua have so far been (illegally) shielded from AFTA's requirements.[212] The fatal development for Proton, however, was the unexpected resignation of Mahathir in 2003. He had made himself Malaysia's one-man industrialisation policy and without him Proton lacked an ideological defender.

Malaysia returned to government by its traditional high-born elite in the form of Abdullah Badawi.[213] In 2005 the new administration chose not to renew Mahaleel's contract and forced Proton to get rid of the recently acquired MV Agusta, and hence its mini car ambitions.[214] With Abdullah telling colleagues, 'I'm not into big projects',[215] but offering no clear statement of intent on industrial policy, morale at Proton sagged and large segments of senior management decided to move on. In the absence of government support, component suppliers were unwilling to risk further capital expenditures, meaning that production upgrades ceased. Proton was stuck with 90 per cent localised manufacturing at uneconomic volumes and no further investment and subsidy. It was forced to cut the number of car platforms from six to three and market share began to erode, from 60 per cent in the early 2000s to 30 per cent today, with the big drop occurring in 2006 right after government support was withdrawn.[216]

Ultimately, without the cash to finance new models, a company which had learned to make its own cars and engines came full circle. It was forced to sign new deals with Mitsubishi to rebadge MMC vehicles as replacements for the indigenous Proton cars it had developed. The next Waja will be a rebadged Mitsubishi Lancer – a newer version of the car that became the original Saga.[217] My genuine Malaysian Waja, sitting stoically in the car park of the Proton headquarters in Shah Alam, is the automotive equivalent of the Last of the Mohicans.

The standard criticism of Proton in Malaysia today is that the business had two decades to prove itself before Mahathir stepped down, and it did

not. Yet when compared with Hyundai's experience in Korea, this judgement may be unfair. Twenty years after the 1973 Korean national car programme was announced, a report by the Boston Consulting Group (BCG)
concluded that the Korean car industry might not see out the decade. In
1992 domestic firms had a production capacity of 3.5 million cars, but sold
only 1.7 million; productivity was still only half the Japanese level; and
Korean cars had a poor reputation for quality in overseas markets.[218] Yet,
with the benefit of hindsight, by the early 1990s firms like Hyundai had
already turned the technological corner in automotive manufacturing and
sales would soon begin to reflect this. All technological learning, like all
education, takes a long time and involves a lot of errors. As one Hyundai
quality control manager put it, the secret of technological progress is 'not
repeating the same mistake' over a very long period of time.[219]

Proton's rate of technology acquisition does not appear to have been
slower than Hyundai's.[220] However, in Korea the government provided an
extraordinary level of protection to auto makers for three decades, from
1970 until 2000, and quite a lot thereafter.[221] In the early 1990s, Hyundai
was able to set up complete knock-down (CKD) kit assembly plants for
light trucks and cars in Malaysia, Thailand, the Philippines and Indonesia.
Such investments by foreigners would have been unthinkable in Korea.[222]
If anything, the story in Malaysia is that government has lacked patience
and tenacity with its industrial policy. This cannot be said to be the fault
of Mahathir alone, although he did fail to empower a bureaucracy with an
institutional commitment to infant industry development, such as existed
in the Economic Planning Board in Korea or MITI in Japan.

Mahathir's major responsibility is for not enforcing export discipline,
and for not fostering more private sector competition, which would have
allowed him to cull and consolidate failing market entrants. The debacle
in steel, where the prime minister's personal performance is particularly
difficult to defend, made things harder in automotive, where Mahathir
and Proton came closer to success. The final verdict must be that Malaysia
learned something under Mahathir's industrialisation policy, but not
enough. Malaysia today is a bit like a country that went to school and
college for twenty years but failed to pay sufficient attention and now
finds itself ill-equipped to live at the economic level to which it aspires.

When Mahathir became prime minister in 1981, he had seen with his own eyes that Korea had the kind of focused industrialisation policy that his country needed. The university-educated headmaster's son knew that, in order to compete, Malaysia had to engage in industrial learning, but he failed to organise the process anything like as effectively as the peasant-born Park Chung Hee. When Mahathir stepped down in 2003, Malaysian GNI per capita was no longer the same as Korea's – it was USD4,160, versus USD12,680 in Korea. That difference of three times has been maintained.[223] Despite this, the directionlessness of the governments that have followed Mahathir has made an increasing number of Malaysians recognise that, despite his depressing flaws, the former premier was right in his instinct that an infant industry policy was essential for economic development.

**A tale of two east Asias**

In Korea, infant industry protection combined with export discipline, plus competition among multiple entrants, made manufacturing policy highly effective in securing technological upgrading. In Malaysia, industrial policy without export discipline and with insufficient attention to the need to foster competition came unstuck. Beyond these two states, other countries in north-east and south-east Asia provide only modest variations on what are two regional stories of success and failure in manufacturing development.

In the north-east, it was Japan that developed Asia's model of infant industry promotion and that country needs little further comment. From the original, rather raw Meiji industrialisation experience to the post-Second World War one, however, there was a shift to a more consensual and social democratic variant on the model, in which relations between labour and management became less confrontational.[224] This is also what happened in West Germany after the Second World War, when labour and capital began to co-operate, in a maturation of social relations. In both countries, post-war corporate leadership became less family-dominated and more impersonally professional – although family business remains important in every economy.

Taiwan featured a greater role for public ownership than in post-war Japan and Korea, and a shortfall of export discipline applied to its biggest firms. This failing can equally be expressed as a lack of support for smaller, private, exporting firms. The situation takes us back to the problems that nineteenth-century Germany and early twentieth-century Japan ran into with dominant companies that did not pull their weight as exporters. And it takes us forward to problems that China could conceivably face in the future. None the less, whatever the caveats, Taiwan and China belong in the category of states which have made profound progress in the acquisition of manufacturing technology. It is the south-east Asian countries we should be worried about.

In south-east Asia's biggest state, Indonesia, Suharto was greatly influenced in the 1980s by Mahathir's Look East industrialisation policy. Unfortunately, he pursued an industrialisation drive which had exactly the same weaknesses as Mahathir's.[225] There was no export discipline and there was very little competition. As in Malaysia, this created an environment in which there was insufficient pressure to push firms up the technological ladder. Edwin Soeryadjaya, from the family that was given a licence to run Indonesia's dominant car assembly joint venture with Toyota, provides a telling anecdote. He recalls a moment of youthful idealism when he tried to convince his father and other directors to develop a truly Indonesian car. He was excited by the launch of the Proton project in Malaysia. 'I said we should steal the technology,' he recalls of his moment of industrial nationalism.[226] This is exactly what government policy should have made his family's firm, Astra, do – just as Hyundai begged, borrowed and stole its technology from Mitsubishi and other firms. Indonesia's market, with 220 million people, was five times bigger than Korea's. However, with no state-enforced discipline to compete and export, Astra's directors quite sensibly told the young Soeryadjaya to shut up and enjoy the domestic profits of tariff protection without competition. Astra has been a cash cow all its life, but has operated with total technological dependency on Toyota.[227]

The ideological driver of Indonesia's industrialisation programme was a German-trained aerospace engineer, B. J. Habibie, who became Minister of Research and Technology, and later vice president, under Suharto. His pet project, Indonesian Aviation Industry (known by its bahasa acronym

IPTN), sought to leapfrog to the development of indigenous aircraft.[228] This was ambitious to say the least. Even the Japanese had failed in their efforts to nurture a successful aircraft making business, although one of Brazil's few industrial policy successes came in this field, in the guise of Embraer.[229] From 1985, IPTN built up a staff of nearly 10,000 people across eighteen business divisions, mostly concentrated in Bandung in west-central Java. However, Indonesia, like Malaysia, failed in its upstream industrial projects to produce basic manufacturing inputs like high-grade steel. The industrial learning that did take place was a loosely connected patchwork of half-skills, in contrast to the web of links that ties together Korean industry from steel, through shipbuilding and automotive, to electronics and semiconductors. Indonesia's capacity to pay for industrial policy was decimated by the Asian financial crisis, little more than a decade after a serious commitment was made in 1985. Since then, industrial projects have been reduced to bare-bones operations and key technical personnel from firms like IPTN have emigrated, often to developed countries. In the past fifteen years, it is probable that Indonesia's technological capacity has actually gone backwards.

Thailand holds the record for the most consistent import substitution industrialisation (ISI) policy in south-east Asia, running from the early 1950s into the 1980s. Industrial policy also was led by probably the most competent, professional bureaucracy in the region. But, as the Japanese scholar of development Suehiro Akira observed, there was almost no pressure for favoured manufacturers to export: 'These industries with no exception,' he wrote, 'belonged to a category of import-substitution industries which exclusively depended upon the domestic market.' Unlike in northeast Asian states, the Thai bureaucracy never brought export discipline to bear because the Thai generals and politicians who ran the country did not prioritise it. Instead, ISI built around low import tariffs on components and high ones for imported finished goods led to assembly joint ventures – mostly with US and Japanese firms – in which there was little technological learning. There were fleeting exceptions, as when a domestic television maker called Tanin began to export sets to Europe in the 1970s. But in the 1980s there was renewed opening to foreign investment, and concomitantly less support for domestic firms. Suehiro writes: 'We may conclude that the presence of the multinational enterprises became large enough to entirely or substantially control the Thai economy.'[230] The only area where industrial policy did lead to strong export growth of domestic, processed products was in agribusiness, but this came at the expense of the long-suffering Thai peasantry. Faced by a mid-1980s recession, Thailand did as Mahathir did and wooed foreign investors to generate exports through low value-added assembly operations. After the Asian crisis and IMF intervention in Thailand, industrial policy and budgets to support it were squeezed even further.

The Philippines abandoned a failed and very corrupt ISI programme in 1962 and thereafter hardly even attempted infant industry promotion. More than anywhere in the region, landowning families dominated post-independence ISI projects and undermined any attempt to foster technological learning; they undertook minimal assembly of multinational companies' products for domestic resale behind steep tariff barriers; the only things they exported were agricultural commodities. Ferdinand Marcos then ran up a large foreign debt, just as South Korea did, but instead of spending the money on export-oriented industrial capacity, he let most of it go on domestic real estate construction, vote buying and non-productive imports. When the regional recession struck in the early 1980s, the Philippine economy collapsed under the weight of unserviceable debt and shrank an astonishing 20 per cent. It only really stabilised in the mid 1990s, and there has been no sustained period of growth since. The Philippines has no indigenous, value-added manufacturing capacity. At the end of the Second World War only Japan and Malaysia had higher incomes per capita in Asia. Then Korea and Taiwan overtook the Philippines in the 1950s. The country slid down past Thailand in the 1980s, and Indonesia more recently. From having been in a position near the top of the Asian pile, the Philippines today is an authentic, technology-less Third World state with poverty rates to match.[231]

## What was not important

North-east and south-east Asia provide small variations around clear themes. What created the Canons, the Samsungs, the Acers and so on in Japan, Korea and Taiwan was the marriage of infant industry protection and market forces, involving (initially) subsidised exports and competition between manufacturers that vied for state support. The north-east Asian states found ways to overcome the problems that afflicted the ISI policies that were promoted in the 1950s (including by the World Bank in its early, 'left-wing' incarnation). Contrary to the claims of many economists, rent-seeking and crony capitalism did not inevitably undermine industrial policy so long as sufficient discipline could be wrapped around infant industry promotion. The mix of plan and market recalls the British development economist Ronald Dore's contemporary observation about foreign perceptions of Japan at the height of its industrialisation: 'Left-wing ... observers come back from Japan convinced they have seen a shining example of state planning,' he wrote. 'Right-wing visitors return full of praise for the virtues of Japan's free enterprise system.'[232] The same, conflicting conclusions have been heard from different visitors to Korea, Taiwan and China.

Unfortunately, the recipe for manufacturing development – which is really not difficult to grasp, even if it varies in its details from country to country – is relentlessly over-complicated and confused by economists. They insist, in their ignorance of history, that efficiency considerations which are important in developed economies should also determine policy in poor countries. Developing states, however, need to invest in learning before they worry too much about efficiency. They must walk before they can run. As a result, many of the things that neo-classical and neo-liberal economists tell us are important variables in development fail to register in a historical review of how countries actually develop.

Such is the case with 'macro-economic stability', the rallying cry of the International Monetary Fund and the World Bank since the 1970s. The term refers in particular to conditions of low debt, low deficits and low inflation. While few people would disagree that, given a choice, such things are desirable of themselves, there is little evidence they are determinants of industrialisation outcomes. This makes sense when we remember that the objective of industrialisation is technological learning, leading to the capacity to originate new technologies indigenously. If a state borrows money or prints money in pursuit of these aims, the question of whether or not this is a good idea is decided by whether the aims are achieved. It is like borrowing money to go to university – the case for it depends on what you learn. The case for debt in a developing country – and for its bedfellows, budget deficits and inflation – is measured in terms of technological progress.

Korea developed with a central bank that took its instructions direct from government, lending to favoured projects irrespective of the prevailing domestic and global economic climate, and showing little concern for an inflation rate that was normally between 15 and 20 per cent a year. Partly as a result of such behaviour, Korea had a low rate of household saving by Asian standards, and funded a large part of its investment needs from overseas borrowing. The country's disdain for macro-economic prudence bordered on the reckless, exasperating its US and multilateral institution advisers. Yet Korea turned out to be a remarkable industrialisation success story.

Taiwan, by contrast, showed the kind of macro-economic discipline the IMF and World Bank champion. The Kuomintang's late 1940s experience with hyperinflation – which was held to have cost the party the civil war on the mainland – caused its leaders to give Taiwan an independent central bank which ran much higher interest rates and much lower inflation than Korea. This encouraged more private saving in the banking system so there was little need for international borrowing. But Taiwan's industrialisation performance was not as good as Korea's.

Macro-economic stability was not a clear determinant of developmental success in north-east Asia, and nor was it in south-east Asia, where there was also notable variation – for instance, between less 'prudent' Indonesia and more prudent Thailand, both of which ended up on the industrialisation rubbish heap. Equally, there is the example of Ferdinand Marcos, who borrowed and printed lots of money like Park Chung Hee and Chun Doo Hwan in Korea, but blew his cash like a drunk in a casino.

Along with macro-economic stability, the IMF and the World Bank have consistently pressed the virtues of private enterprise, and the privatisation of state enterprises. In developed countries, there is considerable evidence that private firms tend to be more cost-efficient than public ones.[233] But in the learning phase of development, the public–private ownership distinction is framed differently, that is, in terms of what kind of company is able to absorb knowledge and make technological progress. When the state's regulatory capacity is weak, it is sometimes easier for governments to pursue industrialisation objectives via state firms. Japan, Korea, Taiwan and China all made rapid technical progress using state-owned companies, particularly at an early stage; China is today making greater use of state firms than any successful developing nation before it. This does not prove that state ownership is superior to private. It merely demonstrates that it is not such an important consideration as developing countries have been told. In failed, autarkic socialist states like the Soviet Union, and India and China in their pre-reform incarnations, the absence of export discipline and competition were the real developmental culprits, not who owned firms' equity.

In a similar vein, the multilateral institutions argue for a linear process of deregulation and opening up in developing countries in order to steadily increase the role of market forces. However, the actual history of successful industrial development in Japan, Korea and Taiwan shows that at critical policy junctures each country increased regulation and protection to defend new industries. This occurred in the early 1960s in Japan, when the country instituted large tariff increases to defend new businesses being nurtured by MITI.[234] And it happened in Korea and Taiwan in the 1970s when those states implemented their heavy industry drives. The same may now be underway, using non-tariff barriers, in China, despite the country's 2001 accession to the World Trade Organisation.

Perhaps the biggest, though rarely voiced, fear among historically literate economists at the IMF and the World Bank is that whenever industrial policy has been successful in the past, it has tended to lead to chronic trade surpluses. These in turn make for damaging imbalances in the global economy. Britain in the nineteenth century, the US in the first two-thirds of the twentieth century, and Germany and Japan from the late twentieth century to this day each ran big, sustained trade and current account surpluses once they became leading industrial powers. Many people suspect that China is heading in the same direction. None the less, however grim the historical pattern, there is no inevitable connection between industrial policy and trade surpluses. In the developmental phase, countries are in fact more likely to run trade deficits to pay for imported technologies they have not yet mastered. Korea, for instance, only produced its first trade surplus in 1977, and did not have consistent surpluses until the late 1980s. The problem of predatory trade and current account surpluses is one of political choice *after* manufacturing development is well under way. Countries choose to run surpluses – typically by maintaining trade controls longer than they are needed, or by restraining domestic consumption such that imports of consumer goods are reduced. However, while it may be tempting to deny developing countries the right to infant industry policies today because of the selfishness of states that used infant industry policies in the past, such an approach is neither fair nor logical. Poor countries have to have access to the same tools of economic development that rich states once used.

## No magic lasts for ever

If manufacturing export discipline, domestic competition and the culling of losers are the closest thing to a magic recipe for industrial development, then the last thing to be stressed is the transience of the magic. Leaving aside the global issue of trade surpluses, poor countries which have used infant industry policies to lever themselves on to the rich man's stage discover that those same policies bring new domestic problems – albeit rich(er) country problems. These can be characterised as the industrial equivalent of Japan's 5 dollar apples – the ultimate outcome of Japan's high-yield, but now grossly over-protected, household farming strategy. In industry as in agriculture, it is one thing to identify the right medicine to cure a poor country's penury, and quite another to quit taking the medicine once the affliction is past. It is worth briefly considering some of the difficulties that north-east Asian states have had to contend with as a result of – or rather, often, despite – their rapid transitions to advanced manufacturing.

The first issue is that while manufacturing plays a special role in economic development, it is not everything. By the late 1970s, Japan was the world's most efficient steel maker and boasted the eight biggest steel mills in the OECD economies. Japan had half the world's industrial robots. And its firms were receiving more US patents than all the western European states combined.[235] Yet Japan today is a rather sorry rich nation, after a 20-year period of repeated recessions and stagnation. Driving around Japan in 2010, I asked myself many times how the world ever lived in fear of Japanese economic hegemony or speculated that this would be 'the Japanese century'. The explanation is that, while its highly effective manufacturing policy nurtured a phalanx of world-class multinationals, most of which continue to prosper, Japan left its small manufacturing firms and its service sector far behind.

Japan's extraordinary post-war progress in large-scale manufacturing gave it the most uneven productivity profile of any rich country: by the late 1980s it outstripped the long-time leader the United States in machinery manufacturing, but was so far behind in services and agriculture (the latter still with high yields but now with low productivity because of the vastly increased incomes of farmers) that it lagged not only the US overall, but Europe as well.[236] At a micro level, this was the difference in manufacturing between Nissan, which at the time of the 1990 Tokyo stock market crash built 40 cars per man year, and Ford, which built 17.[237] On the other hand, in services, Japan's grossly inefficient wholesale trade – which was four times the size of its retail commerce, versus one to two times in the US or UK – bilked consumers by marking up prices again and again. Similar inefficiencies were apparent in services from airlines to tourism. Bill Emmott, in his 1989 book *The Sun Also Sets*, remarked of Japan's legendary army of salary men: 'If these *sararīmen*, as they are called, do work long hours, it is often because they are keen on overtime pay or because of a mixture of peer pressure and inertia. They spend ten hours doing what others manage to do in seven or eight. Many is the office that has an opened bottle of Suntory whisky on the shelf or the annual high school baseball tournament showing on the television.'[238]

There is a limit to what industrial policy can achieve. For several decades, Japan's MITI was superb at structuring competitive, highly transparent fights for industrial licences, staggering the entry of different firms to manage the mix of protection and competition, and forcing businesses to upgrade their production equipment. But as Japan stopped playing catch-up and moved towards the technological bleeding edge, this work became harder. MITI's attempt to organise moves into the technological frontier of biotechnology in the 1980s,[239] for instance, were less successful than the Japanese, Korean or Taiwanese assaults on semiconductors had been, when the technological lie of the land was already visible in the United States. In IT services, MITI was unable to 'plan' the geeky university drop-out who starts a software firm or an internet business in his parents' garage. Japanese academics have warned since the 1980s of a lag in software capability. Equally, MITI has never been able to exert a clear positive effect on small manufacturing business in Japan. The large manufacturers it champions – as is also very much the case in Korea – use their scale to squeeze the margins of smaller, less-favoured suppliers or simply to absorb them in takeovers. The bullying tactics of elite big firms are a perennial problem.

Throughout east Asia, rapid economic growth since the Second World War has encouraged unwarranted political hubris. In Japan, while bureaucrats implemented industrial policy, the country's immature political class was a disaster waiting to happen. After an asset bubble burst at the start of the 1990s, politicians unused to facing difficult decisions failed to clean up insolvent banks and were met with a second round of financial crisis in 1996 and a third one in the early 2000s.[240] Meanwhile property prices outside the big cities collapsed, un- and underemployment increased to previously unimaginable levels, and there was no growth. It did not matter to most families that Japan's large-scale manufacturing remains highly globally competitive because some 50 million out of 60 million members of the workforce are now employed outside manufacturing. Industrial catch-up turned out to be only one part of the self-improvement game that Japan needed to play. Moreover, as Japan's 1980s hubris subsided, its population became aware of the demographic shadow that looms over every developing nation. The young population that made rapid industrial progress possible through its perspiration became older, had fewer kids than its parents, lived for longer and started to consume savings in retirement (what economists call 'dissaving'). Japanese citizens then realised that low growth and the forecast demographic profile of the country meant that the pensions politicians had promised them were unaffordable.

The Japanese experience begs the question as to when a country should transition away from infant industrial policy, and to what. Clearly, Japan did too little to move agriculture from yield-based to profit-based efficiency for too long, and neglected its service sector almost completely. But what might be a better policy? Korea offers one alternative trajectory because of reforms forced on the country in the wake of the Asian financial crisis. The International Monetary Fund insisted on an array of changes that included the deregulation of services and their opening to foreign investment, the introduction of ceilings on corporate debt and an end to debt guarantees among *chaebol* affiliates (which were traditionally used to secure two-fifths of firms' bank credit), the lifting of restrictions on hostile takeovers, and numerous accounting and governance reforms in the interests of minority shareholders. These adjustments were very much in the direction of what is called an 'Anglo-Saxon' economic structure, where financial efficiency and short-term profit considerations are accentuated.[241] The reforms ushered large firms away from overwhelming bank debt finance and towards more of a mix of bank debt, bonds and shareholder equity, with the interests of third party, minority cash investors made more influential.

Some of north-east Asia's most respected development economists predicted the IMF reforms would undermine Korea's ability to continue its acquisition of technological capacity and industrial competitiveness. At the time of the crisis, South Korea was still only a nation with a GDP per capita of USD10,000. Economists Ha-Joon Chang and Jang-Sup Shin wrote: 'Governance reforms put the *chaebol* under serious constraints in operating as business groups, especially through the ban on internal transactions ... Coupled with the stringent regulation of the corporate debt–equity ratio, the restriction on internal transactions has substantially reduced financing options ... In our view, what was needed for Korea after the crisis was not to try a transition to an idealised Anglo-American system but to build what we call a "second-stage catching-up system".'[242] A decade later, however, Korea's biggest firms, led by Samsung, Hyundai and LG, appear to be prospering, with their competitive positions in mobile telephony, cars, electronic goods and chemicals stronger than ever. Gross investment in Korea has fallen significantly, from an average 37 per cent of GDP in 1990–97 to around 25 per cent of GDP, but it is far from clear that this has undermined technological progress in this phase of development. Meanwhile, Korea's GDP per capita in 2010 stood at USD20,600, double the level in 1997; its stock market, thanks to the Anglo-Saxon medicine, is a regional outperformer; and its consumers are finally beginning to enjoy the fruits of development in the form of cheaper consumer goods, better services and foreign holidays.[243]

One hesitates to declare that the timing of the IMF reforms in Korea was good. For one thing, some of the success of the Korean economy in the wake of 1997 reflects the government's continued culling of weaker *chaebol* and effective use of non-tariff barriers to foreign competition, in line with traditional industrial policy.[244] However, it is clear that the timing of the reforms in Korea was vastly better than that of the deregulation and privatisation instituted by the IMF in the Philippines in the 1980s, or in Thailand and Indonesia after the Asian crisis (not to mention IMF-like changes instituted unilaterally in Malaysia since Mahathir's departure in 2003). In South Korea, the IMF may just have done something useful. In south-east Asia, by contrast, the IMF's almost complete undermining of national discretion over industrial policy at an early stage of development threatens to turn the region into an oasis of backwardness in the world's emerging continent. Indeed, this is well under way.

### No alternative

South-east Asian politicians speak increasingly of industrial policy as a lost opportunity to which they cannot return. The argument runs that the region's industrial policy failed, and because the IMF's interventions during the financial crisis made it more difficult for governments to implement effective industrial policy, they should not try. In the same vein as people who argue that land reform is too difficult, however, this reasoning assumes there is a viable alternative to infant industry policy. There is not. As the economic historian Angus Maddison wrote in his book *Explaining the Economic Performance of Nations*: 'Technical progress is the most essential characteristic of economic growth.'[245] If technological progress is to occur in emerging states as part of accelerated economic development – rather than occurring over many, many generations – it requires state-orchestrated industrial policy.

There are those who hope that India, with its much-vaunted IT service sector, represents an alternative to manufacturing-led development. Firms like Infosys and Tata Consultancy Services (TCS) are world-beaters. But twenty years after India launched its current reform agenda in 1991, only 3 million people out of a population of 1.2 billion work in IT – a fraction of 1 per cent of the labour force. The service entrepreneurs, managers and technicians who graduate from the elite Indian Institutes of Technology and run firms like Infosys and TCS create far fewer jobs for others than they would had they been forced to manage factories.[246] Two decades of industrial policy neglect in India have created a situation in which only 14 per cent of the labour force is employed in the manufacturing sector. After twenty years of industry-based development in South Korea, 30 per cent of the working population had already been drawn into industry. There is no way that the specialist IT firms of Bangalore, or the financial services elite of Mumbai, will propel India as a nation to the kind of developmental success seen in Japan, Korea, Taiwan and China. It is not going to happen in a comparable timeframe, and punditry that likens India's economic development to that of the more northerly countries is fatuous.[247]

Governments that are serious about broad-based economic development will continue to cajole domestic entrepreneurs to go into manufacturing and to learn to produce globally competitive manufacturing goods. To this end, subsidy and protection must be extended, but with the ever-present discipline provided by competition. In turn, the best means that has been found to judge competition is the export benchmark – because, like properly supervised school assessments and examinations, exports cannot in the long run be fiddled. Exports provide the critical information flow on which industrial policy decisions about which firms to support, and even more critically which firms not to support, are based. And while vital information is being generated, international trade also introduces firms to new technologies and teaches them flexibility.

Enormous investments over very long periods are required to fund industrial learning and this continues to mean that big business plays a leading role in economic development.[248] Indeed, my sense is that the role of big companies is very much more important than the role of big countries – there are lots of small or low-population countries with big firms, like Belgium or Sweden, that are rich, but no big countries that have become rich off the back of small firms. In turn, the risks to state resources in industrial policy are commensurate with the scale of the companies backed. Big-time entrepreneurs who are not effectively disciplined by a developing country government turn into the oligarchs of south-east Asia – or Russia, or Latin America. Even the north-east Asian entrepreneur who was disciplined effectively to work in the direction of national development continued to pull at his chains. He took his subsidies and, once his business was globally competitive, the entrepreneur – just like businessmen and governments before him – became an evangelical convert to the free market. In Japan, Korea and Taiwan, large firms nurtured by the state have gone on to campaign aggressively for deregulation. They, too, are, to use Friedrich List's phrase, quick to 'kick away the ladder' by which they ascended.

The state never stops disciplining companies by providing the moral framework in which they operate – whether in the more *dirigiste* or more free market phase of economic development. Indeed, the disciplinary challenge becomes more arduous as deregulation proceeds, especially in the financial sector. The real problem is not one of state discipline or no state discipline, but one of the timing of the transition from developmental infant industry policies to policies which stress instead the interests of small businesses, consumers and passive investors. It is clearly possible for states to wait too long before they begin to unpick industrial policy and move to a more open economy. Countries such as Japan in Asia, or Italy in Europe, are the developmental equivalent of adults who refuse to leave home, preferring to stay in their bedrooms rather than confront the next stage of life – or the next stretch of the river, if we switch to the Japanese metaphor. These 'big babies', however, are the less significant issue. Much more striking is that the world is teeming with what can be described as developmental children who have been cast out on to the street at a young age and told to get a job. It is these states, expected to industrialise with no infant industry protection, no state control of financial resources and no state discretion over international capital flows, that point to developmental logic gone haywire.

In a world of few developmental grown-ups and many, many children, the final word should be about the biggest grown-up of all, the United States, and its role in east Asian development. In the north-east, in the context of the Cold War, the US was an idealised responsible adult, supporting not only land reform in Japan, Korea and Taiwan, but also tolerating protectionist infant industry policies over long periods of time. Those economic children grew up, and by the 1980s the US was quite reasonably telling them to stop sponging. In south-east Asia, by contrast, the US did nothing to push land reform and then began to press for inappropriate, rich-country-style industrial and financial deregulation in states where GDP per capita was at most in the low thousands of dollars per year. The deregulation pressure mounted with the end of the Cold War. Today those countries, which were explicit US allies in the Cold War and sent soldiers to die alongside Americans in Korea and Vietnam, are adrift. Meanwhile, two countries which fought wars against the US and have not trusted American developmental advice, China and Vietnam, are in much better shape in economic terms. This rather begs the question as to what it means to be America's friend.[249]

# Part 3

# Finance: The Merits of a Short Leash

*'Demonstrating that an exchange economy is coherent and stable does not demonstrate that the same is true of an economy with capitalist financial institutions ... Indeed, central banking and other financial control devices arose as a response to the embarrassing incoherence of financial markets.'*[1]

Hyman P. Minsky, *Stabilizing an Unstable Economy*

If agricultural policy is important to the development of a country because household farming can provide a quick boost to output in rural-based economies, and manufacturing policy is important because an infant industry strategy offers the fastest way to shift the country's economy towards more value-adding activities, then finance policy becomes important because it can target a nation's limited resources at these two objectives. Indeed, it is the close alignment of finance with agricultural and industrial policy objectives (something that had been much more difficult to achieve before the era of bigger governments and information technology took off in the twentieth century) that has facilitated the unprecedentedly rapid economic development of north-east Asia. At the same time, however, modern finance has greatly increased the risks to developing countries, both from mismanagement of larger domestic capital flows and, particularly, from speculative flows of international capital that are not properly regulated.

Finance policy in north-east Asia recognised the need to support small, high-yield farms in order to maximise aggregate farm output rather than maximising returns on cash invested via larger, 'capitalist' farms. And finance policy recognised the need in industry to defer profits until an adequate industrial learning process had taken place. In other words, financial policy frequently accepted low near-term returns on industrial investments in order to build industries capable of producing higher returns in the future.

The alternative would have been for financial institutions to encourage more consumer lending, which tends to produce higher profits and is the focus of financial systems in rich countries. However, herein lies a far from attractive equilibrium for an emerging economy in which banks become very profitable and industry remains technologically backward. This is the situation in most of south-east Asia and Latin America today. The best banking returns in the east Asian region are produced in the region's most backward countries – the Philippines, Indonesia and Thailand. The case for deregulating, and liberating, finance so that it seeks out the most immediately profitable investments is therefore not strong in the early stages of economic development. Far better to keep the financial system on a short leash for a considerable period of time and make it serve developmental purposes.

This logic, and the precise financial policies it entailed, came naturally to the post-Second World War regimes in Japan, Korea and Taiwan. Each state had recently experienced a loss of control over its financial system with painful consequences. Japan had witnessed pre-war *zaibatsu* business groups own and manipulate banks to profitable but selfish ends, buying upstream raw material businesses and utility providers that squeezed the profits out of downstream manufacturers and thereby inhibited the country's overall manufacturing progress. Korea had privatised banks into *chaebol* groups in the 1950s such that almost all manufacturing development was stymied. And Taiwan's KMT had lost out to the communists in mainland China in part because financial system instability and hyper-inflation had wracked the country in the late 1940s. Post-war governments in each of these north-east Asian states therefore resolved that henceforth money would be made to serve the objectives of national development policy.

Infant industry policy required that funds be directed to industrial projects that were less immediately profitable than either other potential manufacturing investments or consumer lending. Banks were therefore kept under close control. International inflows and outflows of capital were also strictly limited so that domestic capital remained under state control and unregulated flows of foreign funds did not disrupt developmental planning. And the returns that citizens could earn on bank deposits and other passive investments were frequently crimped, increasing the surplus left at the financial system's disposal, which could then be used to pay for development policy and infrastructure. This amounted to a hidden taxation, which was tolerated by people in these societies because they could see the economic transformation taking place all around them. South Koreans, for instance, put up with negative real interest rates on bank deposits because they saw their economy overtake first North Korea, then the south-east Asian states, then even Taiwan in only three decades.

The idea that finance had to be shaped by state-led development policies was consistent with the nineteenth-century European and American experiences. In Germany in the 1870s, industrialisation had been accompanied by the creation of powerful investment banks, described by the economist Alexander Gerschenkron as 'comparable in economic effect to ... the steam engine'.[2] However, the businesses the investment banks backed were framed by state industrial policy, including legal sanction for cartels and for export subsidies. And the banks did not appear until state-sponsored industrialisation was well advanced.[3] Similarly, in the United States industrial progress was fostered by the high tariff policies, railway subsidies and cartel tolerance of the federal government. It was in this context that, at the turn of the twentieth century, banking magnates such as J. Pierpont Morgan invested heavily in the industrialisation process, creating business empires with huge economies of scale. In short, state-directed industrial policy came first, and finance second.

When the state did not provide the right direction to finance, developmental outcomes were different. Nineteenth-century Spain had a large number of investment banks which did nothing to promote industrialisation. This was largely because Spanish company law favoured railroad investment but discriminated against manufacturers. As a result, the Spanish banks financed thousands of kilometres of rail lines, for which all the rolling stock was imported and for which there were no manufactures to transport. After a banking crisis in the 1870s, Spain remained thoroughly un-industrialised.[4] Similarly, Austria had plenty of investment banks and weak infant industry policies; its banks financed only mature firms and government securities, and manufacturing development lagged. In sum, throughout history financial systems have catalysed different developmental outcomes depending on the policy environment that has surrounded them. And it is the governments of successful emerging states that make financial systems support effective industrialisation.

### Finance bulks up

After the Second World War, developing countries were able to put unprecedented financial power behind their development policies.

Almost all governments were becoming bigger and more powerful, and had greater bureaucratic reach than ever. From the 1960s the digital age made possible information management systems that vastly increased the power of financial sectors. And in the early 1970s the Bretton Woods system of fixed exchange rates (which had been the successor to the gold standard) broke down, allowing for vastly increased flows of international capital which could be harnessed – for better or worse – by poor countries. In the late nineteenth century, Germany and the United States had been the first countries to raise their savings and investment ratios to 20 per cent of GDP.[5] In 1960, the American government adviser W. W. Rostow predicted in his influential book *The Stages of Economic Growth* that an unprecedentedly large cohort of developing economies would soon be able to achieve savings and investment rates in excess of 15 per cent.[6] In the event, every one of the nine major east Asian economies, from Japan to Thailand, delivered post-war savings and investment rates of 30 to 50 per cent. And so, in terms of financial clout, there was nothing to prevent any east Asian country – south-east Asian or north-east Asian – from joining the rich world.[7] What caught some countries out was that they financed the wrong policies.

In south-east Asia, high rates of investment were wasted on ineffectual land reforms, industrial policies that lacked competition and export discipline, and expenditures wholly irrelevant to economic development, such as luxury real estate and imported consumer goods. Worse still, as the failings of half-hearted, poorly planned agricultural and manufacturing strategies became apparent from the 1980s, governments were tempted by the siren calls of the incipient Washington Consensus – the free market agenda for economic development that was being pressed on developing countries with increased vigour by the IMF, the World Bank and the US government. The loudest and most evangelical message of these agencies was that deregulating the financial sector could put the development efforts of lagging countries back on track. States were encouraged to privatise existing banks and license new banks, to take a *laissez-faire* attitude to international flows of capital and to expand stock markets. The argument of the Washington Consensus was that liberated capital would then itself identify the right investments to spur economic progress.

What actually happened, in 1997, was a financial catastrophe on a scale similar to that which afflicted Latin America after 1982. Financial sector liberalisation in south-east Asia led not to better allocation of capital, but to control of private banks by business entrepreneurs whose interests, because they were not required to manufacture and were not subject to export discipline, were not aligned with those of national development. As a result, there was a further weakening of already weak financial sector support for agriculture and for industry. Money flowed instead to increasingly speculative, short-term investments, led by luxury real estate. South-east Asian banking systems were 'captured' to selfish ends by entrepreneurs in a manner that echoed what had happened in Latin America following bank privatisation there in the 1970s. Years before the Asian financial crisis, the Korean finance scholar Jung-en Woo warned Asian states about Latin America's IMF-sponsored reforms: 'Privatisation in the Latin American Southern Cone had its conglomerates run amok,' she wrote, 'buying up banks to buy up other enterprises, stacking up loan portfolios with loans made out to affiliated firms ...[It] led to Chilean and Argentine *grupos* profiting like bandits.'[8] Despite the evidence from Latin America about the risks of premature bank deregulation – not to mention what was seen after financial deregulation in Russia in the early 1990s – south-east Asia went ahead with very similar policies. Once again, political leaders knew too little history and were too easily bewitched by economists.

South-east Asian states also got rid of capital controls on IMF advice. Japan had faced formal, repeated demands from the IMF and the secretariat of the General Agreement on Tariffs and Trade (the GATT, the forerunner of the World Trade Organisation) to move to currency convertibility from 1959, but hung on to its highly restrictive Foreign Capital Law until 1980.[9] Korea and Taiwan were similarly recalcitrant in resisting demands to free up capital flows until the 1990s. In south-east Asia, states liberalised far earlier in the development process. The result was escalating short-term foreign debt flows which governments were unable to control. Rich-country money, also with short-term gains in mind, poured into the region chasing relatively high interest rates. Moreover, currencies in southeast Asia were either pegged to the US dollar or appreciating against it, making short-term investment doubly attractive to foreigners – so long as the pegs held.[10] In north-east Asia, Korea faced heavy inflows after lifting capital controls under IMF pressure in 1994. But more of the money than in south-east Asia went to industry. In south-east Asia, international borrowings were used in economies where agricultural and manufacturing policy was failing, in order to finance real estate investment and other non-productive activities such as stock market speculation. Again, there was a similarity to the foreign debt build-up in Latin America prior to its crisis, where too much foreign money was deployed to ends that did not generate foreign exchange.

South-east Asia's armageddon began in July 1997 when the Thai currency was forced off its US dollar peg by international demands for repayment of loans, triggering a global panic over the capacity of other Asian countries to service their debts. The crisis highlighted one clear developmental rule above all: that a state must keep its financial institutions aligned with its development strategy until basic agricultural and industrial policy targets have been achieved. The case for deregulation strengthens as an economy evolves, but the risks of premature deregulation are greater than those of tardy deregulation, especially in our world of globalised financial flows. Indeed, as an economy develops, domestic firms inevitably struggle to break free from state control of finance, creating natural, domestic pressures for deregulation. There is no sense in a state getting ahead of this trend. The deregulation process is difficult enough to handle even once a state has developed its bureaucratic capacity. Japan, Korea and Taiwan each experienced financial crises when liberalising. But what was more important was that these states resisted pressure from the Washington Consensus and held off liberalisation until very substantial developmental progress had occurred.

The key conduits for maintaining financial control in a developing economy have always been capital controls and banking systems – the latter because they are easier for states with limited bureaucratic capacity to manage than stock or bond markets. Banks are beholden to central banks as a source of additional and emergency funds, opening the way for governments to influence them to lend long-term to industry. Stock and bond markets, by contrast, are subject to instantaneous selling by investors in times of panic. They also require more complex regulatory infrastructure and high levels of information transparency to function even moderately well.

Beyond trying to control international capital flows and control banks – whether through public or private ownership – there has been no consistency among successful or unsuccessful states in east Asia in terms of monetary and fiscal policy. At one end of the spectrum, heavy foreign borrowing and loose monetary policy – leading to high inflation and repeated financial crises – did not undermine developmental progress in Korea. At the other end, no amount of monetary prudence, control of foreign debt and low inflation could turn Malaysia into an economic success story. Throughout east Asia, as elsewhere in the developing world, the key was to have finance – whether expansive or conservative – pointed at the right targets.

## Japan feels its way

One of the signs that Japan's path-breaking developmental effort in the nineteenth century was unravelling in the 1920s was that the government lost control of the financial system to *zaibatsu* business groups. This financial system 'capture', along with the reversal of much of the land reform of the 1870s, made gains from economic progress ever more narrowly distributed and helped open the door to military rule in the 1930s.

The problem for the original Meiji policymakers, who learned so much from agricultural reforms and infant industry policies in already-developed states, was that developed nations offered much less clear recipes with respect to financial policy. No country had yet mobilised finance to developmental ends with the efficacy and power that would occur in the twentieth century. Indeed, the role that finance plays in economics would not be seriously explored by economists until the Great Depression and the Keynsian revolution. Japanese governments therefore experimented with different approaches. The earliest Meiji banking legislation was copied from the United States, and allowed scores of private banks to set up and to issue currency. Partly as a result, there was a great deal of inflation in the 1870s, followed by a painful period of deflation in the 1880s. A central bank was therefore set up with a monopoly of note issue, and the state compensated for private banks' hesitancy to lend to industry by funding much early industrial investment from government savings and from public debt secured offshore. Around the turn of the twentieth century, government created several specialised industrial lenders, including Yokohama Specie (1870), Nippon Kangyo (1897), and Industrial Bank of Japan (1902).

Despite this, as in the contemporary United States, vast numbers of small private banks continued to operate – there were around 2,000 in Japan at the start of the twentieth century – and it was this that allowed for widespread capture of banks by business groups, which went into banking to obtain cheap and reliable supplies of funds for their activities. Captive banks ask fewer questions than independent ones and, when regulation is weak, can lend their owners a great deal of money compared with the investment needed to start or buy a bank. In the United States, havoc broke out among under-regulated small banks in 1907, in a crisis referred to as the Panic. In 1927 Japan faced an even greater number of bank runs and failures. Since the most hopelessly conflicted banks were small ones, the Japanese government passed a new Banking Act that forced banks to merge. However, this simply opened the way for a few huge *zaibatsu* lenders to dominate. The four biggest ones came to control the majority of credit, pursuing mostly intra-group lending while denying finance to downstream manufacturers outside their groups. The military dictatorship of the 1930s realigned the *zaibatsu* banks with a new set of military–industrial objectives, but pre-war banking was never closely in tune with manufacturing development objectives and Japan entered the Second World War still at a marked technological disadvantage to Britain and the United States.

After Japan's surrender in 1945, the Supreme Commander for the Allied Powers altered the country's financial structure fundamentally. The driver for the changes was that the *zaibatsu* families had co-operated closely with the military. The largely unintended outcome of the changes was that a financial system was created that was far better suited to the requirements of state-led industrial policy. *Zaibatsu* ownership of banks was ended, and the holding companies through which the families had exercised control were banned. The SCAP acquiesced in the setting up of a powerful Ministry of International Trade and Industry, which provided direction to the banking system and had broad discretion over allocations of foreign exchange. Bank ownership was distributed among diversified groups of corporate owners with the typical investor holding a fraction of 1 per cent. This left agencies like MITI with no competitors in providing direction to the financial system. However, the banks were allowed to retain shareholdings of up to 10 per cent in individual firms.[11] They formed close working relationships with the industrial borrowers they held equity in, nominating officers to sit on companies' boards, sending support staff to work temporarily in their offices, and even taking over the management of firms that appeared to be failing. This so-called 'main bank' system, with its long-term lender–client relationships, supported Japan's industrialisation drive.

The state exercised control over the banking system via a mechanism called rediscounting, whereby the central bank provides loans to commercial banks against loans they have already extended. These 'rediscounts' increase a commercial bank's loan book and therefore its profit potential, but also allow a central bank to set borrowing criteria that must be met. In post-war Japan, qualification for rediscounts depended on the export performance and sectoral focus of the firms that commercial banks ultimately lent to. The generous availability of rediscounts meant that Japanese banks tended to extend more credit than their deposits alone could justify, becoming – in banking parlance – 'overloaned'. They therefore depended on continuing central bank credit to keep them liquid. It was this which allowed the Bank of Japan to turn the screw of moral suasion when issuing 'advice', not just about the use of rediscounted loans but about the priorities of banks' overall loan books. In the 1960s and 1970s, Japanese corporations depended on the banking system for 40–50 per cent of their total funding needs, compared with less than 30 per cent for German firms and less than 20 per cent for British and American ones. (Looked at the other way round, the situation reflected the relative unimportance in Japan of bond and stock markets.)[12] Banks became the critical means for enforcing industrial policy. Their power, and that of agencies like MITI from which they took their cues, was doubly great because the state also controlled access to foreign exchange.

Japan's financial sector was kept on a short, if gradually lengthening, leash for thirty years. MITI bureaucrats were able to develop industrial plans sector by sector in the knowledge that the banking system would deliver what they wanted. As Japanese firms scaled up and became more international in their outlook, however, corporate managers fought a long battle to take control of their finances and to find cheaper sources of funds outside state control. Few companies liked being told what to do by bureaucrats and bankers. An inevitable tension arises in infant industrial policy as it is enforced through the financial system. From the mid 1970s, Japanese firms took advantage of modest acts of deregulation, and found other ways to raise more funds through equity issues and through offshore Eurobond sales[13] (called Eurobonds, confusingly, not because they are denominated in European currency, but because such bond issues were first conducted in Europe). By the mid 1980s, resourceful listed companies were able to get most or all of their non-internally generated funds from the stock market and bond sales. As the economy developed and became more complex and international, the financial leash inevitably lengthened.

A number of factors then contributed to the trend to Japan's bubble economy of the late 1980s. The first was that the banks, losing out on their traditional high-margin business from corporate customers but barred from underwriting share sales, naturally sought to direct more of their funds to real estate and consumer loans. Japan needed to readjust its economic model in favour of less investment and greater consumption; however, a manageable pace of change gave way to a sudden acceleration in financial liberalisation. After three decades of dragging its heels, in 1980 Japan lifted capital controls and then, in 1985, bowed to US pressure over trade surpluses and allowed the yen to appreciate more quickly. The currency's value against the dollar doubled in three years. Financial system deregulation, foreign capital inflows and a rapidly rising currency were bound to produce stresses. What made the transition worse was that the government pursued a loose, almost reckless low interest rate policy to compensate for the export-dampening effects of the appreciating currency. The result was an orgy of previously unthinkable consumer lending. In five years in the late 1980s, urban real estate prices quadrupled and stock prices tripled.[14] It was as if the whole country decided to make up for three decades of developmental graft by going on a speculative binge. This was the period when the eldest son of Nishiyama Kōichi, the diary-writing Niigata farmer, lost the family's entire accumulated wealth playing the stock market.

Financial deregulation, coming after a period of financial 'repression' that focused resources on developmental objectives, had an inevitable wealth effect as asset prices rose. Japan was suckered by this increase in paper wealth into thinking that it was different. The term *nihonjinron*, meaning 'Japanese exceptionalism', was used to justify sky-high asset valuations. But Japan was not different and hubris – that most powerful enemy of sustained economic transformation – derailed its advance, just as it has in so many other societies. From the winter of 1989–90, the asset bubble began to deflate in a process that saw the stock market index fall by three-quarters, real estate values cut by multiples and recurrent, debilitating bouts of consumer price deflation which further discouraged consumption. More than twenty years on, Japan appears still to be in a state of delayed shock that its remarkable post-war developmental performance was not in fact a self-perpetuating miracle.

## Finance as understood by General Park

Japanese financial sector policy in the golden years of development – roughly 1950–1980 – held financial institutions in check, but it was fairly orthodox. Central bank rediscounting kept banks on the hook but it was not sufficient to create high inflation; also, there was not much overseas borrowing and interest rates, although lower than in other industrial countries, were consistently positive. This contrasts with Korea, where a souped-up and, to many contemporary observers, crazed approach to financial management was pursued. Despite its gainsayers, however, Korea showed more than any other country in east Asia that so long as funds are invested in the acquisition of technological capacity – with export discipline providing a quality benchmark – a state can take considerable risks with financial propriety. Park Chung Hee went down to the financial wire in the 1970s with his super-charged heavy and chemical industrialisation drive, but in the end the multi-billion dollar investments paid off handsomely. On the other hand, in south-east Asia several governments showed that, in the absence of the right approach to agriculture and manufacturing, any form of financial loosening can see an economy's wheels spin off completely.

The *dirigiste* tone of Korea's financial sector management during its fast-development phase was set by Park Chung Hee when he renationalised the banks. These had been privatised in 1957 on the insistence of advisers from the US Federal Reserve to the businessmen Park temporarily incarcerated in 1961.[15] Government control plus total attention to the funding needs of heavy industrialisation were Park's idea of an appropriately run financial system. In 1962 a new Bank of Korea Act turned the central bank, in effect, into an arm of the Ministry of Finance. Thereafter, the Bank of Korea used rediscounting of loans extended by the nationalised banks to exert day-to-day control, just as happened in Japan. The difference was that in Korea the policy was much more aggressive. Rediscounting of export loans was unlimited. In other words, any bank that lent against exports – as proven by a letter of credit from a foreign customer – got almost as much money back from the central bank in order to further expand its loan book. There was also unlimited rediscounting of policy loans to other favoured, government-approved projects.

Of course, by creating new money, rediscounting tends to lead to inflation. But Park's government, having never seen the high inflation of Japan pre-1949 or the hyper inflation of China in 1946–50, worried much less about rising prices than did other countries' governments. So long as Korean firms were following the developmental plan and could sell their goods abroad, the banks were told to lend to them. It was in this funding context that exports rose an average 40 per cent a year in the 1960s and over 25 per cent a year in the 1970s, increasing from 3.4 per cent of GDP in 1960 to 35 per cent by the 1980s. Meanwhile, inflation averaged 15–20 per cent annually.[16]

Not only were funds for favoured borrowers abundant, they were effectively free, or very cheap. The cheapest loans went to exporters, typically carrying real interest rates of −10 to −20 per cent. So long as exporters could raise their prices to reflect domestic inflation, they were in effect being paid to borrow. Other favoured industrial projects that were not yet ready to export also received low-cost funds. All this necessarily meant that the interest paid out to depositors was minimal or non-existent. However, there was still money in the banks. The savings of a parsimonious government were kept there. The working capital accounts of large businesses remained there because otherwise they would not be eligible for cheap lending. And a part of household and small business savings was also deposited in the banking system on lousy terms, because the system was the only formal one available. The remaining chunk of private savings found its way into illegal, but tolerated, non-bank financial institutions and freelance lenders known as the 'kerb market'.

From 1974 to 1980, at the height of Korea's heavy and chemical industrialisation drive, the average real borrowing rate in the banking system was −6.7 per cent, versus an average of 18.5 per cent in the kerb market. The loans of the banking system were reserved for exporters, and for larger firms that were leading the technological learning process. As a reflection of the role bureaucratic oversight played, there were 221 different types of preferential loan by the end of the heavy industrialisation period. It was a two-tier system in which any business which could not access funds in the formal banking system had to go to the kerb.[17]

The IMF, the World Bank and the US government – the last of which provided vast amounts of aid to South Korea – did not like General Park's approach to financial management, and their economists tried repeatedly to push him towards more orthodox policies. They had some temporary success in the second half of the 1960s when the government in Seoul agreed to raise real interest rates substantially. However, as the Korea specialist Alice Amsden noted: 'In all, liberalisation amounted to nothing more than a footnote to the basic text of Korean expansion.'[18] In practice in the late 1960s, the single most important financier of industrialisation, the Korea Development Bank (KDB), increased its borrowings of cheaper funds offshore; the KDB also increased guarantees for *chaebol* to borrow internationally, turning a blind eye to the exchange rate risk.[19]

When this risk came home to roost in a major crisis that began in 1969, General Park forgot his promises to US advisers to reward savers and price capital according to the market, enforcing a three-year interest moratorium on kerb lenders that in effect made the general public bail out industry. Ordinary Koreans provided most of the kerb market's funds, while *chaebol* sourced marginal loans there that they could not obtain from banks. By stopping payments on this high interest debt, Park freed up *chaebol* funds to pay their bank debts, and prevented bank collapses. The public lost its interest income from the kerb market, while bank interest rates were cut again.[20]

Such conditions contributed to Korea having a somewhat lower rate of household saving than Japan or Taiwan. But there was not the kind of collapse in individual saving that many economists predicted. In part this was because savers were less sensitive to deposit interest rates than the mathematical models favoured by economists assumed; savers focused instead on the need to hold money against future liabilities in a state with little welfare. In part, savings also held up because it was not easy to consume, especially if this involved using foreign exchange. Imported consumer goods were either banned or enormously expensive due to high tariffs, while stringent capital controls meant that in the 1980s it was still illegal to take a holiday abroad.[21]

Korean families, along with their government and businesses, continued to save, and the shortfall in funds for investment – which remained acute until the first sustained current account surpluses in the late 1980s – was plugged with international borrowing. In the late 1960s and 1970s, Korea had the fastest rate of foreign debt accumulation in the world, even as Latin American states were borrowing heavily. By 1985, Korea was the second most internationally indebted developing country after Brazil, and with a much smaller population; overseas loans amounted to 53 per cent of GNI.[22] However, because of its emphasis on exports, Korea's foreign debt payments relative to its foreign exchange earnings actually declined from 1970. Payments of interest and principal as a share of exports were 28 per cent in that year and only 20 per cent in the early 1980s, even though debt and debt payments increased as a share of GNI. Export discipline was Korea's financial get-out-of-jail card.

## The steamroller approach

In the most investment-intensive era of industrial growth, from approximately 1965 to the early 1980s, there developed a pattern in which each time Korea hit a road block in the form of an external economic shock and/or a domestic financial crisis, government did whatever was financially necessary to maintain developmental momentum. In the early 1970s, in addition to the kerb market interest moratorium, General Park's government forced state banks to swap loans for *chaebol* shares and abandoned the high domestic interest rate policy begun in 1965. It met each crisis with cheaper money. With the first global oil shock, and a deep world recession, from late 1973 until 1975, the government massively increased domestic credit, while foreign debt rose from 31 to 40 per cent of GNI. With the second international oil crisis of 1979, plus increased US interest rates that helped trigger a world recession from 1980, Korea cranked up foreign debt again; the level, which had been pulled back to 30 per cent of GNI before the crisis, was increased to 50 per cent.[23]

Korea grew through a cataclysm which, in 1982, brought similarly indebted Latin American countries, and then the Philippines, to their knees. And Korea kept borrowing through the mid 1980s, when a localised Asian recession saw Mahathir's Malaysia flip-flop away from its infant industry policy to one of dependence on foreign-invested export processing. Korea's determination to stay the industrialisation course was writ large in its attitude to finance. Government invested its way forward, using temporary devaluations to spur exports in slack periods.[24] Throughout, underperforming *chaebol* subsidiaries were culled and merged.

This approach was successful so long as the government had the financial whip hand. Eventually, however, the scaling-up of the *chaebol* into bigger and bigger groups – the level of corporate concentration in Korea was higher than in Japan or Taiwan – meant that the biggest borrowers ceased to fear their lenders. Once the HCI drive was complete in the early 1980s, the *chaebol* were very powerful beasts. In 1983, the three biggest groups, Hyundai, Samsung and Daewoo, were each consuming 10 per cent of credit. With the *chaebol* both huge and heavily leveraged (*average* debt was more than five times equity in the fifty biggest firms) the state banking system could no longer impose its will on businesses whose failure would bring down the banks themselves. The banks were increasingly compelled to lend whatever the *chaebol* wanted. In the 1980s the *chaebol* started to buy up smaller rivals rather than compete with them.[25] They also began to use their cheap bank funds to speculate more heavily in real estate. They themselves lent money to the kerb at high interest. And they used domestic oligopolies to crush smaller competitors they did not buy, and to squeeze consumers ever more effectively. From a force for technological progress, the *chaebol* began to morph into economic bullies whose developmental contribution was much less clear.

The IMF, the World Bank, the US government and a group of Korean economists trained in the US (who had begun to gain influence under President Chun Doo Hwan in the 1980s) all argued that it was time to deregulate finance in order to curb *chaebol* power. This was a view which gained considerable public support after three decades in which ordinary savers had been forced to subsidise big business. In the early 1980s, deposit and lending rates in the banks were raised to positive real levels. The banks were privatised, with a maximum 8 per cent shareholding by any one investor, which ensured some independence from *chaebol* influence. However, the central government continued to set banks' credit quotas and interest rate ceilings, and to appoint senior managers.[26]

Other pro-market reforms did not turn out as the economists predicted. The development of the stock market failed to discipline *chaebol*. When firms listed, the controlling families invariably retained board and management control and a booming late 1980s bourse simply provided additional funds without any shareholder discipline; and the banks' ability to influence large firms' behaviour was thereby further weakened. There was also considerable liberalisation of non-bank financial institutions (NBFIs) – smaller deposit-taking institutions without full banking licences – which had been sanctioned in the 1970s as an alternative to the kerb market. Allowed to multiply, these institutions offered higher interest rates than banks and increased their share of deposits from 25 per cent in 1976 to a dominant 63 per cent in 1989. Unlike with the banks, however, the *chaebol* achieved direct control of many NBFIs – a dangerous development. It was no coincidence that throughout the 1980s and early 1990s the *chaebol* leaders invariably lobbied in favour of financial deregulation.[27]

The situation did not run out of control until 1993, when Kim Young-Sam's government was persuaded by the IMF and its own pro-free market economists to lift capital controls and deregulate short-term offshore borrowing. It was this that led to a flood of short-maturity foreign debt coming into Korea between 1994 and 1997. Overall – and contrary to what is popularly believed – Korea's foreign debt level was not particularly high on the eve of the financial crisis; as a proportion of GNI it was less than half the 1970s and 1980s peaks.[28] But when panic spread from south-east Asia in 1997, and short-term loans were called in rather than rolled over, the liquidity shock was sufficient to trigger a major crisis in Korea.

Despite this, the fact that a relatively smaller proportion of credit in Korea had been directed to non-productive activities like real estate meant that the country began to recover strongly in 1999. As with earlier crises, government orchestrated mergers and business unit swaps among the *chaebol* in order to pare underperforming subsidiaries. It was in this shakeout that Chung Ju Yung's Hyundai obtained control of Kia and, with it, unassailable dominance of the automotive sector.[29] What was different to every preceding crisis was that on this occasion the Korean government heeded IMF advice about structural changes to the financial system. The country acquired north-east Asia's most 'orthodox' financial system, with an independent central bank, wholly independent commercial banks, large foreign-controlled banks and much increased rights for independent investors in stock and other markets. Despite a financial sector wobble over increased consumer debt in the early 2000s, so far the deregulated system has not produced another crisis. However it remains to be seen precisely how well timed Korea's transition to an Anglo-Saxon financial system was.

### Meek Taiwanese do not inherit the Earth

Within the general north-east Asian framework of capital controls, government direction of banks, and export discipline to ensure that borrowers were acceptable credit risks, Taiwan took the most conservative approach to financial management. Compared with Korea, there were higher interest rates, higher savings rates[30] (and hence more domestic money to invest, with less need for foreign borrowing), lower inflation, far fewer non-performing loans and nothing like the repeated banking and balance of payments crises. The Asian financial crisis passed Taiwan by. Yet Taiwan lost its considerable GDP per capita lead over Korea in the 1990s, and by 2010 was USD2,000 behind.[31]

The reason for this is that developmental finance – prudently or, as in Korea, imprudently implemented – is only as good as the policy framework on which it acts. Taiwan did well in agriculture, with rural lending institutions providing effective support to household farming. But in industry the Taiwanese government failed either to discipline large firms to manufacture for export or to support smaller manufacturers to become large as effectively as post-war Korea and Japan did. Instead the island state, in a manner more reminiscent of mid-nineteenth-century Germany or pre-Second World War Japan, relied on smaller companies for most of its exports. Larger, non-export businesses that supplied raw materials and intermediate goods were also able to squeeze downstream manufacturers in a manner that constrained their capacity both for technological upgrading and for scaling up in terms of capital intensity.[32] Consequently, the average Taiwanese manufacturer remained a supplier to more powerful multinational corporations. The situation was bound up with, but not made inevitable by, the Kuomintang's determination to keep most large-scale business under state ownership. Taiwan's problem, in a nutshell, was that the financial policies it adopted catalysed a sub-optimal manufacturing policy.

The Kuomintang nationalised the main Taiwanese banks well before it fled to the island at the end of the Chinese civil war in 1949. Under martial law it also made breeches of capital controls (loosely defined as 'disrupting the money market') an offence punishable by death. But it never used financial system control to implement a manufacturing policy built around big companies. Lending was thinly spread and short term. As one snapshot example, Jung-en Woo has assembled data for 1983 which show that at a time when 400 Korean companies (from 137 *chaebol*) consumed 70 per cent of all bank credit, the top 333 Taiwanese firms took only 30 per cent of Taiwan's bank lending.[33] Longer-term loans for strategic private sector projects were extremely difficult to come by in Taiwan. There was not the kind of highly differentiated preferential bank lending that was used by MITI in Japan and the Economic Planning Board in Korea to support particular manufacturing objectives. And nor was there a 'main bank' system – present in Japan since the Second World War and Korea from the 1970s – whereby a lead institution closely monitored and supported the development of an industrial enterprise.[34] For private firms, banks met little more than their working capital needs, so those businesses had to try to climb the technology ladder using current earnings plus more expensive borrowings from the kerb market. (Despite higher real interest rates in Taiwan, the kerb still played a significant role.)[35] This was extremely difficult.

The Taiwanese government's failure to run more effective industrial policy went hand in hand with its being the most active administration in east Asia in artificially holding down the value of the national currency. The new Taiwan dollar was kept pegged to the US dollar at 40:1 from 1961 all the way to 1985, despite low inflation, persistent trade surpluses from the mid 1970s (much earlier than Korea) and productivity levels which increased by multiples. This combination would normally make a currency appreciate. In order to maintain the exchange rate, the Bank of Taiwan accumulated foreign exchange reserves of USD60 billion by 1987, second in the world to Japan's USD63 billion, despite an economy less than one-tenth the size.[36] Taiwan's 'cheap currency' approach – today echoed in mainland China – supported its heavier dependence, compared with Japan and Korea, on low value-added export processing by multinational firms, which accounted for around a quarter of manufacturing exports in the 1980s, and on relatively lower value-added exports by domestic private firms. A chronically undervalued currency was probably a symptom of the failure to get industrial policy right. The cheap currency, however, was unable to change the fact that by the 1980s the quality and value-added of Korean exports were exceeding Taiwan's, while Korea caught up with and surpassed Taiwan in GNI per capita in the next decade.[37]

In the late 1980s and 1990s Taiwan succumbed to intense international pressure over its currency manipulation and began to deregulate its financial system. As in Korea, the state lost a good part of its capacity to impose industrial policy via the banks. Fifteen new private banks were licensed in 1991, compared with a total of twenty banks in existence to that point. The new owners of private institutions were not responsive to state direction on lending and the central bank did not seek to influence them through rediscounting and overloaning, while the market share of government-linked banks declined steadily from a peak of around 95 per cent in 1980. The stock market, which previously was stifled by Kuomintang control of the listing process, also took off in the 1980s, providing new avenues for financing without government strictures, as did deregulated offshore borrowing. Domestic bank credit fell as a share of Taiwanese firms' total liabilities from an average of over 30 per cent in the 1980s to under 20 per cent by the early 2000s. Meanwhile, the exchange rate appreciated, consumer credit became widely available for the first time and there was an asset bubble, although a less debilitating one than Japan's.[38] Unlike in Japan and Korea, financial deregulation occurred in Taiwan *before* the economy's leading firms had achieved high levels of technological progress and independence from foreign technology suppliers.

**You want error?**

Despite its financial policy underperformance, Taiwan's economy is still a variation on the theme of north-east Asian developmental success. Fundamentally, Taiwan kept its banking system on a short leash until the late 1980s, by which time it was already a USD10,000 per capita plus economy. Capital controls were also maintained to the same point. The timing of the transition to a more open financial system was not optimal, but nor was it a total disaster. If you want to see case studies of financial system calamity, then come to south-east Asia.

Here, there is the same uneven pattern of differing levels of government 'prudence' in managing financial systems as there was in north-east Asia. And the range is at least as great, running from more prudent Malaysia and Thailand through the less orthodox Indonesia to the Philippines, which operated the kind of high foreign debt financial strategy pursued by Korea. The Philippines also followed the Korean path by offering domestic savers typically negative real interest rates, which helped push the gross savings rate down to around a quarter of GNI – the same as in Korea.[39] In none of the south-east Asian countries – prudent or aggressive – however, did the banking system support effective indigenous industrialisation.

The critical variable again here is not who owns the financial system or precisely how it is operated, but the business environment on which it is acting. In each case in south-east Asia the banking system funded an economy in which leading entrepreneurs faced little pressure to manufacture and did not operate under conditions of export discipline. This led to two outcomes: first, there was very little acquisition of technological capability in manufacturing; second, the absence of export discipline meant an absence of the information feedback from exports that enhanced banks' loan quality in north-east Asia. When governments tried, fitfully, to promote industrialisation in south-east Asia – as Mahathir's administration tried in Malaysia – they created relatively more bad debt than in north-east Asia in the course of a less efficient learning process.[40]

The more financially prudent south-east Asian states could potentially have survived their industrialisation missteps and consequent non-performing loans in the lead-up to the Asian financial crisis, just as all the states survived the costs of the earliest attempts at import substitution projects in the 1950s. But from the early 1980s, Malaysia, Thailand and Indonesia each succumbed to the siren call of financial deregulation. This effectively meant handing over increasing control of the financial system to private entrepreneurs whose interests did not tally with those of national development. These same, un-export-disciplined entrepreneurs were also given much increased access to offshore sources of finance. Such developments set the fuse to the deep crises in Malaysia, Thailand and Indonesia that began in 1997, and from which these countries have still not yet fully recovered.

The Philippines, south-east Asia's outlier, had already shown the route to financial disaster in the 1980s, when Latin America too fell apart. For both, the trigger was the 1980 increase in US interest rates to record post-Second World War highs – a move made by the US government to address domestic inflation that had global repercussions.[41] The Philippines, like other countries, could no longer afford its overwhelmingly dollar-denominated debts. As dollar interest rates rose and the Philippine peso's value against the dollar slid, the country faced spiralling costs to roll over borrowings which had not translated into significantly greater export earning potential, especially in manufacturing. Under Ferdinand Marcos from 1965 to 1986, exports as a share of the Philippines' GDP increased from 20 per cent to 26 per cent, but debt service on foreign loans rose more than ten-fold.[42] Moreover, the country had privatised its banking system to oligarchs back in the 1950s, and the banks, as well as the government, were bust. The Philippines was south-east Asia's financial policy path-breaker on the march to the inner circles of developmental hell.

## Korea with a different outcome

It was not the scale of the Philippines' international borrowing that made disaster inevitable. Until shortly before crisis struck in the 1980s, the country's external debts were a smaller share of output than Korea's.[43] If Marcos had done what Park Chung Hee did, and marshalled the banking system to drive an industrial policy kept in check by export discipline, there is no reason why the Philippines could not have turned out like Korea. Instead, the Philippines went from being twice as rich as Korea to eleven times poorer in less than half a century.[44] An absence of a clear focus on manufacturing for export coupled with a willingness to play fast and loose with financial tools led to the worst possible policy combination. With no objective performance standard to meet in the form of exportable goods, the Philippines' entrepreneurial elite manipulated the banking system to such a degree that the country became the closest thing in our study to a kleptocracy.

The tradition of the national elite plundering the financial system began well before the Philippines' independence in 1946. In 1916, Washington devolved financial and most legislative power to its colony, and sponsored the creation of a rather large state-owned investment bank. The Philippine National Bank (PNB) was set up to fund Filipino development in line with the US's own infant industry tradition. The US governor general, Francis Burton Harrison, promised that the bank would be 'capable of sustaining all the government's developmental efforts'.[45] PNB was made the legal repository for all government funds and, within two years, accounted for two-thirds of the assets of the entire banking system.

The problem was, who or what was the PNB going to lend to? The Philippine economy was built around what were dubbed 'free trade' agreements with the United States, but which were in reality protectionist deals that kept the Philippines focused on agriculture.[46] The Philippines agricultural exports to the US entered the market duty-free, while non-colonial competitors faced insuperably high tariffs. Although Filipino shipments of sugar, coconuts and other crops made up four-fifths of the country's total exports in the 1930s, there was no export discipline at work because, without the tariff differential, production was not competitive. (After the US cut tariff-free quotas in the 1970s, the Philippines was left with a thoroughly inefficient agricultural sector.) But the entrepreneurs did not care. The Filipino elite built up its estates and plantations whilst fiercely opposing any political efforts to make entrepreneurs manufacture for export. In these conditions, there were no businesses subject to genuine export discipline for PNB to lend to, no useful information feedback from exports, and hence the state investment bank was a disaster waiting to happen. Only five years after power was devolved to Manila in 1916, PNB was made bankrupt for the first time, having lent huge sums to local oligarchs who failed to repay their loans.

Thus began a pattern of waste and plunder that the Philippines has never escaped. Three years after independence in 1946, the state was again on the point of bankruptcy, having squandered USD620 million in rehabilitation funds provided by the departing colonial power.[47] From the 1950s, the Philippines became east Asia's IMF and World Bank junky, with more programmes and 'efficiency' plans foisted on it than any other state in the region in attempts to stop its financial system from haemorrhaging. Privatisation of the banking system was prescribed in the late 1950s (as it was by US government advisers in Syngman Rhee's Korea in 1957). But in the absence of export discipline, the banks became the personal piggy banks of entrepreneurial families, with the costs of any misadventures picked up by the central bank and the state. By the time Marcos was elected in 1965, there were thirty-three private banks and almost every major business family controlled at least one of them. In 1964 there was the first of an unending series of private bank failures as Republic Bank, which belonged to a distilling-to-lumber entrepreneur, collapsed and had to be taken over by PNB.[48]

Ferdinand Marcos came to power promising radical change. Both as an elected president, and as a dictator from 1972, he made the same political promises to his people as Park Chung Hee, who had been an elected president from 1963 and then became dictator a few weeks after Marcos in 1972.[49] The Philippine leader vowed he would deliver land reform and industrial development, and tame what he called the 'old oligarchs' – what Park referred to as 'liberation aristocrats'. Both men identified the symptom of the problem: entrepreneurs who were contributing very little to national

development. But, unlike Park, Marcos did not enforce export requirements and did not take back control of the privatised banking system. On
his watch, the failings of the financial sector became worse than ever as
entrepreneurs used their private banks to enrich themselves in the most
shameless fashion.

The main ruse was the abuse of preferential credit. As in Korea, the
central bank rediscounted commercial banks' loans – but without any
special focus on exports, and without an industrial strategy that was going
to lead to exports.[50] Two scholars who looked at the Central Bank of the
Philippines in the early 1980s concluded that 'virtually all economic activities can qualify for rediscounting ... the central bank is the "lender of first
resort".'[51] They noted that loans for activities including tobacco trading,
coconut milling and stock trading (the latter following a World Bank–
IMF report calling for the expansion of Filipino capital markets)[52] were
all rediscounted.

In the latter years of Marcos's rule, the banks of his leading cronies
funded a quarter to a half of their assets with central bank money. For
example, one of the banks of Roberto Benedicto, owner of the Hacienda
Esperanza sugar estate we visited in Negros, funded an average of half
its assets from 1979 to the onset of deep crisis in 1984 with central bank
rediscounts. Benedicto did almost no manufacturing and only exported
commodities; other than sugar, his main business interests were in media
and telecommunications. United Coconut Planters Bank, controlled by
Danding Cojuangco – the cock-fighting aficionado and Marcos super-
crony who still thrives in Negros – enjoyed rediscounts *and* interest-free
deposits from a state-mandated levy on coconut production. The latter was
a gargantuan subsidy, with the help of which Danding turned the country's
nineteenth bank by assets in 1976 into its fourth biggest by 1983. But he
contributed nothing to industrialisation (unless one counts beer and rum
production). Marcos himself used central bank-guaranteed foreign loans
to buy Manhattan real estate.[53]

The cause of the Philippines' downfall in the mid 1980s is often blamed
by Filipinos on what is known locally as DOSRI (loans to directors, officers, stockholders and related interests). The financial system collapsed in
an orgy of related-party lending. However, related-party lending was the

*proximate*, not the *ultimate* reason for the crisis. In Korea, the banks also did most of their lending to their owner – the state – and its favoured allies, such as Chung Ju Yung, but this did not result in collapse. Instead of related-party lending, the *ultimate* cause of the financial crises in the Philippines and other south-east Asian countries was the absence of export discipline for domestic firms and therefore the absence of the export information loop in the financial system. These missing components that are automatically in place when a policy of indigenous manufacturing for export is pursued allowed plunder to occur. As the author of the leading study of the Philippine financial sector put it: 'Unlike their counterparts in South Korea and Taiwan, Philippine entrepreneurs could quite easily take the money and run.'[54]

As a murderous financial crisis brewed in the Philippines in the early 1980s, the central bank did ever more rediscounting – pumping money into the economy – because it was the only way to keep the financial system afloat. With US interest rates peaking at 19 per cent and output shrinking, the Philippines could not cover the interest demanded to roll over foreign debt. Marcos instituted a repayment moratorium in October 1983. However, this only caused capital flight to accelerate, facilitated by the fact that most capital controls had been lifted in the early 1970s in line with IMF and World Bank advice. Printing money became the only form of finance left. Like Korea, the Philippines was used to an elevated inflation rate because of rediscounting, but price rises accelerated greatly in the mid 1980s. The inflation rate was 50 per cent in 1984 and the currency slid from 7.5 pesos to the dollar in 1980 to 20 in 1986. Following bank runs, bank nationalisations and the closure of large investment houses in 1981, another four banks had to be shut.[55] In February 1986, amid large-scale protests, Marcos fled on a US government airplane, at the zenith of a crisis in which the Philippine economy shrank by a quarter.[56]

The meltdown signalled the end of the Philippines' association with a particularly perverted form of developmental finance. In 1985, the central bank got rid of its multiple, below-market rediscounting rates that encouraged orgies of 'priority' lending in which the main priority was to plunder. The two big state institutions, Philippine National Bank and Development Bank of the Philippines, wrote down their assets (consisting mostly of loans) by 67 per cent and 86 per cent respectively after years of making 'behest' loans to Marcos's cronies. In 1993, the government moved debts of USD12 billion from the balance sheet of the central bank to that of the treasury. All this was paid for, in large part, by a tripling of domestic government debt in the late 1980s. The debt was deliberately issued in large-denomination bonds, which were beyond the reach of ordinary citizens who continued to keep their funds in the banking system, usually at negative real rates of interest. Banks recovered by borrowing for free from the public and investing the money in high-yield national debt.[57] It was much like Park Chung Hee's interest moratorium in 1972, except that in the Philippines the banking system produced zero developmental upside. Today, banking is dominated by (mostly newly licensed) private and foreign lenders which are kept on a shorter regulatory leash, are not offered rediscounts, and make very good profits. Of course, they still fail to finance industrial upgrading.

None the less, if Filipino governments are incapable of delivering infant industry policy and export discipline, it makes sense that they steer clear of expansive finance. The Philippines suffered everything that neo-classical economists warned in the 1950s and 1960s would come to pass in Korea because of Park Chung Hee's aggressive approach to the banking system. But there was no catastrophe in Korea because Park was spending money to secure technological progress. In the Philippines, it was a case of financial madness without the method. There was a prophetic photograph of Ferdinand Marcos that appeared in Filipino newspapers in late 1978, just when the endgame of his regime was beginning. It features Ferdy, Imelda, finance secretary Virata and central bank governor Licaros all standing with candles inside the national mint at Quezon City while the mint is blessed by a priest. Prominent in the foreground – on top of the printing press, but apparently unnoticed by those present – is a sign that says: 'Hands Off Please'.

### Failure despite prudence

If the Philippines learned that developmental success is not simply about the mobilisation of money, Malaysia and Thailand learned a harsher version of Taiwan's lesson – that financial prudence is less important than an acute focus on technological upgrading.

Malaysia was the most prudent of all the south-east Asian states, in part because of its close historical association (including an abortive two-year union from 1963 to 1965) with Singapore, an offshore financial centre. Offshore centres run conservative monetary and banking systems by their nature, because those attributes (and secrecy) are how they attract funds. Malaysia grew up in this conservative tradition, and did not launch its own currency until 1967; thereafter it maintained a fixed peg to the Singapore dollar until 1973. The central bank, Bank Negara Malaysia, was not truly independent of government, but it was raised in a tradition of orthodox monetary management and close supervision of banks. The institution was led by a single governor, Tun Ismail Mohamed Ali, before and after the currency split with Singapore, from 1962 to 1980.

As in Taiwan, government had all the control of the financial system that would be necessary in order to pursue effective development policy. As well as two large state-controlled banks, the government operated a mandatory central pension fund and other, voluntary savings schemes that could be used to direct savings to developmental objectives. One study put the government-controlled share of not just bank assets but *all* financial assets at a peak of 64 per cent in 1980, the year before Mahathir came to power.[58] However, no Malaysian leader, including Mahathir, used this money to support industrialisation based around exports.

Malaysia's central bank was more than bureaucratically capable of enforcing export discipline through preferential credit policies. But in the absence of political direction to do more, it undertook only a token amount of rediscounting of commercial banks' export loans. The main pro-active role played by Bank Negara Malaysia – one which was demanded by successive governments – was in affirmative action, where it forced subordinate banks to meet minimum lending quotas to *bumiputera* borrowers.[59] When it came to funding his big industrialisation projects, Mahathir circumvented the central bank. Instead he used foreign loans guaranteed by the treasury, and also tapped two domestic state banks, the government-run saving funds and the national oil company, Petronas. None of these institutions enforced export requirements, and over the years each was forced to write off billions of dollars of bad debts. Bank Bumiputera, a state-owned investment bank created in the 1960s, required repeated bail-outs.

Mahathir's uncertain ideological mix of north-east Asian planning *plus* deregulation and privatisation ran through his financial policy as it did his industrial policy. Just as he combined new, state-owned infant industry projects with a privatisation drive for older government businesses, so he combined state mobilisation of funds for his new industrial projects with the freeing up of other parts of the financial sector in a manner that reduced the state's longer-term capacity to shape development. This was particularly the case with banking deregulation and reforms that expanded the local stock market.

Early in his administration, just as he was backing projects like Perwaja and Proton, Mahathir was persuaded to liberalise interest rates. North-east Asian states employed interest rate ceilings throughout their core development periods because when banks are given the freedom to charge what they can, they move in the direction of consumer – as opposed to industrial – lending. This is exactly what happened in Mahathir's Malaysia. The easiest and most attractive place to make higher interest loans after deregulation was by lending for property development and mortgages, and there was an increase in the property sector share of bank credit from just over one-fifth in late 1970s to more than one-third in the 1980s.[60] While it was supposed to be industrialising, Malaysia was actually having a property boom. Kuala Lumpur, with its prematurely built luxury high-rises, contrasted powerfully with the capital of Taiwan, Taipei, which according to the Taiwan scholar Robert Wade still looked like 'a mix of shanty town and transit camp' in the late 1980s.[61] In Taiwan, financial resources were going overwhelmingly to industry.

In 1989, Mahathir's government passed a financial services law which deregulated the stock exchange. This paved the way for the Kuala Lumpur Stock Exchange (KLSE) to grow like topsy – unfortunately, the most prominent expression of Malaysia's development in the 1990s. During a bull run in 1993, the market's capitalisation increased to four times Malaysia's GDP, the highest such ratio in the world. Trading volume that year was more than for the whole of the previous decade and on some days exceeded the New York stock exchange. Even Mahathir's closest political ally, confidant and finance minister, Daim Zainuddin, was drawn to observe: 'Nobody seems to be working. Everyone talks only about shares.'[62]

The market ran out of steam in 1994, and collapsed in 1997. Eventually Malaysians and their government realised that a stock market did not of itself herald the dawn of modernity. It is difficult to see how the KLSE, or indeed any of the east Asian stock markets feted and encouraged by the World Bank and IMF in the 1990s, contributed significantly to developmental outcomes. The market did not, for instance, bring any appreciable shareholder discipline to bear on corporations, which barely noticed the existence of minority investors. Indeed, one reason firms were so keen to take cash from the markets was that those who provided it were less bothersome than bankers. Entrepreneurs frequently used a technique called 'pyramiding', that is, stacking listed companies on top of one another in a manner that allowed them to control firms at the bottom of the pyramid with tiny amounts of equity. They then stripped cash and other assets out of these businesses, ripping off minority investors. In Malaysia, huge insider trading gains were also made out of Mahathir's privatisations. These were allocated, untendered, to private firms, and commonly injected into listed businesses, giving anyone with inside information a chance to profit by buying shares of listed firms which were about to receive asset injections or by selling shares of listed firms which had first been pumped up by false rumours of asset injections.[63]

It was all great fun for insiders and, echoing countries like Russia, Malaysia produced a raft of new millionaire and billionaire financial speculators. But from a developmental perspective, the stock market adventure was at best a pointless diversion. Indeed it was probably worse than this, because lending for stock purchases crowded out industrial finance just like lending for real estate did. In the 1990s, only a quarter of Malaysian commercial bank loans went to manufacturing, agriculture, mining and other productive activities. A firm-level survey of private manufacturers by the central bank found that Malaysian companies met 10–14 per cent of their financing needs from banks, versus 40–50 per cent during the peak 1960s and 1970s industrialisation era in Japan, and more than 30 per cent in Taiwan. Malaysian firms were forced to depend much more heavily on their own retained earnings, a situation which could never meet the costs of sustained technological upgrading or produce firms of real scale.[64]

Malaysia never wanted for investible funds. The country's gross savings rate on the eve of the Asian financial crisis was several percentage points higher than Korea's.[65] But the funds were pointed at the wrong targets, and increasingly so because of the government's declining control over the financial system. Mahathir's stock market obsession was in large part driven by a nationalistic urge to outdo the financial markets of Singapore. The KLSE and the Singapore stock exchange had continued to be closely linked – effectively one market with two geographically separated trading floors – until 1990. Just as Korea was motivated by an historical animus towards Japan, so Malaysia retains one for its divorcee ex-partner of the 1960s. Unfortunately, aping the finance policy of an offshore financial centre, rather than that of an industrial state, was the last thing Malaysia needed to do.

Malaysia survived its poorly conceived industrialisation projects and its stock market and bank deregulation diversions because its monetary policy and bank supervision remained conservative. The central bank took the edge off the government's deregulation impetus, tightening its monitoring of banks in the late 1980s, and again in 1994, while continually pressing for consolidation of small institutions. It attempted to enforce a longstanding 20 per cent cap on individual ownership of banks, even though politicians repeatedly overrode this in the 1990s.[66] Non-bank financial institutions were kept under close control. And the central bank was able to ensure that the flood of foreign debt prior to the financial crisis was on average of a longer maturity than in Thailand and Indonesia, and more widely hedged against currency depreciation.

During the crisis, no Malaysian financial institution had to be shut down, although there were plenty of large bailouts of banks and politically linked companies, involving such traditional cash reservoirs as Petronas and the Employees Provident Fund.[67] In September 1997, Mahathir garnered global publicity when he railed to a joint IMF–World Bank annual meeting in Hong Kong that currency trading should be 'made illegal'. His position was no sillier than that of the IMF, which tried to use the meeting to amend its charter so it could push countries even harder on currency trading deregulation at a time when such deregulation had facilitated a regional meltdown. But the bigger reality was that Mahathir had himself wasted much of his premiership prematurely deregulating the currency trading, banking and financial markets in Malaysia. He showed up in Hong Kong like a bomb-maker protesting the existence of conflict.

## The rewards of obedience

Mahathir's attacks on the multilateral institutions, and Malaysia's belated, temporary reintroduction of capital controls in 1998, turned him into the 'bad boy' of the Asian financial crisis.[68] The Thai government, by contrast, remained the star pupil of the IMF and World Bank. That Thailand has fallen farther than any other country in the region since the crisis is an unfortunate comment on this status. Thailand was also the country where the Asian financial crisis began.

Uniquely among south-east Asian states, Thailand was never colonised. None the less, the country has a long history of accepting bad advice. From the time of the Bowring Treaty with Britain in 1855 until 1926, Thailand was persuaded by British negotiators to run the lowest import tariff in Asia – just 3 per cent. This ensured there could be no protectionist infant industry policy, as a result of which no internationally competitive Thai firms developed. Domestic financial institutions also remained weak, mean-ing that foreign firms dominated any part of the economy that required concentrated capital. This included tin mining, saw mills and shipping – not to mention banking itself. The most capital-intensive activity domes-tic entrepreneurs successfully engaged in before the end of the absolute monarchy in 1932 was rice milling, where the requisite equipment was relatively cheap.

During and immediately after the Second World War, the absence of Europeans and Americans and the presence of a now more developed state bureaucracy allowed local entrepreneurs to enter banking and insurance for the first time. Four substantial Thai financial groups evolved in this period.[69] Indeed, the biggest of these institutions, Bangkok Bank, became the largest bank in south-east Asia. As noted before, Thai governments in this period also began the longest-run strategy of import substitution industrialisa-tion in south-east Asia, with numerous sectoral development campaigns until the 1980s. The private banks financed this, and took small equity positions in many businesses. In the absence of export discipline, however, manufacturers did not make products that were globally competitive.[70]

The powerful banking groups – which were privately controlled but underpinned by military, royal and government equity – were kept in check by south-east Asia's most independent, orthodox and professional central bank. The Bank of Thailand (BOT), set up in 1942, had close relations from the late 1940s with the World Bank and the IMF, which provided ongoing training for its staff.[71] BOT officials came to see themselves as not so much managers of development but as the honest policemen in a country prone to cronyistic business behaviour. As with Bank Negara Malaysia, there was only a modest and non-inflationary amount of rediscounting of bank loans by the central bank, and in Thailand most of this went not to manufacturing but to key export crops, of which much the most important was rice. The share of commercial bank lending going to manufacturing rose only slowly, from 10 per cent in 1958 to around a quarter in the late 1980s. This was roughly on a par with Malaysia. The difference between the two countries' loan profiles until the late 1980s was that the share of Thai lending to the property sector was much lower.[72]

The Thai government's financial policy weakness, however, was that from the 1970s it licensed a substantial number of non-bank finance and securities firms. This was designed to attract additional deposits to higher yield accounts outside the formal banking sector, providing new sources of finance in the straitened decade of the oil crises, and creating more competition for the regular banks. The logic was not dissimilar to that which saw non-bank financial institutions licensed in Korea as replacements for the kerb market in the 1970s, except that in Korea these operated in an export-disciplined economy. In both places, NBFIs were subject to capture by entrepreneurial interests. Unsurprisingly, the results were more immediately negative in Thailand. A series of rescues and finance company closures in the mid 1980s affected institutions that held one-quarter of all financial system assets, and highlighted the risks of financial system capture.[73]

Despite this, the IMF and the World Bank stepped up their campaign for accelerated financial sector deregulation, and the NBFI crisis had no discernible effect on the Thai government's willingness to accept their advice. This tendency was exacerbated by the fact that, by the 1980s, almost all economists recruited to government and the Bank of Thailand were US-trained, and enthusiastic believers in universally applicable, deregulation-focused financial policies. From 1989 to 1991, Thailand's interest rates were almost completely liberalised, with loan and deposit interest ceilings effectively abolished. Together with the licensing of even more non-bank financial institutions, the further loosening of restrictions relating to the stock market and the lifting of most remaining capital controls, this ushered in the kind of consumer-based financial boom that occurred in Malaysia.[74] Except that Thailand experienced even greater financial system capture because its central bank's prudential supervision was undermined by the expansion of non-bank financial institutions, which were easier for entrepreneurs to hijack.

As elsewhere in south-east Asia, the rapid growth of low value-added processing exports by foreign multinationals beginning in the late 1980s helped convince the Thai government that it was managing development competently. And – again as elsewhere in south-east Asia – Thailand was never short of investible funds. From the 1950s on, the rise in bank savings far outpaced economic growth. The aggregate gross savings rate in the period immediately before the 1997 crisis was 35 per cent, on par with that of Korea and only slightly behind Malaysia's.[75] The problem was once again the lack of an effective infant industry policy combined with premature financial deregulation. These two things meant that abundant Thai savings – augmented by unnecessary and speculative foreign capital – ended up in the wrong places, most obviously speculative real estate investments. Thailand became the world's fastest growing economy in the decade 1987–96, but this did not signify long-lasting economic development.[76]

A Thai real estate boom that began in the late 1980s accelerated markedly in the early 1990s. From 1988 to 1996, official figures (which likely understate reality) show that the real estate lending share went from 6 per cent to 15 per cent of bank assets, and from 9 per cent to 24 per cent of finance company assets.[77] A booming Bangkok stock market, whose index rose from 600 in 1990 to over 1,400 in 1996, provided more funds for investment, which often went into the real estate sector. And an unknown proportion of short-term foreign loans, which spiralled to almost a quarter of Thai aggregate investment in the years before the crisis, went to real estate.[78]

The lack of export discipline, and the absence of any defence mechanism based on capital controls, meant that disaster could be seen arriving like an oil tanker appearing over the horizon. As the asset bubble inflated, Thailand acquired an annual current account deficit in the 1990s of between −5 per cent and −8 per cent of GDP. This signal alone was reason enough for currency traders to take short positions against the now freely tradable baht, which it was government policy to hold steady against the dollar. The nation's foreign exchange reserves were expended defending the indefensible, before the government let the currency float on 2 July 1997. That date marked the official commencement of the Asian crisis.

Thailand suffered the worst initial economic contraction of any country in east Asia. As soon as the IMF was called in, it insisted the government imbibe a draught of the anti-spendthrift, anti-inflationary medicine it developed in Latin America in the 1980s. Since Thailand did not have a problem with inflated government budgets, expenditure cuts of around one-fifth and tax rises sent the economy into a tailspin, contracting 14 per cent in domestic currency terms between 1996 and 1998.[79] And the closure of fifty-six of ninety-one non-bank financial institutions in 1997 left both good and bad borrowers without access to working capital. The IMF did not understand what was going on. Part of the problem was the agency's need to come to terms with what a mess its 'star pupil' was really in. The Fund's predictions for Thai economic growth in 1998 shifted from 3.5 per cent just after the crisis broke in August 1997 to −7 per cent a year later – a reflection of how little the institution really knew about the country.[80]

In summer 1998 there were popular protests against austerity (particularly in rural areas) and a voluble campaign against forced sell-offs of Thai companies to foreign interests. Meanwhile, serving and former ministers began to criticise the IMF in the press. In August, the Fund accepted that there had been some misdiagnosis of Thailand's problems, agreeing to let the government run a budget deficit, while the Bank of Thailand began to cut interest rates. There was a modest economic recovery in 1999, but it was not until 2003 that Thailand regained its 1996 GDP. In terms of the privatisation and foreign sale of companies, the government pulled back somewhat from the IMF's original demands. Two banks were sold to foreign interests, others were recapitalised through minority foreign investments, and others still were nationalised.[81]

Overall, if the financial system had not supported an export-oriented manufacturing policy before 1997, it was even less likely to do so afterwards. For the last fifteen years, Thailand has lurched from one political crisis to the next as it has tried to find some route on to the road to development. Since the country was travelling in completely the wrong direction before 1997, this has been no easy task. Instead of globally competitive industry, the financial sector's most striking legacy in the past half century has been the endless square kilometres of drab, low-grade cement construction that confront the visitor when driving through the Bangkok megalopolis. When the equatorial rains come, it can appear unbelievably ugly – as if all the gods were weeping at once over man's developmental failings.

### Journey 5: Jakarta

*And so to our final journey. It takes us to the capital of Indonesia, a country whose post-independence history is dominated by not one, but two gargantuan financial crises. The more recent, 1997 crisis was identified with Suharto, who pursued free market financial reforms in accordance with IMF and World Bank advice. The earlier, 1965 crisis occurred on the watch of the first president, Sukarno, and was the denouement of a socialist modernisation drive. The chaos of that year was made famous by the movie* The Year of Living Dangerously. *In the standard narrative the two financial meltdowns, separated by three decades, were the products of two opposing – capitalist and socialist – approaches to economic development. When viewed through the prism of financial policy and, more generally, the arguments put forward in this book, however, it becomes clear that both crises were precipitated by the same thing: the state's failure to exercise control over the financial system, and to target its efforts at manufacturing and export development. Indonesia's 'socialist' and 'capitalist' catastrophes were really variations on the same deficiency.*

This can be illustrated during a straight, north–south drive across Jakarta. Our route begins not far from the original port that sits on Jakarta Bay on the Java sea in the north. This is Chinatown, the messy commercial heart of old Jakarta before the capital's centre of gravity moved south in the

1980s. Turning into one of the residential lanes off Jalan Gunung Sahari, the driver asks an old man for the house of Om Liem ('Uncle Liem'), as the man who became Indonesia's richest post-independence tycoon is deferentially known. The neighbour slowly points to the far end of the street and we proceed.

Liem Sioe Liong, a billionaire whose companies were reckoned by the 1990s to account for 5 per cent of Indonesian GDP, fled to Singapore during the 1997 crisis, when the mob looted his house and painted 'Suharto's Dog' on the gate. He never moved back to Jakarta. The family still owns the property and occasionally makes use of it. It has been repaired and has a new, higher metal gate. Apart from this, the place is just as it had long been described to me: a modest, rather featureless white bungalow. The window frames are of a cheap and cheerful aluminium variety not associated in the popular imagination with great wealth. Visitors to the house when Om Liem lived here were struck by how little there was in it. Like Chung Ju Yung in Korea, the entrepreneur conserved his capital and did not change his home when he made it big; indeed, he continued to live in a part of town which is today considered distinctly unfashionable. The house, which Liem considered lucky, is a reminder that the nature of entrepreneurs is a constant in development; it is the policies which surround them that vary.[82]

Liem was right to think that he had been lucky. For half a century, under both Sukarno and Suharto, he was granted concessions to own banks and domestic monopolies and oligopolies without ever having to apply his considerable entrepreneurial talents to manufacturing for export or, more broadly, to the technological development of his country. Liem's luck began in the run-up to the nationalist war against the Dutch. A small-time immigrant Chinese trader from Fujian, he was asked by nationalists in Kudus, Java, to provide refuge for Sukarno's dissident father-in-law, Hassan Din. During the war against the Dutch, Liem sold supplies to republican forces.[83] After independence in 1949, he prospered as a well-connected trader, particularly with the military. Like scores of other entrepreneurs, Liem was licensed by Sukarno's government to open private banks. There were 104 in Indonesia by 1957, of which he owned two.

Liem's big break came with Suharto's slow-motion 1965–8 coup. He had come into contact with Suharto through trading activities in central Java, where the future president was an entrepreneurial military commander.[84] After his ascent to the presidency, Suharto showered Liem with monopoly and oligopoly concessions for clove imports (used in the *kretek* cigarettes favoured in Indonesia), flour milling, cement, finished steel products, and more. Most of these deals were in partnership with Suharto family members. As had been the case when Sukarno dispensed largesse, all these concessions came without requirements to develop industrial capabilities or exports. The only significant exports Liem produced were plantation crops and timber; his partners, the president's children, did not even think about competing internationally. Liem became the country's preeminent businessman, sucking out much of the profit from staple businesses like cigarettes, noodle-making and construction materials. His activities did nothing to advance Indonesia's technological progress yet, as many Indonesians observed at the time, before long it was impossible to get through a day without spending money at one of his businesses.

In the 1970s, Om Liem began to expand his banking operations. He recruited Mochtar Riady, an established banker, to build up one of the banks he started in the 1950s. He also took in the Suharto family as his substantial minority partners. Riady, who also had equity, quickly built Bank Central Asia (BCA) into Indonesia's largest private financial institution, creating a neat circle that connected the country's largest supply of private credit to its biggest, and ever-expanding, portfolio of domestic monopolies – firms like national cement maker Indocement; national flour producer Bogosari; car assembler IndoMobil; and the Suhartos toll roads. According to present and former directors, in the run-up to the 1997 crisis, BCA was lending 60 per cent of its funds to Liem businesses, and 30 per cent to Suharto ones.[85]

It seemed that Om Liem had all the angles covered. Although BCA's lending was thoroughly cronyistic – no bank was legally permitted to lend more than 20 per cent of funds to related parties, though they all did – it dealt overwhelmingly with cash-churning monopolies like the flour, cement and toll road businesses that faced no competition. More risky adventures, such as the real estate projects and non-monopoly business investments pursued by Suharto's children, were politely referred to Indonesia's state-owned banks. At the time of the 1997 crisis, BCA had far fewer non-performing loans than other Indonesian banks.[86] The problem, however, was that BCA was part of a larger financial system that targeted credit at non-productive, non-export-oriented activities and one in which rival banks did not have monopolies to lend to. In the era of deregulation, the system therefore financed increasing amounts of speculative activity, particularly real estate, often doing so using foreign debt. Om Liem was very smart and very conservative, but he could not insure against systemic failure.

When the Asian crisis spread from Thailand to Indonesia, there was so much panic that BCA, Liem Sioe Liong, the Suhartos and all their monopolies went down with it. The rupiah's value started to fall at the end of 1997 and it quickly became apparent that the banking system as a whole would be unable to meet its foreign obligations. Bank runs ensued without reference to the particular solvency of individual banks. An extraordinary IDR65 trillion (around USD8 billion)[87] was withdrawn from BCA in two weeks as depositor queues snaked around its branches. Liem Sioe Liong was required to put up collateral assets to cover money the central bank lent BCA to pay out its depositors. He handed over assets he said were worth IDR53 trillion, but, when the businesses and land that comprised them were sold, only IDR20 trillion was raised. By Indonesian standards, this actually turned out to be one of the highest rates of debt repayment. What the country's tycoons could not – or, more often, would not – cover as their banks went bust, was covered by the Indonesian taxpayer. Om Liem lost control of BCA and a large part of his empire, but he kept a decent chunk, living out his days in Singapore.[88] It turned out that even the smartest tycoon in a failed developmental system was not quite smart enough.

### Rewind to Sukarno

In order to reconnect the 1997 crisis back to 1965 – the first of Indonesia's *two* years of living dangerously – we turn off Om Liem's lane, and head further south. The road tracks the easterly of two parallel, north–south canals built by the Dutch. The land between them defines the old city centre of the colonial and Sukarno eras. Turning into this area along Jalan Veteran, one is suddenly awed by the looming, 120,000-capacity Istiqlal national mosque. To the mosque's south-west, surrounded by broad avenues and large state buildings, is the 132-metre Monas pillar at the centre of Independence Square, with its carved flame. We are now among Sukarno's greatest monuments.[89]

Sukarno was trained as an architect and civil engineer, with a curiously dualistic taste for minimalist modernism, on the one hand, and exuberant, baroque sculptures, on the other. He planned, literally, to build a new Indonesia. To the south of Independence Square, he created the spine of a new capital, the long, multi-lane thoroughfare that at different points is called Jalan Thamrin, Jalan Sudirman and Jalan Sisingamangaraja. As we follow this road, it passes Sarinah, a large department store planned by Sukarno and, further south, what used to be the luxury Hotel Indonesia (now the Kempinski), where the journalists drink in the Wayang bar in *The Year of Living Dangerously*. One gets an immediate sense of Sukarno's developmental priorities. Outside the hotel is a roundabout with a giant, heroic sculpture of two exultant figures, reminiscent of the opening scene of *The Sound Of Music*. Then comes the Semanggi bridge intersection, with its feeder lanes cleverly built to create the shape of a four-leaf clover. To the west is the Senayan stadium, constructed for the 1962 Asian Games. Further south, there is another roundabout with another monumental sculpture – a male figure with head raised, holding a large, flat object aloft and known locally as the Pizza Delivery Man.[90] Sukarno's monuments to socialist architectural passion extend some five kilometres from Monas.

Sukarno ran out of money, but not simply because he was a spendthrift when it came to monuments. He had no viable policy for the industrial development of Indonesia, and no interest in exports. In the early 1950s, Sukarno's administration created a central bank, which was authorised to undertake commercial lending, and three other state-owned development banks. These institutions could have been the financial apparatus for effective infant industry policy. But the state banks, which extended the vast majority of domestic credit, actively discouraged exports. The biggest credit line made available in the 1950s was loans to importers, as the government pursued an affirmative action programme called Benteng (the term means 'fortress') to encourage indigenous traders. The policy allowed already-wealthy *pribumi* families – the Indonesian term signifying the indigenous peoples of the archipelago, equivalent to the Malaysian term *bumiputera* – to make huge profits by importing luxury goods, or by selling their trading licences on to the ethnic Chinese or Dutch firms they were supposed to replace (like Om Liem's).[91] At the same time, the government licensed the proliferation of private banks that were unconstrained as to how they lent, and that were also allowed to borrow at will from the central bank. They funded whatever activities their owners saw fit – usually their own.

Indonesia's political and economic conditions deteriorated in the 1950s and Sukarno declared martial law in 1957, promising a more focused, state-led developmental effort. He removed remaining legal guarantees of central bank independence (just as Park Chung Hee would in 1961). He made the state banks almost completely dominant in the allocation of credit and focused them on supporting businesses that he nationalised from the Dutch. Bank Indonesia was told both to lend directly to favoured projects and to rediscount aggressively to the banking system. But credit allocation was still not linked to an industrial policy and to export performance. As an almost inevitable result, funds continued to be provided for wholly unproductive purposes, such as hoarding food staples in times of high inflation in order to sell later for a higher price.

Indonesia in the early 1960s became a zero-discipline financial environment. The central bank fed the beast of credit demand unquestioningly, printing so much money that the economy experienced hyperinflation. Sukarno, however, remained unbowed in his efforts to make the financial system deliver development. As he moved closer to the Indonesian Communist Party (PKI) in his final years, he hatched a last-gasp plan with Jusuf Musa Dalam, the Bank Indonesia governor, to roll all the banks up into a single, giant 'fighting bank'. This would have been in line with the Stalinist and Maoist 'mono-bank' systems. Sukarno called his August 1964 National Day speech 'The Year of Dangerous Living' and told his people to get ready for revolutionary sacrifice. But before this final adventure could be launched, the army and Suharto – following an abortive coup by left-wing army officers in September 1965 – began to curtail Sukarno's power and move towards what they claimed was a fundamentally different model of economic development. And yet it was not.

## Calling in the Berkeley Mafia

To the east of the stretch of Sukarno's Jalan Sudirman between the *Sound of Music* statue and Semanggi bridge lies the area of the city that came to be associated with Suharto's rule. This is the so-called Golden Triangle, enclosed by the thoroughfares Sudirman, Rasuna Said and Gatot Sub- roto. The high-rise district's constant growth in the 1970s, 1980s and 1990s appeared to signal the discovery of a new developmental model. It was, however, a false dawn. Today – just as we saw at the north end of Jalan Sultan Ismail in Kuala Lumpur – the Golden Triangle contains unfinished mega-projects from before the Asian crisis. The most striking are the giant stubs of two I. M. Pei-designed towers for Sjamsul Nursalim's Bank Dagang Nasional Indonesia (BDNI), on the west side of Jalan Sudirman by the Le Meridien hotel. The site has been at a standstill for fifteen years.[92]

Suharto tamed inflation and restored macro-economic stability to Indo- nesia. But he did little more to focus leading domestic entrepreneurs on manufacturing or exports than did Sukarno. Instead, Suharto promoted the Berkeley Mafia, who wooed footloose multinational companies to produce exports. After the Berkeley Mafia returned from the University of California to Indonesia to teach in the 1960s, one of the places they lectured was SESKOAD, the army staff and command college for senior military officers in Bandung. It was via SESKOAD that the group's members, led by Widjojo Nitisastro, came into contact with Suharto. Under Sukarno, they had no influence, but when Suharto formed his first cabinet after he became president in 1968, each of the five core Berkeley Mafia economists received a ministerial post.[93] In these roles, they reined in the central bank, imposed credit ceilings on commercial banks, created hard budget constraints for ministries and oversaw new legislation favourable to multinational firms.

The influence on Suharto of the Berkeley Mafia – and its orthodox financial policy prescriptions – rose and fell over the years depending on the state of the government's budget. Suharto always had his doubts that the answers proffered by his American-trained economists were sufficient for Indonesia's development. But unlike someone like Park Chung Hee, his education and life experience gave him no clear developmental convictions of his own. In the late 1960s, Widjojo Nitisastro and his colleagues were paramount. However, in the 1970s oil boom, when petroleum receipts came to make up two-thirds of the government's budget, contra to their advice Suharto authorised a big increase in central bank preferential credit and a first round of mostly public sector investments in steel, chemicals, fertiliser, aluminium and machine tools. But there was no serious effort to push private entrepreneurs into manufacturing and no export discipline. In the early 1980s the oil price fell precipitously, plunging the budget into deficit and the country into a balance of payments crisis. Suharto turned back to the Berkeley Mafia, who further liberalised foreign investment, cut direct central bank lending, squeezed rediscounting and liberalised interest rates. As the economy picked up amid a foreign investment boom, Suharto began to indulge B. J. Habibie, a German-trained aircraft engineer he appointed Minister for Research and Technology in 1978, with increased budgets. But then came a downturn at the end of the 1980s, when the Berkeley Mafia were allowed to apply their most radical reforms to the financial system. Finally, in the boom immediately before the 1997 crisis, Suharto was leaning towards Habibie again.[94]

The Berkeley Mafia were not hardened ideologues, but they believed that only the market could overcome Indonesia's tendency to crony capitalism. A peripheral member of the group offers an anecdote which helps explain why the economists felt more and more compelled to seek solutions in financial deregulation. Soedradjad Djiwandono, who was governor of the central bank from 1993 until 1998, recalls receiving a letter in late 1996 from Tommy Suharto.[95] The president's youngest son wrote that he had two state banks willing to lend him more than USD1 billion for a car plant. However, such huge loans would breech the central bank's rules on individual banks' exposure to a single project. 'He was asking,' says Soedradjad, '"What can you do for me?"'

Everyone in Jakarta knew that Tommy's Timor car project was a scam that undermined even the very modest infant industry achievements of existing car assemblers. He had been authorised to import 45,000 Kia vehicles and simply rebadge them, before moving on to pure kit assembly.[96] Soedradjad put the letter in a desk drawer and hoped Tommy would go away. Three months later, he was summoned to the president's home on

Jalan Cendana in Menteng, where Suharto had a copy of the letter sitting on
his desk. Soedradjad feigned ignorance, before vaguely recalling the letter
and suggesting that it would be a dangerous signal to the banking system if
Tommy were to receive an exemption from central bank rules. It was clear,
however, that the president wanted his favourite son provided for, however
contrary to Indonesia's interests his car project might be. Soedradjad floated
the possibility of putting together a larger bank consortium that would not
breech central bank guidelines. 'Do that,' Suharto told him. According to
Soedradjad, Bank Indonesia then set out to lend Tommy as little money
as possible. He claims Tommy was asking for USD1.3 billion and ended up
with USD300 million. All the money was written off in the Asian crisis.

It was this context – with Suharto unable to discipline his own family,
let alone proper entrepreneurs – that made the Berkeley Mafia conclude
that moves to financial deregulation were essential. Their logic (and that of
the IMF and World Bank representatives with whom they worked closely)
was that, if it was fully deregulated and privatised, the banking sector would
not indulge people like Tommy. From late 1988, the technocrats therefore
began their final push towards open financial markets. The assault was
led by the finance minister, Johannes Sumarlin, a member of the earliest
Berkeley cadre whose career blossomed late. Sumarlin followed up the early
1980s deregulation of interest rates with a paid-up capital requirement of
just USD16 million for new private banks. He cut the reserve requirement
– the share of a bank's assets it must keep on hold with the central bank,
partly as a matter of prudence – from 15 per cent to 2 per cent. He liberalised rules governing the stock market. And his allies at Bank Indonesia
put a further big squeeze on central bank rediscounting to the state banks.

The net effects were a roster of private banks that increased from sixty-
six in 1988 to 160 in 1993, and a booming stock market. The total number
of local and foreign banks operating in Indonesia by 1993 was 234. Since
the Berkeley Mafia had lifted Indonesia's capital controls way back in the
early 1970s at the end of their first ascendancy, the country was also open to
the full force of international capital flows. Radius Prawiro, Co-ordinating
Minister for the Economy at the time of the late 1980s changes, declared:
'We ... abandoned our own earlier vision of mercantilism ... and, instead,
discovered the wisdom of the market economy.'[97]

## The road to financial hell

The headquarters of Indonesia's old banks such as Bank Central Asia are concentrated near that of the central bank at the north end of Sukarno's north–south spine on the part named Jalan Thamrin. But the road to 1990s financial hell was the Jalan Sudirman stretch of the spine, down through the Golden Triangle and past the Semanggi bridge to the Pizza Delivery Man roundabout. Altogether the stretch is something over three kilometres. It is along this road that the Berkeley Mafia and the real Jakarta mafia – inadvertently assisted by the Rolling Stones' Mick Jagger – brought financial deregulation to a devastating conclusion.

The Golden Triangle part is where most of the scores of new bank headquarters were thrown up beginning in 1988. Many of the banks on this 'Bank Alley' have disappeared since the crisis, but the buildings remain, one after the other down the boulevard. Plus there are the uncompleted projects, like the BDNI twin towers. Further south, much of the land at the farthest reaches of Sudirman, south of the Semanggi bridge, was a squatter slum when the final push on financial deregulation began. This area became the site for a new, purpose-built financial zone known as the Sudirman Central Business District (SCBD).

The story of the SCBD began in the same month that Sumarlin opened up the banking sector, when Mick Jagger (temporarily estranged from the rest of the Rolling Stones) held a concert in the Senayan stadium on the opposite side of the road. It was a Sunday, and thousands of unoccupied youths from the squats turned up to try and crash the gig. While Jagger worked through a set list that included 'Can't You Hear Me Knocking?' and 'Gimme Shelter', the young men from the squats smashed cars, burned tyres and fought running battles with security personnel. In the weeks that followed, the violence provided the impetus – some said, the convenient excuse – for 40 hectares of squatter land to be summarily and ruthlessly cleared. Given the southward push of the mushrooming financial sector, the land was very valuable.

The clearance was undertaken by associates of Tomy Winata, a military-linked entrepreneur popularly believed to control much of Jakarta's gambling, vice and protection rackets. Winata and the army pension fund then became the owners of the giant site. Here, Winata constructed a huge new stock exchange, office buildings for brokerages and even more banks, and a new headquarters for his own bank. Fittingly, the World Bank relocated its operation to Tomy's SCBD. Winata also put up, hard by the stock exchange, what he claimed to be the biggest nightclub in the world, the Bengkel Night Park Entertainment Centre, with room for 15,000 people.[98] The VIP rooms offered full-nudity striptease and the range of drugs that could be had in the club was said to be as good as anything in New York or London. Jakarta was primed for high finance.

Setting the financial pace for Bank Alley, Winata injected his interest in the land into an already listed business, a so-called 'back-door' listing. He raised capital by selling new shares, and later spun off some equity in his SCBD properties by listing another subsidiary.[99] In 1989, the Jakarta stock exchange became the fastest-growing bourse in the world and other entrepreneurs more than matched Winata's flair for financial creativity. The eldest son of Indonesia's number two business dynasty, the Soeryadjayas, took over a tiny private bank in May 1989, offered high interest rates to depositors, and had 150,000 accounts and a USD1 billion balance sheet within two years.[100] The private bank of former oil chief Ibnu Sutowo's family issued USD1 billion of high yield offshore commercial paper.[101] By the mid 1990s, every major business group had one or two banks, and for the first time in post-independence history private banks accounted for the bulk of bank system assets.[102] Bank Alley was humming and Indonesia's tycoons, Tomy Winata, the Berkeley Mafia, the IMF and the World Bank were all happy.

## Gimme shelter

The problem was that, despite the deregulation, nothing had changed to direct the financial system towards more developmentally useful or sustainable lending. The economists of the Berkeley Mafia, the IMF and the World Bank took the view that Indonesia had only a small current account deficit – it was much smaller than Thailand's, at only 3.5 per cent of GDP in 1996 – and so the economy was in good shape. But most exports came from flighty multinational processing operations, which in the mid 1990s were already being tempted by cheaper labour, better infrastructure and better supply chains in coastal China. The Indonesian government did belatedly tell its biggest conglomerates to do more manufacturing for export. But all that happened was Liem Sioe Liong opened some shoe and toy processing operations and the Soeryadjayas shipped batteries, spark plugs and Toyota engines assembled from kits.[103] Such projects did not involve serious technological progress and there was no general export focus to inform credit allocation.

Soedradjad Djiwandono, the central bank governor in the run-up to the crisis, contends that rediscounting to exporters 'was not really needed' because most exports came from small enterprises which self-financed their activities.[104] But this is to miss the biggest lesson that north-east Asia can teach us about financial system management: that governments must use their control of money to lure and cajole leading entrepreneurs into concentrating on manufacturing and international markets. Emil Salim, one of the five original Berkeley Mafia members, retorts with the stock response that the use of export subsidies leads to counter-measures by trade partners. 'They retaliate,' he says.[105] But, as the cases of Japan, Korea, Taiwan and now China testify, trade relationships are not as simple or as symmetrical as that remark implies. It took a very long time for anyone to retaliate against the first three, and the same is proving to be the case with China. Moreover, to act on the basis that what worked for everybody else cannot work for you is – to adapt Friedrich List's metaphor – like kicking away the ladder of progress yourself from below.

Indonesia in the 1990s offered up an exhibition of what happens in deregulated financial markets in developing countries in the absence of export discipline. An ominous trail of disasters began to stack up soon after Sumarlin's October 1988 reform package. In 1992 Bank Summa, started by the Soeryadjaya family's eldest son, collapsed with debts of nearly USD800 million. Summa's loan portfolio, built up in only two years, was a fair proxy for what was happening in a lot of banks. In a rising real estate market, Edward Soeryadjaya bought large tracts of land in Jakarta, Surabaya and Bandung; six luxury hotels; and more property in Singapore and Vietnam.[106] The majority of Bank Summa's assets were real estate. Then interest rates rose, the real estate market corrected, and the bank went bust. The

Soeryadjaya family had to sell the major assets in their conglomerate (the second biggest group in the country) to pay out depositors. In early 1993, Summa was closed down.

In 1994, state bank Bapindo (recently relocated to Tomy Winata's new financial district) went bust. Eddy Tansil – somewhere between a conman and a businessman – had embezzled much of the USD520 million he was able to borrow from the bank using letters of support from Tommy Suharto and two government ministers. In striking contrast to the northeast Asian export letter of credit system as a means to securing a bank loan, Tansil managed to get money as a pre-shipment advance on imports he had not even ordered.[107] Tansil's wife captured the *zeitgeist* of the era when she turned up to his trial wearing a bright red dress with a big dollar sign on the front. Tansil was briefly jailed, escaped prison and fled, leaving his elder brother Hendra Rahardja operating two private banks in Indonesia. These both went bust in the Asian crisis and Rahardja was sentenced to life in prison *in absentia* in 2002 for swindling the central bank out of more than USD200 million. Impressively, a single family managed to loot and destroy both public and private banks.[108]

The next forewarning that a major crisis was brewing occurred when the Sutowos' Bank Pacific could no longer service its USD1 billion of offshore commercial paper. Deregulation had allowed Pacific to sell the kind of short-term 270-day bonds which, in the United States, are only issued by blue chip firms. In the immature east Asian market, a business run by a family with a thirty-year record of fraud and mismanagement could sell such paper. The credulous buyers were mostly other, recently deregulated Asian banks.

By 1996, the central bank was sufficiently nervous to state publicly that seventy commercial banks were exceeding statutory related-party lending limits.[109] But nothing changed. Bankers already operated on the assumption that *everyone* was breaking related-party limits. Loans to non-productive, domestic economy investments – with real estate in the lead – continued apace until the lid blew off the financial system in the second half of 1997. Once the Thai baht was floated in July, foreign lenders stopped rolling over short-term loans around the region. The effect was more than enough to trigger a deep crisis.

**Re-enter the cavalry**

When the crisis broke, and the IMF was called in, Fund experts had no good ideas about what to do because, like Dr Frankenstein, it had been they who had created this new kind of monster with their deregulation policies. Used to the spendthrift governments of Latin America, the IMF prescribed budget cuts and high interest rates, as it had in Thailand. However, the problem throughout the region was not government budgets, but a private sector speculative frenzy made possible by financial deregulation and the absence of effective development policy. IMF austerity merely throttled the real economy.

Financial deregulation had led to a boom in unhedged short-term offshore borrowing by banks and large, non-exporting firms. Such loans outstanding in Indonesia doubled in the eighteen months before the crisis and, as borrowers scrambled for dollars to repay them, they drove the rupiah exchange rate through the floor.[110] An exchange rate which dropped from 2,500 to the dollar in July 1997 to a monthly low of 14,000 in July 1998 meant a collapse of import purchasing power, including for inputs needed by Indonesia's overwhelmingly small-scale manufacturers. The disruption to the banking system left manufacturing firms reaching desperately for barter deals. There was also a physical shortage of containers for export manufacturers in Java because so few containers were arriving and none was manufactured locally. Indonesia's exports, running at USD4.2 billion a month in July 1997, fell to USD1.4 billion in March 1998.

The price for premature financial deregulation was very high. Many manufacturing firms never recovered from the crisis. The economy shrank by a fifth and 15 million people lost their jobs. It took more than a year before the Indonesian government, like the Thai one, began to doubt IMF advice and pumped some money into the economy. Even then, it was not until 2005 that Indonesia regained the level of GDP per capita that it had in 1996.[111] By the time Bank Alley ceased to be Bank Alley, fifty financial institutions had been closed, twenty-six had been taken over by the Indonesian Bank Restructuring Agency (IBRA), twelve had been nationalised, and four out of seven state banks had merged.[112]

The IMF did largely have its way with the restructuring of the financial system. Partly, this was a condition of the USD23 billion funding package the IMF organised, which stabilised the crisis and ensured foreign creditors who fed the borrowing binge were paid out in full. Three substantial state banks were retained, but their activities were circumscribed by a continued absence of preferential credit and by fully deregulated interest rates. The major private banks were all sold off to foreign investors. Om Liem's BCA, initially purchased by a US hedge fund, was later bought out by Indonesian tobacco magnate Budi Hartono, but some of its senior management remains foreign.[113] Overall, the banking system has been structured as one that lends reluctantly (with a bias to consumer lending) and expensively. This produces excellent profits for BCA and the foreign banks, but the system is probably less attuned to industrial development than at any point since independence in 1949. The post-crisis financial system has so far been safe, but it is far removed from what Indonesia needs.

**Financial home truths**

The essential takeaway from east Asian financial history is that all kinds of approaches to both monetary policy and financial system management have been tried, but what finance is acting on has been far more important than the financial arrangements themselves. The financier has not been the decisive element in the economic development puzzle that many economists claim.[114] As a developmental actor, he is defined by and responds to the operating environment around him. It falls to governments to shape that environment and to decide what objectives finance will have.

Control is the key. The successful developing state points financial institutions at the necessary agricultural and export-benchmarked infant industry policies. The state also closes out the possibility that finance will look offshore to alternative opportunities, or that flows of foreign funds will disrupt its plans. It does this by imposing capital controls. The financial deregulation urged by parties to the Washington Consensus does not present a viable alternative to this strategy. Deregulation policies do not empower a 'natural' tendency for finance to lead a society from poverty to wealth, they simply put short-term profit and the interests of consumers ahead of developmental learning and agricultural and industrial upgrading. There is no case for doing this when a country is poor.

At best, the developmental emphasis of the IMF, the World Bank and the US government on financial sector deregulation in recent decades has been a waste of time. More commonly, the policy advice has had clear negative consequences. In forcing the pace of banking deregulation, capital account liberalisation and stock market development, the Washington Consensus has undermined east Asian countries' capacity to shape their development and has greatly increased the risk of financial crises. The risk came home to roost for the Philippines in the 1980s, and for the rest of south-east Asia in 1997. A cult of financial deregulation has taken hold globally in recent decades and has caused plenty of problems in the rich world, but it has caused infinitely greater damage to developing economies.

Financial institutions like banks and bond and stock markets require very long periods of nurture, and considerable bureaucratic and institutional development, before they can be efficient components of a market economy. Even then, financial regulation is the most thorny area of governance for the most sophisticated states. However, the challenges of deregulating finance should not constrain poor countries because efficient financial institutions are not a prerequisite for economic development. Indeed, the danger in describing successful finance in Japan, Korea and Taiwan is that it sounds like it was far more efficient than it was. In reality, governments in north-east Asia directed finance at many wasteful, white elephant projects. Korea was particularly notorious for the bribery that surrounded loan decisions. None the less, with sufficient commitment to manufacturing based on export discipline, the bigger reality was that north-east Asian governments financed enough useful projects to move steadily up the industrial learning curve for several decades, leaving plenty of time to refine financial system performance later.

The easiest way to run developmentally efficient finance continues to be through a banking system, because it is banks that can most easily be pointed by governments at the projects necessary to agricultural and industrial development. Most obviously, banks respond to central bank guidance. They can be controlled via rediscounting loans for exports and for industrial upgrading, with the system policed through requirements for export letters of credit from the ultimate borrowers. The simplicity and bluntness of this mechanism makes it highly effective. Bond markets, and particularly stock markets, are harder for policymakers to control. The main reason is that it is difficult to oversee the way in which funds from bond and stock issues are used. It is, tellingly, the capacity of bank-based systems for enforcing development policies that makes entrepreneurs in developing countries lobby so hard for bond, and especially stock, markets to be expanded. These markets are their means to escape government control. It is the job of governments to resist entrepreneurs' lobbying until basic developmental objectives have been achieved. Equally, independent central banks are not appropriate to developing countries until considerable economic progress has been made.

Ultimately, a finance policy based around control has diminishing returns, just as household farming and infant industry planning do. However, financial control that keeps money aligned with agricultural and industrial policies is essential in the formative stages of development. Retail savers and borrowers have to be asked to pay the price of what economists call 'financial repression' for as long as is necessary to promote basic technological upgrading. The real problem is that we understand so little about how and when nations should optimally move on to more open, deregulated financial systems. There is no doubt that Thailand and Indonesia and, before them, the Philippines were shunted into extremely premature deregulation. Korea, on the other hand, offers an intriguing case study of forced IMF deregulation at a much later stage of industrialisation. At the time of writing, Korea looks to be in good shape and may have positive lessons to impart. However, the biggest lesson of all has long been clear to anyone who has considered history: that economic development is a complex and dynamic process of stages that requires constant and unending adjustment. There are no one-stop solutions to economic progress.

# Part 4

# Where China Fits In

*'The basic point is: we must acknowledge that we are backward, that
many of our ways of doing things are inappropriate, and that we need
to change.'*

Deng Xiaoping, on being confirmed as China's
preeminent leader in December 1978[1]

Can the history of east Asian development tell us something useful about the development of the biggest economy in the region, China's? At a minimum, the wider Asian context helps us frame a useful check-list; more ambitiously, it allows for some tentative projections about China's future. China can be benchmarked against the three basic structural insights brought about by economic development elsewhere in the region: that a country's agricultural potential is most quickly released when its farming is transformed into large-scale gardening supported by agricultural extension services; that the technological upgrading of manufacturing is the natural vehicle for swift economic transformation and is achieved by state direction of entrepreneurs towards state-defined industrialisation objectives; and that finance must be harnessed to both these ends, sometimes temporarily sacrificing short-term efficiency considerations for longer-run developmental gains in the form of technological learning.

The victory of the communists in 1949 gave China a revolutionary government that was no less committed to economic modernisation than governments in Japan, Korea and Taiwan. However, for a long time China was constrained because the Communist Party of China (CPC) was captive to the two great socialist fallacies that undid socialist modernisation programmes in other communist states. The first of these was that agriculture could only be efficient at scale, leading to the collectivisation of farming in the mid 1950s. As we saw in part 1, however, agriculture is not like manufacturing, where scale is essential to low unit costs and to the technological learning process that enables firms to produce more sophisticated products. In agriculture, the product never changes – rice is rice and corn is corn. Yields are maximised by the application of fertiliser and more and more labour, which poor countries have in abundance. Premature mechanisation actually reduces yields and leaves rural inhabitants with nothing to do. In east Asia after the Second World War, mechanisation and communist collectivisation in countries including North Korea, China and Vietnam led to hunger and starvation, as it had already done in the Soviet Union.

The second great communist fallacy that China laboured under was – unlike the scale agriculture prejudice, which was shared by many capitalists – a genuinely socialist one. This was that manufacturing could be developed without trade – through a policy of self-sufficiency, or autarky. In essence, this boils down to a country's people staying home and trying to figure out technological problems on their own. In Asian countries, including China and India, autarky throttled technological development after the Second World War because it removed firms' capacity to buy, borrow and steal already-developed technologies from elsewhere in the world. Each time firms wanted something new they had to, as the saying goes, reinvent the wheel. The legacy of autarky in China was, by the 1980s, all kinds of passable but hopelessly inefficient industrial processes. These included manually loaded kilns for making cement, an alternative Chinese technique for making low-grade glass, domestically developed and very wasteful oil-drilling rigs, tunnel-building techniques that involved digging a hole in the earth and then filling part of it back in, and so on.[2] Through autarky, China failed to develop a single industrial product with which it could compete internationally.

In the era of Deng Xiaoping, China broke out from the two great socialist fallacies. First, household farming was restored. Then, following Deng's visits to the United States, Japan and south-east Asian states in 1979 – which signalled the nation's re-engagement with the world – China opened up to trade and, gradually, to foreign investment, allowing it both to absorb international technology and to begin to benchmark its own products in world markets.

Thereafter, China has benefited from the one characteristic of the CPC that from a developmental perspective has been unambiguously positive. It is that the Party has been relentlessly paranoid. In a world of bad developmental advice, the Chinese government did not make the mistake of south-east Asian states and listen like a patsy to the imprecations of the World Bank, the IMF and the US government to deregulate its economy prematurely. China worked closely with the World Bank – enjoying a great deal of project-specific technical support as well as considerable financing in the 1980s and 1990s – but very much on its own terms. The World Bank's neo-liberal prescriptions for financial deregulation were not entertained.[3]

The IMF, which is more of a macro-economic institution and not set up to offer project-specific advice, was kept on a very short leash. The Chinese government was unwilling to let IMF staffers be seconded to its ministries – access to the Fund has been granted in developing economies in the former Soviet Union, Africa and south-east Asia. The standard Chinese response to IMF efforts to get inside the bureaucracy over the years has been: 'Do us a seminar.' Twice in recent years the Fund has been unable even to publish its annual report about China because of disagreements about the country's use of capital controls. Beijing exercised its right to refuse to authorise publication.[4] In short, China – unlike south-east Asian states – has been paranoid about the advice it has been offered, and has prospered by virtue of its paranoia.

Since 1978, China has posted an impressive developmental record, and has become the second east Asian state after Japan both to fascinate and unnerve western Europe and north America. The country has delivered a near 10 per cent average growth rate for three decades – a rate roughly on par with Thailand's in the ten years before the Asian financial crisis, but sustained over a much longer period.[5] In qualitative terms, China has not matched Taiwan in agricultural performance. It has not matched Korea for the speed and depth of its industrial upgrading. And it has not matched Japan in reinventing the nature of many industrial processes. But because China is so big and so populous – and, more darkly, because it is not an ally of the West – since 1978 it has managed to shake the world. What, then, can we say about the potential limits of Chinese economic development?

**All developmental roads lead back to the countryside**

Agriculture is much the most straightforward piece of the Chinese developmental puzzle. Beginning in the late 1970s, China escaped from its near-genocidal flirtation with collective agriculture, allowing households to farm small plots. After starving to death 30 million mostly rural dwellers as a result of collectivisation and the autarkic development policy of 1958–60 known as the Great Leap Forward, the country managed in the early 1980s to increase its agricultural output by more than one-third simply by letting poor people garden. (This was, of course, a reprise of the 1950s when, some scholars believe, grain output rose as much as 70 per cent under the first, truncated, communist-run era of household farming.)[6] Grain production was 305 million tonnes in 1978 under collective production, and 407 million tonnes in 1984, by which time almost all land had been converted to household agriculture, with average plots of just over one-third of a hectare.[7]

The restoration of household production was not the Communist Party's plan when Deng rose to power in 1978. Instead, the Party leadership, recognising that big communes of hundreds of families were both inefficient and highly unpopular, wanted to make them only somewhat smaller. It was farmers themselves, supported by a few progressive regional Party leaders, who declared their families to be collective units and made household farming a *fait accompli*. As Deng Xiaoping admitted in his turgid autobiography: 'It was the peasants who invented the household contract responsibility system with remuneration linked to output.'[8] This was a fancy way of describing household farming arrangements whereby peasants had to sell a share of their crops at a fixed price to the state – so the government could feed its urban population cheaply – and were then allowed to sell the rest on the open market.

China's grain output went on to exceed 500 million tonnes from the late 1990s. This is despite the conversion of large amounts of agricultural land to commercial and residential use (partly offset by bringing remaining marginal land into agricultural production). And it is despite the conversion of an increasing share of farmland to non-grain crops and animal-rearing. Agriculture has been supported by north-east Asian-style agronomic advice and training in the villages ('extension'), and by state-provided storage and marketing services. Private traders and moneylenders have not been able to corner the profits of farming in the manner of their south-east Asia counterparts, and thereby undermine farmers' incentives to produce more. Today, Chinese rice yields are in line with those of the north-east Asian states and are among the highest in the world. Wheat yields are similarly among the highest in the world, and more than 50 per cent ahead of what is achieved by scale farming in the United States.[9]

China's household farming performance extends to cash crops that require expensive machinery and are commonly, but erroneously, said to necessitate scale production. The country's cane sugar, like that of Taiwan, comes from small farms with yields far in excess of those of Filipino and other south-east Asian plantations, despite having less favourable soil and climatic conditions. In China, most sugar is grown in Guangxi province in the south-east. After the return to household farming beginning in 1978, national sugar output quickly increased 2.5 times by 1985. Today, sugar yields are around 75 tonnes per hectare, just slightly less than Taiwan achieved, and 40–50 per cent higher than in Negros in the Philippines.[10] Chinese sugar farmers share or lease the big tractors they need for deep ploughing. And government ensures that the incentive to produce is not destroyed by monopsony buyers of sugar cane – in other words, the mills.

Under the terms of its accession to the World Trade Organisation in 2001, China cut tariffs and quota restrictions on agricultural imports to levels far below those of Japan, Korea and Taiwan at similar stages of development. Yet only one agricultural commodity has seen a boom in imports. It is soybeans, where imports by value increased from USD3 billion in 2001 to USD25 billion in 2010. Interestingly, Chinese soybean production, concentrated in the northernmost Heilongjiang province, depends for a substantial chunk of its output on large state farms – not on household production. It was decided to retain some collectives in the province as large state units after 1978. As a result, China tries with soybeans to compete at scale with international scale producers (especially US ones) and comes off second best.[11] In 2010, China's 55 million tonnes of soybean imports accounted for 90 per cent of all its overseas 'grain' purchases (soybeans are classified as grain for statistical purposes). With rice and wheat, where the household farming structure is almost ubiquitous, imports were just 400,000 tonnes and 1.2 million tonnes respectively – less than half a percent of China's annual grain consumption. At China's present level of development and incomes, global scale producers of rice and wheat cannot compete with Chinese families gardening their plots.

## Old habits die hard

It would be wrong, however, to think that Chinese farming is some sort of bucolic idyll. Household farming has been fundamental to lifting hundreds of millions of Chinese out of poverty, to priming rural industry, and to creating demand for town-based manufacturers and service providers. But through all this, the Chinese political elite's age-old tendency to see peasants as eminently expendable has never disappeared. Despite a Communist Party with 80 million members (an increasingly smaller percentage of whom are farmers), the country's political commitment to rural–urban equality has been far less enduring than that in post-Second World War Japan, Taiwan and even South Korea. From the early 1990s to the mid 2000s, Chinese leaders looked on as the urban economy took off and the income gap between urban and rural citizens widened dramatically. This was reflected in a national GINI coefficient that moved from something over 0.3 (in line with north-east Asia) to one around 0.45 (in line with south-east Asia). Rural per capita incomes in China are today less than one-third of urban ones, whereas at a similar stage of development in north-east Asian states they were roughly equal.[12]

This large gap opened up because of fiscal and tariff choices. As the urban economy took off, China's central government provided nothing like the subsidies offered to farmers in north-east Asia, while allowing local governments to tax peasants aggressively. They were also made to pay for healthcare, to send their children to school, forced to perform corvée labour, and more. (In China, the bulk of welfare services are managed and funded at the local level.) As the Chinese economy grew under Deng Xiaoping, and then Jiang Zemin, urban bias in national fiscal policy increased greatly. Then, from 2001, China abandoned the bulk of its agricultural protection measures under the terms of its accession to the World Trade Organisation (WTO).

By the time that Hu Jintao took over as president in 2003, there was rising civil unrest in the countryside. At the outset of his term of office Hu based his bid for political legitimacy on his call to create a 'harmonious society', the root of which was a promise to close the gap between town and countryside. It was striking that, in seeking to do so, Hu deployed exactly the language that was used in Japan, Taiwan and Korea by policymakers justifying subsidies for rural dwellers. In 2005, the president gave a keynote policy speech in which he said China had moved from its first stage of modern economic development where 'agriculture supports industry' (by creating surplus, markets, etc.) to a new stage in which 'industry gives nourishment back to agriculture and cities support villages'.[13]

From 2006, a ban was imposed on local government taxation of farmers and significant subsidy increases were provided for agricultural inputs and crop purchase prices. When China launched a RMB4 trillion (USD590 billion) fiscal stimulus programme in 2008 in response to the global financial crisis, a substantial share of the money was targeted at farming infrastructure, as well as at train lines, roads, schools and hospitals in rural areas. The government also announced a ban on all school fees during the years of compulsory education. As a result of these changes, 2006–11 was probably the best period for Chinese farmers since the 1980s.

None the less, the income gap between rural and urban residents remains at more than three times. Only the increase in inequality has been arrested. There remains a much higher political tolerance of inequality in China than was the case in Japan, Korea and Taiwan. More specifically, the critical thing that separates the Chinese farmer from his or her cousins in north-east Asian states is that the Chinese peasant *does not own his or her land*. The historical reason for this is the essentially accidental nature of the reintroduction of household farming after 1978. Land that was divided up among households in that era belonged to collectives created in the 1950s. Since central government never intended a return to private household farming, it did not re-designate farmland as private property. Instead, in 1984 the government granted farmers 15-year 'use' rights for their plots and then, in 1998, issued a Land Management Law that formalised longer, 30-year use rights. Under Hu Jintao's 'harmonious society' drive, a 2007 Property Law made farmers' right to renew these leases a legal one, and clarified that ownership of land is vested in all members of a collective (not just the Party cadres who run the collectives). Legally, too, decisions relating to land must now be agreed by all members of the collective. China, however, is a place where the law and the application of the law are two very different things.

The basic reality of life in the countryside is that land belongs to the collectives, not to individuals, and this has consequences. The most important consequence is that, unlike in Japan, Korea and Taiwan, farmers cannot sell their plots to private buyers. Collective-owned land is unsaleable in law. It can only be converted into government-owned land, in which case compensation is paid to farmers up to a statutory maximum equivalent to thirty years' rental. Local authorities, however, can sell land converted to state ownership for development. This typically occurs at a big mark-up. Thirty years' rent may sound like a lot, but China's historically low yields per person (as opposed to per hectare) have also meant low rents; land redeployed for development or for commercial farming, by contrast, is massively more valuable.

In Japan, Korea and Taiwan, many farmers became rich after the Second World War through the re-zoning of farmland – like Nishiyama Kōichi, who went from peasant to millionaire by virtue of selling some of his land to a developer. In China, this does not happen. Instead, when farmers lose their land it is typically with less compensation than they need to survive independently, while big re-zoning profits are divided between local government fiscal coffers and local government graft. A trend to dispossessing farmers has been escalating for a decade, mainly because central government has never reconciled the supply of local government funding with the responsibilities it places on local governments to provide welfare services. In recent years, Beijing has curtailed local governments' capacity to tax farmers but has not replaced the lost income with central government grants. Instead, local authorities have had to borrow money through off-balance sheet companies they set up.[14] When payments on such debts cannot be met from the profits of the businesses they run themselves, they turn to sale of farmland. The media has focused on the conversion and sale of household farms for real estate and factories. But another fast-rising phenomenon is the leasing of former family farms for commercial agribusiness. Agricultural corporations can be signed up for long leases on collective land without the need for conversion to state land – something that is easier for local governments to finesse (though it is often a stepping stone to later conversion and sale). Agribusinesses not only pay for the leases, they also – unlike individual peasants – pay taxes to local governments.

According to the most authoritative independent surveys, nearly two-fifths of villages have experienced land conversions to non-agricultural uses in the past decade and almost a quarter of villages in China have experienced some switching of household plots to scale agriculture.[15] The pace at which land takings have occurred has accelerated greatly since the early

2000s – the point when central government began to curtail the capacity of local governments to raise money by taxing farmers directly. As of 2010, one in ten Chinese villages was losing land every year, usually against the wishes of its farmers. The average land taking is around 35 hectares (that is, the plots of about 100 families). There are increasing numbers of commercial farm deals running into thousands of hectares.[16]

## Harden your heart already

Does the, by north-east Asian standards, very raw deal being meted out to Chinese farmers matter to the country's overall economic development? Possibly not. Farmers often only give up their land under duress from local government, but they are given some compensation – the average paid to a family in 2010 was RMB13,000 (USD1,900). Since the typical Chinese farmer is now in his or her mid-forties, and has an average thirty years left to live, this translates into about RMB430 a year, or 140 kilos of milled rice at the current price. The payment is not enough even for the nutritional needs of two people; however, the great majority of farm households have children working in towns and cities.[17] Those children are forced to make up the difference between the compensation paid for land conversions and the money that their parents actually need to live. Farmers who lose their land do also find ways to earn some side income, even if the great majority of them are now too old to secure full-time jobs.

China's rural–urban divide is unpleasant, unfair and socially corrosive, but it is not terminal from the perspective of economic development. The farm sector has served its developmental function in terms of priming economic take-off, and continues to meet China's food needs. So long as there is no large-scale civil unrest as a result of land redevelopment and conversion, the main concern for central government in the next few years will be that the rise of commercial farming is leading to reduced output of staple foodstuffs. Aside from the fact that scale agriculture substitutes profit for yield, commercial farming in China also does not cultivate core foods like rice and wheat. Instead it concentrates on more value-added, high-margin, specialist crops, such as vegetables, herbs and flowers – sometimes for export. China's imports of staple foodstuffs are beginning to increase quickly (albeit from a low base) as household farmland disappears. At some point, this will start alarm bells ringing in Beijing about food security – the Chinese Communist Party has a longstanding, and sensible, fear of the country being at the mercy of substantial food imports.

There will likely be a clamp-down on household farm land conversions to commercial agriculture but, unless China's local government funding problem is resolved, the fiscal pressure to squeeze farmers (and their money-remitting offspring) will remain. The Chinese farmer is a long-suffering beast who, down the ages, has been repeatedly mistreated by his urban masters. In recent times, it was his support which ensured the communist revolution. Left to his own devices, he produced a brief output boom, still remembered by older Chinese as a golden era, between the end of the Second World War and the start of collectivisation in 1956. Following various Maoist misadventures, in the 1980s he brought China back from the brink, ramping up agricultural output during an era that also saw the country's most competitive businesses created in rural areas. Huge companies like offroad vehicle maker Great Wall Motor, now China's leading vehicle exporter, leading car parts maker Wanxiang, top beverage firm Wahaha, and Broad Air Conditioning, known for its environmental sensibilities, sprang out of the countryside in the 1980s.[18] And then, at the stage when landowning farmers in Japan, Taiwan and Korea were getting used to four-wheel drive cars and holidays at the seaside, local government started to take away the Chinese farmer's fields to satisfy its fiscal deficit and the greed of village cadres. Central government, which did not finance local government adequately, looked on and said it was all a terrible shame. Now, once again, the Chinese farmer is constrained to fulfill his traditional role and, as the Chinese idiom has it, 'eat his bitterness'.[19]

## The manufacturing conundrum

The story of China's manufacturing policy since 1978 is more complex than that of its agricultural policy because it has taken a series of turns during the reform era. As already mentioned, in the 1980s the central government – identified with the liberal premier Zhao Ziyang – allowed rural industry to flourish off the back of a return to household farming.

As in north-east Asia, the leading entrepreneurs of the period came from the countryside, rural market towns and conurbations. China's big-city state industry continued down its own track, undergoing modest, incremental reforms rather than the privatisation shock therapy which was so damaging to post-communist Russia because it was so readily exploited by insiders. China's development in the 1980s has been aptly described as 'reform without losers'.[20]

In the 1990s, however, parts of the state sector became an increasingly heavy drag on development. The most problematic elements were smaller state firms and downstream state firms. Smaller state manufacturers faced brutal competition from an emergent private sector and from foreign companies, the latter being given much readier access to the market than they had been in Japan, Korea and, to a lesser extent, Taiwan. Compared with the United States' Cold War allies, China had to trade more access to its market in return for access to rich countries' markets; in addition, China's leaders were more ready than those in Japan and Korea to open up the domestic consumer goods sector which they, as socialists, did not regard as being of great 'strategic' industrial significance. By the mid 1990s, state enterprises classified as small and medium-sized were losing increasing amounts of money.

Starting from 1993 under a new and more domineering economic leader, Zhu Rongji, central government pursued a rationalisation programme. This was largely accomplished by pushing responsibility for selling or closing smaller state units on to local governments at the same time that a fiscal squeeze was being imposed on them.[21] The result was that local governments took a hard look at their costs and began to slash loss-making operations. In 1997, the policy was formalised by the CPC at its quinquennial congress and became known as the strategy of 'Grasp the Big, Let Go the Small'. There are no definitive figures, but estimates suggest that some 40 million state workers were laid off between 1995 and 2004.[22]

The Zhu Rongji assault on the state sector surprised many observers (including me)[23] with its scope and its success. Moreover, the cull of loss-making state capacity was combined with a highly effective programme to increase levels of competition among the biggest state firms. Companies which had enjoyed niche monopolies – for instance, China's oil refiners, each with its own product-based turf – were forced to compete with one other. In upstream areas of the economy and in key services, Zhu's economic policy team created oligopolies of two, three or four entrants, which went head to head for market dominance. In oil and gas, petrochemicals, coal, electricity generation and distribution, telephone services, insurance and banking, state sector competition among a small number of big firms was increased dramatically, leading both to higher levels of efficiency and to higher profits. State sector oligopolies maximised returns in a way that state sector monopolies never had.

Across the complete, national-level state sector, the 196 biggest businesses (or, more accurately, groups of businesses) were placed under the control of a new agency, the State Asset Supervision and Administration Commission (SASAC), set up in 2003 in the last year of Zhu's premiership. The remit of SASAC is the consolidation of under-performing units, or culling, and thereby the encouragement of big firms, with powerful economies of scale, that can compete globally. The number of centrally managed firms has shrunk in every year of SASAC's existence, decreasing to 122 groups in 2010; the average group is now bigger than ever, however many loss-making subsidiaries have been closed. SASAC makes firms under its control sign rolling, 3-year contracts stipulating profit targets. Firm bosses are graded (and paid) according to a points system in which 70 out of 100 possible points depend on different profitability measures.[24]

In general, the consequences of state sector reforms have been extremely edifying. From a position of almost no aggregate profitability in the late 1990s, the SASAC-controlled groups were able through the 2000s to deliver annual profits equivalent to 3–4 per cent of Chinese GDP – a sum of RMB1.35 trillion (USD200 billion) in 2010.[25] The bulk of the returns came from just nine upstream and service businesses: PetroChina, Sinopec and CNOOC in oil refining and petrochemicals; China Mobile and China Telecom in telecoms services; Baosteel, the leading steel producer; Chinalco, the dominant aluminium producer; Shenhua Energy, the top coal miner; and the State Electricity Grid. Indeed, around half SASAC firm profits came from just the three oil firms and China Mobile. In short, the government retained full control of the upstream and service businesses which in less successful developing countries fall into the hands of tycoons whose interests are not aligned with industrialization objectives. And the government still made those businesses highly profitable.

### The Zhu inheritance

The Zhu Rongji reforms left China with an industrial economy defined by three structural features. The first is that the group of much more efficient and profitable *upstream* state oligopolies can be used – because of their role as the main importers and processors of raw materials – to cushion the economy against international price shocks. The upstream companies bridle at central government control and would like to break free of it, but have so far had little success in doing so; in the end their managers are stuck with the fact they are public servants.

The second structural legacy is that the state's *manufacturing* policy has become focused on a small number of large, government-linked businesses making producers' goods, that is, products used by other, downstream firms, including everything from metals to machine tools. This echoes Taiwan's public sector-biased industrial policy. However, in the aggregate, China's state firms are probably subject to more competition and export discipline than Taiwan's were. They have posted impressive results in producing increasingly sophisticated goods that compete in world markets, from hydro power turbines to high-speed trains. China holds out the intriguing possibility of producing the most successful state-controlled manufacturing sector yet seen in a developing country – albeit probably not one as all-conquering as some people expect.

The third legacy – and one reinforced by Zhu Rongji's successors – is that the private sector in China has had a fraction of the policy support given to the state sector. Private mainland Chinese firms, which are heavily concentrated in downstream consumer goods sectors, tend to lack the margins, the cash flows and the concentration to break through the technological frontier and emerge as global brand name businesses. Going forward, it is an important and thorny question how much the stymieing of the private sector will constrain China's overall economic ambitions.

Much of the problem in answering this question is to know how big the public and private sectors are, and what 'public' and 'private' really mean, in China. 'Half and half' is a common answer to the first question, but the complexity of the equity structures of corporate groups means that answer is nothing more than a guess. Management of ostensibly public firms is often granted equity that proves to be a powerful motivating force. Many firms that are dubbed public today may have their futures decided by their minority shareholders. On the other hand, more private firms may end up being swallowed by the public sector, a prognosis commonly heard from China's rising middle class. CPC control of politics is black and white, but ownership of business is anything but.

### The gorillas

Among the upstream oligopolies, which are the most clearly state-controlled part of the economy, Zhu Rongji's reforms have created fierce competition between firms fighting for a bigger share of the rents that have accrued from the provision of key raw materials and services. This has made those firms both rich and powerful. However, price controls have so far prevented the upstream businesses from milking their oligopolies to the degree that the cartels of nineteenth-century Germany or the *zaibatsu* of pre-Second World War Japan did. The Chinese government retains bureaucratic price setting for all key upstream inputs into the economy, such as refined petroleum products and electricity. The oligopolies are allowed to make generous long-run profits, but are also used as 'shock absorbers' to cushion downstream enterprises from any big international price changes.[26] This is helpful to all downstream manufacturers, public, private and hybrid.

As one example, when the world crude oil price rose as high as USD140 a barrel prior to the global financial crisis of 2008, China's oil firms were required to take losses on parts of their refining operations in order to protect manufacturers. More recently, as the global crisis slowed China's economy but international coal prices remained at record levels, electricity generators were denied tariff increases that would have reflected their increased input costs. China's government has displayed the same determination seen in north-east Asian states to keep the industrial learning process moving forward irrespective of global economic conditions. The policy tools employed are not always the same, but the objective is.

It is unclear whether close government control can be maintained indefinitely over the steadily rising power of China's upstream oligopolists. Just as Korean *chaebol* battled against state control, despite benefiting enormously from state largesse, so the upstream firms in China are beginning to challenge state power – even though they are state-owned. When world crude prices began their ascent to new highs in 2005–6, Chinese oil companies tried to fight back against price controls by withholding supplies of refined products.[27] More recently, electricity generators ran power plants far below capacity and orchestrated black-outs in protest at low tariffs. The government faced down these rebellions; it seeks to keep the oligopolists responsive to its orders by rotating their bosses, just as it does its army generals. In 2009, for instance, the heads of the three big oil companies were swapped around. What the CPC Organisation Department calls 'personnel adjustment' – *renshi tiaozheng* – keeps the oligopolists dancing to its tune. And Beijing intervenes in other ways to keep the big firms off-balance. Also in 2009, China Mobile, the dominant telephone company, was forced to adopt and develop a new Chinese technical standard, leaving its weaker competitors the relatively easy task of selling phones to customers on the incumbent GSM system.

The central government remains in charge, but the oligopolies are straining constantly to extend their power. Thwarted by price controls, they increasingly use their money and muscle to earn profits through acquisitions rather than competition. Again there are echoes here of Korea in the 1980s. Under the general banner of consolidation, the big state steel and mining firms do not just soak up sub-scale producers, they also use their public sector connections to take down larger private sector challengers. A well-known case was the takeover in 2009 by Shandong Iron and Steel Group of the privately held Rizhao Steel, under considerable bureaucratic duress. Local government leaders orchestrated a hostile takeover of profitable Rizhao by the lossmaking state firm, with Rizhao's owner and China's second-richest businessman, Du Shuanghua, concluding he could not operate independently when the government was against him.

The public sector upstream firms also increasingly use their huge cash flows to acquire businesses in the mid-stream of the economy. For example, the three state-owned oil firms and the electricity generators have made a raft of investments in new energy equipment manufacturers from wind turbine makers to battery companies. It is far from certain the acquisition targets will benefit from being owned by corporations with no manufacturing experience. And the upstream groups seek to extend their control into new areas of trading and distribution. The oil companies recently moved into distribution of natural gas, something they previously left to private firms. Since only the oil majors can import or mine natural gas, they exercise an unfair advantage over the private sector.

All this is part of what the Chinese public and media have dubbed *guo jin, min tui*, or 'the state sector advances, the private sector yields'. The expression reflects a phenomenon almost everyone is conscious of, but one whose limits and implications remain unclear; the equity picture, as already noted, is messy because the state firms do not always take complete control of their acquisition targets. Ultimately, the extending reach of the upstream oligopolies is a matter of cash, which derives from their dominant share of the profits of the state sector. The government's stated intention is to crimp their ambitions by taking more of their cash away. Since 2007, Beijing has extracted small dividends from the big state firms, ranging from 5 to 15 per cent of their net profits depending on the sector. However, the oligopolies are fighting aggressively against paying higher dividends.[28] The managers of the big upstream resources and services firms are not granted the same equity positions as those of some state-linked manufacturers, but they guard their firms' cash jealously; it is their source of power and influence, not to mention non-equity ways of rewarding themselves financially. The government's capacity to siphon off more of the rents of the upstream behemoths and redeploy them to support independent manufacturers will be a key test of its industrial policy. In essence the question is how much the government wants to support independent manufacturers and a pluralistic economy.

## Manufacturing champions

The second structural feature of China's contemporary industrial economy is that its infant industry policy is heavily concentrated on a group of public sector and state-linked manufacturers making producers' goods. North-east

Asian countries had a mixed record employing state sector firms to lead industrial development. State-owned companies were successful in the steel industry in Japan, Korea and Taiwan, steadily raising the quality of output in an industry that seems given to bureaucratic-style public sector control. In Taiwan's state-dominated industrial policy, public firms such as United MicroElectronics and TSMC were also successful in getting to and remaining at the forefront of many types of semiconductor production. However, Taiwan and the rest of north-east Asia had plenty of examples of state firm failure – or at least underperformance compared with private companies. In Taiwan and Korea, for instance, state-owned shipbuilders failed to keep pace with private ones. And private Japanese and Korean chemicals firms beat out state-owned ones from Taiwan in regional competition.

China appears, in the aggregate, to be doing better with its state-owned enterprises. Out of the country's history of socialist industrial planning, and Zhu Rongji's 1990s rationalisation programme, there has developed a roster of substantial mid-stream businesses that are becoming increasingly globally competitive. These public firms are protected from undue market fragmentation by high capital barriers to entry, yet there are enough of them in each industrial segment to make for fierce competition.[29] They indicate that export discipline, and domestic competition combined with the steady culling of losers, are more important than ownership in determining industrial development success. That said, sometimes the key operating units are state group subsidiaries in which managers and other private shareholders hold substantial equity positions. This particularly occurs when existing state units create new manufacturing subsidiaries.

The firms are acquiring international competitiveness in mining machinery, construction machinery, machine tools, aerospace, shipbuilding, thermal, hydro and wind power, telecommunications infrastructure, and more. Even the biggest of the companies – such as China Shipbuilding, China Oilfield, China International Marine Container, Sinovel, or CSR Corp. – are far from household names. Yet in August 2011 the first had a market capitalisation approaching USD20 billion, and the average market capitalisation of twenty-four leading mid-stream state and state-linked manufacturers was USD6 billion. This was well over twice the average value of China's biggest purely private firms.[30]

The state sector producers' goods companies are overseen by a bureau-cratic planning apparatus that has been widely underestimated, not least because it is associated with a communist government. We know little about the inner workings of SASAC or, crucially, the National Development and Reform Commission (NDRC), the key industrial planning agency – far less than we do about equivalent agencies in Japan, Korea and Taiwan. However, with the benefit of hindsight, it is clear that China's bureaucrats have usually made sensible, conservative decisions in nurturing state sector manufacturers, which have also benefited from their links to state-run research institutes.

To give one example, when the NDRC formulated a policy on developing green energy technologies, it advised the government to put the bulk of its subsidy support behind the best-established low-cost technology, wind turbines. Solar panel makers were also screaming for subsidies, but solar power was more expensive and there was concern that the polysilicon-based technology used in China might be superannuated by thin-film technologies under development in the United States. Battery makers, too, wanted money to develop electric vehicles, but here the technological path was even murkier and the market untested. After extensive NDRC analysis, the government went with wind, and state procurement created the biggest wind turbine market in the world. Moreover, policymakers accepted qualified state ownership by allowing managers significant equity in wind turbine subsidiaries started by state units. Sinovel and Goldwind, the biggest wind turbine makers, now have most of their equity in private hands. The combination of conservative, low-risk industrial policy making and market incentives contrasts powerfully with Malaysia's assault on the bleeding edge of steel technology using a single, wholly state-owned firm. China's leading state-linked wind turbine firms are now among the global leaders in their field and export increasing amounts of product.

State producers' goods firms are further supported by NDRC and government campaigns to localise all kinds of machinery used in the economy – something that is easier to influence than the behaviour of individual retail consumers. The move into wind turbines, for instance, was kicked off with a formal NDRC notice in 2005 requiring a minimum 70 per cent local content rate for wind turbines bought with state funds in China. (This was eventually withdrawn under protests from foreign suppliers who pointed out the document was in contravention of China's WTO commitments. By then, however, local and foreign firms' localisation rates had already reached 70 per cent.)[31] In 2009, the NDRC and the government raised the general target for localisation of the entire equipment manufacturing sector from 60 per cent to 70 per cent. The pronouncement did not succeed in convincing every downstream firm to buy Chinese, but the message was listened to given the government's control over the financial system and its huge procurement budget.[32] The state does not lend to or buy from companies that ignore its strictures. It is a story familiar from Japan, Korea and Taiwan.

The biggest enforcer of export discipline on public sector manufacturers is China Development Bank (CDB), China's main investment bank and also the most efficient financial institution in the country. CDB is one of three 'policy' investment banks – *zhengcexing yinhang* – set up in 1994 as part of Zhu Rongji's fiscal and financial overhaul; the policy banks are so called because they are mandated to lend in support of state agricultural and industrial policy. CDB has been run for the past thirteen years by the same highly rated manager, Chen Yuan, son of Chen Yun, the economist who rescued Mao Zedong and Deng Xiaoping from their worst policy follies.[33] The institution built up its balance sheet by supporting large-scale, high-quality domestic infrastructure projects in the 2000s. It thereby also facilitated the growth of mid-stream manufacturers which supplied the projects.[34]

More recently, CDB became the key financial institution pushing mid-stream firms to export. Since 2006 it has financed well over USD100 billion of deals in south-east Asia, Africa, Latin America, Russia and elsewhere.[35] Some of the biggest loans are for straightforward raw material investments by the upstream oligopolies. But many are infrastructure projects in developing countries where CDB provides the finance, Chinese state construction firms do the building work and Chinese mid-stream manufacturers supply and install the hardware.[36] The policy echoes Japan's industrial development through aggressive exports to under-industrialised Asian states at the start of the twentieth century, and Korea's construction service exports to the Middle East and south-east Asia in the 1970s and 1980s. The main difference is that China is operating on a truly global scale. In the past five years, the export discipline brought to bear on Chinese mid-stream firms has rapidly increased the quality of their output.

## All this we can sell you

Among the earliest producers' goods firms that undertook the long march to global competitiveness were manufacturers of thermal electricity generating equipment. Their progress began with a textbook, north-east Asian-style case study of a government reducing technology acquisition costs by centralising the bargaining process with a multinational provider. In the 1980s, China's central government negotiated a market-access-for-technology deal with the US-based power company Westinghouse and diffused the acquired thermal turbine technology (Westinghouse is today only in the nuclear business) among half a dozen state sector engineering firms. In the 1990s, the firms gradually began to produce mid-size turbines, while the government helped them acquire hydropower turbine technology from multinationals like Siemens. The level of competition among the firms and the country's appetite for new electricity generating plants was such that, by the 2000s, China had built up the largest power equipment production capacity in the world. More important, the producers' technology level came within striking distance of the global frontier, while their prices were up to 30 per cent below those of their multinational competitors.[37]

Concessionary financing from China Development Bank and the China Export–Import Bank, another of the policy banks, then encouraged power equipment makers into international markets, starting with other developing states such as India, Pakistan, Vietnam and Indonesia. Chinese manufacturers captured around one-third of the growing Indian market in the late 2000s; in 2010 the biggest firm, Shanghai Electric, signed a 5-year deal to supply India's Reliance Power with equipment for thirty-six power stations in a contract worth USD10 billion. The same year the largest of several 'oil for loans' contracts organised by China's policy banks saw Venezuela being granted a USD20 billion credit line that will finance, among other things, three large Chinese-supplied power stations.

China exported USD9 billion of power equipment in 2009 and is starting to move beyond south Asia, Africa and Latin America to make sales in
eastern Europe. Exports accounted for 20 per cent of total production, in
line with the export share of a company like Hyundai during its key era of
technological upgrading. Export discipline has coincided with firms gradu-
ating from making mid-size thermal turbines to the production of 1,000
megawatt super-high temperature turbines known as 'ultra-supercriticals',
as well as cutting-edge 700 megawatt hydropower turbines (as used on
the world's largest power station, the Three Gorges dam on the Yangtze
river). The three largest Chinese power equipment companies are already
the three biggest producers of thermal turbines in the world.

The common pattern of the Chinese mid-stream businesses is that core
technologies are imported and absorbed during an initial phase of operation in the domestic market. The firms then push up to the global technology frontier during a period of increased export discipline. In shipbuilding,
Chinese yards accounted for less than 10 per cent of global orders until
the end of the 1990s as state firms slowly absorbed basic technologies,
mostly through licensing arrangements. With the China boom of the
2000s, domestic demand grew precipitously and yards also began to bid
for exports. In the international market, Korea won a battle with Japan
at the top end, while China took a rapidly increasing share of orders for
simpler vessels. By the late 2000s China was supplying 40 per cent of the
world's new tonnage, much of it purchased by domestic shipping companies. Chinese shipyards remain dependent on foreign suppliers for many
of their designs, and for up to half the value of ships in terms of purchased
parts and engines, but under export pressure they are quickly climbing the
technology ladder. Leading groups like China Shipbuilding now export
Suezmax ships (the largest vessels that can pass through the Suez canal)
and are moving on to still bigger classes.

In the past five years, the most impressive international growth of Chinese state-linked mid-stream firms has been among manufacturers of construction equipment. The performance of these firms is consistent with the
experience of Japanese companies like Komatsu, Sumitomo and Hitachi
in the 1970s, whose exports of construction equipment jumped from 10
per cent of production to over 30 per cent in a few years, before going on

to account for as much as 70 per cent of output today. Chinese firms like XCMG and Zoomlion have already surpassed the electric power equipment makers by exporting around a third of their production. Sany, an even larger private firm that prospers as the only non-state player in the field, exports a similar proportion of its output; it is, like Sony and Honda in Japan, an example of a 'non-plan' firm that is allowed to survive. All the companies honed their manufacturing skills in a vast but highly price-sensitive domestic market – moving gradually from simple products like wheel loaders to much more complex machines like excavators – and then pushed aggressively into developing country export markets.[38] Around half of China's construction equipment exports go to countries in Asia, and about one-fifth to Africa. However, the US, Europe and Japan are already buying another one-fifth of exports. The Chinese firms have announced targets to export the majority of their production by 2015, in what would be a considerable speeding up of Japanese firms' historic development.

In the telecommunications sector, China's leading equipment firms, Huawei and ZTE, have already shown how far Chinese mid-stream firms can go in international markets. In the 1990s, these two companies acquired increasing shares of domestic telephone infrastructure sales against multinational competition, starting in small towns but eventually accounting for more than half the national market. From 1997, they pushed into developing countries, supported by China Development Bank financing; by 2004, Huawei alone was supported by a USD10 billion CDB credit line; it has had more CDB money than any other Chinese company. More recently, the two firms won breakthrough mobile infrastructure contracts in developed countries, including Spain and Norway, and now operate at the technological frontier. The only remaining technological challenge for Huawei and ZTE is to become standard setters for the next generations of mobile telephone technology, thereby helping to lock in higher profit margins. Unlisted Huawei is by far the most internationally successful Chinese company, ranking second (and not far behind) Sweden's Ericsson as a global vendor of telecoms equipment. The firm reported turnover of RMB185 billion (USD28 billion) in 2010, 65 per cent of which came from overseas markets. Unlike most of China's mid-stream manufacturers, Huawei claims to have a majority of private equity in its ownership; ZTE is a more prototypical state sector offshoot of the Ministry of Aerospace. Huawei says that it is controlled by employee shareholders; however, the company has never provided any proof of this and rumours of major state sector shareholdings abound.[39]

## The limits of the model

The progress of China's telecommunications firms into the front ranks of the global marketplace suggests that its state and state-linked mid-stream 'business-to-business' companies can become the technological leaders of the country's broader industrial development. These firms are the products of a government manufacturing policy that combines domestic competition with export discipline, and which encourages them first to master current technologies, and then to originate new ones. The policy is consistent with what worked in Japan, Korea and Taiwan, and almost certainly an improvement on the state sector variant in Taiwan, because China is, on average, imposing greater competition and export discipline on its public firms than Taiwan ever did. The use of management equity incentives may also exceed what was done in Taiwan, although this is a highly variable, unfolding story in need of much research.

None the less, three caveats should be borne in mind when lauding China's state sector manufacturing policy. The first is that the success of state firms which are backed by industrial policy does not extend beyond mid-stream, business-to-business activities. The most common weakness of publicly owned businesses is that they lack the sensibility and flexibility to succeed in consumer markets, and Chinese public companies have so far been no exception. Mid-stream state-linked companies are succeeding in learning industrial technologies which evolve in a linear and fairly predictable manner, but they are vulnerable when their activities require them to understand retail consumers. In the automotive sector, for instance, large state companies have failed miserably to develop indigenous products that interest Chinese buyers. Instead they rely on foreign joint ventures for technology and designs, exhibiting the same dependency that afflicted Proton in Malaysia. China has more consumer-savvy private car firms that are more able to develop own-brand products, but they are constrained because state firm joint ventures selling foreign models control most of the market. The private firm most likely to succeed may be four-wheel drive specialist Great Wall Motor, in part because state firms do not offer competing products and hence are unable to crowd it out. The other private firms, like Geely and Chery, struggle on wafer-thin margins.

In telecommunications even Huawei – perhaps belying its claim to be a real private company – has struggled to make inroads at the consumer end of its business. Like ZTE, Huawei turns out tens of millions of handsets each year as a contractor to multinationals like Vodafone, but it has so far been unable to become a significant own-brand manufacturer of handsets for international markets. This contrasts with Korea's Samsung, which grew up as a purely private firm and, while it engaged in many business-to-business activities, was always close to consumers. Today Samsung is one of the world's two leading producers of telephony's most value-added consumer product, smart phones. Huawei, by contrast, was started by an ex-military officer, Ren Zhengfei, and grew up selling backbone telecommunications infrastructure to provincial and municipal governments.[40] It then expanded this business to deal with governments and private telephone system operators overseas. Today, the culture of Huawei may be too much that of a business-to-business and business-to-government firm for it to become a top player in handsets.

The second caveat about industrial development based on state-linked manufacturers of producers' goods is that, unlike consumer-oriented business, much of what the Chinese companies sell internationally is subject either to state procurement or to government approval. In developing countries, selling to governments is frequently to China's advantage. The Chinese government has few scruples about which regimes its firms do business with, and China's policy banks attach no political strings to the loans they make. Partly as a result, Chinese firms have bagged major infrastructure deals in countries like Pakistan, Myanmar, Libya and Congo. In developed countries, however, selling to governments or to government-influenced sectors may not always be to China's advantage. Already, Huawei lost out on a USD3 billion sale to Sprint-Nextel in the United States in 2010, and has been blocked from acquisitions which would have yielded it important technology on the basis of 'national security' concerns.[41] Such impediments may affect more Chinese mid-stream firms in the future. Even if national security concerns are not invoked, developed country governments can deploy all kinds of other 'non-tariff barriers' to impede Chinese equipment sales. Since China does not itself operate open tenders for state procurement, and has not acceded to the WTO's General Procurement Agreement (which regulates government purchases), the Chinese government has no legal recourse in such matters. Private firms from Japan and Korea have been able to enter rich countries by appealing direct to their consumers with cars, video cassette recorders and smart phones. China's mid-stream equipment makers are more constrained to go through the political front door.

The third caveat about the mid-stream firms is that, while China seems to be making excellent technological progress, it is impossible to know precisely how real this is in what is a period of extremely aggressive investment. Put simply, China is investing so heavily to acquire technology at present that, superficially, the results are almost bound to look impressive. In some sectors, it will be a few more years before we have a clear sense of the progress that has been made versus the investment laid down. We do not yet know the extent to which China is still merely copying technology from elsewhere, as opposed to beginning to originate its own.

The railway equipment business is one example of this analytical conundrum. In 2007, the government launched an extraordinary USD395 billion programme to construct a 16,000-kilometre high-speed rail network, more than half of which was already complete by the end of 2010.[42] By that point, the Ministry of Railways borrowed over USD300 billion, and provincial governments much more, to fund a network that in four years grew to be three times the size of Japan's *shinkansen* bullet train service and which will soon be five times bigger. To put the Chinese investment in perspective, in 2011 the US government asked Congress for USD53 billion to fund the beginnings of an American high-speed rail network (Congress turned the government down).

In spending such vast sums of money so quickly, it is unclear how cost-efficient the Ministry of Railways' technology acquisition strategy has been. In some respects, the strategy appears to be another textbook operation. Despite mercurial appearances, the ministry researched high-speed rail for fifteen years before it signed its first big technology deals in 2004. Officials followed a proven strategy of luring foreign firms to open offices in China with the promise of a large market, and then spending years talking to them before putting any money on the table. The railway ministry centralised all bargaining with technology providers to reduce costs. However, it also successively entered joint ventures and licensing agreements with each of the world's four leading high-speed rail firms (Bombardier, Kawasaki Heavy Industries, Siemens, Alstom) to allow Chinese rail research institutes to look at all available technologies.[43]

In 2010, the Ministry of Railways announced that the country's two state-controlled locomotive and rolling stock manufacturers not only had digested core high-speed rail technology in only five years, but also were ready to produce even faster trains of their own. The ministry trumpeted the launch of a CRH380 locomotive, with a top speed of 380 kilometres per hour – faster than any train operating in the world. In 2011, however, it became clear that all was not as it seemed. In February, Minister of Railways Liu Zhijun – nicknamed 'Leap Liu' for his promises to leapfrog Chinese railways into global technological leadership – was summarily sacked and placed under investigation for 'severe violation of discipline', a CPC euphemism for corruption. The retired deputy director of the ministry's high-speed department then made unusually candid remarks in the Chinese press, saying that high-speed trains were running faster than those of foreign technology suppliers only because Liu's Ministry of Railways authorised much lower safety tolerances than German or Japanese operators. The core technology, said Zhou Yimin, remained foreign, and there had not been any innovation allowing for higher speeds.[44] A month after Zhou warned of a cavalier attitude to safety, a crash between two high-speed trains in Zhejiang province killed forty people.

It is impossible to know exactly how much technological learning China has achieved in the rail sector. The state bank-backed export discipline phase of development is only just beginning and there is so far little feedback from the international market. Early export contracts for urban light rail and conventional locomotives and rolling stock have been signed in countries including Malaysia, Ghana, Tunisia, Venezuela and Turkmenistan. The first high-speed projects, involving trains and track, have been agreed, but not completed, in Turkey, Venezuela, Argentina and Saudi

Arabia. It is clear China can achieve rail equipment sales in developing countries and that its civil engineering firms, which are leading the construction work, are gaining valuable overseas experience.[45] But the cost of learning about high-speed rail technology has been steep, so the returns will have to be high as well. At home, the Ministry of Railways was forecast to have revenues of RMB200 billion (USD31billion) in 2011, while its repayments of interest and principal on its vast debts were RMB250 billion (USD39 billion).

### The neglected private sector

The discussion of the state-linked mid-stream firms brings us to the final element of China's post-Zhu Rongji industrial structure: a private sector that receives relatively much less policy support. Again, there is a strong echo of the Taiwanese bias in favour of public firms over private ones, reinforced on the mainland by the unchallenged political leadership of the Communist Party of China. But whereas China's national champion public enterprises may be doing better on aggregate than Taiwan's as a result of superior policy implementation, private Chinese firms frequently suffer the same consequences from a deficit of policy support. The problem is particularly acute in the consumer-facing products sector where, as already noted, China's state-linked companies have been found wanting. Just as Taiwan produced no equivalent of a Samsung in consumer electronics, or a Hyundai in automotive, there are doubts as to whether private Chinese companies are capable of becoming global brand-name businesses in consumer industries. Chinese private firms have all the flexibility and entrepreneurial hunger required to compete in consumer markets, but they tend to lack the cash, concentration and subsidy to challenge their multinational competitors.

This is fundamentally an issue of government policy. Since Zhu Rongji's reforms, China has nurtured its stable of state-linked mid-stream companies and encouraged them to export industrial and transportation equipment. By comparison, private firms are constrained because they lack comparable levels of support. They account for the bulk of China's exports – private firms' net exports (exports minus imports) went from zero in 2000 to USD200 billion in 2010[46] – but they are not rewarded by the state for this export performance. In most consumer goods businesses private firms are more open to multinational competition than were their Japanese and Korean cousins at a similar stage of development. They do not enjoy cross-subsidies from other protected non-consumer businesses, such as Hyundai Motor Company had from the *chaebol's* cash-generative shipbuilding subsidiary; in China such non-consumer businesses are in state hands. Private firms enjoy fewer orders for state procurement than their public sector rivals, a big disadvantage in an era when the state is investing so heavily. And in some cases they butt up against entrenched state enterprise competitors which are extremely difficult to displace. The car business is the classic example. The state car firms are doing little for China's technological development because they are dependent on foreign joint venture partners for technology; but they occupy the high margin, larger car segment of the car market, making life for the private firms harder than it would otherwise be. Finally, private firms have less ready access to capital than state ones, although this constraint may be overstated. CDB, for instance, makes large loans to private firms if they are capable exporters. The single biggest constraint for private firms is the relative lack of protection, procurement and subsidy they receive relative to the state sector. Private Chinese companies have to try to develop as rich countries would like them to – in open competition with more experienced, more technologically advanced and far better resourced multinational enterprises.

The most common problem is that private firms lack the cash flows to increase the value-added content of their products. Their margins are too thin, and their credit lines too limited, to fund loss-leading product development over long periods. One manifestation of the cash constraint is that private companies are unable to attack enough of a product's value chain to establish pricing power. This might mean they put together a product but cannot master critical components that command outsize margins, like a car's drivetrain or engine. Or, very commonly, private firms cannot afford to integrate forward to control a product's distribution and sales channels. The pioneering work of the economic historian Alfred Chandler showed how America's original crop of nineteenth-century multinationals all succeeded by dominating distribution and sales of their products, and thereby acquiring pricing power.[47] Those US firms were not subject to the same levels of international competition that Chinese ones are today. In China multinational competitors are able to siphon profit into segments of product value chains where they are strongest, and where they can erect the highest technological and capital barriers to competition.

This is what happened to many private Taiwanese firms that suffered because of the Kuomintang's industrial policy focus on the public sector. One of the island's most famous entrepreneurs, Acer's Stan Shih, dubbed the value chain problem faced by under-supported private companies the 'smiling face'. In the computer and electronics business in which many private Taiwanese firms are active, the highest margins go to either brand-name designers, software firms and chip-makers at one end of the value chain, or to giant retailers at the other. A company like Acer, whose limited resources constrain it to focus on the middle of the chain – the low part of the smile – has seen its operating margins squeezed further and further. The Taiwanese firms' enormous scale of production and global cost leadership do not yield higher returns because upstream firms compete by innovating more quickly while downstream ones control huge chunks of retail distribution. Private Taiwanese companies like Acer needed – and wanted – to make broader assaults on their industries in the global marketplace, but were not supported by their government to do so.

Taiwan made the smiling face famous in electronics. It is possible that China's private sector will extend the smiling face to many more industries. Apart from household consumer goods, where Chinese firms have long manufactured for brand-name multinationals or retailers like Walmart, there are trends towards the smiling face in sectors from motorcycles and cars to photovoltaic (PV) cells.[48] Multinationals calculate that their pace of innovation and marketing muscle can keep the smile in place indefinitely. Taiwan's experience suggests they could be right, and that without more policy support from government China's private sector will not fulfil its potential.

### Chinese sob stories

One well-known example of the problems that private Chinese firms face is the battery, orthodox car and putative electric car maker BYD. The

company was made famous in 2008 when a subsidiary of Warren Buffet's Berkshire Hathaway took a 10 per cent stake in it. BYD started out
in battery making in the 1990s, supported by technical assistance from
European and American mobile phone companies which wanted to lower
costs by diversifying away from battery producers in north-east Asia. The
company's entrepreneurial boss, Wang Chuanfu, then squeezed enough
cash out of a high-volume, low-margin battery business to move into car
making. In the 2000s, BYD reverse-engineered Japanese models and rode
China's boom in car ownership to become the fastest growing and lowest
priced producer. Wang announced he would next marry batteries and cars
to become a global force in electric vehicles. He promised to release a Pure
Electric Vehicle in 2010, and export it around the world from 2011. His
rise was trumpeted by the global media, from *The New York Times* to the
*Wall Street Journal* to the *Economist*.[49]

BYD, however, was only able to compete with cash-rich public sector
auto joint ventures by cutting its prices to the bone. Margins were almost
non-existent, while costs had a floor under them because BYD did not have
the resources to learn the full range of car-making technologies. It bought
the most value-added parts of its vehicles, like chassis and drivetrains, from
international suppliers. And if resources were insufficient for conventional
car making, they were wholly inadequate for a new field like electric vehicles, where complex software and engine management systems present new
technological challenges. The only subsidy BYD obtained was a modest
one from its local government in the southern boom town of Shenzhen,
which it took to reporting as 'profit' in order to shore up its income statement.[50] Without deeper pockets, and having exhausted the cash from a
stock market listing, deadlines to mass produce and export conventional
and electric vehicles came and went. BYD's market capitalisation peaked at
USD25 billion in December 2008, after Buffet's investment, but by summer
2011 the firm was worth less than one-tenth of that.

BYD is the latest in a number of entrepreneurial private manufacturing
firms in China which appear to show enormous promise, and then quickly
wither. Before BYD, the most feted private sector firm was Suntech, the
world's biggest manufacturer of photovoltaic cells used to turn solar rays
into electricity. It was another story of scale without the investment funds

to acquire power over the value chain. Like BYD, Suntech received only modest, provincial-level subsidies and focused on the mid-stream segment of its industry.[51] The bulk of central government subsidy for green energy went to state-linked firms in the wind industry, so Suntech was almost completely dependent on exports for growth. As competition from other Chinese PV cell manufacturers became intense, Suntech discovered that its international upstream polysilicon suppliers, and downstream solar panel installers, were able to capture the lion's share of profits. After the company listed in 2005, its shares were bid up to USD90. In mid 2011, despite its still being the biggest PV cell producer in the world, Suntech's shares were selling for under USD5. The firm's one hope for the future is that in 2011 China's central government began to provide modest subsidies for domestic solar installations, a policy development that may signal an unusual policy tilt towards a private-dominated sector.[52]

As they pursue their unequal struggle, private Chinese firms do have the advantage that in a globalised world it is easier than ever to buy foreign companies, and thereby acquire technology and different parts of a value chain. However, this opportunity is still constrained by inadequate cash flows. Money is required not only to buy firms, but even more so to 'digest' them in a timely manner. In 2010, another private auto firm, Geely, bought troubled Swedish car maker Volvo from Ford for USD1.8 billion. Geely's margins and profits were so thin that in summer 2011 its market capitalisation was only USD2 billion. In other words, it was worth little more than the failed firm whose technology and marketing reach it was trying to absorb. Over time, it may be that with its entrepreneurial determination Geely will absorb everything worth having from Volvo. But by that point the technological frontier that Geely thought it was approaching will have itself moved outwards. When consumer-oriented firms approach the frontier, Japanese and Korean experience suggests they need to race to burst through it, something which requires amounts of cash that private Chinese firms do not have.

Private firms do have access to stock markets to raise investment funds, but China shows what a poor substitute these are for government policy support and long-term bank credit when it comes to nurturing technological advance. The money that private companies can raise from initial public offerings is not nearly enough to fund their progress all the way to the technology frontier. There is a classic mismatch of expectations, with firms seeking long-term funds for technological upgrading and investors looking for short-term returns on a one-off investment. Hence the pattern that, after an initial euphoria, investors realise firms cannot deliver quickly the profits associated with technological leadership, and the stock is sold off. This in turn cuts off stock markets as further sources of investment capital, contributing to private companies' entrapment in low-margin activities. As noted above, in 2011 the average market capitalisation of twenty-four state-linked and policy-supported mid-stream manufacturers in China was USD6 billion. The average market capitalisation of a dozen of the most successful privately controlled manufacturers which do not get the same policy support was USD2 billion – reflecting their smaller scale and, critically, lower expectations of future profit.[53]

### It could be worse

Overall, China's manufacturing policy has the basics in place. Firms in the upstream of the economy have not been allowed to raise mineral, utilities, and services prices such that they undermine the objective of developing advanced manufacturing capabilities. A group of state-linked manufacturers is being both supported by infant industry policies and subjected to export discipline. The detailed policy choices made by China's bureaucrats have usually been conservative, which is as it should be in a developing country that is following an established technological road map.

None the less, the bias against the private sector in China must carry a cost, particularly in consumer-oriented businesses. In this sense China's industrial policy is far from optimal. It is not, however, fair to say that the Chinese government is pursuing a search and destroy mission against private enterprise. Much of its anti-private bias is in fact the policy path dependency of a reforming communist state. In contemporary China, the bureaucracy simply supports the firms it always has done rather than being driven by genuine ideological animus towards private business. The new subsidiaries created by state firms frequently involve significant private equity, even if old, purely state-owned firms like to gobble up private businesses that compete with them. Most importantly, the NDRC and the government do not kill 'off-plan' private firms that succeed despite a lack of state support. Sany is tolerated in construction machinery even though its peers are all state-run. Several big private car makers are allowed to vie with coddled state firms. A private solar industry in which many entrepreneurs are returnees from overseas and hold foreign passports is being grudgingly thrown a lifeline.

It is all rather messy and complicated, which is why the average China watcher swings between periods of optimism and pessimism about the economy on a daily basis. The Sinologist economist Barry Naughton describes the analytical problem as trying to understand the possibilities and the limits of a 're-purposed' Leninist system.[54] It is too early to bring the limitations into clear focus. China is setting a new standard for the performance of state-linked firms in a developing country, but that is not the same thing as saying that China is redefining global industrial standards – there is as yet no Chinese operational innovation that could be compared with Japan's just-in-time and total-quality manufacturing processes, for instance. Manufacturing policy, of course, could change as a result of the transition to a new Chinese leadership in 2012. And it may change drastically in the event of a domestic financial crisis – something common to most emerging economy stories (though not Taiwan's). If the result of such a crisis were to be that firms whose state ownership has not been a success, such as those in the automotive sector, were sold to private entrepreneurs, then it could be the start of a new and even more impressive phase of economic development.

### Where the money comes from

The financial system structure deployed by China's government has so far met the two conditions identified in Japan, Korea and Taiwan as allowing governments to implement effective agricultural and manufacturing policy. First, control has been exercised over banks so that they are not captured by private entrepreneurs whose interests are inimical to national development. And second, capital controls have given the state discretion over the uses of domestic investment funds and the ability to manage foreign capital flows.

China's banks are nationalised. They listed minority equity shares over the past decade, but this has done nothing to reduce control over them by the CPC, which appoints their most senior personnel. The largest institutions, the Big Four – Industrial and Commercial Bank of China, Bank of China, China Construction Bank and Agricultural Bank of China – control around half of system assets. They are not financially sophisticated banks, but they do follow state guidance on lending priorities. The government created more competition for the Big Four by licensing smaller national and city-level banks and allowing them to grow their share of national deposits. However, these institutions are also publicly owned and responsive to political direction; they make up about one-third of bank system assets.

A third group of financial institutions – and the fastest growing by loans extended in the past decade – is the three policy banks created by Zhu Rongji in 1994. China Development Bank (CDB) is much the most important of these. The policy banks' share of loans is around 15 per cent, a very significant slice.[55] CDB alone had almost USD900 billion of loans outstanding at the end of 2011, or 10 per cent of all loans and well over twice what the World Bank lends globally. China's policy banks have become the most focused part of the financial system in terms of financing agriculture and manufacturing policy objectives and enforcing export discipline. Their nearest equivalent in east Asian development experience was the state-owned Korea Development Bank (KDB). However KDB raised much of its money overseas, whereas China's policy banks get all theirs from issuing domestic bonds.

At home, CDB in particular lends against the cash flows from government land sales. (In rural areas around towns and cities, such lending further encourages local governments to dispossess farmers.) CDB loans then often pay for infrastructure development which requires the procurement of subway systems, trains, roads, power stations and so on from China's state producers' goods manufacturers and construction enterprises. Investment in infrastructure has so far kept land prices rising, allowing local governments to service their debts. Internationally, the policy banks secure many loans against mineral rights – oil, gas, coal, copper – and also lend for infrastructure and industrial projects that procure Chinese construction services, transportation equipment, tele-coms equipment, energy generating equipment, wind turbines and much more. A large chunk of policy bank 'foreign' loans in fact go direct to Chinese state-linked companies.[56]

In order to pay for its pro-development financial system China, in the tradition of north-east Asian developmental states, guarantees its deposit-taking banks fat margins by setting minimum lending rates and maximum deposit rates; the commercial banks in turn fund the policy banks by buying policy bank bonds. The margin 'spread' at regular banks was increased sub-stantially from the late 1990s to help the banks write off non-performing loans that were addressed as part of Zhu Rongji's closure of loss-making state enterprises. Some bad loans were bought over by government, while others were gradually paid off with earnings from the gap between lend-ing and deposit rates, which yields tens of billions of US dollars of profit a year.[57] As in Japan and Korea, the manipulation of banking spreads has proven a highly effective means of raising money in a society where the institution of personal taxation is in its infancy. Deposits have not fled the banking system because of this stealth taxation. Fat spreads offset both losses and low margins from following government guidance on lending objectives in support of national development. The major prerequisite of the system is that the government's industrial policy targets are realistic and not too wasteful of funds – something made more achievable by the closure of state sector 'zombie' firms in the 1990s.

Capital controls are the essential adjunct of a financial system that sup-ports China's development objectives because they prevent money leaving the country in search of better returns. The restrictions also prevent interna-tional investors from moving capital in and out of China at will, something which would make the government's job of pointing the financial system at developmental targets much harder. Capital controls are policed by an enormous bureaucracy at the State Administration of Foreign Exchange, which falls under the control of the central bank. It is clear from national balance of payments data that the controls are leaky – crude estimates suggest that sums of money up to 8 per cent of China's GDP move in and out of the country without permission each year.[58] But the logic of capital controls is not that they provide a hermetic seal; rather that, for a developing country, they are infinitely preferable to a free market in the movement of money.

## Two paranoias

Thus far, China's financial system management has worked well in giving government the discretion to run effective developmental policy. However, as north-east Asia's experience has shown, manipulation and repression of a financial system to developmental ends offers only a limited window of opportunity before financial and corporate entrepreneurs, and ordinary citizens, find ways to evade the controls. Commercial banks seek to circumvent rules about how they should lend in pursuit of higher margins. Companies that are being given policy direction bridle at state control; they seek to divert cheap bank funds to high margin activities like real estate or search for non-bank financing options that put them in control. Depositors become increasingly aggressive in looking for higher returns on their savings via investments outside the formal banking sector. And companies, financial institutions and international speculators all try to exploit gaps and loopholes in capital controls. All these tendencies reflect quests for short-term profit that conflict with the state's objective of forcing long-term learning. In the end, the state will always lose the battle for financial control – even in China. The question is whether the state can ensure sufficient developmental schooling occurs before this happens.

Of late there have been suggestions that the Chinese government's control of the banking system is eroding very quickly, while a huge increase in credit outstanding heightens the risk of a domestic financial crisis. On the first point, it is true that a substantial 'shadow banking' system has grown up in China, lending money outside the formal banking system. The supply-side driver for this is a rising class of wealthy Chinese looking for better returns than the state banks offer. The banks themselves, desperate not to lose wealthy clients, help them to find higher yield investments by setting up wealth management funds that evade the government's interest rate controls. According to some estimates, there may now be as much credit outside the banking system in China as there is inside it. However, while this gives rise to anxiety among China watchers, it in fact only parallels the role played by kerb markets in Japan, Korea and Taiwan. Whenever governments repress financial systems in the interests of agricultural and manufacturing development policy, alternative, semi-legal lending and borrowing arrangements spring up.[59]

The growth of non-bank loan finance points to the steady erosion of state power over the financial system. However, it is not the case in China that banks are being captured by private sector business groups in the manner of south-east Asia or Latin America before their financial crises. As with north-east Asian non-bank financial institutions (NBFIs) and kerb markets, investment directed through China's wealth management funds and other shadow bank channels is not, as bank regulators are increasingly keen to remind participants, a liability for the banking system. Any losses – unless the government decides to undertake a public bail-out – belong to the private sector. In theory this could mean that one day depositors in the alternative credit channels take a hit just as they did under Park Chung Hee's kerb market interest moratorium in 1972. When it comes to running developing country financial systems, legal and illegal shadow banking systems are infinitely preferable to allowing the capture of core banking institutions. This reflects another of the pragmatic compromises between plan and market that define successful development policy.

In addition to the shadow banking fear, the concern has been that China's government has become reckless in recent years in using bank lending to prop up growth. This has some justification, but we are not seeing a return to the financial ill discipline of the 1990s, when banks lent to state enterprises that had no revenues and banks' non-performing loans peaked at more than 50 per cent of GDP. In 2009, China did indeed react to the global financial crisis by allowing an extraordinary doubling of bank lending, and today bank loans amount to a very high 140 per cent of GDP. A RMB4 trillion (USD490 billion) stimulus investment programme was largely paid for with bank loans. There were also deep cuts in mortgage rates, deposits required for mortgages and the time that a property has to be held before it can be resold tax-free, leading to an often speculative real estate boom.[60] A substantial chunk of bank lending from the period will never be repaid. However, the proportion of loans that sour will not be as high as when banks were lending to unreformed state enterprises in the

1990s. Unless there is a good deal more unrestrained bank credit in the next few years, the situation should be manageable.

The largest chunk of stimulus lending during the global recession went to local government investment firms undertaking infrastructure projects. Fortunately, China is still in a period where it can throw big money at infrastructure investment and expect not only current stimulus but also significant future gains in terms of economic growth and efficiency. The country is not yet building two bridges where only one is required, in the style of post-bubble Japan. Although income from the new water supplies or underground train systems that have been constructed in recent years is often less than operating costs, there are learning benefits in such projects to the Chinese manufacturers who are supplying them, as well as economic gains to the country at large from adding infrastructure where there was none.[61]

In coming years, the financing gap of local governments will lead to increased bad bank debts, but in the bigger picture this is partly a function of the longstanding, unsatisfactory fiscal relationship between central and local government. Local governments in China are perennially short of funds to run basic public services. The central government prefers that banks lend to them rather than increasing its budgetary transfers, and then has to deal later with what cannot be repaid to the banks. Similarly, the huge loans taken out by the Ministry of Railways – equivalent to 4 per cent of GDP – will have to be bailed out in future. But the part of the investment that needs to be funded from the budget could still be an acceptable price to pay if Chinese railway firms have completed sufficient learning and are selling high-speed train systems around the world.

In the property sector, construction – in particular, speculative construction – has accelerated markedly in recent years, a trend exacerbated by investment funds available from China's growing shadow banking operations. However, government is both determined to rein in real estate speculation and capable of doing so. It was indicative in 2009 that once the economy began to recover from a big fall in exports triggered by the global crisis, Beijing moved immediately to reverse the incentives it had created for the real estate market. A stiff 40 per cent minimum downpayment for mortgages and a minimum 5-year holding period for property prior to tax-free resale were restored at the end of that year. Once again, central government's ability to micro-manage the banking system was important. Loans to households in China, of which mortgages are the largest part, are still equivalent to less than two-fifths of national after-tax income. In the United States before the recent financial crisis, such household debts were 130 per cent of after-tax income. China has experienced the bursting of a few localised property bubbles as a result of recent excesses, but this does not pose an immediate systemic risk. Chinese finance remains on a leash, even if that leash is inevitably, inexorably lengthening.

## Forward march

China's recent reaction to external crises is best viewed, then, not as a sudden loss of financial discipline but in the historical context of the Japanese, Korean and Taiwanese responses to the global currency and oil shocks of the 1970s. The Chinese government has intervened to maintain the momentum of the country's developmental learning process. 'School' has not been suspended because of external economic shocks.

Of course, this does not mean that China has no debt issues. If one adds together different central government debts, local government debts for which Beijing is ultimately responsible and other near-term contingent liabilities (although not long-run liabilities like China's huge state pension fund gap), then public debt is perhaps 80 per cent of GDP.[62] However, some of this debt is offset by readily saleable assets, almost none is owed to foreigners, and capital controls mean that banks do not need to worry about insolvency (that is, their potential losses on bad loans exceeding their capital) because they always have cash on hand. Even as China's structural inflation rate has crept up in recent years, and thereby pushed real deposit rates into negative territory, savings have not fled the banking system *en masse*.[63]

The lessons of north-east Asian finance – ones that were put to a much more extreme test in Korea – are borne out again in China. First, China shows that a financial system can be repressed to serve development policy without causing domestic panic or system instability. Second, this repressed financial system in combination with capital controls has allowed the country to run a high debt level to support development without either creating domestic instability or suffering speculative international attacks. (China's debt profile is less risky than Korea's was in the 1990s because it does not involve borrowing from foreigners.) And third, the acid test of financial policy is how much acquisition of technological capacity can be achieved in industry before the window of opportunity afforded by financial repression closes. China has made considerable gains, but there is much more to be done.

The main problem for China is that its structural rate of growth is beginning to slow as it gets richer and reduced population growth is cutting the supply of new labour to the workforce. This means the government will be less able to rely on growth going forwards to shrink its debts relative to the size of the economy. In turn, with annual growth dropping from 10 per cent to perhaps 7 per cent in the next few years, and a somewhat more open financial system, financial crisis risk increases. Another way of putting this is to say that China's investment-led industrial learning process needs to be less wasteful in the future. The country cannot afford to create as much debt relative to output as before because it cannot run away from the debt as quickly. The best days of industrial policy-led development are therefore already gone.

### A financial repression too far

Finally, it should be said that there is one element of financial system policy in China that has almost certainly been unnecessarily inefficient. Again, it is something which echoes past Taiwanese practice: the aggressive under-valuation of the exchange rate. By 1987, when Taiwan was finally forced by international pressure to undertake substantial upward revaluation of its currency, its central bank had accumulated foreign exchange reserves of USD60 billion, second only to Japan in the world and massively more relative to the size of Taiwan's economy. Most of the reserves were built up by the central bank buying up foreign exchange inflows at fixed rates to suppress the value of the Taiwan dollar. At the time, economists estimated the Taiwan dollar was undervalued against trade partner currencies by around 25 per cent.[64] China has done something very similar. A crude adjustment for price changes and the relative size of the Chinese economy suggests Taiwan's USD60 billion of reserves in 1987 were equivalent to China having something over USD2 trillion today. In mid 2012 China actually had USD3.3 trillion in foreign reserves.[65]

An undervalued exchange rate is a form of subsidy. Subsidies are essential to nurturing world-class firms in developing economies, but an undervalued exchange rate is a very blunt one. It helps all firms to export, whereas subsidies delivered through a banking system and other targeted means support only firms whose technologies have been prioritised as part of infant industry policy. Suppressed exchange rates subsidise low-value added domestic manufacturers which are not pushing national technological capacity forward and, worse, support the processing operations of multinational businesses.

There are also substantial costs attached to undervaluing a currency. The value of foreign exchange reserves that are accumulated eventually has to be marked down because trade partners will ultimately force appreciation. In addition, there are ongoing costs. The Chinese central bank pays interest on the renminbi bonds it issues, and reserves it sequesters, in order to reduce the inflationary impact of China's foreign exchange surplus.[66] In the 1980s, many people said Taiwan's extraordinary reserves were a symbol of its success as a developing economy. Still more is said of China's foreign exchange pile today. But if Taiwan is a guide, China will come to be seen as further proof that acute and chronic currency manipulation is not a useful long-term addition to the industrial policy tool cupboard.[67] In fairness to China, however, it should be said that the country's undervaluation of its currency has not been as rigid as Taiwan's was and the renminbi has been allowed to appreciate modestly since 2007.

## Good dragon, bad dragon

Overall, China's government has lined up most of the ducks necessary to enable rapid economic development. However, there is little to suggest that China offers qualitative improvements to policies which have been used before. While the leading role of the state sector provides the strongest evidence yet that ownership is not a critical issue in industrial policy if competition and export discipline are in place, no one has suggested that China's anti-private sector bias is an advantage. Contemporary chatter about the rise of a 'Beijing consensus' on development policy is a perversion of historical facts. The true break-out example in successful Asian development was Meiji Japan, and China is simply a follower in that tradition.

China's development is exceptional not because of the tried and tested land reform, infant industry and financial repression policies that made it possible, but because of its scale. At more than ten times the population of Japan, anything that happens in China has an amplified effect on the world. The country's GDP per capita is still only USD5,000 per person, yet it is already the biggest market for everything from minerals to telephones to cars (with the important caveat that the average price and sophistication of products consumed in China is well below that in rich countries). It is the size of China, not the originality of its development policies, that has shaken the world.

Is China's continued rise inevitable and without limits? Not at all. Many people believe that the scale of the country and its domestic market guarantee success. But the size of China also makes it a difficult place for central government to run effective industrial policy and to curtail waste. China has yet to create truly world-beating firms, and history suggests that a state's size is no great advantage in this respect. Many of the world's most successful firms were created in rather small countries in Europe. Most big states – Brazil, India, Indonesia, Russia – are relative economic failures (even if the United States is not). This is because it is the quality of governance and policy-making that determine a country's prospects. China will be no exception.

In this respect, recent political developments are not particularly encouraging. The country's government is tending towards a form of self-interested, consensual rule by a CPC elite that depends increasingly on birthright rather than on performance and merit. In the new politburo standing committee announced in November 2012, three of the seven leaders are sons of former senior party figures and one married into a political dynasty.[68] This 'princeling' polity tends to look to its own and is less and less inclined to take difficult economic policy decisions. It is all but impossible to imagine today a Zhu Rongji figure driving through the kind of policy changes that Zhu implemented in the 1990s and early 2000s. Unfortunately, however, as a country grows richer the need for difficult decisions does not decrease. As 1980s Japan showed, when countries think they have discovered the mythological 'secret' of wealth creation and stop adjusting they become vulnerable.

Even if China avoids a financial crisis in the next decade, demographic trends will take the edge off the more outlandish claims made for the country's economic potential. China is already exiting the most favourable demographic period for economic development, when workers are abundant and retirees few. The average age of the working population is starting to grow older, and the cohort of workers will slowly begin to shrink in a few years, as the proportion of retirees rises. The bargaining power of Chinese workers is already increasing, something which is well overdue but which is closing the gap between productivity gains and wage gains that has characterised development thus far. The economy can no longer be run simply by adding more and more people and investment each year. China has to adapt to a different demographic environment. In a comparison with Japan, Korea and Taiwan, the main point of interest is that China is reaching population stabilisation and demographic aging at a relatively lower level of GDP per capita, which may mean its long-run economic outlook is more challenging. There will be around 300 million pensioners by 2030 consuming savings, not creating them, and the population will be falling, having peaked at under 1.5 billion.

Apart from the demographic shift, the other easy prediction to make about China is that its very slow pace of institutional development will create ever more friction in society and, eventually, produce a significant economic cost. Political pluralism, separation of powers, judicial independence and the like have long been consigned to the back burner. For thirty years the democratisation of village elections has been presented as the means by which the CPC will roll out the democratic future it claims it is committed to. Too little has been done, and less and less in the past decade. After making some progress in developing the legal system in the late 1990s and early 2000s, in recent years the CPC has rolled that progress back. And the repression of dissenting voices, no matter how measured the criticism, is as aggressive and brutal as at any point since 'reform' began.

Since 1978, the CPC has learned the importance of competition in economic development, but it does not understand or entertain its role at a social and political level, despite the enormous changes that have occurred in China – ones which demand greater political sophistication.

As well as a country of technological capacity, China needs to become a country of institutional systems. It is only a combination of the two that can take the country to the front rank of nations and allow Chinese people to be genuinely proud of where they come from. Thus far, institutional deficiency has not been a significant drag on China's economic growth. But it will catch up with it eventually. The Chinese government already spends more money trying to micro-manage people's lives through its domestic security apparatus than it does on defence.[69] On its present trajectory, China is set to be a middle-income per capita, but profoundly institutionally retarded state. At an economic level, this gives leading nations nothing to fear. At a political level the outlook is more tricky. We must hope that the fact that China is more cosmopolitan, and its military more subject to civilian control, than nineteenth-century Germany or inter-war Japan makes it a less threatening rising power. In the coming years, the world's developed nations will need to remain engaged with a more assertive China, and to press their political and humanitarian principles. Of course, this would be a whole lot easier if we could only be a little more honest about the real nature and drivers of economic development.

# Epilogue:
# Learning to Lie

An historical review of east Asian economic development shows that the recipe for success has been as simple as one, two, three: household farming, export-oriented manufacturing, and closely controlled finance that supports these two sectors. The reason the recipe worked is that it has enabled poor countries to get much more out of their economies than the low productive skills of their populations would otherwise have allowed at an early stage of development. Governments manipulated economies which thereby forged ahead and created wealth that paid for people – who cannot be neatly transformed by government policy – to catch up.

Neo-classical economists do not like political intervention in markets. They claim that markets are inherently efficient. But history shows that markets – with the primordial exception of what the institutional economist Ronald Coase dismissed as 'individuals exchanging nuts for berries on the edge of the forest' – are created.[1] Which is to say that in a functioning society markets are shaped and re-shaped by political power. Without the dispossession of landlords in Japan, Korea, Taiwan and China there would have been no increased agricultural surplus to prime industrialisation. Without the focus on manufacturing for export, there would have been no way to engage tens of millions of former farmers in the modern economy. And without financial repression, it would not have been possible to pay for an accelerated economic learning process. In all of the above, markets and competition were made to serve development.

The message that east Asia – and indeed an historical understanding of development around the world – sends to economists is that there is no one type of economics. At a minimum, there are two. There is the economics of development, which is akin to an education process. This is where the people – and preferably all the people – who comprise an economy acquire the skills needed to compete with their peers around the world. The economics of development requires nurture, protection *and* competition. Then there is the economics of efficiency, applicable to a later stage of development. This requires less state intervention, more deregulation, freer markets, and a closer focus on near-term profits. The issue is not whether there are two kinds of economics that exist at different stages of development. The question is where these two stages meet. This is the difficult and interesting subject to which economists could more productively apply themselves.

Unfortunately, the intellectual tyranny of neo-classical 'efficiency' economics – the natural subject matter of rich countries – means that it is all but impossible to have an honest discussion about economic development. Poor states can only be successful by lying. They have to subscribe publicly to the 'free market' economics touted by the rich while pursuing the kind of interventionist policies that are actually necessary to become rich in the first place. It is a very hard thing to recommend lying, but in this instance one has to. The alternative – to rail against Western intellectual hegemony and to stick your rhetorical finger in the eye of its leader, the United States, as Mao, Sukarno and Mahathir did – is pure folly. Far better to take a page out of Park Chung Hee or contemporary China's book: make public pronouncements about the importance of free markets, and then go quietly about your *dirigiste* business.

It must be said, however, that there are problems on both sides of the argument about appropriate economic development policy. In countries that have successfully combined household agriculture, manufacturing and financial repression since the Second World War there has been an unwillingness or an inability to recognise the limitations of the model. In the richest countries that employed the one, two, three approach after 1945 – Japan in east Asia and Italy in Europe[2] – there has been a pronounced resistance to economic deregulation until long after it was needed. In Korea, it required the Asian crisis and a fortuitously well-timed intervention by the IMF to introduce reforms that otherwise would not have occurred. The one, two, three approach only gets an economy – not to mention a society – so far. If policies do not change, the economic sclerosis of contemporary Japan or Italy beckons.

Secondly, governments which have used one, two, three to develop in east Asia have frequently, and disingenuously, pretended that economic development is the only thing that defines the progress of a society. This stance is tied up with rhetoric about 'Asian' values, suggesting that 'Asian' (who are *they*?) people do not want the same things as people in rich countries. This is rubbish. Economic development is only one part of a society's development. The other parts, to do with freedom and the rights of the individual, are no less important. In China today, another government is claiming racial exceptionalism to justify deliberate institutional backwardness. China is putting off the creation of an independent legal system and more open, representative government until well after they are warranted. This is not what the Chinese people want. It does not matter that you can afford a small car or a motorbike if your friend or relative disappears into one of the country's extra-legal 'black jails'.[3] Nor does a new kitchen seem so pleasant if the food you eat in it is poisoned for lack of environmental controls or by the addition of some low-cost but toxic ingredient, the use of which has been covered up with official connivance. Emerging countries could themselves help to frame a more honest debate about economic development by setting and meeting benchmarks for the other components of overall development. In China's case, its government's unwillingness to actively discuss political and social progress scares rich, free countries so much that a sensible discussion of the requirements of economic development becomes all but impossible.

Will we witness an economic transformation like Japan, Korea, Taiwan or China's again? The answer is quite possibly not, for one simple reason. Without effective land reform it is difficult to see how sustained growth of 7–10 per cent a year – without fatal debt crises – can be achieved in poor countries. And radical land reform, combined with agronomic and marketing support for farmers, is off the political agenda. Since the 1980s, the World Bank has instead promoted microfinance, encouraging the rural poor to set up street stalls selling each other goods for which they have almost no money to pay. It is classic sticking-plaster development policy.

The leading NGO promoting land reform, US-based Landesa, is today so pessimistic about the prospects for further radical reforms in the world's poor states that it concentrates its lobbying efforts on the creation of micro plots of a few square metres. These plots supplement the diets and incomes of rural dwellers who work in otherwise unreformed agricultural sectors. From micro interventions, however, economic miracles will not spring.

South-east Asia (like India) is a region in which serious land reform is off the political agenda, even if the farce that is the Philippine reform programme continues. Given this, can the Philippines, Indonesia, Malaysia and Thailand do anything else to improve their economic performance? Most obviously they could make the Association of South-East Asian Nations (ASEAN) work as a vehicle for effective industrial policy. There is no reason why the four core economies of ASEAN (and indeed Vietnam, the important economy omitted from this book) could not run an effective manufacturing infant industry policy in what is a market of 500 million people.[4] But there is no sign of this happening. Rather than raising barriers and promoting exports to nurture local manufacturing enterprise, ASEAN is engaged in signing free trade agreements with industrially more developed states, including China. There is very little cohesion, or substantive dialogue, between the political leaders of the Philippines, Indonesia, Malaysia, Thailand and Vietnam. And the considerable influence of the offshore financial centre of Singapore in ASEAN is developmentally deeply unhelpful. It is as if Switzerland or Monaco had been granted a seat at the table when post-war European industrial policy was being planned in the 1950s. South-east Asia remains a beacon for what not to do if you want economic transformation. Allow landlordism and scale farming despite the presence of vast numbers of underemployed peasants capable of growing more. Do not worry too much about export-oriented manufacturing, which can happily be undertaken by multinational enterprises. Leave entrepreneurs to their own devices. And proceed quickly to deregulated banking, stock markets and international capital flows, the true symbols of a modern state. That is how its politicians constructed the south-east Asian region's relative failure.

The rich world cannot be expected to save poor countries from bad politicians. But the likes of Mahathir and Suharto were not so terrible. What seems most wrong in all this is that wealthy nations, and the economic institutions that they created like the World Bank and the International Monetary Fund, provided lousy developmental advice to poor states that had no basis in historical fact. Once again: there is no significant economy that has developed successfully through policies of free trade and deregulation from the get-go. What has always been required is proactive interventions – the most effective of them in agriculture and manufacturing – that foster early accumulation of capital and technological learning. Our unwillingness to look this historical fact in the face leaves us with a world in which scores of countries remain immiserated; and in which rural poverty nourishes terrorist groups that echo those suppressed in south-east Asian countries, but which now directly threaten the citizens of rich nations. It is not easy to implement the policies discussed in this book, especially land reform. However I repeat what others concluded after the Second World War: that to turn away from such policies indicates that the world is acceptable to us as it is. Take a look at south Asia, the Middle East and Africa, and ask yourself if it is.

# Notes

## Introduction

1. *World Development Report 1987* (Washington: World Bank, 1987). Apart from the inclusion of the offshore financial centres, the economic modelling was weak because it considered industrial policy and protection only at the national level, not at the sectoral level. Sectoral manufacturing policy varied enormously within most countries, especially in Japan, South Korea and Taiwan during their fast-growth phases. In addition to the modelling, the report's review of economic history was highly controversial. It highlighted British economic deregulation in the mid nineteenth century after the country became the world's technological leader, but said nothing of the country's protectionist policies deployed while it was ascending to this position. US protectionism during its rise in the nineteenth and early twentieth centuries was glossed over; only the country's tariff low point of around 24 per cent in 1857 was mentioned, when the average American tariff across the whole period was nearer 40 per cent. In Europe there was very little discussion of German industrial policy and industrial cartels. Instead there was much discussion of nineteenth-century France's *laissez-faire* economic policy – which left it in an economic condition far inferior to that of Germany. See especially, pp. 38 and 77. *World Development Report 1983* was in some respects the intellectual forerunner of this publication, staking a first and highly dubious claim that South Korean development was the result of free markets.

2. *The East Asian Miracle: Economic Growth and Public Policy* (New York and Oxford: Oxford University Press for the World Bank, 1993). The report's inconsistencies were neatly captured by two contradictory statements made by the World Bank president in the foreword. On the one hand, Lewis T. Preston conceded: 'The eight economies studied used very different combinations of policies, from hands-off to highly interventionist. Thus, there is no single "East Asian model" of development.' A few lines later, however, he got back to the World Bank's central ideological message: 'The authors conclude that rapid growth in each economy was primarily due to the application of a set of common, market-friendly economic policies, leading to both higher accumulation and better allocation of resources.' This internal inconsistency continues throughout the report.

3. The term was first used by the economist John Williamson in 1989. The headquarters of the three agencies are all located in Washington, D.C. Williamson listed ten policies which he said constituted the consensus. Among them, policies of particular interest for this book will be the use of market interest rates, freely determined exchange rates (inferring no capital controls), trade liberalisation, openness to foreign investment, privatisation of state enterprises, and deregulation.

4. Chalmers Johnson is quoted from *MITI and the Japanese Miracle: The Growth of Industrial Policy, 1925–75* (Stanford: Stanford University Press, 1982), p. viii. Alice H. Amsden is quoted from *Escape from Empire: The Developing World's Journey through Heaven and Hell* (Boston: MIT Press, 2009), p. 9. It is not clear why she mentions only Thailand among the south-east Asian states. W. W. Rostow is quoted from *The Stages of Economic Growth* (Cambridge: Cambridge University Press; third edition, 1991), p. xvii.

5. See Michael Spence, ed. *The Growth Report* (Washington: World Bank Commission on Growth and Development, 2008). The publication lists thirteen states that have grown at least 7 per cent a year for twenty-five years since the Second World War. I omit three offshore financial centres (Hong Kong, Singapore and Malta), a tiny oil state (Oman) and another tiny state overwhelmingly dependent on a diamond mine (Botswana). The other seven fast-growth states, all in east Asia, are listed below.

6. Korea and Taiwan reported GDP per capita of USD21,000 and USD19,000 respectively in 2010. Malaysian GDP per capita was USD8,000. According to the World Bank's World Economic Outlook database, in 1962 (the first year for which records are available) Indonesia, Thailand and South Korea each had GNI per capita around USD100. The World Bank does not break out data for Taiwan. Apart from Japan (USD610), the most prosperous states in terms of GNI per capita in 1962 were Malaysia (USD300) and the Philippines (USD210).

7. Yoshihara Kunio, *The Rise of Ersatz Capitalism in South-East Asia,* (Singapore and Oxford: Oxford University Press, 1988). In the same period, another Japanese economist, Suehiro Akira, confirmed and expanded many of Yoshihara's south-east Asia-wide observations with respect to the Thai kingdom in *Capital Accumulation in Thailand* (Tokyo: Centre for East Asian Cultural Studies, 1989).

8. The HDI is derived from a combination of GNI per capita, life expectancy and average years in education.

9. The exceptions to the rule of 'agricultural drag' are the handful of low-population, large cultivable area agricultural super-specialists: Denmark, Australia and New Zealand. But even these states are not clear exceptions, as much of their success depends on the industrial processing of their agricultural output.

10. The British Empire's treasury understood the logic of offshore centres and consistently argued the case for them in preference to larger colonies, which were favoured by aggrandising politicians and entrepreneurs who wanted government to subsidise their activities by paying for infrastructure and the like. Today's offshore financial industry

is rooted in the string of little islands that were beloved of the accountants of an economically predatory empire. (Not all the small islands of the British Empire have remained as offshore financial centres. Bombay and Lagos were originally settled by the British because they were islands. In south-east Asia, Penang gave way as the original offshore centre to Singapore.) Among major studies of development economics, Ha-Joon Chang's *The East Asian Development Experience: The Miracle, the Crisis and the Future* (London: Zed Books, 2007), p. 18, Alice H. Amsden's *Asia's Next Giant: South Korea and Late Industrialisation* (Oxford: Oxford University Press, 1989), p. 4; Robert Wade's *Governing the Market: Economic Theory and the Role of Government in East Asian Industrialization* (Princeton, NJ: Princeton University Press, 2003), p. xv, all explicitly reject the inclusion of Hong Kong or Singapore in the debate about developmental policy in east Asia. 'They are city states,' writes Wade, 'and not to be treated as economic countries.'

11. See, for instance, Angus Maddison, *Explaining the Economic Performance of Nations*, 1820–1989 (Canberra: Australian National University, 1993) p. 117.

12. All data for Cuba are from the United Nations HDI, 2009. Cuba's gross school enrolment rate as a percentage was 100.8 (gross enrolment can exceed 100 because of re-enrolment of children who drop out of school). The GDP per capita figure for that year was USD6,876 at purchasing power parity (PPP). Many Cuban doctors have gone to Venezuela, which is able to pay them with oil revenues.

13. On Taiwan's education system, see Wade, *Governing the Market*, pp. 64 and 190. A National Youth Commission survey in 1983 showed that one-quarter of all Taiwanese graduates since 1960 were engineers. Engineers were earning 11 per cent more on average than law graduates.

14. See David Landes, 'Japan and Europe: Contrasts in Industrialization', in William W. Lockwood, ed., *State and Economic Enterprise in Japan: Essays in the Political Economy of Growth* (Princeton, NJ: Princeton University Press, 1965), p. 108. Vocational and apprentice schools accounted for only 7 per cent of the education of Japanese boys of secondary school age in 1900. In 1930, only 9 per cent of university students graduated in engineering, rising to 16 per cent at the end of the decade. Until the Second World War, universities focused on humanities subjects.

15. Masayuki Kondo, 'Improving Malaysian Industrial Technology Policies and Institutions' in K. S. Jomo and Greg Felker, eds., *Technology, Competitiveness and the State* (London: Routledge, 1999).

16. The Japanese committees were usually elected. The Taiwanese ones were appointed, but according to criteria which ensured members were representative of ordinary farmers' interests.

## Part 1 – Land: The Triumph of Gardening

1. W. A. Dolph Owings, ed., *The Sarajevo Trial* (Chapel Hill, NC, USA: Documentary Publications, 1984), pp. 54.

276                                                                                           NOTES

2. With respect to weeding in Asian household farming, Ronald Dore notes that rice
   in Japan is traditionally weeded three times per crop, or up to nine times a year. See
   Ronald Dore, *Land Reform in Japan* (London: Athlone, 1984), p. 5.
3. Calculations based on an average US yield per hectare of 8.5 tonnes and a price per
   tonne of USD300.
4. See Shirley Kuo, Gustav Ranis and John Fei, *The Taiwan Success Story* (Boulder,
   CO: Westview Press, 1981), p. 57.
5. Data average 1953–2007. Data sourced from Taiwan Council of Agriculture and
   Philippines Sugar Research Institute Foundation. Taiwan was a major sugar producer
   in the 1950s and 1960s; however, sugar is today no longer an important crop.
6. With respect to Malaysia, see Lim Teck Ghee, *Peasants and Their Agricultural
   Economy in Colonial Malaya, 1874–1941*, East Asian Historical Monographs
   (Kuala Lumpur and New York: Oxford University Press, 1977), pp. 90–95, and his
   discussion of British colonial efforts to discourage smallholders from competing
   with plantation rubber. With respect to Kenya and Zimbabwe, see Bill Freund,
   *The Making of Contemporary Africa* (Bloomington, IN: Indiana University Press,
   1984), p. 111. He references colonial Kenya's subsidies to scale (white) agriculture,
   including tea, to keep it profitable, and the fact that in Southern Rhodesia, peasant
   smallholders continued to supply most urban foodstuffs from small plots despite
   the seizure of half of cultivable land by white settlers. Freund concludes: 'Peasants
   were actually more productive in per-acre use of the land.' Klaus W. Deininger,
   *Land Policies and Land Reform* (Washington DC: World Bank Publications,
   2004), p. 16, also highlights the imposition of colonial era laws in Zimbabwe to
   make the subdivision of large tracts of land difficult and impede black smallholder
   agriculture.
7. A classic example is W. W. Rostow's 'stages' view of development in which
   agriculture plays the initial capital accumulation role in Stage 1. See Walt Whitman
   Rostow, *The Stages of Economic Growth : A Non-communist Manifesto* (Cambridge:
   Cambridge University Press, 1960).
8. Toyota and Nissan both adapted truck chassis to carry car bodies and went on to
   lead the global four-wheel drive market. China's most successful international firm,
   Huawei, got its earliest breaks supplying rural telecommunications equipment.
9. Michael Lipton, *Why Poor People Stay Poor* (Harvard: Harvard University Press,
   1977).
10. More recently Michael Lipton, in *Land Reform in Developing Countries* (London:
    Routledge, 2009), p. 275 noted that the worst poverty remains rural in Latin
    America and is largely due to extreme and inefficient land inequality.
11. The estimate for Taiwan is from K.T. Li, *Economic Transformation of Taiwan*
    (London: Shepheard-Walwyn, 1988), chapter 21.
12. Or as Deininger puts it: 'there is a strong negative relationship between initial
    inequality in asset [land] distribution and long-term growth' and 'inequality [in

land distribution] reduces income growth for the poor, but not for the rich'. In Deininger's data set, long-term growth refers to the period from 1960 to 1992. The only other developing countries he found that grew an average of more than 2.5 per cent with very unequal land distribution (defined as having a land distribution Gini coefficient of more than 70) are Puerto Rico (a small and anomalous part of the United States) and Israel. See Klaus Deininger and Lyn Squire, 'New Ways of Looking at Old Issues: Inequality and Growth', *Journal of Development Economics*, vol. 57, no. 2 (1998), pp. 259–87.

13. Tang land management was in fact more complex than stated here because small parcels of land were also granted to farmers in perpetuity. The bureaucratic requirements were extraordinary for a pre-modern state. See S.A.M. Adshead, *T'ang China* (London: Palgrave Macmillan, 2004), pp. 90–91. The system broke down (like much else in Tang) from around 750, but until then Adshead remarks that it did 'establish a class of highly competent micro-managers, smallholders, female as well as male, with a mixture of usufruct and ownership, a possible optimum for the Chinese peasantry'.

14. The Meiji land tax reform began in July 1873 and ended in 1876. See Kozo Yamamura, 'The Meiji Land Tax Reform and Its Effects', in Marius B. Jansen and Gilbert Rozman (eds.), *Japan in Transition* (Princeton, NJ: Princeton University Press, 1986).

15. The Japanese population was around 35 million in 1868, rising to 70 million on the eve of the Second World War. On the absence of food imports prior to 1900, see Penelope Francks, Johanna Boestel and Choo Hyop Kim, *Agriculture and Economic Development in East Asia* (London: Routledge, 1999), p. 52.

16. See Lipton, *Why Poor People Stay Poor*, p. 35. Lipton references fifteen countries that were already wealthy at the time of the Meiji restoration; their populations, when faster growth and industrialisation took off, were 35–70 per cent urban. (Britain was 36 per cent urban in 1811. See C. M. Law, 'The Growth of Urban Populations in England and Wales, 1801–1911', *Transactions of the Institute of British Geographers*, no. 41 (June 1967), p.128.)

17. Lipton, *Why Poor People Stay Poor*, p. 24.

18. Francks *et al.*, *Agriculture and Economic Development in East Asia*, p. 63.

19. Based on estimates given by Wolf Ladejinsky in the Atcheson-Fearey Memorandum of 1945, one of the key official documents which led to post-Second World War land reform in Japan. Farm household debt is given as JPY135 per household prior to the First World War, rising to JPY1,000 in 1937. At its peak, interest on farmer debt was estimated to consumer one-third of total net farm income. Reprinted in Wolf Isaac Ladejinsky and Louis J. Walinsky (ed.), *Agrarian Reform as Unfinished Business* (New York: Oxford University Press on behalf of the World Bank, 1977), p. 570.

20. Quoted in Dore, *Land Reform in Japan*, p. 49.

21. See Francks *et al.*, *Agriculture and Economic Development in East Asia*, p. 20.

22. See Dore, *Land Reform in Japan*, chapter 3, for more on the rebellion.

23. Now called the Northern Culture Museum, Niigata.

24. Life expectancy cited in Louis G. Putterman, *Continuity and Change in China's Rural Development* (New York: Oxford University Press, 1993), p. 9. Land ownership data from Carl Riskin, *China's Political Economy* (Oxford: Oxford University Press, 1987) and William Hinton, *Fanshen* (New York: Monthly Review Press, 1966), chapter 2. Details of Deng home from author visit and interviews, August 1994.

25. R. H. Tawney, *Land and Labour in China* (London: George Allen & Unwin, 1932; reprinted Boston, MA: Beacon Press, 1966), p. 66. I have changed the romanisation Shensi to the pinyin Shanxi.

26. Hinton, *Fanshen*, chapter 1.

27. There is an echo here of events in the late 1970s and early 1980s, when farmers returned to household farming long before this was given general sanction by the CPC in 1983.

28. Reprinted as Appendix A, Hinton, *Fanshen*, p. 615.

29. Most estimates have ranged from 1 million to 5 million. Part of the discrepancy depends on whether the calculation is limited to deaths attributable to land reform, or whether it includes deaths resulting from other political struggles around the time of 'liberation', such as that against Nationalist anti-revolutionaries. According to Denis Twitchett and John K. Fairbank (eds.), *The Cambridge History of China* (Cambridge: Cambridge University Press, 1978–91), in many parts of the country there was a policy to execute at least one landlord in every village.

30. Hinton, *Fanshen*, p. 200. The preceding paragraphs draw on Hinton, chapters 14, 20, and 21.

31. There are no national data from the start of the war against Japan in 1937 to the end of the Chinese civil war in 1949. The likelihood is that in the 1940s output increased markedly in areas subject to land reform that were not heavily affected by the Japanese war or the civil war. From 1949 to 1952, output increased considerably. Early official Chinese data claimed that grain output rose by more than 40 per cent. Estimates by Thomas Wiens suggested more like 25 per cent, based on evidence that official data understated output for the 1949 base year. Chinese data published in the 1980s indicate grain production rose a further 20 per cent from 1952 to 1957 and these numbers are generally accepted by scholars. In absolute terms, the best recorded pre-1949 harvest, 1936, was around 139 million tonnnes; 1952 was 155 million tonnes; 1957 was 195 million tonnes. See Carl Riskin and Thomas Wiens, 'The Evolution of Policies and Capabilities in China's Agricultural Technology', in *Chinese Economy Post-Mao* (Washington DC: US Congress, Joint Economics Committee, 1978). Zhang Gensheng, *Rural Reform in China* (Shenzhen: Haitian Publishing House, 2001), p. 324, is one of those who uses the official Chinese data published in the 1980s which may understate 1949 output. He writes (without giving a source) that

grain production in 1949 was 113.2 million tonnes, in 1953 was 166.8 million tonnes, and in 1956 (on the eve of collectivisation) was 192.7 million tonnes. Zhang is a former deputy director general of the State Council's Development Research Center and vice chairman of the NPC's Finance and Economics Committee. His numbers infer a 70 per cent increase in grain output in seven years.

32. Nicholas R. Lardy, *Agriculture in China's Modern Economic Development* (Cambridge: Cambridge University Press, 1983), Christopher Bramall, *Living Standards in Sichuan, 1931–78* (London: Contemporary China Institute, SOAS, 1989).

33. The JCRR was part of the Economic Co-operation Agency set up under the China Aid Act (1948). The first meeting of the JCRR was held in Nanjing in October 1948 at a time when the final rout of nationalist forces by Mao's communists was already under way.

34. Ladejinsky and Walinsky (ed.), *Agrarian Reform as Unfinished Business*, p. 289. The remark occurs in a letter to George Gant of the Ford Foundation.

35. See 'Too Late to Save Asia?', first published in the *Saturday Review of Literature*, 22 July 1950, and reprinted in Ladejinsky and Walinsky (ed.), *Agrarian Reform as Unfinished Business*, above. Ladejinsky was in mainland China for only about one week, around the time of the final communist victory in October 1949. See also James Putzel, *A Captive Land* (New York: Monthly Review Press, 1992), p. 72.

36. The Atcheson-Feary Memorandum, 26 October 1945, reprinted in Ladejinsky and Walinsky (ed.), *Agrarian Reform as Unfinished Business*, p. 575. Robert A. Feary was a pro-land reform State Department official working in its Office of Far Eastern Affairs. George Atcheson Jr was the State Department representative at MacArthur's headquarters in Japan.

37. SCAP Directive 411 on Rural Land Reform, 9 December 1945, reprinted in Ladejinsky and Walinsky (ed.), *Agrarian Reform as Unfinished Business*, p. 579.

38. See Dore, *Land Reform in Japan*, chapter 6, p. 129. The sequence of events was as follows: the Japanese diet drafted its own bill; MacArthur instructed land reform to be undertaken; the draft bill was passed; the occupying forces rejected the first reform bill; a second reform bill was passed in October 1946. The higher retention limit of the first bill was about 5 hectares, compared with 3 hectares in the second bill. This 2-hectare change was the difference between expropriating 100,000 landlords versus more than 1 million landlords. MacArthur's role in pushing through radical land reform should not be overstated. A Soviet demand for a lower retention limit expressed via the Allied Council for Japan, an advisory body to the SCAP, was important, as was British support for Ladejinsky's suggestion of a 3-hectare retention. For an excellent discussion, see Putzel, *A Captive Land*, chapter 3.

39. There was a small cash component.

40. Dore, *Land Reform in Japan*, pp. 172–3. The estimate for the number of cases in which landlords tried to evade expropriation is cited in Dore, pp. 151–2.

41. Japan's Economic Planning Board estimated that in 1954 the index of rural consumption hit 136 compared with a base of 100 in the mid 1930s, versus only 94 in urban Japan. Cited in Dore, *Land Reform in Japan*, p. 202.

42. Francks *et al.*, *Agriculture and Economic Development in East Asia,* chapter 4.

43. Wolf Ladejinsky, 'Chosen's Agriculture and Its Problems', first published in *Foreign Agriculture* (1940), reprinted in Ladejinsky and Walinsky (ed.), *Agrarian Reform as Unfinished Business*, p. 49. (Chosen is an old name for Korea.)

44. Putzel, *A Captive Land*, p. 80, highlights this point.

45. John P. Powelson and Richard Stock, *The Peasant Betrayed: Agriculture and Land Reform in the Third World* (Washington DC: Cato Institute, 1990), p. 179.

46. See Anthony Y. C. Koo, *The Role of Land Reform in Economic Development* (New York: Praeger, 1968), p. 8.

47. Koo, *The Role of Land Reform in Economic Development*, p. 44.

48. Koo, *The Role of Land Reform in Economic Development*, p. 38. There were 195,000 separate transactions under land to the tiller in Taiwan. See 'Table 12: The Rise of Ownership – Taiwan Before and After Land Reform'.

49. Kuo, Ranis and Fei, *The Taiwan Success Story*, p. 53.

50. Kuo, Ranis and Fei, *The Taiwan Success Story*, chapter 5. Data from various income surveys in Taiwan are consolidated in a table on p. 45. A global survey of sixty poor countries by economist Hollis Chenery in 1964 concurred that in Taiwan the income share of the bottom 40 per cent of the population was the highest to be found.

51. For instance, in 1953 agricultural products made up 14 per cent of Taiwan's exports, processed agricultural products 78 per cent, and industrial products only 8 per cent.

52. Taiwan Sugar Corporation (TSC) also inherited some former Japanese landholdings planted to sugar, which for the most part continued to be farmed in small plots by households. TSC managed to avoid being subjected to land reform; however, the rental terms it offered household farmers were better than under Japanese colonialism and the state company also undertook considerable extension work.

53. Data for JCRR activity are from E. Thorbecke, 'Agricultural Development' in W. Galenson (ed.), *Economic Growth and Structural Change in Taiwan* (Ithaca and London: Cornell University Press,1979), pp. 182–3. Data for agricultural extension workers from Kuo, Ranis and Fei, *The Taiwan Success Story*, p. 54. In 1960, there were 79 per 100,000 population, compared with 60 in Japan, 4.7 in Thailand, 1.6 in the Philippines and 1.2 in India.

54. Koo, *The Role of Land Reform in Economic Development*, chapter 8, calculates that in constant 1935–7 Taiwan dollars, farm income was TWD276 million in 1950, rising to TWD577 million in 1960.

55. High US tariffs on imported sugar have been used to protect domestic producers, including politically influential Cuban exiles, for decades. The special import quota given to the Philippines has been reduced in recent decades and is now only 50,000

tonnes per year. See Suresh Gawali, 'Distortions in World Sugar Trade', *Economic and Political Weekly* 38, no. 43 (25 October 2003), pp. 4513–5.

56. Mark Cleary and Peter Eaton, *Tradition and Reform* (New York: Oxford University Press, 1996) estimate that in the early 1990s 55 per cent of Filipino farmers were landless, while they classified a further 26 per cent as 'near landless', meaning they controlled less land than could keep them above the poverty line. These estimates are roughly in line with those from the Philippine Institute for Development Studies. See 'Post 2008 CARP: Extension with Critical Reforms', *Development Research News*, vol. 26, no. 3, (2008), which estimates that 8.5 million out of 11.2 million farmers are landless.

57. This section employs an exchange rate of PHP46.15 to USD1 prevalent in late 2009.

58. See Jeffrey Reidinger, *Agrarian Reform in the Philippines* (Palo Alto, CA: Stanford University Press, 1995), chapter 3 and Putzel, *A Captive Land*, chapter 3.

59. The Bell Mission report was commissioned in 1950 and prepared by Daniel Bell, undersecretary of the US Treasury. The Hardie Report was commissioned in 1951 by the US Mutual Security Agency (a Cold War successor to the Economic Co-operation Agency which had overseen the Marshall Plan) and prepared by Robert S. Hardie, who worked on land reform in Japan. See Putzel, *A Captive Land*, p. 84.

60. For an overview of land legislation in the past hundred years, see Department of Agrarian Reform, Republic of the Philippines, 'Philippine Agrarian Reform', 3 March 2006.

61. Marcos, quoted in Reidinger, *Agrarian Reform in the Philippines*, p. 8. With respect to the little land reform Marcos did achieve, his key rivals, the Aquinos, were among the first to be expropriated. To this day, some household farmers in Luzon remain extremely grateful to Marcos. In addition to their acquiring land, for which they typically paid nothing, agricultural extension work there in the 1960s was often of high quality. See Reidinger, p. 91.

62. NPA membership, which includes both political officers and guerrillas, from Reidinger, *Agrarian Reform in the Philippines*, p. 55. In South Vietnam, Thieu came to power following the assassination of Ngo Dinh Diem, under whose long rule the US had done almost nothing to support land reform. Cumulative land reform in the Philippines 1980–86 estimated in Reidinger, p. 97.

63. Quoted in Reidinger, *Agrarian Reform in the Philippines*, p. 139.

64. Earl G. Parreño, *Boss Danding* (Quezon, Philippines: Earl G. Parreño, 2003), p. 72. This is a difficult book to obtain. Written by a Filipino journalist it has been sold only through a handful of bookshops in the Philippines, perhaps because of the political influence of the Cojuangco family. The PHP7 million loan to buy Hacienda Luisita came from the Government Service Insurance System with the proviso that 'the lots comprising the Hacienda Luisita shall be subdivided by the applicant corporation

among the tenants who shall pay the cost thereof under reasonable terms and conditions'; the Philippine central bank extracted a similar undertaking in signing off the foreign exchange aspects of the acquisition. The Luisita affair is discussed in several other publications, including Walden Bello *et al.*, *The Anti-development State* (London and New York: Zed Books, 2005), chapter 2.

65. Philippine Institute for Development Studies, 'Post 2008 CARP: Extension with Critical Reforms'.

66. Saturnino M. Borras Jr, 'The Philippine Land Reform in Comparative Perspective: Some Conceptual and Methodological Implications', *Journal of Agrarian Change*, vol. 6, no.1, (January 2006), p. 80, and n. 17, p. 80.

67. See Borras, 'The Philippine Land Reform in Comparative Perspective', p. 93, which notes that the same problem is alleged to have occurred in Latin American land reforms. Saturnino M. Borras Jr and Jennifer C. Franco, 'Struggles for Land and Livelihood: Redistributive Reform in Agribusiness Plantations in the Philippines', *Critical Asian Studies vol.* 37, no.3 (2005), pp. 331–61, provide several case studies of direct landlord–tenant deals which made tenants worse off than ever, including a scheme offered to banana farmers in Mindanao by the US multinational Dole.

68. The estimate for the total area of cultivable land in the Philippines is from the UN Food and Agriculture Organisation. In addition to the effective exemption of large, commercial farms, Reidinger, *Agrarian Reform in the Philippines*, p.160, calculates that a 5-hectare retention limit exempted three-quarters of all smaller farms from land reform. The World Bank commented in a 1987 report on the proposed CARL legislation that it 'would encourage evasion, leave out a high proportion of tenants and landless, and add to the administrative burden' (see Reidinger, p.165). The figures for landlessness are from the Philippine Institute for Development Studies, 'Post 2008 CARP: Extension with Critical Reforms'.

69. The following section is based on author interviews, 11 and 12 November 2009. Thanks to Ted Lopez, Executive Director of Alter Trade Foundation, for setting up the interviews and giving up his time to accompany me.

70. Six thousand hectares is a conservative estimate and close to the hectarage Danding declared to the Department of Agricultural Reform. Some press and NGO estimates of his holdings range as high as 20,000 hectares.

71. Reidinger, *Agrarian Reform in the Philippines*, p.134. Parreño, *Boss Danding*, p. 183 cites rumours that Danding's private armies, spread over numerous estates, comprised 3,000 men and received training from Israeli military officers.

72. Parreño, *Boss Danding*, pp. 98 and 125.

73. Danding even regained control of San Miguel after his return to the Philippines. See Parreño, *Boss Danding*, p. 15. Danding's party is the Nationalist People's Coalition (NPC). The NPC briefly supported Cory Aquino's successor, Fidel Ramos, then backed Joseph Estrada (before he was impeached), and then backed Gloria Macapagal Arroyo. Parreño, p. 208, states that in Negros Occidental in

the mid 2000s Danding loyalists accounted for six out of seven congressmen and twenty-eight out of thirty-two mayors. One of Danding's two sons, Charlie, served the maximum three terms for Negros' Fourth Congressional District.

74. Bello *et al.*, *The Anti-development State*, p. 54. Much of the political cover for Danding's 'land reform' came during the presidency of his close political ally Joseph 'Erap' Estrada, who was president from 1998 until his impeachment trial in 2001. There have been numerous reports from tenants that Danding subsequently offered them small cash payments to buy back full title to his land – illegal under the terms of the CARL – and other reports of farmers being asked to sign blank sheafs of legal documents. According to Parreño, *Boss Danding*, p. 200, a tape recording was made of one meeting of 1700 farm workers, on 27 September 1998, at which Danding declared he had bought his land back.

75. See 'Regional Dynamics: Rise and Decline of the CPP–NPA in Negros Occidental' in Rosanne Rutten (ed.), *Brokering a Revolution* (Quezon City: Ateneo de Manila University Press, 2008).

76. The man killed was Diony Gaylan. He died on 6 March 2004.

77. Provincial Government of Negros Occidental, 'An Evaluation of CARP Implementation in Negros Occidental', December 2007.

78. 'Pressure from the People: The Task Force Mapalad Experience in Defending Agrarian Reform', presentation prepared for the First Visayas Area-specific Development Program (ASDP) Conference Workshop, Lahug, Cebu City. 26 May 2005.

79. Provincial Government of Negros Occidental, 'An Evaluation of CARP Implementation in Negros Occidental'.

80. 45 per cent of the Philippines' population lived at less than USD2 per day during 2000–2007, according to UNDP data. Raw sugar prices from World Bank Commodity Prices Review Online. The rest of this paragraph is drawn from Michael S. Billig, *Barons, Brokers and Buyers* (Honolulu: University of Hawaii Press, 2003), pp. 61 and 75.

81. Figures for yields per hectare from FAOSTAT 2009. Survey data cited in Putzel, *A Captive Land*, p. 33. China's 1985 value-added per hectare, updated according to the US consumer price index, would be USD5,000 in 2009. This can be very loosely compared with the retail value per hectare that would be obtained by the best home gardeners in rich countries, as discussed at the beginning of the chapter. Roger Doiron's home garden produced food with a shop value equivalent to USD135,00 per hectare.

82. See Ladejinsky and Walinsky (ed.), *Agrarian Reform as Unfinished Business*, p. 325.

83. See Gary E. Hansen (ed.), *Agricultural and Rural Development in Indonesia* (Boulder, CO: Westview Press, 1981), p. 5. The 1973 Indonesian agricultural census showed the average landholding on Java to be just 0.64 hectares, with most owners holding less than half a hectare. Rural landlessness (excluding tiny garden plots) has

increased subsequently in Java and is today reckoned to account for at least 70 per cent of the farming population. Java has about 9 million hectares of cultivable land.

84. Roy Prosterman, Robert Mitchell and Timothy Hanstad (eds.), *One Billion Rising: Law, Land and the Alleviation of Global Poverty* (Amsterdam: Amsterdam University Press, 2009), p. 135.

85. For Ladejinsky's estimates of Indonesian land redistribution, see Ladejinsky and Walinsky (ed.), *Agrarian Reform as Unfinished Business*, pp. 341–2. Quotation from a letter to A. T. Mosher, executive director of the US Council on Economic and Cultural Affairs (ECA), in Ladejinsky, p. 297.

86. For a description of Sukarno and Suharto era attempts to increase yields, see Hansen (ed.), *Agricultural and Rural Development in Indonesia*, pp. 7–43.

87. The interests of plantation owners are much more closely aligned with those of factory or mine operators than is popularly perceived. Plantations are a kind of (low-efficiency) agricultural factory.

88. Powelson and Stock, *The Peasant Betrayed*, p. 219. Sugar plantations covered about 75,000 hectares at the time of nationalisation.

89. The Tebu Rakyat Intensificasi (TRI) programme. See Powelson and Stock, *The Peasant Betrayed*, p. 221.

90. Michael Lipton, 'Towards a Theory of Land Reform', in David Lehmann (ed.), *Peasants, Landlords and Governments* (New York: Holmes and Meier, 1974), p. 272.

91. Cleary and Eaton, *Tradition and Reform*, p. 95. The period 1979–84 was that of the third Indonesian five year plan under Suharto (known as Repelita III); in the preceding plan period, 1974–9, just under half a million settlers were sponsored. The earliest sponsored migration in Indonesia occurred under the Dutch colonists in the first two decades of the twentieth century.

92. As anyone who visits rural Java will see, it is not only what is grown in people's tiny gardens, but also the chickens and other food animals that wander around which contribute to the high output. There is a detailed discussion in Prosterman *et al.* (eds.), *One Billion Rising*, p. 176 and, generally, chapter 4. The efficiency of home gardens has led campaigners like Prosterman, who doubt that effective land reform is possible in most countries today, to promote garden-style micro-plots as a policy alternative for those who do not have them. Micro-plots, however, will not create the kind of rural surplus that drove development in north-east Asia.

93. A. Vandenbosch (1933) in Ladejinsky and Walinsky (ed.), *Agrarian Reform as Unfinished Business*, p. 59, estimated that Dutch interests were earning around USD160 million a year in the early twentieth century from Indonesia; using the US consumer price index to adjust the sum to 2010 US dollars, it is equivalent to USD2 billion a year. Malaysian plantation hectarage is taken from Lim Teck Ghee, *Peasants and Their Agricultural Economy, 1874–1941*, p. 128.

94. See Lim, *Peasants and Their Agriciultural Economy, 1874–194*, pp. 90 and 127 and K. S. Jomo, *A Question of Class* (Singapore: Oxford University Press, 1986), p. 55.

Roads in colonial Malaysia were like railways in the central and western United States in the role they played in opening up the country. Quotation at Lim, *Peasants and Their Agricultural Economy, 1874–1941*, p. 94.

95. Lim, *Peasants and Their Agricultural Economy, 1874–1941*, pp. 149–51. The campaign for restriction was led by the Rubber Growers' Association, which essentially represented plantation interests and had members in the two key rubber-growing British colonies: Malaysia and Sri Lanka. A survey of 537 plantations in the Federated Malay States in 1923 showed an average yield among 426 of those estates of 375 pounds per acre per year.

96. Lim, *Peasants and Their Agricultural Economy, 1874–1941*, p. 143 gives a detailed description on which this section is based.

97. The report was commissioned by the British Colonial Office and published in 1948. P.T. Bauer, the report's author, estimated that Malaysian smallholders lost GBP30 million as a result of the 1922 Stevenson scheme and GBP10 million as a result of the 1930s international restriction scheme. The total GBP40 million was equivalent to roughly two years of total Malaysian production at 1940 levels. If one adjusts the figure in line with the UK GDP deflator since 1930, it is equivalent to GBP2.1 billion. The colonial government of what was by then the Malayan Union rejected Bauer's estimates of losses to smallholders when the report was in draft, but he stood by them. He concluded (p. 37): 'Rubber is a crop ideally suited to the needs of Asiatic smallholders.' However the Rubber Research Institute of Malaya, paid for by an export tax on all producers, worked almost exclusively to support estate agriculture. As a result (p. 88): 'The rubber growing smallholder has been the stepchild of the Malayan administrations for the last 20 or 30 years; his efficiency and importance are generally overlooked ...The treatment [of smallholders], and the planting provisions of rubber regulation which have already been mentioned, were a clear breach of certain definite moral obligations.' P.T. Bauer, 'Report on a Visit to the Rubber Growing Smallholdings of Malaya, July–September 1946' (London: His Majesty's Stationery Office, 1948).

98. See Lim, *Peasants and Their Agricultural Economy, 1874–1941*, p. 125. A similar pattern of high-yield market gardens feeding urban and mining populations was apparent in African colonies, like Rhodesia, with a pro-scale bias in agricultural policy. See Freund.

99. See K. S. Jomo, *A Question of Class*, pp. 77 and 123–4. In addition, Shireen Madziah Hashim, *Income Inequality and Poverty in Malaysia* (Lanham, MD and Oxford: Rowman & Littlefield, 1998), p. 202, states that the export tax, research levy and replanting levy to which rubber was subjected in the 1980s amounted to a combined tax of 13 per cent of crop value.

100. On land concentration, see Jomo, *A Question of Class*, p. 113. According to Jomo, tenancy is more prevalent in rice farming than in rubber; landlessness rates range up to 40 per cent. On falling yields, see Cleary and Eaton, *Tradition and Reform*, p. 75. Rice yields began to decline in the 1970s.

101. Zahir Ahmed, *Land Reforms in Southeast Asia* (New Delhi: Orient Longman, 1975), p. 188.
102. Where there is little export processing activity in Malaysia – for instance in Sabah – poverty rates remain the highest. The rate is 80 per cent for Sabah rice growers. See Shireen Madziah Hashim, *Income Inequality and Poverty in Malaysia*, p. 219. For further detail on unused agricultural land, see Cleary and Eaton, *Tradition and Reform*, p. 75.
103. Ronald J. Herring, *Land to the Tiller* (New Haven and London: Yale University Press, 1983), p. 284.
104. Pasuk Phongpaichit and Chris Baker, *Thailand: Economy and Politics* (Kuala Lumpur and New York: Oxford University Press, 1995; second edition, 2002), pp. 16 and 41. The yield figure is based on data for 1950, but would not have changed much from the 1930s. The comparison with post-land reform north-east Asia refers to yields following land reforms after the Second World War, not Meiji Japan.
105. Pasuk and Baker, *Thailand*, pp. 31–2.
106. Pasuk and Baker, *Thailand*, p. 36.
107. Peter Vandergeest, 'Displacements in Neoliberal Land Reform: Producing Tenure (In)securities in Laos and Thailand', in Peter Vandergeest *et al.* (eds.), *Development's Displacements: Ecologies, Economies, and Cultures at Risk* (Vancouver: University of British Columbia Press, 2007). The Act set up an Agricultural Land Reform Office (ALRO), which ever since has concentrated on distribution of publicly owned lands, most of which are already occupied by squatters. This is consistent with the focus on public lands in the Philippines, Indonesia and Malaysia instead of actual redistribution of existing private agricultural land. Similarly, a 1974 Land Rent Control Act in Thailand was generally not enforced because of opposition from landlords and local government officials.
108. Pasuk and Baker, *Thailand*, p. 45.
109. Note that the delta and central plain areas are not themselves particularly fertile by south-east Asian standards. Their heavy clay soils are much less agriculture-friendly than other parts of the region.
110. Thailand's Bank of Agriculture and Agricultural Co-operatives (BAAC) was set up in 1966. From 1975, commercial banks were also mandated to make a minimum share of their loans to agriculture; they preferred to lend to large agribusinesses or major cultivators, as was the case with BAAC.
111. The author has his doubts. Despite vast amounts of international media attention, CP Group, the leading Thai agribusiness, has not emerged as a truly world-class business. In the 1980s it diversified into Thai telecommunications services (under government protection) and retailing and has not become a focused industrial enterprise. No south-east Asian state has produced a real, value-adding branded agribusiness which can compete with firms like Dole at a global level.
112. Pasuk and Baker, *Thailand*, pp. 64–5.

113. On *phleng luk thung*, see Pasuk and Baker, *Thailand*, p. 79. Data on rural incomes from Pasuk and Baker, p. 89.

114. It is notable that when Thaksin's younger sister, Yingluck, won an election and became prime minister in 2011, the first thing her administration did was to scrap new wealth taxes on land and property initiated (ironically) by the previous, army-backed government. The Thaksin family signalled that its alliance with the rural poor is now on the back burner. Thaksin Shinawatra was never fundamentally interested in reshaping the Thai political economy; what he realised was that the rural north-east vote was there for the taking. For further detail on Thaksin, see Joe Studwell, *Asian Godfathers* (London: Profile Books, 2008) and Pasuk and Baker, *Thailand*, p. 200. At the time of writing, Shinawatra remains in exile.

115. Zahir Ahmed, *Land Reforms in South-east Asia* (New Delhi: Orient Longman, 1975), p. 170.

116. A brief discussion of American agricultural history and farm consolidation can be found in Bruce L. Gardner and Gordon C. Rausser (eds.), *Handbook of Agricultural Economics* (Amsterdam: Elsevier, 2007), Volume 1A.

117. Francks *et al.*, *Agriculture and Economic Development in East Asia*, pp. 79 and 87. The price the government paid for a standard 60 kilogram bag of rice was JPY4,162 in 1960, JPY8,272 in 1970 and JPY17,674 in 1980.

118. JPY300 million in 1987, adjusted for Japan's GDP deflator, is JPY292 million today (less because of the deflation that followed the bubble era). The sum is then converted into US dollars at the average 1987 exchange rate of JPY144 to USD1.

119. The complete diary has not been translated into English. The above is based on a discussion of the diary in Nishida Yoshiaki, 'Dimensions of Change in Twentieth-century Rural Japan', in Ann Waswo and Nishida Yoshiaki (eds.), *Farmers and Village Life in Twentieth-century Japan* (London: Curzon Routledge, 2003) and on an interview with Professor Nishida, November 2009.

120. Agricultural import restrictions are discussed in Francks *et al.*, *Agriculture and Economic Development in East Asia*, p. 146.

121. The exact proportion of the farm share of exports was 58 per cent in 1965 and 17 per cent in 1975. See Francks *et al.*, *Agriculture and Economic Development in East Asia*, p. 192.

122. OECD estimates for agricultural 'producer support' are located at http://www.oecd-ilibrary.org/agriculture-and-food/producer-support-estimates-subsidies_20755104-table1. There are three low population European states on par with Japan and Korea – Norway, Iceland and Switzerland.

123. On the Japan visit described in this chapter in November 2009, I ate two apples, paying JPY400 in Tokyo and JPY300 in Chichibu (they were big apples). In Tokyo, I balked at the offer of ten strawberries in a styrofoam package for JPY1000, a very small honeydew melon for JPY1000 and a very small watermelon for JPY3000.

124. Lipton, *Why Poor People Stay Poor*, p. 23.

125. Japan was a little different from the other north-east Asian states and China, because its initial take-off coincided with a weaker land reform. The leading business role in the Meiji era was taken by the samurai warrior class. When deeper land reform was instituted after the Second World War, Japan already had a class of urban entrepreneurs. None the less, some important businessmen like Soichiro Honda were from farm families while the leading auto-maker, Toyota, was very much a rural-based business.

126. James Rorty, 'The Dossier of Wolf Ladejinsky', *Commentary*, April 1955, pp. 326–34.

127. *The New York Times*, 23 December 1954.

128. 'Indentured' labour, subject to long-term contracts, was the 'liberal' nineteenth-century replacement for slavery in the British Empire.

129. Michael Lipton, 'Towards a Theory of Land Reform', in David Lehmann (ed.), *Agrarian Reform and Agrarian Reformism* (London: Faber & Faber, 1974), p. 288, observes: 'There is now abundant evidence that 'output per unit of land is inversely related to farm size.' He provides a long list of academic studies to support this assertion, covering east and south Asia and Africa. Interestingly, even a World Bank study of South Africa stated that 'the literature contains no single example of economies of scale arising for farm sizes exceeding what one family with a medium tractor could comfortably manage'. See Hans P. Binswanger and Klaus Deininger, 'South African Land Policy: The Legacy of History and Current Options', in Johan van Zyl, Johann Kirsten and Hans P. Binswanger (eds.), *Agricultural Land Reform in South Africa* (Cape Town: Oxford University Press, 1996).

130. Wolf Ladejinsky, 'Agrarian Revolution in Japan', in Ladejinsky and Walinsky (eds.), *Agrarian Reform as Unfinished Business*, pp. 286–7.

131. Putzel, *A Captive Land*, p. 81. After seeing his draft bill emasculated by Rhee's cabinet, Cho Pong-am left government and tried to build a political opposition to Rhee. This led to his demise.

## Part 2 – Manufacturing: The Victory of the Historians

1. Paul Bairoch, *Mythes et paradoxes de l'histoire économique* (Chicago: University of Chicago Press, 1993; Paris: Editions La Découverte, 2005).

2. The academic debate over the relative productivity performance of manufacturing versus services revolves around the reasons for the 'de-industrialisation' of rich countries. However, many of the theoretical considerations are the same as for developing states. See, for instance, Robert Rowthorn and Ken Coutts, 'De-industrialisation and the Balance of Payments in Advanced Economies', *Cambridge Journal of Economics*, 28: 5, 2004, p. 767 and Robert Rowthorn and Ramana Ramaswamy, *Deindustrialization – Its Causes and Implications* (Washington DC: International Monetary Fund, 1997).

3. Share of services trade in total international trade from the World Bank's World Development Indicators. Separately, it is notable in east Asia that even the offshore

port financial centres of Hong Kong and Singapore had considerable manufacturing sectors in the early stages of their economic take-off, and Singapore still does today. Other than the micro oil state of Brunei, the only place in east Asia to have developed successfully based on services without (much) manufacturing is Macau, which focused on gold smuggling and gambling and which had a population of less than 200,000 at the end of the Second World War. India is sometimes held up as an economy developing through services because of its well-known information technology (IT) sector. In reality, India's IT sector currently employs only 3 million people in a population of 1.2 billion. The India case is revisited at the end of this chapter.

4. UK manufacturing output is measured by the Office of National Statistics' inflation-adjusted Index of Production series, which began in 1948. Employment in UK manufacturing is today just over 2.5 million workers, or 8 per cent of the labour force, versus 9 million workers, or 35 per cent of the labour force, in 1960.

5. The term 'picking winners' originates among early neo-liberal thinkers writing about continental European economies in the 1960s and 1970s; it grew into something of a term of abuse and has subsequently been widely used among scholars and in the media with reference to east Asia.

6. The original agency was the Commerce and Industry Deliberation Council, set up in 1927. The post Second World War agency was the Industrial Rationalisation Council, which subsequently became the Industrial Structure Council. These institutions are discussed further on page 74. See Chalmers Johnson, *MITI and the Japanese Miracle: The Growth of Industrial Policy, 1925–1975* (Stanford, CA: Stanford University Press, 1982), p. 94.

7. See Ha-Joon Chang, *The Political Economy of Industrial Policy* (New York: St Martin's Press, 1994), p. 123. Only three of the top ten *chaebol* in 1966 were among the top ten in 1974, and only five of the top ten in 1974 were in the top ten in 1980. Paik *et al.* (1988), p. 352 (cited in Chang) state that six of the 1980 top ten were still in the top ten in 1985. In Taiwan, where the state interfered in the private sector much less than in Korea, the roster of leading private firms appears to have been more stable. Of the fifteen biggest private industrial firms in 1971, twelve were still in the group in 1980. See Robert Wade, *Governing the Market: Economic Theory and the Role of Government in East Asian Industrialisation* (Princeton: Princeton University Press, 1990), p. 69.

8. Sahashi was head of MITI's key Enterprises Bureau from 1961 and later vice-minister for MITI.

9. The most powerful of these bureaucracies were MITI and the EPB. Taiwan's IDB and China's NDRC have faced more competition from other ministries and never enjoyed the same influence over bank credit. However, both Taiwan and China have another elite group of senior political leaders to oversee all aspects of economic and developmental issues: the Economic and Financial Special Group in Taiwan and the Central Economic and Financial Leading Group in China.

10. Holland is sometimes proposed as a country that developed without policies that can be identified as protectionist. Holland, however, grew up as a larger-than-average offshore trade and finance centre serving continental Europe, particularly Germany, whose most important river, the Rhine, meets the sea at Holland. Other low population states in Europe like Denmark, Sweden and Switzerland conform to the protectionist pattern of industrialisation.

11. In some periods the export of raw wool was not just taxed but banned. There were at least sixteen parliamentary acts in the sixteenth century banning or limiting clothing imports. So-called 'sumptuary' restrictions focused on luxury goods, while nine Acts of Apparel during the reign of Elizabeth I (1558–1603) had more general application.

12. Paul Bairoch, *Economic and World History* (Brighton: Wheatsheaf, 1993), p. 23.

13. Quoted in Tessa Morris Suzuki, *A History of Japanese Economic Thought* (London: Routledge, 1989), p. 60.

14. 'My Six-year-old Son Should Get a Job', chapter 3, Ha-Joon Chang, *Bad Samaritans* (London: Random House, 2007).

15. In modern economics the term 'learning by doing' was popularised by the Nobel Laureate Kenneth Arrow's 1962 paper 'The Economic Implications of Learning by Doing'. To my mind, however, Arrow hijacked a concept that makes much more sense in its everyday usage. Arrow's paper asserts that the fact that everyone learns by doing means that the learning of new technologies is an automatically generated part of the economic process. Learning by doing thereby becomes another pillar of the win–win ideas of modern economics in which the market takes care of everything. Historically, however, effective learning by doing has always required government intervention.

16. Before becoming provisional president of the new Chinese republic in 1911, Sun Yat-sen lived for almost a decade in Japan, just when industrialisation was starting to yield impressive results.

17. The Meiji leaders came from the rural Satsuma and Choshu *han*, not the more open, internationally minded Tokyo seaboard. Their rural background was very much like that of the Prussian Junkers. The German territory lost to France came back with Napoleon's defeat by the British in 1815, but the Prussians never forgot their humiliations at the battles of Jena and Auerstadt. They finally had their revenge in the 1870 war with France.

18. Friedrich List, *The National System of Political Economy* (London: Longmans, Green, 1885), pp. 368–9. List claimed that the British prime minister William Pitt carried a copy of *The Wealth of Nations* around with him and used its arguments in negotiations with the French 'who were destitute of all experience and political insight' to convince them that 'by nature France was adapted for agriculture and the production of wine'.

19. Tariff protection in the United States pitted manufacturers in the north (in favour) against exporters of agricultural raw materials in the south and west (against). Over

time, most of the battles were won by the protectionist camp, although Hamilton initially lost out to Thomas Jefferson, who was partly free trade and partly anti-industry in his views. In 1816 Congress passed a substantial tariff, with an average rate around 25 per cent, which greatly assisted domestic manufacturers. Tariffs were then cut from 1833 to 1842 before being raised again. As would be the case in north-east Asia, individual tariff rates were particularly important – a high US tariff on steel railways, for instance, supported the development of the US steel industry against British competition.

20. Britain, for instance, banned the export of woollen cloth from its colonies in 1699 and banned the import into Britain of finished cotton cloth from India in 1700. In the early eighteenth century the government of Robert Walpole barred the American colonies from building steel capacity which competed with Britain.

21. List, *National Political Economy*, p. 127.

22. The so-called Iwakura mission visited the United States followed by more than ten European countries; the group was away almost two years. Minister of Civil Affairs Okubo Toshimichi was responsible for determining a list of pilot industrial projects based on the tour's findings.

23. Hirata's translation was published in 1897. See Keizō Shibusawa, *Japanese Society in the Meiji Era* (Tokyo: Ōbunsha, 1958), p. 73. The first Japanese translation of List came not from the German original but from an English translation and was published in 1889; the translator was Ōshima Sadamasu.

24. The papers of finance minister Okubo Toshimichi and the first ambassador to the US, Iwakura Tomomi, contain much praise for Prussia. See George. M. Beckman, *The Making of the Meiji Constitution; The Oligarchs and the Constitutional Development of Japan, 1868–91* (Lawrence, KS; University of Kansas Press, 1957), chapter 1. Among Kenneth B. Pyle's works, see 'Advantages of Followership: German Economics and Japanese Bureaucrats, 1890–1925', *Journal of Japanese Studies*, vol. 1, no. 1, Autumn 1974, p. 143.

25. Britain outlawed both the export of production machinery and the emigration of skilled artisans until the mid nineteenth century. None the less, a British parliamentary enquiry in 1825 estimated that 2,000 technicians were illegally 'aiding' industrial projects around Europe. In the 1780s Graf von Reden, the industrial czar in charge of many early Prussian state investments, went in person to tour Britain in search of technology and personnel. He obtained technology for iron puddling and coke furnace operation and brought over the brother of the English ironmaster John Wilkinson to manage the state iron works in Silesia, and a Scot, John Baildon, to run the coke furnaces. In the early 1800s John Cockerill and a group of English technicians were lured by the Prussians to Aachen to create one of Europe's most advanced machine building plants. Less than a decade after the Meiji Restoration, the Japanese already had hundreds of foreigners on the government payroll. But foreigners did not stay indefinitely. As one example, a key shipping firm, Nippon

Yusen Keisha, was set up in 1884 with 174 foreign staff, including mariners. By 1895 there were 224 foreigners, but by 1920 there were none. See William Lockwood, *The Economic Development of Japan: Growth and Structural Change, 1868–1938* (Princeton, NJ: Princeton University Press, 1954), p. 329, and David Landes, 'Japan and Europe: Contrasts in Industrialization', in William Lockwood (ed.), *State and Economic Enterprise in Japan: Essays in the Political Economy of Growth* (Princeton, NJ: Princeton University Press, 1965), p. 93.

26. Lockwood, *The Economic Development of Japan*, p. 330.

27. Toyoda, of course, is the firm known today as Toyota, the car maker. Sakichi Toyoda, the founder, patented his first loom in 1891 and continued to innovate until, in 1924, he produced the Type-G, which changed thread without stopping. The money raised from selling this technology to the UK helped to fund the start-up of the car business.

28. Again, this echoes European experience where governments in Prussia, other German states, France and Austria all started state-owned pilot factories in the eighteenth and nineteenth centuries. Anecdotal evidence suggests that most of these production units took a long time to become profitable, as the industrial learning process began. Frequently the European plants were also sold on to private entrepreneurs.

29. Two critical constitutional rules which Japan copied from Prussia were, first, that in the event that parliament should fail to agree a new budget the existing budget automatically remained in force, much reducing political control over the bureaucracy; and, second, that it was the emperor who chose the prime minister without reference to parliament.

30. In the run-up to the First World War Germany was importing just under half the ore for its vast iron and steel sector, mostly from French Lorraine and Sweden. Germany's rate of investment in fixed assets increased from 14 per cent of GNI in the 1851–70 period to 24 per cent in 1891–1913. Around two-thirds of this investment went on industry and transportation. See Clive Trebilcock, *The Industrialization of the Continental Powers, 1780–1914* (London: Longman 1982), p. 62.

31. See Johannes Hirschmeier, 'Shibusawa Eiichi: Industrial Pioneer', in Lockwood (ed.), *State and Economic Enterprise in Japan*, p. 209.

32. Estimates by Kamekichi Takahashi for 1928 are Mitsui 6.5 per cent, Mitsubishi 4.5 per cent, Sumitomo 1.4 per cent, Yasuda 2.8 per cent, totalling an aggregate 15.2 per cent of paid-up capital. William Lockwood, 'Japan's New Capitalism', p. 494, in Lockwood (ed.), *State and Economic Enterprise in Japan*, states that the Big Four made up one quarter of paid-up capital by the Second World War.

33. Trebilcock, *The Industrialization of the Continental Powers*, p. 72.

34. The group not only handled export subsidy payments among its own members but also negotiated further rebates with raw material cartels, like the coal miners. See Trebilcock, above, p. 72.

35. Electrical engineering, for instance, was by 1910 a duopoly of Siemens-Schuckert and AEG, which were created by the mergers of more than twenty large companies over two decades. Chemicals was split between Hoescht-Casella and the triple alliance of BASF, Bayer and the Aniline Dyes Manufacturing Co.

36. Chalmers Johnson's observation about the descent into fascism, war and post-war that 'from the point of view of the history of industrial policy ... the 1940s are one continuous era' can justifiably be extended to an even longer formative period. See Johnson, *MITI and the Japanese Miracle*, p. 195.

37. The relevant laws were the 1925 Exporters Association Law and the 1925 Major Export Industries Assocation Law. The new ministry, however, remained rather weak.

38. Expressions like 'industrial rationalisation', 'irrational economic structure' and 'irrational competition' have been used in Japanese, Korean and Chinese ever since to explain the need for the state to cull losers. I remember hearing such terms in China as a young journalist in the early 1990s and not bothering to think clearly about what they meant.

39. The Important Industries Control Law of April 1931.

40. It is notable that the *zaibatsu* families were deeply unpopular with the public, which regarded them as 'crony capitalists' with only their own interests at heart. In part, popular support for the military reflected a view that politicians failed to control the *zaibatsu* and were involved in a squalid and corrupt alliance with them. A significant part of the bureaucracy supported the military based on the same outlook.

41. MITI's power derived from a number of sources. During the war the MCI became the Ministry of Munitions and when it reverted to being the MCI (and then MITI) it managed to retain control of its industrial planning role, plus oversight of strategic sectors including electric power and aircraft manufacturing. After the war, the 1949 Foreign Exchange and Foreign Trade Control Law (which the SCAP regarded as very temporary but which remained in force until 1980), gave MITI its single most important tool: control over foreign exchange allocations for business. MITI also controlled vast sums of money outside its formal budget, by approving credit at the Japan Development Bank, the Export–Import Bank, the Small Business Finance Corp., the Bank for Commerce and Industrial Cooperatives, the Japan Petroleum Development Corp., the Productivity Headquarters and more. In the mid 1950s, the MITI press club calculated that MITI controlled funds around twenty times its official budget. See Johnson, *MITI and the Japanese Miracle*, p. 78. MITI had 21,000 employees in 1949, reduced to 14,000 by 1974.

42. On MITI's centralised licensing of technology, see William Lockwood, 'Japan's "New Capitalism"', p. 459, in Lockwood (ed.), *State and Economic Enterprise in Japan*. In the 1950s the Industrial Structure Council was known as the Industrial Rationalisation Council. Some important ideas employed by the Industrial Structure Council originated with emerging American management gurus like Peter Drucker. There is a curious paradox in the way so many people see business

engineering as good and scientific, whereas any form of state industrial policy is bad and pseudo-scientific. Johnson discussed the Drucker influence on MITI in *MITI and the Japanese Miracle*, p. 216.

43. Kawasaki Steel was given 3 million square metres of free land in Tokyo Bay, where it built the world's most sophisticated integrated steel plant in 1953.

44. Japan's GNI growth averaged 9.2 per cent in 1953–60. This compares with 4.1 per cent in 1886–98, 6.1 per cent in 1906–19, and 6.8 per cent in 1931–8. See Lockwood (ed.), *State and Economic Enterprise in Japan*, p. 89.

45. Most of the industrial plants themselves were located in what is now North Korea, but the legacy was also contained in the personnel of the colonial military, bureaucracy and institutions like banks.

46. Park Chung Hee, *Our Nation's Path: Ideology for Social Reconstruction* (Seoul: Hollym Corp.; second edition, 1970), p. 218.

47. Park, *Our Nation's Path*, p. 214, and Park Chung Hee, *The Country the Revolution and I* (Seoul: Hollym Corp.; second edition, 1970), pp. 120–21.

48. The Spinners and Weavers Association of Korea brought together fifteen integrated textile firms in a cartel, operating much like the Japan Cotton Spinners Association did in the 1910s by forcing its members to upgrade equipment, consolidating marketing activities and, critically, buying raw cotton as a single unit. See Alice Amsden, *Asia's Next Giant: South Korea and Late Industrialisation*, pp. 61 and 66. In Korea in the early 1960s there were also big currency devaluations which spurred exports – of 100 per cent in 1961 and 50 per cent in 1964. However, Amsden shows that production subsidies offered by the government to textile firms increased by even more, spurring them to lead the export drive. By the late 1960s the government was desperate to promote synthetic textiles because the cost of subsidising a low value-added business based on imported cotton was becoming untenable.

49. Data from the World Bank's World Development Indicators series.

50. Amsden, *Asia's Next Giant*, p. 69.

51. On interest rates for exporters, see Jung-En Woo, *Race to the Swift: State and Finance in Korean Industrialization* (New York: Oxford University Press, 1989), p. 162.

52. Chosen was the Japanese colonial name for Korea. The Industrial Bank was one of the few places where the Japanese allowed native Koreans to get anywhere close to the centre of economic power. By the Second World War, half the staff was Korean. See Woo, *Race to the Swift*, p. 30.

53. Quoted in Woo, *Race to the Swift*, p. 131.

54. World Bank, *Korea: Managing the Industrial Transition, Vol. 1* (Washington DC: World Bank, 1987), p. 45.

55. See Wade, *Governing the Market*, p. xlvi, n. 47.

56. The GDP per capita in 1975 of South Korea and Guatemala was just under USD500.

57. The main moment at which Park did do something was when he switched to higher interest rates in 1965, a policy that was reversed in the 1970s. This is discussed in

part 3. In general Park ignored the US and the multilateral agencies, and failed to heed numerous IMF demands to end export subsidies. However, unlike other east Asian leaders like Sukarno or Mahathir, Park never sought public fights with the US or the multilateral agencies.

58. The contents of this section are drawn from William Kirby, *Germany and Republican China* (Stanford: Stanford University Press, 1984) and William Kirby, 'Continuity and Change in Modern China: Economic Planning on the Mainland and on Taiwan, 1943–58', in the *Australian Journal of Chinese Affairs*, no. 24, July 1990.

59. Around one-fifth of Chinese exports went to Germany in 1936 under this arrangement. German advisers were withdrawn from China in spring 1938.

60. Kirby, 'Continuity and Change in Modern China', p. 128.

61. See Wade, *Governing the Market*, p. 208.

62. See R. Short, 'The Role of Public Enterprises: An International Statistical Comparison', International Monetary Fund Department Memorandum Series 83/84, 1983. Based on 1970s data used in the study, Taiwan's SOEs accounted for around one-third of gross investment. In addition to starting new state firms, the KMT in Taiwan hung on to most of the businesses it took over from Japanese colonial interests; in South Korea, by contrast, these firms were sold off.

63. In 1957, for instance, the interest rate for exporters was 11.9 per cent versus a non-export rate of 19.8 per cent. Subsidised export credit, however, was much less widely available than in Korea, accounting for about 6 per cent of total credit in Taiwan in the 1960s and early 1970s. See Wade, *Governing the Market*, p. 59 and Shirley Kuo *et al.*, *The Taiwan Success Story: Rapid Growth with Improved Distribution in the Republic of China, 1952–1979* (Boulder, CO: Westview Press, 1981), p. 79. One study of the period 1962–76 estimated that all the different kinds of export subsidy in Taiwan were equivalent in value to 10.6 per cent of the economy's total export receipts. See Tibor Scitovsky, 'Economic Development in Taiwan and South Korea', in L. Lau, ed., *Models of Development: A Comparative Study of Economic Growth in South Korea and Taiwan* (San Francisco: Institute for Contemporary Affairs, 1986), p.160.

64. The best known are United MicroElectronics, which is state-controlled but with five private partners, and TSMC, the government joint venture with Holland's Philips which in 1986 invested in a first ASICs foundry in Taiwan. See Wade, *Governing the Market*, p. 103.

65. See Kuo *et al.*, *The Taiwan Success Story*, p. 109. The authors calculated that exports accounted for 22.5 per cent of increased manufacturing production in 1956–61 and 68 per cent in 1971–6.

66. See Wade, *Governing the Market*, p. 70. Although he does not make the connection, Wade notes elsewhere that from the 1970s the Taiwanese economy exhibited higher levels of market concentration than the Korean one, meaning fewer firms commanded more control. This suggests that not only were big Taiwanese SOEs

doing less exporting than Korean *chaebol*, they may also have faced a less competitive environment at home. For details of exports by small and medium-sized firms in Japan in the 1920s, see Johnson, *MITI and the Japanese Miracle*, p. 97. The sources Johnson quotes estimated that smaller firms accounted for somewhere between half and 65 per cent of exports.

67. Data for Korea and Taiwan are from the IMF's World Economic Outlook database. The latest numbers, for 2010, put Korea's GDP per capita at USD20,800 and Taiwan's at USD18,600.

68. See Wade, *Governing the Market*, p. 323. ITT sold its telecommunications division to Alcatel-Lucent in 1989. GTE merged with Bell Atlantic in 2000 and became Verizon.

69. By the 1980s the (overwhelmingly domestic) sales of Taiwan's six biggest state industrial firms were equal to the (more export-oriented) sales of its fifty biggest private firms. See Wade, *Governing the Market*, p. 178.

70. Fortune 500, 1981. If one compares large private firms, Korea's Hyundai was already turning over USD8 billion a year in the early 1980s, versus less than USD2 billion at Formosa Plastics.

71. For instance, the net profit margin of Taiwan's biggest electronics firm, Hon Hai (which does vast amounts of manufacturing for Apple, HP and Dell), was 3.5 per cent in 2009. This compares with a net profit margin of 7 per cent at Samsung in 2009 and 9.75 per cent in 2011.

72. Wade, *Governing the Market*, p. 34.

73. The just under 50 per cent increase in Japan's farm output occurred between 1953 and 1963. This compounded the approximate doubling of output between 1880 and 1915 in the Meiji era.

74. Johnson, *MITI and the Japanese Miracle*, p. 230.

75. Kazushi Ohkawa and Henry Rosovsky 'A Century of Japanese Economic Growth', in Lockwood (ed.), *State and Economic Enterprise in Japan*, p. 71. Park Chung Hee followed the same logic when greatly increasing agricultural investment after his coup: 'Since farmers constitute a market which plays an important role in economic progress, I believe the increase of farmers' income is vital' (*Our Nation's Path*, p. 222).

76. Tokyo University (abbreviated to Todai), and its law school, have been the preeminent suppliers of top bureaucrats since the Meiji Restoration. Note that the history department at Todai comes under the law faculty. A survey by the National Personnel Authority in 1965 found that 73 per cent of MITI officers at the level of department chief or above had graduated from Todai Law.

77. Quoted in Johnson, *MITI and the Japanese Miracle*, p. 108.

78. Johnson, *MITI and the Japanese Miracle*, p. 25. Johnson observed of developed, market-based countries versus ones running developmental industrial policy: '[The] difference between the market-rational and the plan-rational state is that

economists dominate policy-making in the former while nationalistic political officials dominate it in the latter.'

79. Wade, *Governing the Market*, p. 203.

80. Dodge never went to college and was not formally trained in any profession. However, his banking career lent him many of the views associated with neo-classical economics – demands for free markets, low inflation and balanced budgets.

81. Among the American economists sent to Korea were Edward Shaw, Ronald McKinnon, and Hugh Patrick. Park's response to the demands is typified by import restrictions, where tariff rates were selectively reduced and formal import quotas liberalised, but where a mass of non-tariff barriers remained in place. For a discussion, see Woo, *Race to the Swift*, p. 102.

82. Rostow taught economic history successively at Oxford and Cambridge and at the Massachusetts Institute of Technology before entering government service. His most senior government position, held under Lyndon Johnson, was the post known today as National Security Advisor. *The Stages of Economic Growth* was published in 1960; its pointed subtitle is: *A Non-communist Manifesto*. Other than Rostow, it is worth mentioning Arthur Lewis, the West Indian development economist, for his policy influence in the 1950s and 1960s and his history-based outlook.

83. Economic grants and aid from the US to South Korea between 1946 and 1978 were USD6 billion, compared with USD15 billion for the whole of Latin America. Taiwan received USD2.4 billion between 1946 and 1978. In the peak period of the 1950s, US aid to Korea was equivalent to about 15 per cent of GNI, versus 6 per cent for Taiwan. In south-east Asia, the Philippines received USD2 billion in grants and aid between 1946 and 1978, and Thailand USD800 million, but these countries did not use the funds to structure an effective industrial policy or impose rigorous export discipline. A similar point can be made about pre-1949 Nationalist China, which was the single biggest recipient of US aid in the 1940s. Data about US grants and aid are contained in an annual report to Congress, commonly known as the Greenbook, and can be accessed online at http://gbk.eads.usaidallnet.gov/ On Arthur D. Little, see Wade, *Governing the Market*, p. 182, n. 28, and p. 208. Little is the oldest management consultancy in the world, but in recent decades has been eclipsed by larger peers.

84. Wade, *Governing the Market*, pp. 225–6.

85. Woo, *Race to the Swift*, p. 190.

86. The term refers to Widjojo Nitisastro, Mohammad Sadli, Subroto, Ali Wardhana and Emil Salim, all of whom served as ministers. One should stress that the early academic influences on this group were not neo-classical economists, but ones like Ragnar Nurske and Arthur Lewis; however, they proved much more biddable before IMF and World Bank advice than did policymakers in north-east Asia. The Berkeley Mafia's main teacher in America was Bruce Glassburner of the University of California, Davis. Emil Salim reappears in part 3 of this book.

87. The other promises were democracy, class unity, social equity and an end to 'evil customs'.

88. Except, of course, that Malaysia was much richer. The World Bank's World Development Indicators series gives GNI per capita in current dollars in 1962 as: Korea USD110, Malaysia USD300. This was the first year in the series.

89. The term animal spirits originated with David Hume. It was also employed by John Maynard Keynes. Keynes defined animal spirits as the 'spontaneous urge to action rather than inaction' which often make human beings, particularly entrepreneurs, more optimistic and quick to act than a perfect weighing of mathematised probabilities would lead them to be.

90. A cab to the airport in Seoul costs about USD50 to travel 74 km, versus USD50 in Taipei to travel 40 km. Cab fares are not a bad guide to the equality differential, since governments set the fares and hence largely decide what cab drivers are going to earn.

91. Park, *The Country, the Revolution and I*, p. 159. Park liked to quote Goethe's maxim 'Genius is the crystallisation of perseverance.'

92. With respect to his physical aggression and hobbies, see Donald Kirk, *Korean Dynasty : Hyundai and Chung Ju Yung* (Armonk, NY: M. E. Sharpe, 1994), p. 20 and chapter 2. With respect to his hobbies, Kirk notes that Chung, like Park Chung Hee, read a lot of history books, although he was mainly interested in biographies of 'leaders', including Churchill, Genghis Khan, Lincoln and several Japanese industrialists. Kirk sums up Chung's sex life, p. 285, as follows: 'his cold public demeanour belied his wild private life, an extra-curricular existence as rich and improbable as his career in business and industry'.

93. The brother, In Yung, was taken on as a translator by a US lieutenant in the 8th Army. In time, Hyundai Construction got a lock on most of the 8th Army's construction work. When most US forces pulled out after the Korean War, Chung bought up large amounts of heavy engineering equipment on the cheap.

94. And the businesses of other leading entrepreneurs. Lee Byung Chull of Samsung, for instance, was in rice milling, sugar refining, real estate and trading before Park Chung Hee focused him on manufacturing. As we shall see later in part 2, the pre-Park business profiles of such entrepreneurs will be familiar to anyone who knows the business structures of south-east Asia.

95. Seodaemun was finally closed in 1987, the year of Roh Tae Woo's declaration of democracy.

96. Although Park was always the power behind the coup, it was fronted for the first six weeks by General Chang Do Yung. Park placed Chang under house arrest, and then in Seodaemun, before eventually releasing him.

97. Lee Hangu, *The History of Korean Chaebol* (Seoul: Dae Myeong Press, 2004). Available only in Korean, it names twelve leaders of the country's biggest firms, including Samho Group, Gaepong Group, Daehan Group, FarEast Group, Donglip Industry and Donghwa Industry, as having been arrested in the days following 28 May. Lee

also names three other senior businessmen, including Samsung's Lee Byung Chull, for whom arrest warrants were issued. Kim Hyung-A in *Korea's Development under Park Chung Hee* (London: RoutledgeCurzon, 2004) writes that fifty-one businessmen were arrested on 28 May and most were released on 30 June However, he adds, the senior group of thirteen businessmen was not released until 14 July after having agreed to set up the PCER (see next page), which was formally inaugurated on 17 July. Stephan Haggard, Byung-kook Kim and Chung-in Moon in 'The Transition to Export-led Growth in South Korea, 1954–66', *Journal of Asian Studies*, vol. 50, 4 November 1991, write that as well as the elite group of thirteen *chaebol* owners, 120 other businessmen also came under investigation. Kim Jong Pil, a leading figure in the junta, claimed that the strategy to scare and redirect the businessmen, rather than simply to punish them, was largely his. It should also be noted that some industrial planning groundwork had been done under the Syngman Rhee government and the short-lived Chang Myon administration that followed it, and that in this sense the Park group did not start with an entirely blank canvas.

98. Kim, *Korea's Development under Park Chung Hee*, p. 81.

99. Kim, *Korea's Development under Park Chung Hee*, p. 83.

100. Hyundai's original cement plant opened at Tanyang in 1964 and exported its first cement to Vietnam in 1965, the year that US combat troops arrived. See Kirk, *Korean Dynasty*, p.56. The US financing for the cement plants came from USAID, the successor to Washington's Economic Co-operation Administration, and was a loan, but on concessionary terms. Hyundai obtained USD4.25 million.

101. See Kirk, *Korean Dynasty*, chapters 5 and 6, p. 56, and Richard M. Steers, *Made in Korea: Chung Ju Yung and the Rise of Hyundai* (New York and London: Routledge, 1999), p. 47. It was Vietnam where Hyundai won its biggest contracts in the 1960s. The same brother, Chung In Yung, who had built the relationship with the 8th Army in Korea dealt with the US military in Vietnam. The Chungs were up for anything to earn export dollars: in Vietnam this included being the US army's main laundry and dry-cleaning contractor. One of the key Hyundai executives handling the original Thai highway project was the recent ROK president Lee Myung Bak.

102. Steers, *Made in Korea*, p. 67.

103. Kirk, *Korean Dynasty*, p. 61. Exports as a share of GDP went from under 5 per cent to 15 per cent in the same period.

104. The following is based on interviews and a plant visit on 12 July 2010.

105. See the POSCO museum site at http://museum.posco.co.kr/museum/docs/eng/s91b0060001i.jsp

106. See Amsden, *Asia's Next Giant*, p. 296. She cites a report by the Korea Steel Association giving construction cost per tonne of steel produced at plants analysed of USD1,750 in Brazil, USD820 in the US, USD590 in Japan and USD400 at Pohang.

107. See Amsden, *Asia's Next Giant*, p. 302. Nippon Steel was formerly called Yawata. Other technology providers included Fuji and NKK.

108. The World Steel Association gives 2009 crude steel output of the world's biggest producers as ArcelorMittal 78 million tonnes, Baosteel 31 million tonnes, POSCO 31 million tonnes, Nippon Steel 27 million tonnes. ArcelorMittal is Indian-controlled inasmuch as the controlling shareholder is Indian; however the firm is headquartered in London and much of its production capacity is outside India as a result of debt-financed acquisitions. The group is part manufacturer, part leveraged investment vehicle, with four times the debt to equity ratio of POSCO in 2012.

109. The bestselling Sonata sedan has its own factory on the west coast.

110. Author visit 13 July 2010. The same is true at the manufacturing headquarters of Samsung, presently Korea's most valuable company. The last of its original, and rather Dickensian, factories was bulldozed in 2010. The replacements are glass structures with carefully tended green spaces and basketball courts. The 28,000 staff at the renamed Samsung Digital City no longer even have to wear a uniform, which is unusual in Korea. Hyundai, long the most conservative *chaebol*, still requires blue windbreakers and official company attire.

111. The International Labour Office (ILO) gave the average Korean work week between 1976 and 1985 as 53.3 hours. No other country it surveyed averaged more than fifty hours. The average working week is now shorter, with most large firms having moved to a two-day weekend.

112. Quotation at Kirk, *Korean Dynasty*, p. 125. Kirk met the the now-deceased brother in charge of HMC, Se Yung, on many occasions. He was particularly struck that Se Yung showed no passion for the product that HMC learned to make so well.

113. See Kirk, *Korean Dynasty*, p. 134. In the mid 1970s Park authorised USD100 million of borrowings by HMC – USD72 million offshore and USD28 million onshore – at a time when its paid-in capital was USD5 million. In others words, doing what the government wanted was worth cheap loans twenty times the equity that the owners had put down for the business.

114. It was the EPB which set domestic prices for all kinds of products where it was concerned to foster Korean technological learning. The effect of having fixed domestic prices was that it forced private companies to compete not on price but on quality, on exports (which were subsidised by high domestic prices) and on other standard-raising activities like winning quality and service awards. The EPB set domestic car prices based on engine size.

115. Chung Ju Yung revealed the export target the week after production began. See Kirk, *Korean Dynasty*, p.135 and Steers, *Made in Korea*, chapter 5. In another major Hyundai project from the 1970s, the vast Jubail port facility in Saudi Arabia built by Hyundai Construction, one of the project managers told Kirk that Chung Ju Yung ordered his team to cut the bid price by USD100 million as Chung had to be certain of meeting his export and foreign exchange targets. 'We have to secure it. Otherwise I cannot face Park' was the instruction Chung reportedly gave the manager. After the low-ball bid, Hyundai Construction put so much pressure on

its construction crews in Jubail to work fast that they rioted, and the Saudi army was called in. See Kirk, p. 83.

116. The initial Mitsubishi stake was 10 per cent, rising to 12.6 per cent.

117. The most important case was Kim Jae Ik, Minister for Economic Affairs in the early 1980s, who thought that there was no way Korea could develop a globally competitive car sector given the tiny scale of its domestic market. In the early 1980s, the Korean market for cars was smaller than Malaysia's, despite a larger population. Kim was killed by a North Korean bomb in 1983; he had wanted to merge HMC with Daewoo.

118. See Amsden, *Asia's Next Giant*, p. 269. When Hyundai Heavy Industries, the shipbuilder, was unable to meet overly ambitious delivery targets that had helped it win early orders, Hyundai Merchant Marine bought up several ships that buyers used their contractual rights to refuse delivery of. HHI obtained much of its technical support from Scottish engineers and bought its early designs from a yard that was approaching bankruptcy in Govan, Scotland.

119. Among some of the Asian examples are Daewoo in Korea, all the firms which went into car making (and failed) in Taiwan, all the state auto firms in China (which are in joint ventures with multinationals in Changchun-Tianjin, Beijing, Shanghai, Wuhan, Chongqing, Guangzhou), Proton in Malaysia, Siam Motors in Thailand and Astra in Indonesia. In the official *History of Hyundai Motors*, published in 1987, Chung Ju Yung wrote on p. 165 that a joint venture at HMC would 'severely impede creativity and independence and the future prospect of a local enterprise', while a new car firm seeking to export 'should not allow foreign capital participation to a significant degree'.

120. There was a short-lived Ford–HMC fifty–fifty joint venture to make engines, one of the toughest technological challenges for an aspiring car maker. However HMC soon switched to the more favourable deal offered by Mitsubishi for engine technology.

121. Just when the Chungs were negotiating with Mitsubishi over the HMC deal, they were also talking to another Mitsubishi unit for technology to start their shipbuilding arm, HHI. In the latter case Mitsubishi was more nervous of Hyundai's potential, and refused anything better than a joint venture to make small vessels under 50 dwt. The Chungs walked away, obtaining their technology from foreign consultants and from European shipping firms on the edge of bankruptcy. See Kirk, *Korean Dynasty*, pp. 98 and 132 and Steers, *Made in Korea*, p. 94. At HMC, Amsden, *Asia's Next Giant*, p. 175, identified eighteen different technology transfer deals in the run-up to the launch of the Pony. Another thirty technology transfer deals were done before HMC's export drive began in the 1980s, a good number of which proved to be failures. As with the shipbuilding venture, much of the basic organisational work for HMC was entrusted to managers brought in from Hyundai Construction.

122. On early quality issues at HMC, see Kirk, *Korean Dynasty*, p. 134. Wade, *Governing the Market*, p. 309, states that in the early 1980s the domestic retail price of the Pony was USD5,000 versus an export retail price of USD2,200.

123. Sales of the Pony took off after HMC's new factory was completed in 1980. Most sales were in the heavily protected (and now fast-growing) Korean market, but there were also some cut-price Pony exports to Africa, Latin America and Canada. In 1985, the last full year before the US Excel launch, HMC sold more than 200,000 cars worldwide. See Steers, *Made in Korea*, p. 84.

124. Hyundai's north American subsidiary lost hundreds of millions of dollars between 1987 and the mid 1990s. The low point was 1992, when the US–Canada unit posted a USD140 million loss. From 264,000 in 1987, HMC sales in the US fell to under 100,000 in 1992. However, HMC's capacity to compete in the US augured well for Europe, where car prices at the time were about one-fifth higher while safety standards (and hence costs) were lower. HMC sold 111,000 cars in Europe in 1992, up by more than half on 1991 and an indicator of things to come.

125. Shinjin entered a fifty–fifty joint venture with GM in 1972. Daewoo did try to obtain technological independence from GM, one reason why the joint venture was always fractious. The American side sold out its interest in 1992 for USD165 million.

126. Following the restoration of democracy in the late 1980s, Chung undertook a vain and unsuccessful run for the Korean presidency in 1992, during which he made highly personal attacks on the eventual winner, Kim Young Sam. Chung had already fallen out with Kim's predecessor and mentor, Roh Tae Woo, the first democratically elected president since Park Chung Hee ended elections and declared martial law in 1972. One effect of Chung's worsening political relations was a reduction in Hyundai's access to state bank credit. At the same time, Daewoo bought General Motors out of its joint venture in 1992 and began a very aggressive attack on HMC's position in the domestic market.

127. Renault–Nissan bought a 70 per cent stake in Samsung's auto subsidiary, since increased to 80 per cent, during the crisis. The SAIC takeover of SsangYong was abandoned in 2009 when the Chinese side walked away.

128. Author interview, 13 July 2010.

129. At the time of writing Ford had yet to confirm its 2010 global sales figures, but the difference with HMC–Kia was expected to be a matter of a few thousand units. Of the three biggest groups by sales in 2010, Toyota and GM each sold 8.4 million units and VW sold 7.1 million. Hyundai sales in 2010 came to 3.6 million from HMC and 2.1 million from Kia. See *Automotive News*, 26 January 2011.

130. See Steers, *Made in Korea*, p. 84.

131. One can argue the case that Thailand in the 1960s, 1970s and early 1980s came closer than Malaysia to instituting effective industrial policy. The Thai bureaucracy was a more effective supporter of industrial policy than the Malaysian one, not least because Mahathir undermined the Malaysian bureaucracy. However, my view is that the concentration of Malaysian industrial planning under a single leader, and its focus on a number of very high-profile projects, makes it the best case study for analysis. For a comparison of Thai and Malaysian industrial policy in the

post-Second World War eras, see Greg Felker, 'The Politics of Industrial Investment Policy Reform in Malaysia and Thailand', in K. S. Jomo (ed.), *Southeast Asia's Industrialization; Industrial Policy, Capabilities and Sustainability* (Basingstoke: Palgrave Macmillan, 2001), chapter 6.

132. Off the record interview with a local billionaire who provided at least one unrepayable 'loan' to the Tunku.

133. Quoted in Barry Wain, *Malaysian Maverick: Mahathir Mohamad in Turbulent Times* (Basingstoke: Palgrave Macmillan, 2009), p. 3.

134. Mahathir's own racial make-up is uncertain; he himself appears to obfuscate about it. He told his biographer Barry Wain that it could have been his grandfather or great-grandfather who came to Malaysia from India and described his grandmother on that side as 'Penang Malay', implying she had no Indian blood. The author goes with Barry Wain's working assumption that it was Mahathir's grandfather who immigrated, and that Mahathir probably knows this. While he was prime minister the Malaysian press avoided any mention of his Indian connection. There is plenty of foreign blood in the Malaysian aristocracy – the Tunku's mother was Thai – but Malaysia's racial politics require that leaders appear to be pure Malay. For further discussion of Mahathir's roots, see Wain, *Malaysian Maverick*, p. 5.

135. Park Chung Hee's analysis was not entirely non-racial – he reserved special developmental praise for the German 'people'. However, Park was mainly concerned with the practical lessons of history. By contrast, the introduction to Mahathir's *The Malay Dilemma* begins: 'My early thoughts on problems affecting the Malays were first set down in arguable form in response to a challenge made by Professor Ungku Aziz, Professor of Economics (now Vice-Chancellor) of the University of Malaya. In 1966, at a seminar in Kuala Lumpur to discuss the reasons for the poor examination results of Malay students, I brought up the question of hereditary and environmental influence as being among the factors contributing towards the problem.' The book continues in a not dissimilar fashion and contains little structural economic analysis. Mahathir Mohamad, *The Malay Dilemma* (Singapore: Donald Moore for Asia Pacific Press, 1970), p. 1.

136. The official death toll from rioting in Kuala Lumpur on 13 May 1969 was 196, with 439 wounded. Unofficial reckonings claimed higher figures.

137. 'Entrepreneurial' Mahathir had gone into all kinds of sideline businesses since graduation, including property speculation, a pharmaceutical trading business, a franchise petrol station and a limousine service operating between Kuala Lumpur and the city airport. Mahathir's first trip to Japan was in 1962. He comments: 'The dedication and the drive of the Japanese were clear to see. Anyone would have seen that Japan was doing something right in order to rebuild the country. Upon becoming Prime Minister I decided to adopt Japanese and Korean strategies and methods for developing Malaysia.' Mahathir's description of Japanese progress in

cultural terms is immediately noticeable. Written response to questions put to Mahathir, 7 March 2011.

138. Author interview, 9 July 2010.

139. Malaysia's GNI per capita in 1981 was USD1570, Korea's was USD1560.

140. Anwar Ibrahim, Mahathir's former deputy, calls Mr Suzuki 'a very key guy' in helping form Mahathir's developmental thinking. Interview 8 July 2010. Mahathir himself comments: '[Suzuki's] personal knowledge of the workings of Mitsui was invaluable during the implementation of Malaysia's development plans.' Written response to questions put to Mahathir, 7 March 2011.

141. Mahathir described Look East as 'emulating the rapidly developing countries of the East [i.e. north-east Asia] in the effort to develop Malaysia'; in technological terms he defined the policy as 'a move up the technology ladder to basic industries such as steel making'. See K. S. Jomo and Tan Kock Wah (eds.), *Industrial Policy in East Asia: Lessons for Malaysia* (Kuala Lumpur: University of Malaya Press, 1999), pp. 249–50. On the particular link with the HCI drive in Korea, see p. 278.

142. Their puritanism and autocratic personalities are obvious similarities between Park and Mahathir. Just as Park began by shutting down a large number of bars and nightclubs in Seoul which represented the decadence of the old elite, so Mahathir railed against the drinking, smoking, gambling and golf of the Malay upper classes and civil service. However, while Mahathir grew up in a semi-rural area, he never had much interest in or understanding of rural life, something which set him apart from the peasant Park. Indeed, the underlying logic of Mahathir's *The Malay Dilemma* is that the original '*bumiputera*' Malaysians are backward *because they are rural*.

143. When Mahathir became prime minister, control of HICOM (created in 1980) was shifted to the prime minister's office. For a description of its investments, see Chee Peng Lim, 'Heavy Industrialisation', in K. S. Jomo (ed.), *Japan and Malaysian Development: In the Shadow of the Rising Sun* (London: Routledge, 1994).

144. Mahathir's own National Agricultural Policy, published in January 1984, was only thirteen pages long. In 1985, Malaysian banks lent more than four times as much to real estate projects as to agriculture. See K. S. Jomo, *Growth and Structural Change in the Malaysian Economy* (Basingstoke: Macmillan, 1990), pp. 207, 210.

145. Written response to author questions put to Mahathir, 7 March 2011.

146. The 22-volume IMP, produced by the Malaysian Investment Development Authority (MIDA), working with the United Nations Industrial Development Organisation (UNIDO), has been generally praised by industrial policy experts. However, it was not ready until early 1986, by which time Mahathir was already facing problems with the Proton and Perwaja projects. Mahathir's love affair with all things Japanese began to wane in 1984. See Kit G. Machado, 'Proton and Malaysia's Motor Vehicle Industry', in Jomo (ed.), *Japan and Malaysian Development*, p. 291.

147. See Jomo and Tan (eds.), *Industrial Policy in East Asia*, p. 279.

148. For more on the exclusion of the private sector, see Lim Chee Peng, 'Heavy Industrialisation', in Jomo (ed.), *Japan and Malaysian Development*, p. 249.

149. Asked why Proton could not license technology, as Hyundai did, instead of entering a joint venture, Mahathir responded: 'We had practically no knowledge or experience in the automotive industry. The best way was to have a partner experienced in that field. Mitsubishi Motors was willing to help us build a national car, and not just a replica of their car.' The author's view is that Malaysia in the early 1980s had at least as much experience in the automotive sector as Korea in the early 1970s – there were eleven car assemblers in Malaysia by 1980 and the local market was much bigger than Korea's a decade earlier. Asked why Malaysia started with only a single domestic car firm, Mahathir responded: 'We had to continue the import and assembly of foreign cars to avoid public criticisms.' The idea that Mahathir made policy in response to public criticisms will not fit with the recollection of many Malaysians. Other questions put to Mahathir were evaded or avoided. Written responses from Mahathir 7 March 2011.

150. The term *bumiputera*, meaning 'sons of the soil', refers not only to Malays but to other ethnic groups native to what is now Malaysia. I prefer not to use the term 'indigenous' since there are today very few Malaysians who were born outside the country.

151. Author interview, 9 July 2010.

152. Off the record interview, 9 July 2010.

153. Results of amendments to the Investment Coordination Act and the Promotion of Investments Act. Mahathir allowed investments by Wholly Foreign-Owned Enterprises (as opposed to joint ventures), suspended requirements for foreign firms to grant equity to *bumiputeras*, and created a one-stop permit shop for foreign investors. Foreign direct investment approvals were RM525 million in 1986 versus RM6.2 billion in 1990.

154. Just as Mahathir offered the new incentives, the Industrial Master Plan of 1986 stated unequivocally that multinational processing operations wooed by Malaysia in the late 1960s and 1970s had failed to meet technological objectives in terms of upgrading the economy. Much the biggest source of investment in the late 1980s was Japan, whose currency began to appreciate rapidly against those of its trading partners following the 1985 Plaza Accords with the United States. For further discussion, see Jomo, *Growth and Structural Change in the Malaysian Economy*, p. 134. At current prices, Malaysian exports were USD22.7 billion in 1980, USD29.6 billion in 1985 and USD53.9 billion in 1988.

155. In the peak investment period of 1981–5, the investment share of GDP hit a record 36 per cent, with state investment half of this. From 1986 to 1988, the investment share of GDP dropped to 26 per cent, and the public sector investment share to just 11 per cent. See Jomo, *Growth and Structural Change in the Malaysian Economy*, p. 47.

156. Asmat was secretary general of MITI from 1992 to 2001. Author interview, 9 July 2010. '[Mahathir] reads one book and he's an expert,' snorts Mahathir's former

deputy, Anwar Ibrahim. Anwar, who was subjected to arrest and a show trial by Mahathir after the Asian financial crisis, has good reason to put the boot into his former boss. But in this instance, numerous persons around Mahathir concur that his thinking was heavily influenced by a single book. Anwar's own reputation for perspective and level-headedness is far from stellar. Author interview, 8 July 2010.

157. Says the MSC's own website: 'The Multimedia Super Corridor (MSC) is a government-designated zone, designed to leapfrog Malaysia into the information and knowledge age. Originally, it includes an area of approximately 15 km by 50 km, which stretches from the Petronas Twin Towers to the Kuala Lumpur International Airport, and also includes the towns of Putrajaya [a grandiose new administrative capital] and Cyberjaya. It has since been expanded to include the entire Klang Valley.' The government bailed the project's developers out at the time of the Asian financial crisis. Many larger MSC firms are multinational companies which have been lured there from other sites in Malaysia with fiscal incentives. There is little evidence that the MSC has so far created significant value-added for Malaysia. Unlike, for instance, the Korean government's plan to make local firms players in high-volume semiconductor manufacturing, it has never been clear what the MSC is supposed to do.

158. Of course the Waja cannot compare with the latest, fifth generation Elantra. The fair comparison is with the first generation Elantra of 1991 or the second generation Elantra of 1995–2000. The Elantra and the Waja are cars of the same, 1.6 litre engine size in their standard models.

159. HMC began kit assembly operations in 1968 and produced its first in-house engine in 1991 (the same year the Elantra debuted). Proton began operations in 1983, starting with kit assembly, and produced its first in-house engine in 2005, which was then fitted to the Proton-designed Waja that had launched in 2001. Measuring from inception to in-house engine, HMC required twenty-three years and Proton twenty-two years.

160. Estimates of the annual return on the first IPP range between 14 and 25 per cent. The deal required Tenaga, the state power firm, to buy a minimum 72 per cent of the output from two gas-fired power plants for twenty-one years – what is called 'take or pay'. Since Tenaga had intended to build the plants itself, the Yeohs obtained the sites with much of their infrastructure (gas pipes in, electricity transmission lines out) put in place by the state at taxpayers' expense. They obtained a starting price of 15.2 Malaysian sen per kilowatt hour (compared with 11.5 sen in subsequent IPP deals) with payment every two weeks. Superficially, the Yeohs' net return on operations was about 14 per cent per year, but some analysts calculated the return on equity as high as 25 per cent. There are two main reasons for this: firstly, the extremely generous take or pay arrangement allowed higher than normal gearing for the project, pushing up the return on invested cash (as opposed to the return on total equity and debt invested); and secondly, some construction and service work was done by private YTL subsidiaries, raising the temptation for the owners to skim off profit from the

project through high-priced contracting and service contracts – although this is of course merely a theoretical possibility. YTL's own website is surprisingly candid about what it describes as its 'lucrative deal', although there is no discussion of rates of return. Like almost all Malaysian privatisations, the Yeohs IPP deal was not openly tendered. See http://www.ytl.com.my/getnews.asp?newsid=12843

161. Between 2004 and 2010 YTL did take over, in several tranches, all the equity in one of the two original cement plants built under Mahathir's Look East policy. YTL already had cement interests on the less-developed east coast of Malaysia and, by adding the large Perak Hanjoong plant, became the number two player in cement in the country. However, unlike Chung Ju Yung, who learned to build cement plants, the Yeohs have throughout acquired all their technology on a turnkey basis, mostly from South Korean suppliers.

162. For Chung's war trading activities, which spanned both the Second World War and the Korean War, see Kirk, *Korean Dynasty*, p. 27. Lim admits to bid rigging, citing a Singapore auction of fourteen bulldozers, in his autobiography *My Story: Lim Goh Tong* (Kuala Lumpur: Pelanduk, 2004), p. 24.

163. Lim took as his partner in the venture Mohamad Noah Omar, father-in-law to both Malaysia's second premier, Abdul Razak, and its third, Hussein Onn, and grandfather of the current premier, Najib Razak. The casino has traditionally provided sinecure posts for Malaysia's powerful police force, including its most senior members.

164. The Singapore resort is called Resorts World Sentosa; Universal Studios has provided the creative input through a joint venture. Other major offshore investments include the acquisition of the betting firm Stanley Leisure in the United Kingdom and gaming operations in the United States, as well as various cruise ship businesses.

165. Lim's construction firm Kien Huat, once one of the biggest in Malaysia, became a passive holding firm for the Lim family's equity in Genting.

166. See Wain, *Malaysian Maverick*, p. 93. The successful Japanese bid was RM313 million; the best local bid was RM71 million lower. A Malaysian engineering firm was retained by the Japanese, but its management said later that they had experienced no technology transfer.

167. Lim, *My Story*, unpaginated foreword.

168. Syed Mokhtar did come to control DRB-HICOM after the death of Proton boss Yahaya Ahmad in a helicopter crash (see below). By this point DRB-HICOM had sold its interest in Proton but retained investments in automotive components manufacturing.

169. Khoo's sin was to have been too close to Mahathir's political rival, Razaleigh Hamzah. Unlike when Chung Ju Yung quarrelled with Korean president Kim Young Sam, Khoo had no real business stature independent of his political sponsors and he faded away. South-east Asian tycoons never escape their dependence on politicians, whereas in north-east Asia they can outgrow these relationships.

170. A protégé of former finance minister Daim Zainuddin, Wan Azmi's Land & General corporation went bust. He still works out of Rohas Perkasa.

171. Krishnan's key businesses are headquartered at Menara Maxis, on the Twin Towers site, while Mahathir, since he left the premiership, has occupied a capacious 86-floor office at the Towers.

172. Krishnan is the only oligarch who managed to be genuinely close to both Mahathir and his arch-enemy Razaleigh Hamzah whom Mahathir defeated in a vicious and hugely expensive UMNO internal election in 1987. Post-Mahathir, Krishnan has already prospered under two more premiers.

173. As estimated by *Malaysian Business*, February 2011. The same source is used for Robert Kuok's wealth, below.

174. Although Kuok's senior executives in Malaysia work out of Wisma Jerneh, named for his insurance business, back down near Francis Yeoh junction.

175. Basically the north side of the Royal Selangor Golf Club. The only other choice for the super-rich and royals is Bukit Tunku (known in English as Kenny Hills) on the west side of the city.

176. Tan is the Malaysian billionaire every other billionaire loves to hate – perhaps because it makes them feel better about themselves. His core cash flow comes from untendered government privatisations, including a state lottery. At least three other billionaires have described him to me in less than glowing terms, but I am not sure he is as different from them as they would like to think.

177. Hussain's business was the RHB Group.

178. Across from Vision City, the older Sheraton hotel was built by the UMNO-linked Renong Group whose debt-laden boss, Halim Saad, was bailed out by the government during the crisis and relieved of his post.

179. Interview with Anwar Ibrahim, who was one of the ministers present, 8 July 2010. Mahathir held a cabinet meeting in the morning with a full day of Japanese cultural training to follow.

180. According to the account given by the Secretary General of the Communist Party of Malaya, and the CPM field commander Siew Ma, after Gurney's Rolls-Royce had been halted by gunfire he climbed out of the car and 'began walking calmly and directly towards our high bank ambush positions'. Ching Peng, *My Side of History* (Singapore: Media Masters, 2003), p. 288.

181. Part of the firm founded by the late Lee Kong Chian, which used to be the biggest plantation and commodity processing business in south-east Asia.

182. The current owners (see below) declined either to meet the author or organise a plant tour.

183. Malaysia's supply of domestic gas did make gas DRI attractive as a technology, but to choose a partner with no relevant experience and then to fail to check that partner's proposals adequately appears reckless. Mahathir took personal charge of the negotiations with Nippon Steel.

184. In April 1987, the Japanese side agreed compensation of RM467 million against project costs around RM1.3 billion. Unfortunately, since the Yen had soared against the Ringgit since 1985, the Ringgit cost to Malaysia of the part of the project not covered by compensation soared.

185. Author interview, 7 July 2010. Dr Tan is the managing director of Penang-based Southern Steel. The other two members of the team were Wan Abdul Ghani Wan Ahmad, former managing director of one of Malaysia's existing downstream steel producers, Antara, and Choo Kin Hean, CEO of the state-owned Malayawata Steel mill. Their report was submitted to Mahathir but never made public.

186. Written response to author from Mahathir, 7 March 2011.

187. Mahathir attended the opening of the plant at Gurun and mentioned automotive steel in his speech, which strongly suggests Chia was telling him it would be among the plant's output. In correspondence, Mahathir himself was evasive on this point. In the period the Gurun plant opened, Mahathir also allowed ASM boss William Cheng, against explicit civil service advice, to open new flat steel capacity after Cheng told him he would supply industrial and automotive demand. Cheng built the plant but sold all the output to the domestic construction sector in competition with Perwaja's flat products. This story is confirmed both by civil service and industry sources.

188. This is capital expenditure plus operating losses from inception to the point when Chia left the business in August 1995; at that point outstanding bank debt was RM5.7 billion and accumulated operating losses were RM 2.5 billion. There had been additional financing from non-bank sources. Some of the numbers are brought together in Wain, *Malaysian Maverick*, p. 173, which puts Perwaja's total costs at the point of Chia's departure at 'RM 15 billion or more'.

189. Perhaps the most egregious of many cases concerned RM957 million in untendered contracts with the Man Shoon Group and companies affiliated with Kok Mew Shoon, a long-time associate of Chia's. Auditor PWC was so concerned by what it found at Perwaja that it printed only three copies of its 1996 report on the firm: one for Mahathir; one for Anwar; and one for the governor of the central bank. Although PWC identified Man Shoon Group's untendered contracts, it did not mention the connection between Mr Kok and Eric Chia, which was revealed by journalists after the report was leaked. Wain, *Malaysian Maverick*, p. 174, provides a long list of Chia's dirty laundry. After Mahathir left power in 2003, Chia was sent to trial by the government of Abdullah Badawi on a single criminal charge of breach of trust. He was acquitted.

190. A long-time senior employee of Abu Sahid describes Chia as having been his 'mentor'. Off the record interview, Kuala Lumpur, July 2010.

191. According to Perwaja's own website, the two new DRI reactors came on stream in 1993, while new furnaces and other equipment for steel making were commissioned in 1996. Of the RM1.3 billion 'price' for Perwaja, RM800 million was debt owed to

the state-owned Perbadanan National Berhad (PNB) and RM530 million was the agreed cash component.

192. Off-the-record interviews, Kuala Lumpur, July 2007, and subsequent correspondence. In the first half of 2010, Abu Sahid was paying RM2 million a month to the government, having paid nothing for an extended period; he still owed a substantial part of the RM500 million, even after more than a decade. According to Anwar Ibrahim, the Malaysian government also gave Abu Sahid 'a huge chunk of land in Johor and a big contract' because Perwaja was such a 'tough' deal to take on. Author interview, 8 July 2010. Accounts published when Abu Sahid sold some equity in Perwaja in 2006 show that the firm owed Tenaga RM310 million.

193. Ever the asset traders, Abu Sahid and his partners retained warrants, called Irredeemable Convertible Unsecured Loan Stock (ICULS), giving them a free option to buy back control of Perwaja at any point in the next ten years.

194. Abu Sahid started out trading auto parts for public sector buyers including the police, army and welfare state. This was his entrée into transportation, which in turn was his business connection with Perwaja.

195. Biographical details from Perwaja's website at http://www.perwaja.com.my/ home/home.php

196. Amsden, *Asia's Next Giant*, p. 291 gives the budgeted cost of Pohang's initial 9.1 million tonne facility, built in four phases, as USD3.6 billion. Work started in 1970. This sum, adjusted in line with the US consumer price index (CPI), is equivalent to USD19.9 billion in 2009 terms. Adjusting the RM10 billion written off in 1996 to cover most of Perwaja's costs to date, using the same US CPI index, yields a 2009 figure of USD5.5 billion. Steel output capacity has remained at around 1.5 million tonnes. Barry Wain, Mahathir's biographer, estimates the full cost of Perwaja was at least USD8 billion.

197. In 1984, Malaysia already had one car for every twenty-one people (the highest penetration in south-east Asia outside of Singapore), compared with one car for every 146 people in South Korea and one for every fifty-one people in Taiwan. This was largely a function of Malaysia's greater inequality which allowed a relatively richer minority to own cars at an earlier stage of development compared with north-east Asian states. See K. S. Jomo (ed.), *Industrialising Malaysia: Policy, Performance, Prospects* (London: Routledge, 1993), p. 275. According to the World Bank's World Development Indicators, which contain more recent car ownership data, Korea caught up with the Malaysian rates of car ownership in 2005 – at around one car for every four people – by which time the Korean car market was twice the size of the Malaysian one because of its bigger population.

198. That Mahathir did not see domestic competition as helpful to his industrial development plans is borne out by this statement: 'Proton was the first national car. When it was doing reasonably well we started a second national car company which should produce only small 600 c.c. cars which would not compete with the

bigger Proton cars.' Written response to questions put to Mahathir, 7 March 2011. Superficially, Perodua had a major private sector shareholder in the form of United Motor Works, which held 38 per cent in 1993. However, UMW was ultimatately controlled by state-owned Perbadanan National Berhad; other state agencies held 30 per cent and Daihatsu 32 per cent. Proton had been established with 70 per cent equity held by HICOM and 30 per cent by Mitsubishi.

199. Mahathir reached an outline deal with Mitsubishi on a trip to Japan in October 1981. Mahathir began discussions with Daihatsu on another trip to Japan in 1991. The trading house Mitsui, then managed in Malaysia by Mahathir's long-time confidant Kazumasa Suzuki, handles much of Daihatsu's international trading activity.

200. In 1982, long after the original MMC technology transfer deal had been agreed, Hyundai did sell a 10 per cent stake to the Japanese to raise cash; this subsequently rose to 12.6 per cent, but remained a purely passive investment.

201. Written response to questions put to Mahathir, 7 March 2011.

202. For Mahathir's personal forays into businesses in real estate, taxis and trading, and his home workshop where – among other things – he invented a new Islamic toilet, see Wain, *Malaysian Maverick*, pp. 15–16 and p. 55 respectively.

203. For a more detailed discussion, see K. S. Jomo, 'The Proton Saga: Malaysian Car, Mitsubishi Gain' and Kit G. Machado, 'Proton and Malaysia's Motor Vehicle Industry', in Jomo (ed.), *Japan and Malaysian Development*, chapters 11 and 12. Most of the sheet steel needed by Proton came from Mitsubishi's own steel subsidiary in Japan. With respect to content localisation at Proton, Nadzmi Mohd Salleh, the current Proton chairman who was on the original national car project team and has been involved with the business on and off for twenty-five years, recalls visiting potential component partners recommended by MMC in the early 1990s. He says MMC executives in Kuala Lumpur gave the impression these were independent firms, but it soon became clear that they were all MMC suppliers over which the car maker had leverage. 'I was a young man. I was so naive,' he says of his expectations of the Japanese partner. Author interview, 5 July 2010. With respect to Mahathir, there was further proof of his naivete in the mid 1990s when he almost signed up to a joint venture to manufacture engines and cars in China that would have seen Malaysia commit more than a billion dollars of public money. According to persons close to the deal, Mahathir was encouraged by Mitsubishi and its consultants to believe that the investment was funding a Proton project that would produce vehicles with Proton engines. In reality, Mitsubishi was looking to sell a production line for a commercially failed engine of its own in a project where all the cash would be provided by Malaysia. The deal was on the point of being signed in China's Great Hall of the People in Beijing when the reality behind it was explained to Mahathir and he pulled out, instead inking a non-binding memorandum of understanding that was subsequently forgotten about. The key consultant pushing the deal, Rin Kei Mei, had played a significant role in the original, deeply flawed Proton–Mitsubishi agreement in Malaysia.

204. The MMC contract was never made public. On US export plans, see Jomo (ed.), *Industrialising Malaysia*, p. 280. Entrepreneur Malcolm Bricklin had agreed with Mahathir to sell the Proton Saga in the US but had failed to obtain the necessary federal and state approvals.

205. Proton was exempt from a 40 per cent tariff on knock-down car kits imported into Malaysia and paid only half of the tariff on other components. In 1989, the year after the Japanese management takeover, Proton showed a first profit, but this was largely a result of a bookkeeping adjustment by which the firm raised the prices charged to its distributor and thereby moved earnings on to its own profit and loss account.

206. *Sunday Times* economy car ratings 1989, quoted in Jomo (ed.), *Industrialising Malaysia*, p. 280. Jomo states, p. 260, that Proton's first year sales in the UK were a record for a new entrant in that market.

207. Proton and Yahaya Ahmad acquired a combined 80 per cent of Lotus in October 1996 for GBP51 million.

208. Author interview with Mahaleel Bin Tengku Ariff, 5 July 2010. He said the peak parts spend with Mitsubishi was around RM2 billion a year. Proton paid EUR70 million for MV Agusta in December 2004. The Italian firm was developing a low-cost mini car body that did not require moulds and Mahaleel believed he could launch a Malaysian mini car costing only RM10,000.

209. Author interview, 5 July 2010.

210. Author interview, 5 July 2010.

211. During the crisis the heavily indebted shipping interests of Mahathir's son Mirzan were bought over by Malaysian International Shipping Corporation, which in turn required a bail-out and takeover by national oil and gas firm Petronas. The mechanism was typically murky but the upshot was another bill for taxpayers.

212. Under AFTA, Japanese plants in Thailand should have preferential access to a market like Malaysia based on only 40 per cent local content, whereas by 2003 Proton was 90 per cent localised but not yet globally competitive. Proton and Perodua secured an official exemption from the terms of AFTA until 2008 and then continued to enjoy an informal rebate of half of Malaysian excise duty (which should not now be differentiated), enjoying a subsidy equivalent to around 15 per cent of a car's retail price. AFTA, like all things ASEAN, lacks an enforcement mechanism beyond bilateral negotiation.

213. Abdullah is a slight variation on the theme in that he is the son of a prominent religious figure from the independence era. There was a complete return to sociological form in 2009, however, when Abdullah was succeeded by Najib Razak, the banker son of Malaysia's second prime minister.

214. The business had been bought in December 2004 for EUR70 million; it was sold a year later in a fire sale for a token €1 plus the business's debts.

215. S. Jayasankaran, 'The New Way: Think Small', *Far Eastern Economic Review* (6 November, 2003), p. 15.

216. The Malaysian winner in all this is the Daihatsu joint venture Perodua, where Daihatsu (like Mitsubishi before it sold out of Proton in the 1990s) resisted government demands to localise content and export. The firm sells a token 5,000 units a year overseas at a loss as a sop to the Malaysian government, compared with a peak of 38,000 exports at Proton. In the wake of the financial crisis, Mahathir allowed Daihatsu to increase its equity and management control at Perodua, leaving the Malaysian side as an ever more passive partner. Since Mahathir's departure, Perodua has continued to import around 30 per cent of its component supply while still enjoying 'national car' tax breaks. Perodua's market share overtook that of Proton in the mid 2000s.

217. The new Waja/Lancer is to be called the Proton Inspira.

218. See Kirk, *Korean Dynasty*, p. 171. As Kirk notes, no one in Korea listened to BCG.

219. Quoted in Amsden, *Asia's Next Giant*, p. 281. The manager in question was attached to Hyundai's shipbuilding subsidiary, but the point is a general one.

220. The difference was production volumes. Because of Korea's export focus, HMC produced its first 5 million vehicles by 1992 – within twenty years of inception. Both Malaysian producers combined, Proton and Perodua, produced their 5-millionth vehicle around twenty-five years after Proton started.

221. Even since the Asian financial crisis and IMF-mandated market opening, non-tariff barriers have continued to be employed to considerable effect. Korea's use of idiosyncratic environmental and other standards to stymie car imports is a major reason that the US–Korea Free Trade Agreement, under negotiation since 2006, was not agreed and ratified until the end of 2011. When talks started in 2006, the US was exporting around 6,000 cars a year to Korea versus more than 700,000 Korean cars (including ones assembled in US plants) sold in America.

222. The deal in Malaysia was concluded in 1993 by Chung Ju Yung personally. It involved assembly of HMC trucks with imported HMC engines and Malaysian-stamped body parts. The other south-east Asian deals were concluded around the same time. See Kirk, *Korean Dynasty*, p. 175.

223. When Mahathir assumed the premiership in 1981, Malaysia's GNI per capita was USD1570 and Korea's was USD1560. In 2008, they were USD7,250 and USD21,530 respectively.

224. At least after the late 1960s. There were still a lot of strikes – often violent – in the 1950s and early 1960s.

225. Emil Salim, a long-time economic adviser to Suharto and one of the five members of the so-called Berkeley Mafia of Indonesian technocrats, says: 'Mahathir had already done Proton. That was a big influence. Suharto's reaction was "What is going on when a country of twenty-five million can do this?"' The other trigger, however, says Salim, was Indonesia's long-awaited achievement of rice self-sufficiency in 1985: 'Suharto called everyone in and said, "What is our next target?" It had to be industrialisation.' Author interview, 19 December 2010.

226. Author interview, 19 December 2010. Astra has long been reckoned the best-run business in Indonesia.

227. During the Asian financial crisis British conglomerate Jardine Matheson gained control of Astra and, as of 2010, derived most of its worldwide profit from the business. Jardine likes to keep quiet about this, since the average Indonesian might find the situation upsetting. It was interesting that on my visit to Perodua in Malaysia, which is technologically captive to Toyota affiliate Daihatsu, Malaysian managers told me that whenever they pass on government complaints that exports are minimal they are told that their quality and productivity lags Astra in Indonesia and that they must first match that standard before being capable of serious export volumes. But of course Astra itself has never done any serious exporting either. Edwin Soeryadjaya, who remains extremely respectful of the Toyota managers he worked with when his family controlled Astra, says of Toyota's capacity to keep the technological whip hand over its joint venture partners: 'Not for nothing are they the most successful car company in the world.' Author interview, 19 December 2010.

228. Habibie did a degree and doctorate in aerospace engineering in Germany and then worked there in aerospace for around ten years. IPTN was created in 1985 from P. T. Nurtanio, an aviation enterprise which Habibie ran after his return to Indonesia from Germany in 1974. After the Asian crisis, IPTN changed its name to Dirgantara or Indonesian Aerospace Inc. and its workforce was cut to under 4,000. It continues to make small aircraft, to assemble helicopters from kits, to manufacture components for Airbus and Boeing, and to produce military goods, but the firm's major ambitions have been shelved.

229. Japan is an important sub-contractor in the production of certain complex aircraft parts for Boeing and Airbus. Even a failed industrial policy produces some technological return.

230. Suehiro Akira, *Capital Accumulation in Thailand, 1855–1985* (Tokyo: Centre for East Asian Cultural Studies, 1989), p. 185 and p. 208 this quotation. Separately, the president of the Federation of Thai Industries, Paron Issarasena, wrote of the late 1980s wave of foreign investment in Thailand: 'These industries will come to use Thailand's generalised system of preferences (GSP) and then leave for other countries which offer them better privileges, leaving nothing for Thailand.' He was pretty much right. *Bangkok Post*, 12 January 1989.

231. The Philippines' GNI per capita was USD210 in 1962 and still USD210 in 1970, by which time Taiwan and Korea were better off. The Philippines was ahead of Thailand in 1980, but by 1990 its GNI per capita was USD690 versus USD1410 in Thailand. Indonesia caught up with the Philippines before the Asian financial crisis, was then knocked back, and has since caught up again. The GNI per capita of both states was just under USD1900 in 2008.

232. Ronald Dore, *Flexible Rigidities: Industrial Policy and Structural Adjustment in the Japanese Economy 1970–80* (London, Athlone, 1984), p. 27. In a similar vein, the influential economist Albert Hirschman described successful economic development as a 'multi-dimensional conspiracy'.

233. See William Megginson and Jeffry M. Netter, 'From State to Market: A Survey of Empirical Studies on Privatisation', *Journal of Economic Literature* 39 (2001), pp. 321–89.

234. The Japanese tariff increases date from 1961. In part they compensated for an easing of foreign exchange controls demanded by the IMF and the OECD, which Japan joined in 1964. Lockwood (ed.), *State and Economic Enterprise in Japan*, p. 491, describes the tariff increases as 'a sweeping upward revision of tariffs ... quietly begun'. The point about increased protection in the midst of the development process extends to other historical examples – Germany increased levels of protection from 1878 in a critical phase of her industrial development.

235. Dore, *Flexible Rigidities*, introduction and chapter 3. On steel, see Jang-Sup Shin, *The Economics of the Latecomers: Catching Up. Technology Transfer and Institutions in Germany, Japan and South Korea* (London: Routledge, 1996), p. 49.

236. Angus Maddison, *Explaining the Economic Performance of Nations: Essays in Time and Space* (Aldershot: E. Elgar, 1995), p. 124.

237. Bill Emmott, *The Sun Also Sets: Why Japan Will Not be Number One* (London: Simon & Schuster), p. 157.

238. Emmott, *The Sun Also Sets*, p. 26.

239. MITI's biotech section was set up in 1982. Another area in which MITI has had limited success, mentioned in passing earlier, is aerospace.

240. In 1996 the highlights of the second round were the collapse of one of the country's fourteen city banks as well as the number four securities firm, Yamaichi. The government was forced to nationalise two banks (now called Shinsei and Aozora), but again balked at a comprehensive clean-up of the banking sector. In 2003, a still weak banking sector embroiled the government once more as it was forced to pump funds into Resona Bank.

241. For a fuller discussion, see Ha-Joon Chang and Jang-Sup Shin, 'Evaluating the Post-crisis Corporate Restructuring in Korea', in Ha-Joon Chang (ed.), *The East Asian Development Experience: The Miracle, the Crisis, and the Future* (London: Zed Books, 2006).

242. Ha-Joon Chang and Jang-Sup Shin, 'Evaluating the Post-crisis Corporate Restructuring in Korea', in Chang (ed.), *The East Asian Development Experience*, pp. 301, 304.

243. Korean consumers are also experiencing the pressures of personal indebtedness. Just as the Korean household savings rate has fallen from one-quarter of disposable income before the Asian crisis to under 5 per cent in 2011, so average household

debt, most of which is mortgage borrowing, has reached American levels, at around 140 per cent of annual income.

244. As noted above, Korea's use of non-tariff barriers such as technical standards to block imports already held up the signing and ratification of a free trade deal with the US for more than five years.

245. Maddison, *Explaining the Economic Performance of Nations*, p. 124.

246. There are sixteen Indian Institutes of Technology. They operate as independent universities and have a combined student population around 15,000 undergraduates and 12,000 post-graduates.

247. Another way of looking at India's economic structure is to consider that the country's manufacturing trade deficit is around 5 per cent of GDP whereas its vaunted service sector produces a surplus of less than 1 per cent. Services cannot compensate for what manufacturing should be doing at India's stage of development.

248. The work of Alfred Chandler on the role of big business is perhaps the best known. Scholars who stress the role of big business in east Asia include Peter Nolan.

249. Alice Amsden captured the two faces of the United States rather well when she stated that since the Second World War there have been two different policies towards global development: 'The first lifted all boats, the second lifted all yachts.' Alice Amsden, *Escape from Empire: The Developing World's Journey through Heaven and Hell* (Cambridge, MA: MIT Press, 2007), p. 1.

### Part 3 – Finance: The Merits of a Short Leash

1. Hyman P. Minsky, *Stabilizing an Unstable Economy* (New Haven, CT: Yale University Press, 1986; reissued New York: McGraw Hill, 2008), p. 106.

2. Alexander Gerschenkron, *Continuity in History and Other Essays* (Cambridge, MA.: Harvard University Press, 1968), p. 137.

3. German development was already gathering pace in the 1830s, while there were no joint stock banks before 1848 and only a significant number after 1870. It was later still that the banks became specialised by industry.

4. See Gabriel Tortella, 'Spain 1829–74', in Rondo Cameron (ed.), *Banking and Economic Development: Some Lessons of History* (New York: Oxford University Press, 1972). A new banking law that encouraged the opening of investment banks in Spain was passed in 1856, but their activities were very much framed by existing company law. Tortella estimates that by the mid 1860s about fifteen times as much capital had been invested in railways as in industry.

5. Savings and investment, plus imported or minus exported capital, are equal in the accounting system used by economists. In other words, if there are no international flows of capital, every dollar of investment must be financed by a dollar of savings.

6. W. W. Rostow, *The Stages of Economic Growth: A Non-communist Manifesto* (Cambridge: Cambridge University Press, 1960; third edition, 1990), p. 36. Rostow says that 10 per cent is the minimum requisite for what he calls 'take-off': 'The

difference between a traditional and a modern society is merely a question of whether its investment rate ... has risen up to 10 per cent or over.'

7. According to the World Bank's World Development Indicators series, peak pre-Asian crisis gross savings rates as a percent of GNI were: Japan, 41 per cent (1970); Korea, 39 per cent (1988); Malaysia, 39 per cent (1996, increasing during the financial crisis to 42 per cent in 1998); Thailand, 36 per cent (1996); Indonesia and the Philippines were somewhat lower at 33 per cent (1989) and 28 per cent respectively (1977 – before the Philippines' mid-1980s crisis, since when the savings rate rose to a new peak of 35 per cent in 2000). The World Bank does not provide data for Taiwan.

8. Jung-En Woo, *Race to the Swift: State and Finance in Korean Industrialization* (New York: Columbia University Press, 1991), p. 195. In addition to Argentina and Chile, Uruguay also privatised banks in the 1970s, resulting in 'capture' by local business groups. In Mexico after the Latin American foreign debt crisis of 1982, the Salinas government privatised banks to local business groups. In Russia, all the oligarchs who came to dominate the post-Soviet economy rose through their initial control of financial institutions, before using these institutions to acquire mineral resources. On Russia, see David E. Hoffman, *The Oligarchs: Wealth and Power in the New Russia* (New York: Public Affairs, 2002). For more on bank privatisation in south-east Asia, see Joe Studwell, *Asian Godfathers* (London: Profile, 2007).

9. Various sops to the international community were offered along the way. For instance, in 1963 Japan signed up to Article 11 of the IMF charter, committing it to not imposing trade controls because of balance of payments shortfalls. Chalmers Johnson called Japan's efforts to meet international demands for deregulation in the 1960s 'a purely cosmetic public relations gesture'. See Chalmers Johnson, *MITI and the Japanese Miracle: The Growth of Industrial Policy, 1925–1975* (Stanford, CA: Stanford University Press, 1982), p. 279.

10. The relatively high interest rates were the nominal rates. Unlike domestic investors, who are concerned with 'real' inflation-adjusted interest rates, foreigners repatriate their money. So they are only concerned with their home inflation rates. However, when it became clear the Asians pegs could not be defended, foreigners wanted their money back.

11. Reduced to 5 per cent in 1987. See Masahiko Aoki and Hugh Patrick (eds.), *The Japanese Main Bank System* (Oxford and New York: Oxford University Press, 1994), chapter 1.

12. See Aoki and Patrick, *The Japanese Main Bank System*, Table 1.6, p. 37.

13. The government deliberately made domestic corporate bond issues difficult and expensive to buy in order to retain its leverage through the banking system. It was this that made Eurobonds so attractive in the 1980s. For more on changing financing patterns in the period, see Aoki and Patrick, *The Japanese Main Bank System*, p. 9.

14. Rapid currency appreciation dated from the US–Japanese Plaza Accord of September 1985. The yen strengthened from around 250 to the US dollar to 125 in 1988. The

official discount rate of the central bank dropped from 7 per cent to 2 per cent in the same period. The Nikkei 225 Index was 3.1 times higher at its peak of just under 39,000 at the end of 1989 than in September 1985. The Urban Land Price Index peaked in September 1990 at just under four times the September 1985 level.

15. See Woo, *Race to the Swift*, p. 43. It was the US advisers who also oversaw the creation of an independent central bank which Park made very un-independent.

16. The consumer price index increased an average 17 per cent annually in the 1960s and 19 per cent annually in the 1970s. The peak of rediscounting was during the HCI drive in the late 1970s.

17. See Woo, *Race to the Swift*, pp. 113 and 157. She cites a 1980 survey which suggests that 70 per cent of household savings at that point were kept with illegal kerb lenders. The kerb financial system in the 1970s was perhaps 30 per cent of the size of the formal banking system (which also held corporate and government deposits), with the vast majority of loans from the kerb going to businesses. On preferential loans, see Woo, p. 11 and Stephan Haggard, Chung H. Lee and Sylvia Maxfield (eds.), *The Politics of Finance in Developing Countries* (Ithaca: Cornell University Press, 1993), p. 33. The role of preferential loans peaked at around 70 per cent of formal bank lending in the late 1970s under the HCI programme, up from less than 40 per cent in the 1960s.

18. Alice Amsden, *Asia's Next Giant: South Korea and Late Industrialization* (New York: Oxford University Press, 1989), p. 78.

19. See Woo, *Race to the Swift*, p. 103. Woo calculates that between 1965 and 1969, adjusting for interest rate changes, the London inter-bank offered rate (LIBOR) was an average 13 percentage points lower than the Korean inter-bank rate. Korea's foreign borrowing in this period increased from 4 per cent of GNI to 21 per cent.

20. The presidential decree on the kerb market was part of the concluding phase of the crisis and came on 3 August 1972. After the moratorium expired, lenders were allowed to collect a much-reduced rate of interest on the debt. In the context of a devaluation and an interest holiday, Korean industry bounced back in 1973 with a 73 per cent rise in exports. See Amsden, *Asia's Next Giant*, p. 96.

21. On capital controls in Korea, see Ha-Joon Chang, 'The Political Economy of Industrial Policy in Korea', *Cambridge Journal of Economics*, vol. 16, 1993, p. 139.

22. Korea borrowed most heavily from US banks, whose boards figured their government would never let its ally go bust. An American banker was quoted in the 13 December 1976 edition of the *Wall Street Journal* as saying: '[T]he American government is the guarantor of the whole South Korean government, lock, stock, and barrel.'

23. The increases in foreign debt were also connected with the need to stabilise the domestic banking system at different points. From the mid 1960s to the Asian financial crisis there were four separate bank bail-outs in Korea, two of them in the long first crisis, in 1969–70 and 1972, one with the second oil crisis, during 1979–81,

and one with the mid-1980s Asian recession, in 1986–8. See Haggard *et al.* (eds.), *The Politics of Finance in Developing Countries*, p. 23.

24. There were temporary devaluations in 1971 and others during the mid-1970s and early 1980s recessions. Permanent devaluations would of course have made the foreign debt load unmanageable.

25. This was reflected in the fact that the sales of the ten biggest *chaebol* in 1979 were the equivalent of one-third of GDP, and in 1984 to two-thirds of GDP. See Robert Wade, *Governing the Market: Economic Theory and the Role of Government in East Asian Industrialization* (Princeton: Princeton University Press, 2004), p. 306.

26. Interest rates were raised but still regulated in the 1980s. The debt levels of the *chaebol* meant there was no way they could afford market rates. The first bank privatisation was in 1981; in the course of the decade, the five national commercial banks were each privatised and new banks were licensed. See Haggard *et al.* (eds.), *The Politics of Finance in Developing Countries*, p. 23 and Woo, *Race to the Swift*, p. 195.

27. In opening Korea's stock market to foreign investors, a sensible precaution was taken. As in Taiwan, and now China, government set a maximum amount of foreign capital which could enter the market at any one time and selected foreign institutional investors to manage this allowance. Such Qualified Foreign Institutional Investor (QFII) schemes limit a country's risk in the event sentiment suddenly turns heavily negative – as happened in the Asian crisis – and foreign funds seek to exit the market *en masse*. With respect to Korea's NBFIs, see Haggard *et al.* (eds.), *The Politics of Finance in Developing Countries*, p. 45. The earliest NBFIs dated from the kerb moratorium period in 1972. The *chaebol* always managed to control these institutions. Dozens more were licensed in 1982–3. The importance of NBFIs in the Korean financial system has its closest east Asian parallel in Thailand. On the *chaebol* lobbying for financial deregulation, see Amsden, *Asia's Next Giant*, p. 135. By 1996 the Korean Federation of Industries, the main *chaebol* association, was so enamoured of deregulation that it prepared a report calling for the abolition of all government ministries bar defence and foreign affairs. The report was never published. As already noted, from the 1980s on, the *chaebol* grew almost exclusively by acquisitions.

28. Total South Korean public debt was only 25 per cent of GNI on the eve of the Asian crisis in 1997. However, the absolute amount of foreign debt increased from USD44 billion in 1994 to USD120 billion in 1997, and almost all of it was short-term and hence subject to recall at a few weeks' notice. See Ha-Joon Chang (ed.), *The East Asian Development Experience: The Miracle, the Crisis and the Future* (London: Zed Books, 2006), p. 269.

29. The five biggest *chaebol* were dealt with in what were dubbed the Big Deals, affecting seventeen major subsidiaries across eight business sectors.

30. The average total (household, business and government) savings ratio to GDP was 30.5 per cent in Taiwan in the 1970s, versus 17.5 per cent in Korea. See Wade,

*Governing the Market*, p. 59. The difference between Taiwan and Korea came down to different levels of household saving.

31. Taiwan was more than USD3,000 per capita better off than Korea in the early 1990s. The differential shrank steadily to under USD1,500 by 1996 before increasing temporarily during the Asian financial crisis. The differential began to decrease again from 1999 and since 2005 Korea has led. The difference was a little over USD2,000 in 2010.

32. Wade, *Governing the Market*, p. 67 notes that although the average Taiwanese firm was less than half the size of the average Korean one in terms of employee numbers in the 1970s, Taiwan's upstream suppliers were notably more concentrated than Korea's – in other words, the Taiwanese upstream firms were more oligopolistic.

33. On credit distribution, see Woo, *Race to the Swift*, p. 170. For Taiwan she gives a figure of 18 per cent of total domestic credit for the 333 firms, which the author estimates would approximate to around 30 per cent of bank credit. Depository institutions were two-thirds of total financial system assets at the time. Taiwan's Bank of Communications and China Development Corp. were set up in the 1960s with the stated aim of doing industrial finance and long-term credit respectively. However, in practice both acted more like regular commercial banks.

34. Note that India operated a main bank system through the 1970s and 1980s, but it did not lead to the kind of industrial upgrading seen in Korea and Japan. India lacked export discipline. See V.V. Bhatt, 'Lead Bank Systems in India', in Aoki and Patrick, *The Japanese Main Bank System* above. Bhatt writes: 'An export-oriented strategy imposes a certain discipline not only on the lead bank and the enterprise, but also on the government whose policies have to be in accord.'

35. Taiwan's central bank estimated that between 1965 and 1988 private firms obtained around 55 per cent of their domestic borrowing from financial institutions and around 35 per cent from the kerb market. Data quoted in Haggard *et al.* (eds.), *The Politics of Finance in Developing Countries*, p. 79.

36. It was 1987 when exchange controls were lifted under pressure from trade partners, especially the US. Taiwan's second highest foreign reserves in the world were followed by West Germany's at USD56 billion. Most foreign exchange reserves were acquired by the Taiwan central bank because it forced the financial system to hand over foreign exchange at a pre-determined exchange rate, paying for it with domestic currency. The inflationary effects of issuing large amounts of domestic currency can be controlled by paying with bonds issued by the central bank, or by crediting the banks with an increase in their reserves held at the central bank while not allowing them to draw on those reserves. In the 1980s, as well as building huge foreign exchange reserves, the Bank of Taiwan increased the share of deposits banks were required keep on reserve to a very high 24 per cent. China's central bank has more recently increased reserve requirements to similar levels as it pursued a cheap money policy.

37. See, for instance, D. Rodrik, 'Industrial Organization and Product Quality: Evidence from South Korean and Taiwanese Exports', mimeo, Kennedy School of Government, Harvard University, June 1988.

38. The share of bank loans going to individuals doubled from 20 per cent to 40 per cent from 1980 to 1990. Taiwan's housing price index rose five fold between the start of 1987 and late 1990. The Taiwan Stock Exchange Index went from a little over 600 points in 1985 to 12,000 in early 1990. In subsequent years the housing index remained at much higher levels while the stock index exhibited extreme volatility.

39. Data from the World Bank's World Development Indicators series. In the key development decade of the 1970s, the average gross savings rate for Korea was 24.1 per cent of GNI; for the six years of the decade for which WDI has data for the Philippines, gross savings averaged 24.8 per cent of GNI.

40. This is very much a *relative* observation. Governments in north-east Asia created lots of bad debt through infant industry policy anchored by export discipline – all learning is wasteful – but they created relatively less debt for every dollar of investment compared with south-east Asia.

41. The US federal funds rate peaked at 19 per cent.

42. From the World Bank's World Development Indicators series. Foreign debt service (repayments of interest and principal) data are not available for the Philippines until 1970, when the annual disbursement was USD307 million in current dollars; in 1986 payments totalled USD3 billion in current dollars.

43. As noted earlier, Korea's foreign debt peaked at over 50 per cent of GNI in 1985. The Philippines was well below this level in the first fifteen years of Marcos's rule and only reached it in 1981, as the economy was beginning to crash. As economic crisis took hold, and output and exports contracted, foreign debt spiralled to over 90 per cent of GNI in Marcos's last year, 1986. The debts were rescheduled under the same Brady Plan used in Latin America and have remained a heavy burden on the Philippine economy ever since. See Jeffrey Sachs and Susan Collins (eds.), *Developing Country Debt and Economic Performance, Volume 3: Country Studies – Indonesia, Korea, Philippines, Turkey* (Chicago: University of Chicago Press, 1989). Available at http://www.nber.org/books/sach89-2

44. Philippine GNI per capita was USD210 in 1962 and USD1890 in 2008. Korean GNI per capita was USD110 in 1962 and USD21,530 in 2008.

45. Remember that in the half century prior to 1914 the United States was the most heavily protected economy in the world, with an average tariff double that of European states. Prior to the setting-up of PNB, banking in the Philippines was dominated by British banks which engaged only in low-risk trade finance. The quotation from Harrison is at Paul D. Hutchcroft, *Booty Capitalism: The Politics of Banking in the Philippines* (Ithaca, NY: Cornell University Press, 1998), p. 66.

46. In fact there were three consecutive bilateral free trade agreements, each of which structured the economic relationship in same way. The 1909 Payne–Aldrich Tariff

Act established free trade between the US and the Philippines. It was followed by the Bell Trade Act in 1946 and the Laurel–Langley Act in 1954. In essence, these agreements embedded the Philippines comparative advantage in sugar and coconut production that had existed in the nineteenth century. In the 1930s, the Philippines' agricultural exports to the US were about 80 per cent of all the country's exports.

47. On PNB's first bankruptcy, see Hutchcroft, *Booty Capitalism*, p. 67. On the 1949 debacle, see Hutchcroft, pp. 30 and 71.

48. Overseas Bank of Manila failed in 1967, GenBank in 1976, and four more banks in the mid 1980s. There were many other significant failures of non-bank financial institutions.

49. Park regarded Marcos's move as a useful precedent. After winning three, not entirely transparent, elections, he ruled as dictator under the so-called Yushin Constitution until his assassination in October 1979.

50. In 1967, 'export production' was added to the list of top priorities for rediscounting, but only at the same level of precedence as 'industrial or agricultural products' in general. See Paul Hutchcroft, 'Selective Squander: The Politics of Preferential Credit Allocation in the Philippines', in Haggard *et al.*, *The Politics of Finance in Developing Countries*, p. 183. Hutchcroft concludes there was an 'utter absence of selectivity' in rediscounting. In addition to rediscounts, the Philippines deployed other forms of preferential credit as well, the most important of which were foreign loan guarantees, currency swap arrangements by which the central bank assumed exchange rate risk on foreign loans, and forced government deposits in specified banks (such as those which made Danding rich).

51. Eli Remolona and Mario Lamberte, 'Financial Reforms and Balance of Payments Crisis: The Case of the Philippines, 1980–83', *Philippine Review of Economics and Business* 23 (1986), p. 113.

52. A joint World Bank–IMF study group visited the Philippines in 1979 to address its worsening economic problems. One recommendation was the further development of the stock market and other non-bank sources of finance. World Bank–IMF, *The Philippines: Aspects of the Financial Sector* (Washington, DC: World Bank, 1980).

53. The data in this paragraph refer to Benedicto's Republic Planters Bank; he also controlled Traders Royal Bank. Marcos's main direct bank vehicle was Security Bank, which obtained more central bank largesse than any other institution. See Hutchcroft, *Booty Capitalism*, pp. 164–5.

54. Hutchcroft, *Booty Capitalism*, p. 80.

55. The 1981 crisis began with the flight of the infamous Dewey Dee, who had both been involved in banking himself and left behind USD85 million (in contemporary value) of unpaid borrowings from other banks. True to form, Filipinos had a great name for Dee and his partners: they were known as the 'Four Horsemen of the Apocalypse'. Four banks were nationalised in this period. The banks that failed

between 1984 and 1987 were Banco Filipino, Pacific Bank, Philippine Veterans Bank, Manilabank.

56. GNI per capita fell from USD700 in 1982 to USD520 in 1986.

57. On state bank write-downs, see Hutchcroft, *Booty Capitalism*, p. 188. Government domestic debt was PHP88 billion in 1986 and PHP291 billion in 1990.

58. Natasha Hamilton-Hart, *Asian States, Asian Bankers: Central Banking in Southeast Asia* (Ithaca, NY: Cornell University Press, 2002), p. 119.

59. From 1975 a minimum 20 per cent of bank lending had to go to *bumiputera* borrowers. On the very limited rediscounting for export loans, see Hamilton-Hart, *Asian States, Asian Bankers*, p. 117.

60. In 1977, the property sector share of credit was 22 per cent; in 1988 it was 36 per cent. See K. S. Jomo, 'Malaysian Debacle: Whose Fault?' in Ha-Joon Chang and Gabriel Palma (eds.), *Financial Liberalisation and the Asian Crisis* (Basingstoke: Palgrave, 2001), p. 105.

61. Wade, *Governing the Market*, p. 42.

62. Malaysia's 1989 financial reform law was the Banking and Financial Institutions Act; it was followed by the 1992 Securities Act. Daim Zainuddin, quoted in Joe Studwell, 'After the Gold Rush', *Asia Inc.*, December/January 1995/6.

63. The Kuala Lumpur Composite Index did not regain its 1997 level until 2007. The World Bank and IMF push on stock market development in poor countries is particularly associated with the World Bank's 1989 World Development Report, *Financial Systems and Development*. For a fuller discussion of pyramiding and other financial games, see Studwell, *Asian Godfathers*, chapter 5, 'Banks, Piggy Banks, and the Joy of Capital Markets'.

64. Figures for Malaysia from Jomo, 'Malaysian Debacle: Whose Fault?' in Chang and Palma (eds.), *Financial Liberalisation and the Asian Crisis*, p. 106. For Japan and Taiwan, see earlier in this chapter.

65. According to the World Bank World Development Indicators database, in 1996 in Malaysia, gross national savings were 39 percent of GNI versus 35 per cent in Korea.

66. The equity cap for individuals or related groups applied to all new banks, and any existing bank subject to merger. But it was ignored in cases relating to PhileoAllied, Hong Leong and DCB–RHB where it should have applied.

67. In the wake of the crisis, Bank Negara Malaysia, the central bank, orchestrated the consolidation of twenty-one commercial banks, twelve investment banks and twenty-five finance companies into ten financial groups.

68. Capital controls were reintroduced from September 1998. Most controls were lifted again in 2004 and 2005 after Mahathir stepped down from the premiership.

69. The groups centred on their core banks, Bangkok Bank, Bangkok Metropolitan Bank, Bank of Ayudhya and Union Bank of Bangkok. In the 1970s, Union Bank was superseded in importance among privately controlled bank groups by that centred on Thai Farmers Bank. See Suehiro Akira, *Capital Accumulation in*

*Thailand, 1855–1985* (Tokyo: Centre for East Asian Cultural Studies, 1989), pp. 157, 248 and 287.

70. One can argue that the reason Bangkok Bank became a very important regional financier in countries like Malaysia and Indonesia was precisely because government policy was not aggressively directing its funds to support export-led Thai industrialisation. For more on Bangkok Bank, see Studwell, *Asian Godfathers*, p. 94.

71. On relations between the central bank and the World Bank and IMF, see R. Doner and D. Unger, 'The Politics of Finance in Thai Economic Development', in Haggard *et al.* (eds.), *The Politics of Finance in Developing Countries*, pp. 97 and 104.

72. Figures for Thai commercial bank credit by sector come from Doner and Unger, 'The Politics of Finance in Thai Economic Development', p. 105. The share of credit going to construction and real estate was only 11 per cent in 1988 and 16 per cent in 1990.

73. Between 1983 and 1986, thirty-two finance companies had to be bailed out by the central government and fifteen were closed down; there were also three bank recapitalisations.

74. Thailand adopted IMF Article VIII, which covers currency convertibility, in May 1990.

75. Suehiro, *Capital Accumulation in Thailand 1855–1985*, p. 245, calculated that Thai bank deposits rose 7.6 times in 1957–67, and 6.6 times in 1967–77, while GDP in current prices rose about 2.5 times in each of these periods. The aggregate savings rates are taken from the World Bank World Development Indicators series.

76. Real GDP growth in Thailand averaged 9.2 per cent in 1987–96, versus 6.5 per cent in 1951–86.

77. On real estate lending, see B. Renaud *et al.,* 'How the Real Estate Boom Undid Financial Institutions: What Can Be Done Now?' in J. Witte and S. Koeberle (eds.), *Competitiveness and Sustainable Economic Recovery in Thailand* (Bangkok: National Economic and Social Development Board and World Bank Thailand Office, 1998).

78. According to calculations by Peter Warr, the average short-term capital inflow as a share of total savings/investment was 2.1 per cent in 1973–86, and 22.8 per cent in 1987–96. See Peter Warr, 'Boom, Bust and Beyond' in Peter Warr (ed.), *Thailand Beyond the Crisis* (Oxford: RoutledgeCurzon, 2005), p. 13.

79. See Warr (ed.), *Thailand Beyond the Crisis*, p. 5 and, with respect to budget cuts, Pasuk Phongpaichit and Chris Baker, 'Thailand's Crisis: Neo-liberal Agenda and Local Reaction', in Chang and Palma (eds.), *Financial Liberalisation and the Asian Crisis*, p. 89. VAT was raised from 7 per cent to 10 per cent, petrol tax was put up, as were some utiility prices. In the first half of 1998, sales of non-durable goods in Thailand fell 10–15 per cent, while those of durables fell 50–75 per cent. The IMF made its demands under the terms of a USD17.2 billion emergency loan facility.

80. The 3.5 per cent figure was contained in the IMF's first Letter of Intent with the Thai government in August 1997, the –7 per cent figure in a fifth Letter of Intent signed in August 1998. LOIs are the formal mechanism by which the IMF agrees

to make funds available to members. Both sides write down what they will do and exchange the signed documents.

81. Between July 1997 and July 1999, seven banks and eleven financial companies were nationalised.

82. Liem was still alive at the time of this visit to his Jakarta home. He passed away in 2012.

83. Liem arrived in Java in 1938, aged 22, and worked with a brother. See Jamie Mackie, 'Towkays and Tycoons: Chinese in Indonesian Economic Life in the 1920s and 1980s', in Audrey Kahin and Virginia M. Barker (eds.), *The Role of the Indonesian Chinese in Shaping Modern Indonesian Life* (Ithaca, NY: Cornell Southeast Asia Program, 1991).

84. Suharto's ascent to power began with the 30 September 1965 assassination of senior generals by a rival army faction, leaving him as one of two senior surviving generals (his superior, Abdul Haris Nasution, was less politically adroit). His rise continued through anti-communist purges – which left perhaps half a million, possibly more, people dead – to Suharto's promotion to acting president in 1967, and his confirmation as president in March 1968. Back in the mid 1950s, Suharto had been Diponegoro Division commander in central Java. In this capacity he ran or condoned unauthorized army businesses, something for which he was punished by being sent to SESKOAD, the army staff college in Bandung, in 1959–60. Om Liem was not particularly close to Suharto in the 1950s, but he made his vital connection, paying regular contributions to army 'foundations' run by the future president.

85. Siti Hardijanti Rukmana, Suharto's eldest daughter, known as Tutut, and Sigit Harjojudanto, his oldest son, controlled the Suhartos' 30 per cent interest in BCA (600,000 of 2 million issued shares) at the time of the Asian crisis; Mochtar Riady had 18.7 per cent before he sold out to the Salims in 1990. The levels and division of related-party lending at the bank were confirmed by several senior current and former BCA directors in interviews, December 2010. Many loans were disguised by the use of nominee shell companies.

86. Even in the most speculative period in the lead-up to the 1997 crisis, BCA's loan book remained fully serviced in terms of both interest and principal payments. Mochtar Riady ran BCA conservatively until he resigned to run his own financial group in 1990, and if anything the bank became more conservative under Liem's son Andree in the 1990s. In 1997, BCA's exposure to real estate was only just over 15 per cent of its portfolio, well below that of other banks.

87. This employs the average exchange rate of USD1: IDR8,000 for the five years from July 1997, rather than the much higher dollar figure that would have resulted from the exchange rate before the crisis.

88. The valuation of what Liem's assets raised at sale is an estimate. According to central bank governor Soedradjad Djiwandono, there is no authoritative record of the funds received from the sale of the Liem (or other) assets because assets were

sold by the Indonesian Bank Restructuring Agency (IBRA) but proceeds went into the government budget and no formal reconciliation was ever published. Press estimates of how much the Liem assets raised all put the recovery rate at around 40 per cent of the headline value. A PhD thesis calculated a higher rate of 48 per cent. See Marleen Dieleman, *How Chinese are Entrepreneurial Strategies of Ethnic Chinese Business Groups in Southeast Asia? A Multifaceted Analysis of the Salim Group of Indonesia* (Leiden: Leiden University Press, 2007), p. 161.

89. Sukarno was a master of the grand gesture. He was the chairman of the jury that selected Frederich Silaban, a Christian architect, to design the national mosque. He placed the Monas in the middle of the old Dutch Konigsplein military parade ground.

90. Officially, this is the Youth Monument, and the previous one the Welcome (Selamat Datang) Monument.

91. Sukarno's three development banks were Bank Industri Negara, Bank Negara Indonesia and Bank Rakyat Indonesia. On credit allocation, see Andrew J. MacIntyre, 'The Politics of Finance in Indonesia', in Haggard *et al.* (eds.), *The Politics of Finance in Developing Countries*, p. 129. Bank Indonesia data show that, for instance, in 1956 credit allocation to importers was IDR1.3 trillion versus less than IDR400 million to exporters. From 1953 to 1957, loans to importers averaged approximately double those to exporters.

92. Nursalim was perhaps the worst of all the tycoons in not repaying funds provided to support his bank during the Asian crisis. He remains holed up in Singapore. It was his wife who wanted the I. M. Pei towers, after admiring the Bank of China building Pei designed in Hong Kong. A model of the planned project can be viewed at http://www.lera.com/projects/id/

93. During Suharto's long rule the five key members of the Berkeley Mafia went on to hold many different ministerial posts.

94. In the 1970s, major projects included Krakatau Steel, the Dumai oil refinery and the Asahan aluminium smelter. Direct central bank lending and rediscounting averaged around half of all bank credit outstanding from the mid 1970s until 1983, before such credit was forced relentlessly down to less than 20 per cent by the end of the 1980s. When Suharto turned to Habibie for the last time at the end of his regime, he was appointed vice president and Suharto's designated successor.

95. Author interview, 17 December 2010. Soedradjad's US PhD came not from Berkeley but from Boston University. However, he was close, intellectually and personally, to the Berkeley Mafia. His father-in-law was Widjojo Nitisastro's mentor, Sumitro Djojohadikusumo.

96. No prudent bank such as BCA, in which Tommy's family invested, would lend to Tommy because he was so unreliable. Suharto's children were all close to the managing directors of the state banks. It has been claimed, but never proven, that state bank lending was often on the basis of so-called *surat sakti* – 'sacred letters'

– which effectively instructed loans be made, and which originated with Suharto. This would not be surprising. Park Chung Hee in Korea used just such letters. There is one on display in the POSCO museum in Pohang demanding complete bureaucratic and financial support for its boss, Park Tae Joon. The difference is that in Korea a forced loan came with an export requirement.

97. Radius Prawiro, 'Back to the Wisdom of the Market Economy,' speech to the Indonesian Institute of Management Development, 1989, p. 13. Quoted in Adam Schwarz, *A Nation in Waiting: Indonesia's Search for Stability* (St Leonards: Allen & Unwin, 1999), p. 56. The decision to lift almost all capital controls in 1971 is discussed in Andrew J. MacIntyre, 'The Politics of Finance in Indonesia', in Haggard *et al.*, *The Politics of Finance in Developing Countries*, p. 139. Bank data in this paragraph are from J. Soedradjad Djiwandono, *Bank Indonesia and the Crisis: An Insider's View* (Singapore: Institute for South-East Asian Studies (ISEAS), 2005), p. 53.

98. Winata's father built barracks for the army although, like many south-east Asian tycoons, he prefers to offer a more hard-scrabble back story, telling journalists he got his start selling ice lollies and washing cars. His deep relations with the military give him great power, not least with the Jakarta police. It is often said that the army runs Tomy and Tomy runs the (Jakarta) police. It should be stressed that in private Winata is always careful to deny that he has ever had any involvement with the drug trade. Today the Bengkel is a shadow of its former self.

99. The back-door listing was a takeover of a government company that owned the Borobudur Hotel. The development project was then spun out as Jakarta International Hotels & Development (JIHD). The Jakarta stock exchange did not start trading from the new Sudirman Central Business District (SCBD) site until 1995; before then it continued to operate from the Danareksa building on Jalan Merdeka Salatan near Monas in the north.

100. See Joe Studwell, 'Inside the Summa-Astra Affair', *Asia Inc.*, April 1993.

101. Sutowo left national oil company Pertamina with USD10.5 billion in debts when he was eased out in 1976. The private fiefdom he created included Bank Pacific, which he handed over to his daughter Endang Mokodompit, and which had to be bailed out by the government in 1995 after reckless, illegal related-party lending. See Kevin O'Rourke, *Reformasi: The Struggle for Power in Post-Soeharto Indonesia* (Crows Nest, NSW: Allen & Unwin, 1998), p. 47.

102. This change happened very fast. From 1949 to the mid 1980s, state banks and the central bank consistently accounted for 75–90 per cent of bank credit. By the end of 1990, local private banks already made up 36 per cent of credit, and with foreign banks, 42 per cent. Private lenders became dominant around 1992. See Andrew J. MacIntyre, 'The Politics of Finance in Indonesia', in Haggard *et al.* (eds.), *The Politics of Finance in Developing Countries*, p. 138.

103. For some further discussion, see K. S. Jomo (ed.), *Southeast Asia's Industrialization*, chapter 11, p. 292. By the early 1990s, manufacturing exports constituted the bulk

of Indonesian exports for the first time, but this disguised the weakness of the underlying export structure and the predominance of low value-added processing by foreign firms. From a macro-economist's perspective, of course, all exports are regarded as equal.

104. Author interview, 17 December 2010.

105. Author interview, 19 December 2011. Emil Salim is a very open and engaging gentleman. However, the author was struck by how often his comments in the course of a two-hour discussion used the 'efficiency' language of neo-classical economics and how he did not seem to conceptualise Indonesia's economic plight in structural terms. The contrast with the traditional north-east Asian and Chinese outlook was striking.

106. Studwell, 'Inside the Summa-Astra Affair', p. 42.

107. See O'Rourke, *Reformasi*, pp. 57 and 285–6 and Hamilton-Hart, *Asian States, Asian Bankers*, p. 54.

108. The Suhartos did the same thing, but for them it was easy. Hendra Rahardja's banks were Bank Harapan Sentosa and Bank Guna International. The money he owed the central bank was liquidity credits extended during the crisis. He fled Indonesia and never served time.

109. Hamilton-Hart, *Asian States, Asian Bankers*, chapter 3.

110. Private foreign debt was USD55 billion (16 per cent of GDP) by July 1997. Of this, more than USD34 billion had a maturity of less than one year. Data from the Bank for International Settlements.

111. GNI per capita increased marginally in 1997, to USD1130, because the Asian crisis struck Indonesia late in the year. In 1998, GNI per capita fell to USD680. It was USD1,170 in 2005.

112. See Luc Laeven, 'Risk and Efficiency in East Asian Banks', Policy Research Working Paper 2255 (World Bank Financial Sector Strategy and Policy Department, December 1999).

113. Indonesia's three biggest banks are still state-owned. After BCA at number four, banks five to fifteen by assets are all in foreign ownership. There are still more than a hundred very small private banks; these survive by concentrating on high-margin consumer lending. Competition among banks in the post-crisis, IMF-designed system has not driven lending rates down. In December 2010, Indonesian banks were able to charge firms 13–14 per cent on short-term loans, despite a central bank base rate of 6.5 per cent.

114. The most famous exposition of this view is perhaps Schumpeter's. The banker, he wrote, 'is essentially a phenomenon of development ... He makes possible the carrying out of new combinations, authorizes people, in the name of society as it were, to form them. He is the ephor [the senior magistrate in ancient Greece] of the exchange economy.' Joseph Schumpeter, *A Theory of Economic Development*, translated by Redvers Opie (Cambridge, MA: Harvard University Press, 1934), p. 74.

## Part 4 – Where China Fits In

1. Li Xiangqian and Han Gang, 'Xin faxian Deng Xiaoping yu Hu Yaobang deng sanci tanhua jilu' ('Newly Discovered Record of Three of Deng Xiaoping's Talks with Hu Yaobang and Others'), *Bainianchao*, no. 3 (1999): 4–11, reprinted in Xie Chuntao, ed., *Deng Xiaoping xiezhen* (*A Portrait of Deng Xiaoping*) (Shanghai: Shanghai cishu chubanshe, 2005), p. 192.

2. The hugely polluting cement kilns developed in China are a form of vertical kiln into which ingredients are loaded by hand before ignition. The glass-making process is known as the Luoyang technique. For more on China's 'alternative' technologies, see Joe Studwell, *The China Dream: The Elusive Quest for the Last Great Untapped Market on Earth* (London: Profile, 2002), p. 192.

3. To be fair to the World Bank, it was instrumental in organising conferences in the 1980s which introduced Chinese policymakers to different economic ideas and policy alternatives. However, China dictated the terms of interaction in a manner that filtered out any possible neo-liberal influence. My personal sense is that some World Bank staffers were only too happy for this to happen. In a period when the Bank's annual World Development Reports were becoming more and more stridently neo-liberal, the China mission brought economists sympathetic to planning and government intervention to Chinese conferences and even organised, in 1987, a high-level team from Korea to explain to Chinese economists that country's ideas on 'plan and market'; once again, this was at the request of the Chinese side. China showed none of the intellectual dependency on the West exhibited by south-east Asian governments.

4. In 2007 and 2008. China is unusual, but not unique, in refusing publication of its annual IMF consultation.

5. China's average GDP growth was 9.9 per cent in the twenty-eight years from 1980 to 2008. Thai growth was 9.5 per cent in the decade 1987–96, but only 7.3 per cent in the twenty-eight years prior to 1996.

6. As discussed in Part 1, there is no good data on this period. The 70 per cent figure results from official Chinese data published in the 1980s. See, for instance, Zhang Gensheng, *Rural Reform in China* (Shenzhen: Haitian Publishing House, 2001), p. 324. He states that grain production was 113.2 million tonnes in 1949, 166.8 million tonnes in 1953, and 192.7 million tonnes in 1956 (on the eve of collectivisation). Zhang is a former deputy director general of the State Council's Development Research Centre. Other, non-Chinese scholars think that 1949 output was higher than 113 million tonnes and therefore the output growth of the 1950s, while significant, was less. Though no expert, I am inclined to this latter view if only because I suspect quite a lot of yield gains were already achieved under household farming in 'liberated' areas of China in the 1930s and 1940s.

7. Data from the National Bureau of Statistics (formerly State Statistics Bureau), quoted in Studwell, *The China Dream*, p. 33. Grain production statistics in China

include foodstuffs such as potatoes and soybeans which are not technically grain, but which are staple foodstuffs in the Chinese diet. Average farm size of 5.6 Chinese mu (3730 square metres; 1 mu equals 666.6 square metres) is based on recent Landesa farm surveys, see n. 14 below, which cover China's seventeen most important agricultural provinces. Some other, less productive provinces have larger average farm sizes.

8. *Selected Works of Deng Xiaoping*, vol. 3 (1982–1992) (Beijing: People's Publishing House, 1993), p. 370.

9. According to UN Food and Agriculture Organisation (FAO) data for 2009, Chinese rice yields were 6.59 tonnes/ha versus a world average of 4.2 tonnes/ha. Chinese wheat yields were 4.75 tonnes/ha versus 2.99 tonnes/ha in the US, and a world average of 3.02 tonnes/ha.

10. With respect to sugar in the early 1980s in China, see Studwell, *The China Dream*, p. 33. Latest data on Guangxi sugar yields are from the CEIC database. In the 1990s, when sugar was still a significant crop in Taiwan, average yields were over 80 tonnes/ha, versus around 55 tonnes/ha in the Philippines.

11. Chinese soybean import values are from the CEIC database. The discussion here is a simplification of a complex subject. Some Chinese scale soybean farming is now in private hands. US soybean producers farm high-yield, genetically modified soy varieties, which are not available in China. And the Chinese soybean sector has been disrupted historically by changing government policy, leading to relocation of soy production further north and also much less effective extension, processing and marketing support than with other crops.

12. GINI data are per the Standardized World Income Inequality Database (SWIID) and the University of Texas Estimated Household Income Inequality data set. The latter attempts to adjust for some methodological weaknesses in the SWIID series. In trend terms, both data sets tell a very similar story. Rural income data per the Landesa 2010 China survey.

13. From '*nongye zhichi gongye*' to '*gongye fanbu nongye, chengshi zhichi nongcun*'. Hu's 2005 speech was entitled 'Constructing a Harmonious Society and Advancing New Rural Construction'. See Ethan Michelson, 'Public Goods and State–Society Relations: An Impact Study of China's Rural Stimulus', working paper no. 4, Indiana University Research Centre for Chinese Politics and Business, February 2011.

14. Local governments in China are prohibited in law from raising funds directly, so they use investment companies to borrow from banks or undertake bond issues.

15. US NGO Landesa, in co-operation with China's Renmin University, has conducted five large-scale sample surveys in China since 1999, the most recent in mid 2010. The latest round interviewed nearly 1,600 rural households in seventeen major agricultural provinces. The survey indicates that 37 per cent of villages had experienced land taking for non-agricultural purposes between the second half of the 1990s and 2010, up from 27 per cent in the 2005 survey. By 2010, 24 per cent

of villages had experienced leasing out of tracts of land, typically for commercial agriculture.

16. The Landesa 2010 China survey estimates the mean land taking at 560 mu (37 hectares). However, it is very difficult to collect accurate data. Household farmers who are surveyed are aware when land conversions are going on, but they rarely know the full details (even when it is they who are being expropriated). Local governments have no incentive to admit how much land they are converting because it draws central government attention to them. All we know for sure is that the pace of land conversions by local governments has accelerated rapidly.

17. Average compensation from the Landesa 2010 survey. The law allows a maximum thirty years' rental as compensation. Based on the average farm size of 5.6 mu, and the median annual rental of Rmb290 per mu, this translates to a theoretical maximum Rmb48,000. The milled rice price at the time of writing was Rmb1.5 per jin or Rmb3 per kilo. In Landesa surveys, more than 80 per cent of farm families have at least one member in non-farm employment.

18. Great Wall hails from Baoding in Hebei province and started in agricultural machinery repair; Wanxiang is from Yuhang in Zhejiang province and started by making agricultural machinery; Wahaha began in Shangcheng district on the outskirts of Hangzhou in Zhejiang; Broad was started in Chenzhou in Hunan province. All but Wanxiang, which had a precursor business in the 1970s, were founded in the 1980s.

19. To be fair to the government, China is so big that it could never hope to decant its surplus rural population into non-farm employment as quickly as Taiwan and Korea did. Going foward, the slowing growth of the Chinese workforce should give rural labour more wage bargaining power. However it remains the case that at a policy level China has never, in the post-1978 era, prioritised the welfare of the rural population in the way that Japan, Taiwan and Korea did.

20. Lawrence Lau *et al*, 'Reform without Losers: An Interpretation of China's Dual-track Approach to Transition', *Journal of Political Economy* 108, no. 1 (February 2000), pp. 120–43. Yasheng Huang, *Capitalism with Chinese Characteristics: Entrepreneurship and the State* (Cambridge: Cambridge University Press, 2008), also contains useful descriptions of the 1980s economy and its rural drivers.

21. Zhao Ziyang was ousted during the political turmoil of 1989. The premier in 1993 was Li Peng. Zhu Rongji became a vice-premier that year and – largely because Li Peng was not trusted by Deng Xiaoping to run the economy – Zhu took on that role, which normally falls to the premier. In January 1994, Zhu overhauled China's tax system, redirecting a large part of national fiscal income away from the provinces and to the centre. In 1998, Zhu succeeded Li Peng as premier, serving until 2003.

22. It was after the 15th Communist Party Congress in September 1997 that local governments knew they had considerable licence in dealing with their local state

enterprises. Official data indicate that the number of state enterprise workers fell from more than 70 million in the mid 1990s to under 30 million by the mid 2000s.

23. The big lay-offs in the state sector occurred in the period (1998–2001) when I was writing *The China Dream* and the failure to recognise the depth and significance of these cuts is one of the book's major weaknesses.

24. See 'Provisional Methods for Assessing Performance of Responsible Managers of Central Enterprises', 30 December 2006, available at: http://www.sasac.gov.cn/gzjg/yjkh/200701310039.htm

25. In turn, SASAC firms account for the bulk of all SOE profits. In the pre-global financial crisis peak year of 2007, SASAC firm profits were 4 per cent of GDP, versus 4.2 per cent for all state sector firms both centrally and locally controlled. In 2010, SASAC firm profits of Rmb1.35 trillion were a smaller share of total SOE profits of Rmb2 trillion.

26. The shock absorber term is Arthur Kroeber's. The scale of the long-run profits of the resource and service oligopolies is reflected in their market capitalisations (China has listed a minority share in each), which massively outstrip anything in the manufacturing sector. Market capitalisations of fifteen leading state oligopoly firms on 30 September 2011 were: Petrochina, USD225 billion; Sinopec, USD93 billion; CNOOC, USD75 billion; China Mobile, USD200 billion; China Unicom, USD49 billion; China Telecom, USD52billion; China Life, USD66billion; Ping An, USD43 billion; ICBC, USD207 billion; BOC, USD114 billion; CCB, USD155 billion; Bank of Communications, USD41 billion; China Merchants Bank, USD37 billion; Shenhua Coal, USD79 billion; Chinalco, USD14 billion.

27. Sinopec was the most aggressive, cutting off gasoline supplies to Guangdong province.

28. By way of comparison, the average dividend paid by listed US companies in the post-Second World War era is around half of net profits.

29. For instance, in each of thermal power equipment, construction equipment and machine tools, around a dozen big state firms compete with each other. In shipbuilding and telecommunications infrastructure, there are half a dozen major players. The rail sector has only two major manufacturers.

30. Market capitalisations of twenty-four state-linked industrial companies at 23 August 2011: Offshore Oil (coal mining/oil machinery) USD3.3 billion; China Oilfield (coal mining/oil machinery) USD8.7 billion; Changsha Zoomlion (construction equipment) USD12.6 billion; XCMG (construction equipment) USD7.3 billion; Xi'an Aircraft (Defence/Aerospace) USD4.1 billion; China First Heavy (general industrial machinery) USD4 billion; Nari Technology (general industrial machinery) USD6.2 billion; China International Marine Container (general industrial machinery) USD7.1 billion; Shandong Weigao (medical equipment) USD2.1 billion; Mindray Medical (medical equipment) USD2.6 billion; Sinovel (wind turbines) USD8.5 billion; Xinjiang Goldwind (wind turbines) USD5.1 billion; Dongfang Electric (power equipment) USD6.4 billion; TBEA (power

equipment) USD4.3 billion; China XD (power equipment) USD3.5 billion; Baoding Tianwei (power equipment) USD3.3 billion; Zhejiang Chint (power equipment) USD2.8 billion; Shanghai Electric (power equipment) USD5.5 billion; CSR Corp. (railway equipment) USD7 billion; CNR Corp. (railway equipment) USD6 billion; China Shipbuilding (shipbuilding, etc) USD17.6 billion; China CSSC (shipbuilding, etc) USD6.6 billion; YangziJiang (shipbuilding, etc) USD3.2 billion; ZTE (telecom equipment) USD9.3 billion.

31. NDRC document No.1204 of 2005. NDRC policy documents start from zero each calendar year, an indication of how many are produced. The more sensitive ones offering 'guidance' to Chinese firms are not made public. Indeed, the contents may be classified as state secrets.

32. In the industrial equipment sector there are also more, sector-specific targets. For the period of the Eleventh Five-year Plan (2006–10), for instance, the NDRC set targets for coal industry mechanisation to reach 95 per cent in large mines, 80 per cent in mid-size mines and 40 per cent in small mines.

33. It was the elder Chen who, in a speech at a Party plenum in 1980, described the correct approach to economic reform as 'crossing the river by feeling the stones' (*mozhe shitou guohe*). The phrase is frequently and erroneously ascribed to Deng Xiaoping.

34. CDB was a major funder of the Three Gorges hydropower project, the 'South–North' water diversion project, and many other big power and road projects. Remarkably for a development bank, CDB boasts the lowest rate of non-performing loans (NPLs) in the country. The reported NPL rate was 0.94 per cent in 2009, versus 1.5–4.3 per cent at the big four commercial banks. CDB has the most rigorous loan approval systems in China. Chen Yuan signs off personally on all major loans.

35. CDB's foreign loan balance was USD18 billion at the end of 2007, USD65 billion in 2008 and USD98 billion in 2009. Export–Import Bank is also a significant provider of foreign loans to support Chinese mid-stream firms. In a typical deal in December 2009, Ex-Im Bank lent Pakistan's Ministry of Railways USD203 million to support the purchase of 277 Chinese-made locomotives.

36. China's state construction firms are commonly specialised in different activities, such as China Railroad Construction and China Road and Bridge Corporation, and now come under the control of SASAC.

37. In what may turn out to be a case of *déjà vu*, Westinghouse (now controlled by Japan's Toshiba) in 2010 won a deal to supply China with four third-generation AP1000 nuclear reactors on the basis of substantial technology transfer. The company reportedly handed over 75,000 technical documents after signing the contracts. See *Financial Times*, 23 November 2010.

38. Sany specialised in concrete pumps, which was a major reason why it could build up scale and then enter the wheeled machinery sector dominated by in-plan state players. This was akin to Honda's forcing its way from motorcycles into cars despite

Japan's Ministry of International Trade and Industry not wanting any more car makers.

39. The *Washington Post* reported that in the era of its domestic expansion Huawei received significant financing for its buyers from China Construction Bank, some of which was never repaid. This suggests government contacts beyond what private firms can normally count on. See John Pomfret, 'History of Telecom Company Illustrates Lack of Strategic Trust between U.S., China', *Washington Post,* 8 October 2010.

40. The firm says that Ren Zhengfei now owns less than 2 per cent of the business.

41. Huawei was forced to give up a takeover of US firm 3Com in 2008, of Motorola's wireless network division in 2010, and to divest patents from 3Leaf, a small US firm it did buy, in 2011. National security concerns have also been raised by the UK, Indian and Australian governments with respect to Huawei sales in those markets.

42. This investment is only for high-speed rail; hundreds of billions more dollars are being spent to expand other parts of the network. Major high-speed lines opened in 2011 included Guangzhou–Shenzhen, Beijing–Shanghai, Beijing–Wuhan and remaining pieces of the Shanghai–Chengdu line. It now takes 4.5 hours to travel 1,400 kilometres by train between Beijing and Shanghai.

43. Central government negotiators moved successively from deals with Bombardier to Kawasaki Heavy Industries to Siemens to Alstom as they planned different phases of manufacturing and technology acquisition. In 2010, a ministry official boasted to the national news agency that Germany's Siemens, which lost out in the earliest tenders, cut its price for a technology transfer licence by more than half before it was granted a contract. The person explained that 'any big global player entering the Chinese market had to agree to all-round technology transfer, localised production, the creation of a Chinese brand and reasonable prices'. He claimed that China acquired 'forty years of high-speed railway development in just five years'. Interview in Chinese at http://news.xinhuanet.com/video/2010–07/02/c_12291007.htm China's two train manufacturers are China North Locomotive and Rolling Stock Corp.(CNR) and China South Locomotive and Rolling Stock Corp.(CSR).

44. Zhou Yimin quoted in *21st Century Business Herald*, 21 June 2011.

45. For instance, China Railway Group is leading the high-speed project in Venezuela, China Railway Construction Corp. the high-speed project in Turkey. The learning of these firms in overseas markets feeds back to the equipment makers in a virtuous circle.

46. Overall, state sector net exports turned heavily negative in this period, moving from a small surplus in 2000 to minus USD153 billion in 2010. This reflects a huge increase in imports of commodities like oil, iron ore and coal processed by upstream state firms, as well as equipment purchases by manufacturers. Whether the data also reflect a more fundamental weakness in China's state sector-oriented industrial policy is an open question.

47. See Thomas K. McCraw, *Essential Alfred Chandler: Essays toward a Historical Theory of Big Business* (Boston, MA: Harvard Business School Press, 1988) and Alfred D. Chandler, *Strategy and Structure: Chapters in the History of the Industrial Enterprise* (Cambridge, MA: MIT Press, 1962).

48. For instance, when private equity firm Cerberus controlled Chrysler it was in active discussion with Chinese local-government owned car maker Chery to subcontract small car production. In solar cells, BP has shut down all its own production and is subcontracting it to Chinese suppliers.

49. BYD grew its conventional car sales in China to half a million vehicles a year. The *New York Times* story can be accessed at: http://www.nytimes.com/2009/01/13/business/worldbusiness/13chinacar.html?scp=7&sq=BYD&st=Search

50. For its 2008 accounting year, BYD booked RMB359 million (just over USD50 million) of 'grants and subsidies' from the Shenzhen government as one-quarter of its pre-tax profit. The firm has received similar subsidies in subsequent years. All data from published profit and loss statements.

51. The main subsidies Suntech received were start-up funds in the form of an investment by the Wuxi municipal government and cheap land to site its production facilities and headquarters.

52. China introduced its first national solar feed-in tariff in 2011 which subsidises the cost of solar installations with a grid purchase price above that for electricity from non-renewable sources. As a result, domestic solar installations were on course in mid-2012 to increase from 1.5 gigawatts in 2011 to 4 gigawatts in 2012 (versus forecast total global installations of 30 gigawatts).

53. Market capitalisations of leading private firms on 19 August 2011: Sany (construction equipment) USD19 billion; Geely (autos) USD2.2 billion; Great Wall Motor (autos) USD3.9 billion; BYD (autos) USD2 billion; Yingli Green Energy (photovoltaic) USD824m; Suntech (photovoltaic) USD919m, Haier Shanghai (household appliances) USD1.3 billion; Haier HK (a separate household appliance business) USD2.7 billion; BYD Electric (mobile phone batteries and peripherals) USD0.6 billion; Lenovo (computers) USD6 billion; Huiyuan (non-alcoholic beverages) USD0.84 billion; Mengniu (foodstuffs, dairy products) USD7 billion; New Hope (fertiliser, agricultural feedstuff) USD1.1 billion.

54. See Barry Naughton, 'China's Distinctive System: Can It be a Model for Others?', *Journal of Contemporary China*, June 2010. Naughton notes that total assets of China's state firms are 1.5 times GDP, compared with 30 per cent in supposedly *dirigiste* France.

55. The policy banks are only about 8 per cent of total bank assets because they do not have many bonds on their balance sheets, unlike the commercial banks. The policy banks sell bonds to commercial banks to fund themselves. China's three policy banks are China Development Bank, Export–Import Bank and Agricultural Development Bank. Their combined loans outstanding at the end of 2011 were

RMB8.3 trillion versus total bank system loans of RMB55 trillion. Data from the policy banks' annual reports.

56. On CDB, see Henry Sanderson and Michael Forsythe, *China's Superbank: Debt, Oil and Influence – How China Development Bank is Rewriting the Rules of Finance* (Singapore: John Wiley, 2012).

57. As the state enterprise closure programme advanced in the late 1990s, the central bank opened up a 4 percentage point gap between loan and deposit rates, which has been maintained since. About 1.5 percentage points of this gap accounts for bank profits, a reminder that the banks are very inefficient by international standards. Cumulative profits of Chinese banks hit a record USD165 billion in 2011, according to calculations by Reuters, 18 February 2012.

58. This figure is reached by a very crude calculation and is merely indicative. It takes China's foreign exchange reserves and subtracts the current account balance and net foreign direct investment. It appears that significant unauthorised outflows occurred in the late 1990s, and significant inflows have occurred since.

59. Financial analysts' estimates of the scale of China's shadow banking system are given in Henny Sender, 'Chinese Finance: A Shadowy Presence', *Financial Times*, 31 March 2011. China's own central bank has started to publish a series for total 'social financing', which aims to capture not just bank credit but other forms of off-balance sheet lending as well. This echoes the manner in which the central banks in Japan, Korea and Taiwan monitored both legal and kerb market credit. Figures from China's central bank put all forms of non-bank loan financing at around half total credit in recent years; the biggest non-bank lenders are trust companies charging about twice the bank interest rate.

60. Domestic currency lending by the banking system was RMB9.6 trillion (USD1.4 trillion) in 2009, versus RMB4.9 trillion in 2008. Mortgage rates were cut from 0.85 to 0.7 times the relevant state-set interest benchmark, cash down-payments were cut from 40 per cent to 20 per cent, and minimum holding time before a tax-free resale was cut from five years to two years.

61. Other temporary subsidies introduced in 2009 which helped Chinese manufacturers included cutting by half the 10 per cent tax on vehicles with small-displacement engines. In addition the government allocated RMB45 billion in subsidies to rural residents trading in old vehicles and home appliances for new ones. The major beneficiaries of these subsidies were domestic manufacturers.

62. See the debt reckoning compiled in the *China Economic Quarterly (CEQ)*, June 2011, p. 41. Like any such tally, the calculation required many subjective judgements. The liabilities listed by the *CEQ* are official treasury debt of 17 per cent of GDP in 2010, accumulated off-balance sheet debt related to previous bank restructurings of 9 per cent of GDP, Ministry of Railways debt of 4 per cent of GDP, debt issues used to fund the three policy banks equivalent to 13 per cent of GDP, sterilisation

treasury bills equivalent to 10 per cent of GDP, debts of local investment companies of local governments estimated at 27 per cent of GDP.

63. China has had negative one-year deposit rates since the start of 2010. Savings have been exiting the banks in 2011 and 2012, but not at a rate that poses an immediate risk.

64. The Taiwan dollar rate against the US dollar barely changed from 1961 to 1986. The rate was fixed at NTD40:USD1 in 1961, adjusted to NTD38 in 1973 and NTD36 in 1978, when the government instituted a 'managed float' of the currency. The exchange rate moved little until the US forced a free float in 1987.

65. China's foreign exchange reserves were equivalent to 65 per cent of GDP in September 2012, Taiwan's were 58 per cent of GDP at the end of 1987. However, allowance should be made for the fact China has twice as much export capacity accounted for by foreign firms. Export processing of goods for re-export inevitably generates a foreign exchange surplus. Around half China's exports are accounted for by foreign-invested enterprises, versus about one-quarter in Taiwan in the 1980s.

66. An increase in required reserves has the same effect as the central bank selling bonds because it ties up loanable funds. The ongoing costs of these interventions – known as 'sterilisation' – become painful when domestic inflation rises, requiring government to pay higher domestic interest rates, but interest earned on investments of foreign reserves is lower. This is the situation China confronts in the wake of the global financial crisis.

67. Taiwan ran big current account surpluses for most of the 1980s; its record was 21 per cent of GDP in 1986 during an economic downturn. China's biggest current account surplus to date was 10.1 per cent of GDP in 2007. It should be noted that I am arguing against a *substantially* undervalued exchange rate. Overvalued exchange rates are not a good thing either, as China and many other east Asian countries discovered in the more distant past.

68. Xi Jinping, Yu Zhensheng and Zhang Dejiang were born to high-ranking Party families; Wang Qishan married into one.

69. The Chinese Finance Ministry's budget for 2012 shows the government plans to spend USD111 billion on domestic security, including police, the state security apparatus, armed militia, courts and jails, versus USD106 billion on national defence. The domestic security budget represents a year-on-year increase of 14 per cent.

## Epilogue – Learning to Lie

1. R. H. Coase, 'The Institutional Structure of Production', *American Economic Review*, 82, no. 4, (September 1992), p. 713. The article is in fact the acceptance speech Coase gave in 1991 when he was awarded the Nobel prize for economics.

2. Italy introduced a significant land reform programme in 1950, backed by heavy investment in irrigation, rural infrastructure and agronomic extension. This was coupled with export-oriented manufacturing development and financial system repression. The Italian economy expanded faster than that of any other European state in the 1950s and 1960s, growing an average 5.8 per cent a year from 1950 to 1963 and 5.0 per cent a year from 1963 to 1973. For a treatment of the economic development similarities between Italy and Japan, see Richard J. Samuels, *Machiavelli's Children: Leaders and Their Legacies in Italy and Japan* (Ithaca, NY: Cornell University Press, 2003).

3. Black jails – *hei jianyu* – are a network of extra-legal detention centres in China used to detain citizens outside the already highly repressive formal judicial system. The existence of black jails is denied by the government, but there are so many of them that citizens commonly not only know of their existence, but also their locations.

4. Half a billion people across the five states, including Vietnam.

# Bibliography

The bibliography in this book is necessarily rather long. Directly below are listed in order of publication a number of particularly useful works that relate to east Asian development, followed by the main bibliography.

Friedrich List, *The National System of Political Economy* (London: Longmans, Green 1885). List wanders off message from time to time, but this is good, combative stuff from the man who took on Adam Smith. A few outstanding anecdotes and *bons mots*. List, of course, focused on Europe and north America's economies.

William Lockwood, *The Economic Development of Japan: Growth and Structural Change*, 1868–1938 (Princeton, NJ: Princeton University Press, 1954). The classic historical account of the economy of Meiji Japan, where it all began.

Walt Whitman Rostow, *The Stages of Economic Growth: A Non-Communist Manifesto* (Cambridge: Cambridge University Press, 1960). My favourite treatise on economic development, because it is short and to the point.

Wolf Isaac Ladejinsky and Louis J. Walinsky (ed.) *Agrarian Reform as Unfinished Business: The Selected Papers of Wolf Ladejinsky* (New York: Oxford University Press on behalf of the World Bank, 1977). Ladejinsky's correspondence and papers open up the world of agricultural development with some very funny observations about hapless politicians. This man was special.

Michael Lipton, *Why Poor People Stay Poor: Urban Bias in World Development* (Harvard: Harvard University Press, 1977). An academic classic.

Chalmers Johnson, *MITI and the Japanese Miracle: The Growth of Industrial Policy, 1925–1975* (Palo Alto, CA: Stanford University Press, 1982). The first of the trilogy of classic works that explained the nature of successful post-war development in Japan, Korea and Taiwan. The second was Amsden's, and the third was Wade's (see below).

K. S. Jomo, *A Question of Class: Capital, the State and Uneven Development in Malaya* (Singapore: Oxford University Press, 1986). South-east Asia has not produced the same classic texts on development as north-east Asian states, but this old book by the prolific Jomo is well worth reading.

Alice H. Amsden, *Asia's Next Giant: South Korea and Late Industrialization*, (New York: Oxford University Press, 1989). What Johnson did for the understanding of Japan, Amsden did for South Korea.

Stephan Haggard, Chung H. Lee and Sylvia Maxfield eds., *The Politics of Finance in Developing Countries* (Ithaca, NY: Cornell University Press, 1993). The best multi-country collection of essays about financial systems and their impact on development.

Ha-Joon Chang, *Kicking Away the Ladder: Development Strategy in Historical Perspective* (London: Anthem, 2002) A Cambridge economist turns to history to explain why most economists are wrong. This book was followed by Chang's bestselling *Bad Samaritans: Rich Nations, Poor Policies and the Threat to the Developing World* (London: Random House, 2007).

Robert Wade, *Governing the Market: Economic Theory and the Role of Government in East Asian Industrialization* (Princeton, NJ: Princeton University Press, 2004). Wade's subtitle implies that the book is about east Asia. In fact it is really about Taiwan.

Joe Studwell, *Asian Godfathers: Money and Power in Hong Kong and South-east Asia* (London: Profile Books, 2008).

Barry Naughton, 'China's Distinctive System: Can It be a Model for Others?' in *Journal of Contemporary China*, June 2010. A short and sweet examination of China's development policy by an economist who knows his history.


S. A. M. Adshead, *T'ang China: The Rise of the East in World History* (London: Palgrave Macmillan, 2004).

Zahir Ahmed, *Land Reforms in South-east Asia* (New Delhi: Orient Longman, 1975).

Alice H. Amsden, *Asia's Next Giant: South Korea and Late Industrialization* (New York: Oxford University Press, 1989).

Alice H. Amsden, *Escape from Empire: The Developing World's Journey through Heaven and Hell* (Cambridge, MA: MIT Press, 2007).

Masahiko Aoki and Hugh Patrick (eds.), *The Japanese Main Bank System* (Oxford and New York: Oxford University Press, 1994).

Paul Bairoch, *Economic and World History* (Brighton: Wheatsheaf, 1993).

Paul Bairoch, *Mythes et paradoxes de l'histoire économique* (Chicago: University of Chicago Press, 1993; Paris: Editions La Découverte, 2005).

Chris Baker and Pasuk Phongpaichit, *A History of Thailand* (Cambridge: Cambridge University Press, 2005).

Arsenio M. Balisacan, 'Agrarian Reform and Poverty Reduction in the Philippines', *Policy Dialogue on Agrarian Reform Issues in Rural Development and Poverty Alleviation* (30 May 2007).

P. T Bauer, 'Report on a Visit to the Rubber Growing Smallholdings of Malaya, July–September 1946' (London: His Majesty's Stationery Office, 1948).

George. M. Beckman, *The Making of the Meiji Constitution: The Oligarchs and the Constitutional Development of Japan, 1868–1891* (Lawrence, KS: University of Kansas Press, 1957).

Walden Bello et al., *The Anti-Development State: The Political Economy of Permanent Crisis in the Philippines* (London and New York: Zed Books, 2005).

V.V. Bhatt, 'Lead Bank Systems in India' in Masahiko Aoki and Hugh Patrick (eds.), *The Japanese Main Bank System* (Oxford and New York: Oxford University Press, 1994).

Michael S. Billig, *Barons, Brokers, and Buyers: The Institutions and Cultures of Philippine Sugar* (Honolulu: University of Hawaii Press, 2003).

Hans P. Binswanger and Klaus Deininger, 'South African Land Policy: The Legacy of History and Current Options', in Johan van Zyl, Johann Kirsten and Hans P. Binswanger (eds.), *Agricultural Land Reform in South Africa (World Development Report 1987* (Washington: World Bank, 1987; Cape Town: Oxford University Press, 1996)).

Raymond Bonner, *Waltzing with a Dictator: The Marcoses and the Making of American Policy* (New York: Vintage, 1988).

Saturnino M. Borras Jr, 'The Philippine Land Reform in Comparative Perspective: Some Conceptual and Methodological Implications', *Journal of Agrarian Change*, vol. 6, no. 1 (January 2006).

Saturnino M. Borras Jr and Jennifer C. Franco, 'Struggles for Land and Livelihood: Redistributive Reform in Agribusiness Plantations in the Philippines', *Critical Asian Studies*, vol. 37, no. 3 (2005).

Chris Bramall, 'Living Standards in Sichuan, 1931–78', Research Notes and Studies no. 8 (London: Contemporary China Institute, SOAS, 1989).

Loren Brandt and Thomas G. Rawski (eds.), *China's Great Economic Transformation* (Cambridge and New York: Cambridge University Press, 2008).

Rondo Cameron (ed.), *Banking and Economic Development: Some Lessons of History* (New York: Oxford University Press, 1972).

Alfred D. Chandler, *Strategy and Structure: Chapters in the History of the Industrial Enterprise* (Cambridge, MA: MIT Press, 1962).

Ha-Joon Chang, 'The Political Economy of Industrial Policy in Korea', *Cambridge Journal of Economics* 16 (1993).

Ha-Joon Chang, *The Political Economy of Industrial Policy* (New York : St.Martin's, 1994).

Ha-Joon Chang (ed.) *The East Asian Development Experience: The Miracle, the Crisis and the Future* (London: Zed Books, 2006).

Ha-Joon Chang and Jang-Sup Shin, 'Evaluating the Postcrisis Corporate Restructuring in Korea' in Ha-Joon Chang (ed.), *The East Asian Development Experience: The Miracle, the Crisis, and the Future* (London: Zed Books, 2006).

Ha-Joon Chang, *Bad Samaritans: Rich Nations, Poor Policies and the Threat to the Developing World* (London: Random House, 2007).

Ha-Joon Chang and Gabriel Palma (eds.) *Financial Liberalisation and the Asian Crisis* (Basingstoke: Palgrave Macmillan, 2001).

Ching Peng, *My Side of History* (Singapore: Media Masters 2003).

Mark Cleary and Peter Eaton, *Tradition and Reform: Land Tenure and Rural Development in South-east Asia* (New York: Oxford University Press, 1996).

R. H Coase, 'The Institutional Structure of Production', *American Economic Review* 82, no. 4 (September 1992).

Klaus W. Deininger, *Land Policies and Land Reform* (Washington DC: World Bank Publications, 2004).

Klaus W. Deininger, *Land Policies for Growth and Poverty Reduction* (Washington DC: World Bank Publications, 2003).

Klaus Deininger and Lyn Squire, 'New Ways of Looking at Old Issues: Inequality and Growth', *Journal of Development Economics*, vol. 57, no. 2 (1998).

Deng Xiaoping, *Selected Works of Deng Xiaoping, vol. 3 (1982–1992)* (Beijing: People's Publishing House, 1993).

Department of Agrarian Reform, Republic of the Philippines, 'Philippine Agrarian Reform: Partnerships for Social Justice, Rural Growth and Sustainable Development', 3 March 2006.

Marleen Dieleman, *How Chinese are Entrepreneurial Strategies of Ethnic Chinese Business Groups in Southeast Asia? A Multifaceted Analysis of the Salim Group of Indonesia* (Leiden: Leiden University Press, 2007), available at https://openaccess.leidenuniv.nl/bitstream/handle/1887/12076/Thesis.pdf;jsessionid=AE9DC528BA72429D09 929BBB8B671B38?sequence=1

J. Soedradjad Djiwandono, *Bank Indonesia and the Crisis: An Insider's View* (Singapore: Institute for South-East Asian Studies, 2005).

R. Doner and D. Unger, 'The Politics of Finance in Thai Economic Development' in Stephan Haggard, Chung H. Lee and Sylvia Maxfield (eds.) *The Politics of Finance in Developing Countries* (Ithaca, NY: Cornell University Press, 1993).

Ronald Dore, *Land Reform in Japan* (London: Athlone, 1984).

Ronald Dore, *Flexible Rigidities: Industrial Policy and Structural Adjustment in the Japanese Economy, 1970–80* (London: Athlone, 1986).

R. E. Elson, *Suharto: A Political Biography* (Cambridge: Cambridge University Press, 2008).

Bill Emmott, *The Sun Also Sets: Why Japan will Not be Number One* (London: Simon & Schuster, 1989).

Greg Felker, 'The Politics of Industrial Investment Policy Reform in Malaysia and Thailand' in K. S. Jomo (ed.), *Southeast Asia's Industrialization; Industrial Policy, Capabilities and Sustainability* (Basingstoke: Palgrave Macmillan, 2001).

Penelope Francks, Johanna Boestel and Choo Hyop Kim, *Agriculture and Economic Development in East Asia: From Growth to Protectionism in Japan, Korea, and Taiwan* (London: Routledge, 1999).

Bill Freund, *The Making of Contemporary Africa: The Development of African Society since 1800* (Bloomington, IN: Indiana University Press, 1984).

Bruce L. Gardner and Gordon C. Rausser, *Handbook of Agricultural Economics* (Amsterdam: Elsevier, 2007).

Suresh Gawali, 'Distortions in World Sugar Trade', *Economic and Political Weekly* 38, no. 43 (25 October 2003).

Zhang Gensheng, *Rural Reform in China* (Shenzhen: Haitian Publishing House, 2001).

Alexander Gerschenkron, *Continuity in History and Other Essays* (Cambridge, MA.: Harvard University Press, 1968).

Dharam Ghai *et al.*, *Agrarian Systems and Rural Development* (London: Macmillan, 1979).

Edmund Terence Gomez (ed.), *Political Business in East Asia* (Abingdon: Routledge, 2002).

Stephan Haggard, Byung-kook Kim and Chung-in Moon, 'The Transition to Export-led Growth in South Korea, 1954–66', *Journal of Asian Studies*, vol. 50, no. 4 (November 1991).

Stephan Haggard, Chung H. Lee and Sylvia Maxfield (eds.), *The Politics of Finance in Developing Countries* (Ithaca, NY: Cornell University Press, 1993).

Natasha Hamilton-Hart, *Asian States, Asian Bankers: Central Banking in Southeast Asia* (Ithaca, N|Y: Cornell University Press, 2002).

Paul M. Handley, *The King Never Smiles* (New Haven, NJ: Yale University Press, 2006).

Gary E. Hansen (ed.) *Agricultural and Rural Development in Indonesia,* Westview Special Studies in Social, Political, and Economic Development (Boulder, CO: Westview Press, 1981).

Shireen Mardziah Hashim, *Income Inequality and Poverty in Malaysia* (Lanham, MD and Oxford: Rowman & Littlefield,1998).

Ronald J. Herring, *Land to the Tiller: The Political Economy of Agrarian Reform in South Asia* (New Haven and London: Yale University Press,1983).

William Hinton, *Fanshen: A Documentary of Revolution in a Chinese Village* (London: George Allen & Unwin, 1932; reprinted Boston: Beacon Press, 1966)).

Albert O. Hirschman, *Rival Views of Market Society* (New York: Viking Penguin,1986).

Johannes Hirschmeier, 'Shibusawa Eiichi: Industrial Pioneer' in William Lockwood (ed.), *State and Economic Enterprise in Japan: Essays in the Political Economy of Growth* (Princeton, NJ: Princeton University Press, 1965).

David E. Hoffman, *The Oligarchs: Wealth and Power in the New Russia* (New York: Public Affairs, 2002).

Yasheng Huang, *Capitalism with Chinese Characteristics: Entrepreneurship and the State* (Cambridge: Cambridge University Press, 2008).

Paul D. Hutchcroft, 'Selective Squander: The Politics of Preferential Credit Allocation in the Philippines', in Stephan Haggard, Chung H. Lee and Sylvia Maxfield (eds.), *The Politics of Finance in Developing Countries* (Ithaca, NY: Cornell University Press, 1993).

Paul D. Hutchcroft, *Booty Capitalism: The Politics of Banking in the Philippines* (Ithaca, NY: Cornell University Press, 1998).

Paul D. Hutchcroft, 'Reflections on a Reverse Image: South Korea under Park Chung Hee and the Philippines under Ferdinand Marcos' in Byung-Kook Kim and Ezra F. Vogel (eds.), *The Park Chung Hee Era: The Transformation of South Korea* (Cambridge, MA: Harvard University Press, 2011).

Marius B. Jansen and Gilbert Rozman (eds.) *Japan in Transition: From Tokugawa to Meiji* (Princeton, NJ: Princeton University Press, 1986).

S. Jayasankaran, 'The New Way: Think Small', *Far Eastern Economic Review* (6 November 2003).

Yoong-Deok Jeon and Young-Yong Kim, 'Land Reform, Income Redistribution, and Agricultural Production in Korea', *Economic Development and Cultural Change*, vol. 48, no. 2 (January 2000).

Chalmers Johnson, *MITI and the Japanese Miracle: The Growth of Industrial Policy, 1925–1975* (Palo Alto, CA: Stanford University Press, 1982).

K. S. Jomo, *A Question of Class: Capital, the State, and Uneven Development in Malaya*, East Asian Social Science Monographs (Singapore: Oxford University Press, 1986).

K. S. Jomo, *Growth and Structural Change in the Malaysian Economy* (Basingstoke: Macmillan, 1990).

K. S. Jomo (ed.), *Industrialising Malaysia: Policy, Performance, Prospects* (London: Routledge, 1993).

K. S. Jomo (ed.), *Japan and Malaysian Development: In the Shadow of the Rising Sun* (London : Routledge, 1994).

K. S. Jomo, *Southeast Asia's Industrialization: Industrial Policy, Capabilities and Sustainability* (Basingstoke : Palgrave Macmillan, 2001).

K. S. Jomo, 'Malaysian Debacle: Whose Fault?' in Ha-Joon Chang and Gabriel Palma (eds.), *Financial Liberalisation and the Asian Crisis* (Basingstoke: Palgrave Macmillan, 2001).

K. S. Jomo and Tan Kock Wah (eds.), *Industrial Policy in East Asia: Lessons for Malaysia* (Kuala Lumpur: University of Malaya Press, 1999).

Charles Hsi-Chung Kao, 'An Analysis of Agricultural Output Increase on Taiwan, 1953–64', *The Journal of Asian Studies*, vol. 26, no. 4 (August 1967).

Kim Hyung-A, *Korea's Development under Park Chung Hee* (London: RoutledgeCurzon, 2004).

William Kirby, *Germany and Republican China* (Palo Alto, CA: Stanford University Press, 1984).

William Kirby, 'Continuity and Change in Modern China: Economic Planning on the Mainland and on Taiwan, 1943–58', *Australian Journal of Chinese Affairs*, no. 24 (July 1990).

Donald Kirk, *Korean Dynasty : Hyundai and Chung Ju Yung* (Armonk, NY: M. E. Sharpe, 1994).

Masayuki Kondo, 'Improving Malaysian Industrial Technology Policies and Institutions' in K. S. Jomo and Greg Felker (eds.) Technology, Competitiveness and the State (London: Routledge, 1999).

Anthony Y. C. Koo, *The Role of Land Reform in Economic Development: A Case Study of Taiwan, Praeger Special Studies in International Economics and Development* (New York: Praeger, 1968).

Shirley W. Y. Kuo, Gustav Ranis, and John C. H. Fei, *The Taiwan Success Story: Rapid Growth with Improved Distribution in the Republic of China, 1952–79* (Boulder, CO: Westview Press, 1981).

Dan Kurzman, *Kishi and Japan: The Search for the Sun* (New York: I. Oblensky, 1960).

Wolf Isaac Ladejinsky and Louis J. Walinsky (ed.), *Agrarian Reform as Unfinished Business: The Selected Papers of Wolf Ladejinsky* (New York: Oxford University Press on behalf of the World Bank, 1977).

Luc Laeven, 'Risk and Efficiency in East Asian Banks', *Policy Research Working Paper 2255* (World Bank Financial Sector Strategy and Policy Department, December 1999).

David Landes 'Japan and Europe: Contrasts in Industrialization' in William W. Lockwood (ed.), *State and Economic Enterprise in Japan: Essays in the Political Economy of Growth* (Princeton, NJ: Princeton University Press, 1965).

Nicholas R. Lardy, *Agriculture in China's Modern Economic Development* (Cambridge: Cambridge University Press, 1983).

Lawrence Lau (ed.), *Models of Development: A Comparative Study of Economic Growth in South Korea and Taiwan* (San Francisco: Institute for Contemporary Affairs, 1986).

Lawrence Lau *et al.*, 'Reform without Losers: An Interpretation of China's Dual-track Approach to Transition', *Journal of Political Economy*, vol. 108, no. 1(February 2000).

C. M. Law, 'The Growth of Urban Population in England and Wales, 1801–1911', *Transactions of the Institute of British Geographers* 41 (June 1967).

Lee Hangu, *The History of Korean Chaebol* (Seoul: Dae Myeong Press, 2004).

J. D. Legge, *Sukarno: A Political Biography* (Harmondsworth: Penguin, 1973).

David Lehmann (ed.), *Peasants, Landlords, and Governments: Agrarian Reform in the Third World* (New York: Holmes & Meier, 1974).

David Lehmann (ed.), *Agrarian Reform and Agrarian Reformism: Studies of Peru, Chile, China and India* (London: Faber & Faber, 1974).

Arthur W. Lewis, *The Theory of Economic Growth* (London: Allen & Unwin, 1955).

K. T. Li, *Economic Transformation of Taiwan* (London: Shepheard-Walwyn, 1988).

Lim Goh Tong, *My Story: Lim Goh Tong* (Kuala Lumpur: Pelanduk, 2004).

Lim Teck Ghee, *Peasants and Their Agricultural Economy in Colonial Malaya, 1874–1941*, East Asian Historical Monographs (Kuala Lumpur and New York: Oxford University Press, 1977).

Lim Chee Peng, 'Heavy Industrialisation' in K. S. Jomo (ed.), *Japan and Malaysian Development: In the Shadow of the Rising Sun* (London : Routledge, 1994).

Michael Lipton, 'Towards a Theory of Land Reform' in David Lehmann (ed.) *Peasants, Landlords and Governments* (New York: Holmes and Meier, 1974).

Michael Lipton, *Why Poor People Stay Poor: Urban Bias in World Development* (Harvard: Harvard University Press, 1977).

Michael Lipton, *Land Reform in Developing Countries: Property Rights and Property Wrongs* (London: Routledge, 2009).

Friedrich List, *The National System of Political Economy* (London: Longmans, Green 1885).

William Lockwood (ed.), *State and Economic Enterprise in Japan: Essays in the Political Economy of Growth* (Princeton, NJ: Princeton University Press, 1965).

William Lockwood, *The Economic Development of Japan: Growth and Structural Change, 1868–1938* (Princeton, NJ: Princeton University Press, 1954).

Kit G. Machado, 'Proton and Malaysia's Motor Vehicle Industry' in K. S. Jomo (ed.), *Japan and Malaysian Development: In the Shadow of the Rising Sun* (London : Routledge, 1994).

Jamie Mackie,'Towkays and Tycoons: Chinese in Indonesian Economic Life in the 1920s and 1980s', in Audrey Kahin and Virginia M. Barker (eds.), *The Role of the Indonesian Chinese in Shaping Modern Indonesian Life* (Ithaca, NY: Cornell Southeast Asia Program, 1991).

Angus Maddison, *Explaining the Economic Performance of Nations, 1820–1989* (Canberra: Australian National University, 1993).

Mahathir Mohamad, *The Malay Dilemma* (Singapore: Donald Moore for Asia Pacific Press, 1970).

Thomas K. McCraw, *Essential Alfred Chandler: Essays toward a Historical Theory of Big Business* (Boston, MA: Harvard Business School Press, 1988).

William Megginson and Jeffry M. Netter, 'From State to Market: A Survey of Empirical Studies on Privatisation', *Journal of Economic Literature* 39 (2001).

Ethan Michelson, 'Public Goods and State–Society Relations: An Impact Study of China's Rural Stimulus', Working Paper no. 4 (Indiana University Research Centre for Chinese Politics and Business, February 2011).

Hyman P. Minsky, *Stabilizing an Unstable Economy* (New Haven, CT: Yale University Press, 1986; reissued New York: McGraw Hill, 2008).

Barry Naughton, *Chinese Economy: Transitions and Growth* (Cambridge, MA: MIT Press, 2007).

Barry Naughton, 'China's Distinctive System: Can It be a Model for Others?', *Journal of Contemporary China* (June 2010).

Kazushi Ohkawa and Henry Rosovsky 'A Century of Japanese Economic Growth' in William Lockwood (ed.), *State and Economic Enterprise in Japan: Essays in the Political Economy of Growth* (Princeton, NJ: Princeton University Press, 1965).

Kevin O'Rourke, *Reformasi: The Struggle for Power in Post-Soeharto Indonesia* (Crows Nest, NSW: Allen & Unwin, 1998).

W. A. Dolph Owings (ed.), *The Sarajevo Trial* (Chapel Hill, NC: Documentary Publications, 1984).

Park Chung Hee, *Our Nation's Path* (Seoul: Hollym Corp.; second edition, 1970).

Park Chung Hee, *The Country the Revolution and I* (Seoul: Hollym Corp., second edition, 1970).

Earl G. Parreño, *Boss Danding* (Quezon, Philippines: Earl G. Parreño, 2003).

Philippine Institute for Development Studies, 'Post 2008 CARP: Extension with Critical Reforms', *Development Research News 26*, no. 3 (2008).

Pasuk Phongpaichit and Chris Baker, *Thailand: Economy and Politics* (Kuala Lumpur and New York: Oxford University Press, 1995; second edition, 2002).

Pasuk Phongpaichit and Chris Baker, 'Thailand's Crisis: Neo-liberal Agenda and Local Reaction', in Ha-Joon Chang, Gabriel Palma and D. Hugh Whittaker (eds.), *Financial Liberalization and the Asian Crisis* (Basingstoke: Palgrave Macmillan, 2001).

Pasuk Phongpaichit and Chris Baker, *Thaksin: The Business of Politics in Thailand* (Copenhagen: Nordic Institute of Asian Studies, 2004).

John P. Powelson and Richard Stock, *The Peasant Betrayed: Agriculture and Land Reform in the Third World* (Washington DC: Cato Institute, 1990).

Roy Prosterman, Robert Mitchell and Timothy Hanstad (eds.), *One Billion Rising: Law, Land and the Alleviation of Global Poverty* (Amsterdam: Amsterdam University Press, 2009).

Provincial Government of Negros Occidental, 'An Evaluation of CARP Implementation in Negros Occidental' (December 2007).

Louis G. Putterman, *Continuity and Change in China's Rural Development: Collective and Reform Eras in Perspective* (New York: Oxford University Press, 1993).

James Putzel, *A Captive Land: The Politics of Agrarian Reform in the Philippines* (New York: Monthly Review Press, 1992).

Kenneth B. Pyle, 'Advantages of Followership: German Economics and Japanese Bureaucrats, 1890–1925', *Journal of Japanese Studies*, vol. 1, no. 1 (Autumn 1974).

Jeffrey Reidinger, *Agrarian Reform in the Philippines: Democratic Transitions and Redistributive Reform* (Palo Alto, CA: Stanford University Press, 1995).

Eli Remolona and Mario Lamberte, 'Financial Reforms and Balance of Payments Crisis: The Case of the Philippines, 1980–83', *Philippine Review of Economics and Business* 23 (1986).

B. Renaud *et al.*, 'How the Real Estate Boom Undid Financial Institutions: What Can Be Done Now?' in J. Witte and S. Koeberle (eds.), *Competitiveness and Sustainable Economic Recovery in Thailand* (Bangkok: National Economic and Social Development Board and World Bank Thailand Office, 1998).

Carl Riskin and Thomas Wiens, 'The Evolution of Policies and Capabilities in China's Agricultural Technology' in *Chinese Economy Post-Mao* (Washington DC: US Congress Joint Economics Committee, 1978).

Carl Riskin, *China's Political Economy: The Quest for Development Since 1949* (Oxford: Oxford University Press, 1987).

D. Rodrik, 'Industrial Organization and Product Quality: Evidence from South Korean and Taiwanese Exports', mimeo, Kennedy School of Government, Harvard University (June 1988).

James Rorty, 'The Dossier of Wolf Ladejinsky: The Fair Rewards of Distinguished Civil Service', *Commentary*, April 1955.

Walt Whitman Rostow, *The Stages of Economic Growth: A Non-Communist Manifesto* (Cambridge: Cambridge University Press, 1960).

Robert Rowthorn and Ken Coutts, 'De-industrialisation and the Balance of Payments in Advanced Economies', *Cambridge Journal of Economics* 28, no. 5 (2004).

Robert Rowthorn and Ramana Ramaswamy, *Deindustrialization – Its Causes and Implications* (Washington, DC: International Monetary Fund, 1997).

Rosanne Rutten (ed.), *Brokering a Revolution: Cadres in a Philippine Insurgency* (Quezon City: Ateneo de Manila University Press, 2008).

Jeffrey Sachs and Susan Collins (eds.), *Developing Country Debt and Economic Performance, Volume 3: Country Studies – Indonesia, Korea, Philippines, Turkey* (Chicago: University of Chicago Press,1989).

Richard J. Samuels, *Machiavelli's Children: Leaders and Their Legacies in Italy and Japan* (Ithaca, NY: Cornell University Press, 2003).

Henry Sanderson and Michael Forsythe, *China's Superbank: Debt, Oil and Influence – How China Development Bank is Rewriting the Rules of Finance* (Singapore: John Wiley, 2012).

Joseph Schumpeter, Redvers Opie (trans.), *A Theory of Economic Development* (Cambridge, MA: Harvard University Press, 1934).

Adam Schwarz, *A Nation in Waiting: Indonesia's Search for Stability* (St Leonards: Allen & Unwin, 1999).

Tibor Scitovsky, 'Economic Development in Taiwan and South Korea' in L. Lau (ed.), *Models of Development: A Comparative Study of Economic Growth in South Korea and Taiwan* (San Francisco: Institute for Contemporary Affairs, 1986).

Keizō Shibusawa, *Japanese Society in the Meiji Era* (Tokyo: Ōbunsha, 1958).

Jang-Sup Shin, *The Economics of the Latecomers: Catching-up, Technology Transfer and Institutions in Germany, Japan and South Korea* (London: Routledge, 1996).

R. Short, 'The Role of Public Enterprises: An International StatisticalComparison', *International Monetary Fund Department Memorandum Series* 83/84 (1983).

Michael Spence (ed.), *The Growth Report* (Washington DC: World Bank Commission on Growth and Development, 2008).

Richard M. Steers, *Made in Korea: Chung Ju Yung and the Rise of Hyundai* (New York and London: Routledge, 1999).

Joe Studwell, *The China Dream: The Elusive Quest for the Greatest Untapped Market on Earth* (London: Profile, 2002).

Joe Studwell, *Asian Godfathers: Money and Power in Hong Kong and South-east Asia* (London: Profile Books, 2008).

Suehiro Akira, *Capital Accumulation in Thailand, 1855–1985* (Tokyo: Centre for East Asian Cultural Studies, 1989).

Tessa Morris Suzuki, *A History of Japanese Economic Thought* (London: Routledge, 1989).

R. H. Tawney, *Land and Labour in China* (London: George Allen & Unwin, 1932; reprinted New York: Octagon Books, 1972).

Jay Taylor, *The Generalissimo's Son: Chiang Ching-kuo and the Revolutions in China and Taiwan* (Cambridge, MA: Harvard University Press, 2000).

E. Thorbecke, 'Agricultural Development' in W. Galenson (ed.), *Economic Growth and Structural Change in Taiwan* (Ithaca, NY and London: Cornell University Press, 1979).

Gabriel Tortella, 'Spain 1829–74' in Rondo Cameron (ed.), *Banking and Economic Development: Some Lessons of History* (New York: Oxford University Press, 1972).

Clive Trebilcock, *The Industrialization of the Continental Powers, 1780–1914* (London: Longman, 1982).

Denis Twitchett and John K. Fairbank (eds.), *The Cambridge History of China* (Cambridge: Cambridge University Press, 1978–91).

Peter Vandergeest, Pablo Idahosa, and Pablo S. Bose (eds.), *Development's Displacements: Ecologies, Economies, and Cultures at Risk* (Vancouver: University of British Columbia Press, 2007).

Adrian Vickers, *A History of Modern Indonesia* (Cambridge: Cambridge University Press, 2005).

Ezra F. Vogel, *Deng Xiaoping and the Transformation of China* (Cambridge, MA: Belknap Press, 2011).

Robert Wade, *Governing the Market: Economic Theory and the Role of Government in East Asian Industrialization* (Princeton, NJ: Princeton University Press, 2004).

Barry Wain, *Malaysian Maverick: Mahathir Mohamad in Turbulent Times* (Basingstoke: Palgrave Macmillan 2009).

Peter Warr (ed.), *Thailand Beyond the Crisis* (London: Routledge, 2004).

Ann Waswo and Nishida Yoshiaki (eds.), *Farmers and Village Life in Twentieth-century Japan* (London: Curzon Routledge, 2003).

Thomas Wiens, 'The Evolution of Policies and Capabilities in China's Agricultural Technology', *Chinese Economy Post-Mao* (Washington DC: US Congress, Joint Economics Committee, 1978).

J. Witte and S. Koeberle (eds.), *Competitiveness and Sustainable Economic Recovery in Thailand* (Bangkok: National Economic and Social Development Board and World Bank Thailand Office, 1998).

Jung-En Woo (now Meredith Woo-Cumings), *Race to the Swift: State and Finance in Korean Industrialization* (New York: Columbia University Press, 1991).

World Bank, *Korea: Managing the Industrial Transition* (Washington: World Bank, 1987).

World Bank, *World Development Report 1987* (Washington, DC: World Bank, 1987).

World Bank, *The East Asian Miracle: Economic Growth and Public Policy* (New York and Oxford: Oxford University Press for the World Bank, 1993).

World Bank–IMF, *The Philippines: Aspects of the Financial Sector* (Washington, DC: World Bank, 1980).

Kozo Yamamura, 'The Meiji Land Tax Reform and Its Effects' in Marius B. Jansen and Gilbert Rozman (eds.), *Japan in Transition* (Princeton, NJ: Princeton University Press,1986).

Nishida Yoshiaki, 'Dimensions of Change in Twentieth-century Rural Japan' in Ann Waswo and Nishida Yoshiaki (eds.), *Farmers and Village Life in Twentieth-century Japan* (London: Curzon Routledge, 2003).

Yoshihara Kunio, *The Rise of Ersatz Capitalism in South-East Asia* (Singapore and Oxford: Oxford University Press, 1988).

Yoshihara Kunio, *Capital Accumulation in Thailand* (Tokyo: Centre for East Asian Cultural Studies, 1989).

Zhang Gensheng, *Rural Reform in China* (Shenzhen: Haitian Publishing House, 2001).

Johan van Zyl, Johann Kirsten and Hans P. Binswanger (eds.), *Agricultural Land Reform in South Africa: Policies, Markets and Mechanisms* (Cape Town: Oxford University Press, 1996).

# Acknowledgements

*How Asia Works* was commissioned by Andrew Franklin at Profile Books in London and Morgan Entrekin at Grove Atlantic in New York. I am grateful for their continuing support. Sally Holloway was, for the third time, my main and highly efficient editor, aided by important interventions from Andrew Franklin and constant oversight from Penny Daniel. Jamison Stoltz in New York was the editor responsible for creating the North American edition. The distillation process for this book was not quick; thank you to everyone, and to my agent, Clare Alexander, for your good humour throughout.

*How Asia Works* could not have been written without friends who provided free lodging during the research process. Thanks to Marcus Consolini in Tokyo; Arthur Kroeber and Debbi Seligsohn, Matt Forney and Paola Zuin, and David Cantalupo and Fu Jia in Beijing; Simon and Miho Cartledge in Hong Kong; Josh Green and Lorien Holland in Kuala Lumpur; and Ivo Philipps and Tracy Forster in Singapore. Ted Lopez of the Alter Trade Foundation went out of his way to facilitate my research in the Philippines. In addition, the Daiwa Foundation generously provided a grant to cover some field work expenses in Japan.

The Judge Business School at the University of Cambridge and the Economic and Social Research Council kindly allowed me to intermit the completion of a doctoral thesis to write this book. I would also like to thank Peter Nolan for encouraging me to return to academic study, and Jane Davies and Peter Williamson who supervise my research on Chinese industrialisation. Some of the ideas in this book were worked out while taking a Master's course in development economics at Cambridge. Thanks to Peter Nolan, Ha-Joon Chang, Gabriel Palma, Michael Kuczynski, Ajit Singh and Geoff Harcourt for their inspiration.

As I wrote the manuscript I benefitted – not for the first time – from the comments and support of Arthur Kroeber, Jonathan Anderson and my wife, Tiffany Bown. Among people who helped in the research phase, one or two prefer not to be named. But most can: Ann Waswo, Yoshiaki Nishida, Ronald Dore, Marie Conte-Helm, Donald Kirk, Harry Bhadeshia, John Swenson-Wright, Young-Jun Jang; Alanis Qin, Janet Zhang and everyone else at Dragonomics; Carl Riskin, William Kirby, K. S. Jomo, Edmund Terence Gomez, Henry Barlow, Barry Wain, Asgari Stephens, Steve Hagger, Tan Tat Wai, Jamie Mackie, Kevin O'Rourke, Adam Schwarz, Endy Bayuni, John McBeth, Edwin Soeryadjaya, Gene Galbraith, Paul Hutchcroft, Rosanne Rutten, Philip Bowring, Roy Prosterman and Li Ping. Lucy McMahon and Will Rowlands began the process of turning large amounts of academic material I collected into what I hope will become a published academic addendum to this book. Updates about this will be posted at www.howasiaworks.com.

# Index